W Shrubsole

Christian Memoirs

Or, a review of the present state of religion in England: in the form of a new pilgrimage to the heavenly Jerusalem

W Shrubsole

Christian Memoirs
Or, a review of the present state of religion in England: in the form of a new pilgrimage to the heavenly Jerusalem

ISBN/EAN: 9783337288808

Printed in Europe, USA, Canada, Australia, Japan

Cover: Foto ©Lupo / pixelio.de

More available books at **www.hansebooks.com**

CHRISTIAN MEMOIRS;

OR, A

REVIEW OF THE PRESENT STATE

OF

RELIGION IN ENGLAND;

IN THE FORM OF

A NEW PILGRIMAGE

TO THE

HEAVENLY JERUSALEM:

CONTAINING,

BY WAY OF ALLEGORICAL NARRATIVE,

A GREAT VARIETY OF DIALOGUES

ON THE MOST INTERESTING SUBJECTS,

AND

ADVENTURES

OF EMINENTLY

RELIGIOUS PERSONS.

By W. SHRUBSOLE.

Which Things are an Allegory.—Gal. iv. 24.

ROCHESTER:
Printed and Sold by T. FISHER;
Sold also by J. MATTHEWS, in the Strand; SIMMONS and VALLANCE, Cheapside; and W. HARRIS, St. Paul's Church yard, London.
MDCCLXXVI.

THOSE PROTESTANTS OF EVERY DENOMINATION,

WHO, IN THEIR FAITH AND PRACTICE,

RECEIVE AND ADORN

THE DOCTRINAL ARTICLES OF

THE ESTABLISHED CHURCH OF ENGLAND;

AND, ESPECIALLY,

TO THOSE AMONG THEM,

WHO HAVE HONOURED THE AUTHOR,

BY SUBSCRIBING TO THIS PUBLICATION;

THE FOLLOWING MEMOIRS

ARE MOST RESPECTFULLY DEDICATED,

BY THEIR VERY SINCERE FRIEND,

AND MUCH OBLIGED SERVANT,

IN THE GOSPEL OF CHRIST,

WILLIAM SHRUBSOLE.

To the READER.

THE following narrative was first taken in hand to divert my mind from melancholy reflections which arose, from a too great attention to what might be the fatal consequences of an accident, that befel me in *October* 1773. And it had the desired effect: for my thoughts were so engaged by the variety of incidents which occured to me; that, after some time, I was again favoured with my usual peace and chearfulness. At my beginning to write, I had no design of forming such a work; but as I advanced, the scene so gradually and pleasantly opened to me; that I not only rejoiced to find my mind relieved from the former distressing ideas; but became so insensibly attached to the story, that I determined to prosecute the subject, until I had brought the Pilgrims to their desired rest.

It is observable, that the histories of nations, and lives of eminent persons, contain a perpetual fund of entertainment, notwithstanding human nature has been the same in all nations and ages. So in the divine life; altho' true religion, or the way to the *Heavenly Jerusalem,* hath continued invariably the same, among all men to whom it has been revealed; yet the different complexions and circumstances of the persons who walk in this path, and the trials with which the *great God* sees it expedient to exercise them, are so various, that they will ever furnish an interesting and engaging series of incidents, to such as seek for real improvement in writing or reading religious memoirs.

For this reason, in the following work, I have kept nearly in the good old path, trod by the Pilgrims of the last century, and so eminently displayed in *Mr. Bunyan's Progress.* But the late great revival of religion among us, and the many distinguished

characters

characters engaged in that glorious work; together with the present abounding of error, immorality and infidelity, afford memoirs so very interesting; that I hope the reader, throughout the narrative, will find his attention so agreeably fixed on the dialogues, descriptions, and adventures which successively follow each other, as to prevent its being tedious or disgustful.

It has been my endeavour to avoid the imputation of too great severity, even towards such professors as I was obliged to censure: and, in all these cases, it will appear, that the reproofs are not given on account of any particular mode in their religious worship; but, for their deserting and opposing those grand doctrines, which so peculiarly distinguish the Christian religion from all others. For, throughout this narrative, I have been solicitous to enforce the fundamental principles of the Gospel, to discountenance bigotry to any forms of worship, or non-essential points of doctrine, and warmly to recommend love, candour, and communion to those of every party, who hold the doctrines of grace, and possess the life and power of christianity.

It is, undoubtedly, with great concern, that every friend to religion and his country must take notice, of the prevailing passion among us for novels, romances and sentimental folly and obscenity; which has almost generally seduced the youth of both sexes into such a giddy and triffling behaviour, as is unworthy of rational beings. Nor are those which are called the best novels wholly to be excepted from this censure: for even *they* not only present such delusive and inflammatory scenes to the mind, as tend to divest young ladies of that modesty and sensibility which are both their honour and safety; but they also furnish our *wealthy and titled felons*, those murderers of beauty, honour, innocence and peace, with many execrable methods of seduction, which might

never

never have occured to their minds; and have proved a terrible retribution on the ladies, for that paffionate and criminal fondnefs with which they inceffantly read thofe enfnaring compofitions.

Far lefs pernicious was ancient Gothic romance, which was remarkable for ftrictly keeping within the bounds of decency and every hero was an enthufiaft in defence of the honour of the fair fex. Their *Genii, Fairies, Talifmans, and Enchanted Caftles,* tho' chiefly the works of imagination; were yet more fuitably adapted to the elevated expectations and powers of the foul; and much better calculated to ferve the interefts of morality; than are the vicious, groveling, fceptical and foppifh fcenes, of the greater part of the entertaining books of this day.

In the following pages, the public will be prefented with a work entirely free from fuch poifon, yet I hope both inftructing and entertaining; and not lefs fo, for appearing in a religious character. Without putting on the forbidding appearance of a fyftematic divine, or a grave moralift; I have endeavoured to forward the work of both, by recommending, in a free focial manner, the bleffed Redeemer of men, as the *Alpha* and *Omega,* the *Firft* and the *Laft* of religion, both as to faith and practice. And fhall think myfelf honoured if I am made at all ufeful in difplaying the glory of his divine perfon, the compleatnefs of his excellent work, and the riches of his free grace; fo as to induce any perfon to efteem him the more by reading thefe memoirs. Should I be thought to have gone too far in this path; I muft profefs I think it not poffible, while due care is taken to guard the facred *Palladium of Gofpel Holinefs.* For this reafon, I have introduced the *Town of Illumination,* inhabited by *Antinomians*; and in that inftance, as well as in many others

others, hope I have sufficiently shewn my detestation of any licentious principles or practices. But should the characters of such backsliders as Messrs. *Serious, Goodman,* and *Trueman* be objected against me in this respect: let it be considered, whether they are drawn more strongly than those of *David* and *Peter* in holy writ. However *that* may be, they are copied from matters of fact, with which I am so well acquainted that I can never forget them. And how terrible soever the instance of *Mr. Serious,* in particular, may appear; yet, it is certain that, both the fall and repentance of that unhappy Pilgrim, were attended with circumstances far more affecting, than could be described by the most masterly writer.

It may be thought by some, that there is too much severity manifested towards *Arius, Socinus,* and *Deist,* at least to the two former. But I can make no distinction between those who absolutely deny divine revelation, and those, who, by corrupting a part of it, subvert the whole. I regard both parties as fatally criminal, in rejecting and perverting a revelation, in which *God's only begotten son* is set forth, as labouring and dying for sinners of the human race; confirming his mission by many astonishing miracles; and uttering prophecies which have been fulfilled in all the following ages, and are still compleating with wonderful exactness. Such a blaze of evidence as hath shone from the earliest age of Christianity, and such glorious gospel light as at present illuminates *Great Britain*, will not be opposed, slandered, and ridiculed by the lovers of darkness and sensuality, whether infidels or professed Christians, without the severest rebukes from the *Almighty*. Nor will the boasted moral actions of such criminals, which, in general, originate from caprice, complexion, pride, and a thousand other selfish motives,

NAMES

OF THE

SUBSCRIBERS.

A

THE Rev. John Andrews, *Marden, Kent.*
The Rev. Mr. Andrew, *Rochford, Essex.*
Mr. ―― Abdy, *London.*
Mr. ―― Abington, *London.*
Mr. Thomas Adamson, *New-Cross.*
Mr. Henry Alexander, *Maidstone.*
Mr. Mark Allister, *Egerton.*
Mr. William Amhurst, *Portsmouth.*
Mr. John Amner, *Sheerness.*
Mrs. Mary Ancell, *Sheerness.*
Mr. George Anderson, *Sheerness.*
Mrs. ―― Angel, *Bear-lane, Christ-church.*
Mr. ―― Archer, *Deal.*
Mr. Arthur, *Dartford.*
Mr. David Atkins, *Sheerness.*
Mr. William Atwood, *Dover.*

B

The Rev. David Bradberry, *Ramsgate.*
Mr. Alde man Baker, *Rochester.*
Mr. Richard Baker, *Sheerness.*
Mr. James Baker, *Sheerness.*
Mrs. Mary Barham, *Sheerness.*
Mr. Zacharias Barnes, *Liverpool.*
Mr. John Bartholomew, *Portsmouth.*
Mr. Thomas Bassett, *Sheerness.*

Mr. ―― Bayless, *London.*
Mr. Richard Beaton, *Minster, Sheppy.*
Mr. Thomas Bell, *Norwich.*
Mr. William Berry, *Chatham.*
Mr. Abraham Bigsby, *Deptford.*
Mr. ―― Binks.
Mr. William Bishop, *Sheerness.*
Mr Henry Bishop, *Sheerness.*
Mr. Samuel Blackmur, *Sheerness.*
Mr. J―― Blasson, *London.*
Mr. William Borne, *Maidstone.*
Mr. Henry Bourne, *Dalby.*
Mr. John Bourne, *Dalby.*
Mr. Robert Bowden, *Petty-France, Westminster,* 3 books.
Messrs. Bowley and Moggs, *Soho,* 6 books.
Mr. Joseph Boyden, *Chatham.*
Mr. John Boys, *Dover.*
Mr. James Bright, *Sheerness.*
Mr. ―― Brooshoost.
Thomas Smalley Browning, Esq; *Greenwich.*
Mr. George Brown, *Portsmouth.*
Mr. John Bullock, *Tottenham-court-Road.*
Mr. ―― Bunnell.
Mr. Edward Burch, *Chatham.*
Mr. Daniel Burford, *Sheerness.*
Mr. Edward Burford, *Woolwich.*
Mr. Spencer Burgess, *Ratcliff-cross.*
Mr. ―― Burt.

The

(xiv)

C

The Rev. Dr. Conyers, *St. Paul's, Deptford.*
The Rev. Samuel Cooper, *Loxley, Warwickshire.*
Mrs. Elizabeth Caile, *Greenwich.*
Mr. Joseph Cansfield, *Greenwich.*
Mr. John Carpenter, *Sheerness.*
Miss Eliz. Carpenter, *Sheerness.*
Mr. James Carrington, *Sheerness.*
Mr. —— Chambers, *London*
Mr. Samuel Chancellor, *London.*
Mr. Thomas Cheesman, *Sheerness.*
Mr. Edward Clarke, Surgeon, *Sheerness,* 4 books.
Mr. —— Clark, *Egerton.*
Mrs. Sarah Cl——, *Norwich.*
Mr. John Coker, *Portsmouth.*
Mr. Thomas Coley, *Homerton Academy.*
Mr. John Collingwood, *Sheerness.*
Mr. William Collingwood, *Greenwich.*
Mr. Samuel Collingwood, *Gravesend.*
Mr. Thomas Comber, *London.*
Mr. John Comber, *Tonbridge.*
Mr. George Conquett, *Sheerness.*
Mr. —— Constable,
Dr. John Cook. *Leigh, Essex.*
Mr. Edward Cook, *Sheerness.*
Mr. Philip Cooper, *Deptford.*
Mr. —— Cope, 2 books.
Mr. Edward Corry, *Woolwich.*
Mr. George Coveney, *Dover.*
Miss Susan Cox, *Greenwich.*
Mr. Thomas Creasy, *Greenwich.*
Mr. William Creasy, *Gravesend.*
Mr. ——Crowther, *Staplehurst.*
Mr. Matthew C——, *Norwich*
Capt. Thomas Curling, *Ramsgate.*
Mr. Samuel Curry, *Sheerness.*

D

The Rev. Charles De Coetlogon, *London.*
Mr. Richard Dadd, *Chatham.*
Mr. Thomas Davies, *Boughton Malherb.*
Mr. —— Davies.
Mr. —— Davies, *Serjeant's Inn.*
Mrs. —— Davis.
Mrs. —— Dawson, *Norfolk-street, Southwark.*
Mrs. Susannah Daydon, *Norwich*
Mr. William Dean, *Milk-street, London.*
Mr. John Deedy, *Greenwich.*
Mr. Robert Dickie, *Greenwich.*
Mr. Charles Doleson, *Greenwich*
Mrs. —— Dornford, *Deptford.*
Mr. William Draper, *Deptford.*
Mr. James Duckenson, *Portsmouth.*
Mr. William Dun, *Norwich,* 3 books.
Alexander Duncan, Esq;
Mr. John Duncan, *Chatham.*
Mrs. —— Duppa, *London.*
Jonathan Durden, Esq; *Petty-France, Westminster.*
Mrs. —— Dyer, *Norfolk-street, Southwark.*

E

The Rev. Thomas Eade, *London,* 2 books.
The Rev. John Edwards, *Leeds*
Mr. John Edmonds, *Sheerness,* 2 books
Mr. Parker Edwards, *Sheerness.*
Mrs. Sarah Edwards, *Greenwich*
Mr. John Egelsham, *Gravesend.*
Mr. John Elgar, *Portsmouth.*
Mr. Richard Everal, *Rochester.*
Mr. George Everest, *Sheerness.*
Mr. Thomas Exabee, *Sheerness.*

F

Lady Mary Fitzgerald.
Mr. James Fanten, *Greenwich.*
Mr. Charles Fern, *Brompton.*

Mr.

(xv)

Mr. William Finch, *Deptford.*
Mr. Nathaniel Finckell, *Charlton.*
Mr. John Fisher, *Liverpool.*
Mr. Thomas Fletcher, *Woolwich.*
Mr. James Ford, *Deptford.*
Mr. Norris Fox, *Chatham.*
Mr. Daniel Friend, *Ramsgate.*
Mr. James Fuller, *Sheerness.*
Mr. Samuel Fuller, *Lenham*

G

The Rev. Cradock Glascott, 2 books.
Mr. Isaac Gammon, *Deal*, 2 books.
Mr. Alexander Gardiner, *Dover*
Mr. —— Garlick, *London.*
John Garrat, Esq; *Ellington, in Thanet.*
Mr. George Gibson, *Loampit-hill, Deptford.*
Miss Gideon, *Knightsbridge.*
Mr. Thomas Gilbert, *Chatham*, 2 books.
Mr. —— Giles.
Mr. Benjamin Glandfield, *Dover.*
Mr. Daniel Golden, *Strand*, 6 books.
Mrs. Elizabeth Goodeve, *Portsmouth.*
Mr Sampson Gooding, *Lenham.*
Mr. George Gooding, *Smarden.*
Mr. Stephen Goodson, *Ramsgate.*
Mr. Joseph Goslett, *Malden, Essex.*
Hr. Henry Gosling, *Sheerness.*
Mr. John Griffiths, *New-Cross.*
Mr. Joseph Grigsby, *Sheerness.*
Mr. —— Grindley, *London.*
Mr. William Grinstead, *Sheerness.*

H

The Rt. Hon. Countess Dowager of Huntingdon, 12 books.

The Rev. John Harris, *Hull.*
Mr. John Hales, jun. *Gravesend.*
Miss —— Halt head, *Chatham.*
Mr. Thomas Harper, *New-road, London.*
Mr. Samuel Harris, *Greenwich.*
Mr. Francis Harrison, *Chatham*
Mr. Thomas Haycraft, *Deptford.*
Mr. —— Haylay, *Deptford.*
Mr. Matthew Hervey, *Malden, Essex.*
Mr. —— Hexter, Schoolmaster at *Ealing.*
Mr William Hill, *Deptford.*
Mr. William Hills, *Sandwich.*
Mr. John Hodges, *Brompton.*
Mr. —— Hodgkinson, *London.*
Mr. Thomas Hodgson, *Sheerness.*
Mr. —— Hog, *Leeds.*
Mr. Bernard Holbrook, *London.*
Mr. Robert Holbrook, *Sheerness.*
Mr. —— Holden, *Staplehurst.*
Mrs. Catharine Hooper, *Ramsgate.*
Mr. William Hopkins, *Greenwich*, 7 books.
Mr. James Hovey, *Sheerness.*
Mr Morris Hughes, *Inner-Temple, London*, 6 books.
Mr. Robert Hugill, *Sheerness.*
Mr. Henry Hunt, sen. *Wells-street, Oxford-road.*
Mr Henry Hunt, jun. *ditto.*
Mrs. Mary Hunt, *ditto.*
Miss Elizabeth Hunt, *ditto.*
Mr. John Hunt, *Sheerness*, 2 books.
Mr. —— Hunter, *London.*
Mrs. Mary Hurst, *Broadstairs.*
Mr. William Hurwood, *Sheerness.*
Mr. William Hurwood, *St. Ann's, Soho.*
Mr. John Hurwood, *Rotherhithe.*

c 2 Mr.

(xvi)

Mr. James Hurwood, *Westminster*.
J.
Mr. —— Jackson, *Dartford*.
Mr. Thomas Jacobs, *Sheerness*.
Mr. James Jagger, *Malden, Essex*.
Mr. —— Jarvis.
Mr. William Jefferies, *Sheerness*
Mr. John Jeffery, *Sheerness*.
Mrs. Elizabeth Jeffs, *Sheerness*.
Messrs. Jenkins, *Rochester*.
Mr. —— Johns, *Dover*.
Mrs. Johnston, *Westminster*.
Mr. John Jones, *London*.
Mr. William Jones, *Portsmouth*.
Mr. —— Jones, *London*.
Mrs. —— Jordan, *Deptford*.
K
The Rev. Andrew Kinsman, *Plymouth*, 14 books.
Robert Keen, Esq; *Minories*, 50 books.
Mr. Edward Keigwin, *Chatham*.
Mr. Ambrose Kidwell, *Sheerness*.
Mrs. Mary Knight, *Chatham*.
Mr. James Knott, *Dover*.
Mr. John Knott, *Chatham*.
L.
The Rev. Francis Leicester, 2 books.
T. Lacey, Esq; 6 books.
Mr. —— L——, 2 books.
A young Lady at *Greenwich*.
Mr. John Lambeth, *Sheerness*.
Mr. John Langman, *Sheerness*.
Mrs. Eliz. Langman, *Sheerness*.
Mr. Langston, *London*.
Mr. Thomas Leech, *Greenwich*.
Mrs. —— Leggatt, *Wapping-Old-stairs*.
Mr. Samuel Lepine, *Canterbury*.
Mr. Thomas Lindsey, *Norwich*.
Mr. Bartholomew Lindsey, *Norwich*.
Mr. Edward Love, *Sheerness*.

Miss Caroline Lowe, *London*.
Mr. Joseph Lucas, *Portsmouth*.
Mrs. Elizabeth Luke, *Sheerness*.
Mr. —— Lunchen, *Woolwich*.
M
Lady Robert Manners.
The Rev. Henry Mead, *London*
The Rev. Samuel Medley, *Liverpool*.
Mr. William M'Cullock, *Gravesend*.
Mr. William Maddock, *Sheerness*.
Mr. Daniel Mannock, *Egerton*.
Mr. John Martyr, *Yalding*.
Mr. James Martyr, *Otford*.
Mr. William Mason, *Rotherhithe*.
Mr. Samuel Mason, *Greenwich*.
Mr. Lewis Masquirier, *Coventry-street, Westminster*.
Mr. —— Matravers, *Vere-street, Clare-market*.
Mr. J. Matthews, *Strand*, 25 books
Mr. Richard Maxfield, *London*.
Mr. John May, *Malden, Essex*.
Mr. —— Mayor, 2 books.
Mr. William Meredith, *Rochester*.
Mr. John Meyer, 2 books.
Mr. John Mitchell, *Sheerness*.
Mr. William Mitchell, *Chatham*
Mr. Joseph Moore, *Maidstone*, 2 books
Mr. John Moore, *Maidstone*.
Mr. Ralph Morris, *London*.
Mr. —— Morris, *London*.
Mr. Joshua Morton, *Sheerness*.
Mr. John Moulden, *Chatham*.
Mr. John Munn, *Maidstone*.
Mr. —— Munn, *Egerton*.
Mr. William Myhill, *Norwich*.
N
Mr. William Newcomb, *London*
Mr. Thomas Newland, *Deptford*.
Mr. Joseph Norwood, *Ramsgate*

The

(xvii)

O
The Rev. John Olding, *Deptford.*
Mr. William Oats, *Maidstone.*
Mr. Olney, 2 books
Mr. Jacob Outrim, *Sheerness.*
P
The Rev. Edward Peronett, *Canterbury.*
Mrs. Elizabeth Paddon, *Greenwich.*
Mr. —— Parker, *King's Mews.*
Mr —— Parker, *London.*
Mr. Thomas Parker, *Sheerness.*
Mr. Henry Parkin, *Sheerness.*
Mrs. Anna Parkins, *Ratcliffe-highway.*
Mr. John Parlby, *Portsmouth.*
Mr. Robert Pattison, *Malden, Essex.*
Mr. Henry Pattison, *ditto.*
Mr. George Pearce, *Chatham.*
Mrs. Jane Pearson, *Sheerness.*
Mr. John Perdue, *Greenwich.*
Mr. John Peterson, *Sheerness.*
Mr. Thomas Phillips, *Norfolk-street, Southwark,*
Mr. Robert Piercy, *Bedworth, near Coventry.*
Mr. J. W. Piercy, Printer, *Coventry.*
Mr. William Pitman, *Sheerness.*
Mr. William Porter, *Sheerness*
Mr John Prat, *Deptford.*
Mr. William Prats, *Portsmouth.*
Mr. —— Preston, *Dartford.*
Mr. William Prouting, *Deptford.*
Mr. Elias Pullen. *Gravesend.*
R
Mr. —— Ramsdale.
George Rainier, Esq; *Ramsgate.*
Mr. James Rawbone, *Malden, Essex.*
Mr. Adam Reed, *Woolwich.*
Mr. James Richards, *Greenwich.*

Mr. Thomas Richardson, *Norwich.*
Mr. —— Rickand, *Egerton.*
Mr. William Rickards, sen. *Woodnesborough*
Mrs. —— Ridout
Mr. Richard Roper
Mr. James Rule, *Portsmouth*
Mrs. Mary Rumble, *Gravesend*
Mr. John Rumsey, *Portsmouth*
Mr. Thomas Russell, *Woolwich*
Mr. John Russell, *Dover,* 4 books
Mr. Richard Russell, *ditto*
Mrs. Sarah Russell, *ditto*
Mr. —— Russell, *London*
Mr. Anthony Rymold, *London*
S
Mr. John Sadd, *Malden, Essex*
Mr. Jacob Sadler. *Greenwich*
Mr. —— Sanders, *London*
Mr. Charles Sandys, *Greenwich*
Mr. Samuel Savage, jun. *Deptford*
Mr. James Saxton, *Greenwich*
Mr. John Scurries, *Park-street, London*
Mr. William Searles, *Deptford*
William Shepherd, Esq; *Plymouth,* 6 books
Mr. James Shepherd, *Sheerness*
Mrs. Mary Shepherd, *Rochester*
Mr. Richard Shirley, *Milton*
Mr. George Shirley, *ditto*
Mr. —— Shoolbred, *London*
Mr William Shrubsal, *Minster, Sheppy,* 3 books
Mr. Samuel Silver, *Sandwich*
Mr. William Simcock, *Rochester*
Mr. Thomas Simms, *Portsmouth.*
Mr. Henry Sifley, *Sheerness:*
Mr. William Sloman, *Greenwich.*
Mr. —— Smart, Attorney, at *Malden, Essex*
Mr. William Smith, *Guildhall, Westminster*
Mr. George Smith, sen. *Sheerness*

Mr.

Mr. Charles Smith, *Woolwich*.
Mr. George Smith, *Westminster*
Mr. Robert Smith, *Sheerness*, 2 books
Mr. William Smith, *Sheerness*
Mr. Thomas Smith, *Cornhill, London*
Mrs. Agnes Smith, *Greenwich*
Mr. Luke Smithett, *Dover*
Mr. Thomas Souard, *Rotherhithe*
Mr. John Sowerby, *Liverpool*.
Mr Austin Spearpoint, *Dover*
Mr. Mark Spicer, *Greenwich*
Mr. Daniel Spring, *Hornmonger-lane, Southwark*
Mr. Robert Staples, *Sheerness*.
Mr. Alexander Steill, *Portsmouth*
Mr. Andrew Sterne, *Sheerness*
Mr. Thomas Stiles, *Rochester*
Mr. John Stone, *Sandwich*
Mr. Thomas Storey, *Liverpool*
Mr. John Stunt, *Sheerness*
Mr. Walter Stunt, *Maidstone*
Mr. John Stunt, *Norwich*
Mrs. —— Sutherland, *Sheerness*
Mr. James Sutton, *Malden, Essex*.
Mr. John Sutton, *Liverpool*.

T.

The Rev. Thomas Tuppen, *Portsmouth*
Mr. Nowell Taylor, *Woolwich*, 3 books
Mr. William Taylor, *Portsmouth*
Mr. William Taylor, *Woolwich*
Mrs. Margaret Taylor, *Sheerness*
Mr. Henry Temple, *Sandwich*
Mr. William Temple, *Sheerness*
Mr. Joseph Thomas, *Dover*

Mr. John Thompson, *Rotherhithe*
Mr. William Thomson, *Portsmouth*
Mr. William Thresher, *Talgarth-College, Wales*
Mr. Thomas Tong, *Sheerness*
Mr. John Tovery, *Deptford*.
Mr. Nicholas Tucker, *Sheerness*

V & U.

Mr. George Viney, *Harrietsham*
Mr. —— Umpage, *Gravesend*.
Mr. —— Underwood, *London*
Unknown, *Deptford*.

W.

The Rev. John West, *Margaret-street, Saint Mary-le-Bone*, 6 books
The Rev. Mr. Wilmshurst, *Malden, Essex*
The Rev. Richard Woodgate, and the Church in *Jewin-street, London*, 50 books
Daniel West, Esq; *Islington*, 50 books
Mr. Richard Walker, *Maidstone*, 2 books
Mr. Edward Walk, *Sheerness*
Mr. Joseph Walley, *Liverpool*
Mr. Daniel Walter, *Bear-lane, Christ-church*
Mr. Henry Watkins, *Holborn-bridge*, 3 books
Mr. Abel Watson, *Chatham*
Mr. James Whiscard, *Greenwich*
Mrs. —— Whitehead
Mr. Thomas Whitewood, *Portsmouth*
Mr. Francis Wickenden, *Sheerness*.
Mr. Thomas Wignell, *Greenwich*.

Mr.

Mr. —— Wild, *London*
Mr. Thomas Williams, *Norwich*
R—— Wilson, Esq; 6 books
Mr. Alexander Wilson, *Greenwich*
Mr. Joseph Withers
Mr. Richard Wood, *Snow's-fields, Southwark*

Mr. Joseph Wood, *Queenborough*.
Mr —— Wood, *London*
Mr. —— Woolaston, *ditto*.
Mr. Godfrey Wragg, *St. Ann's, Soho*
Mr. Thomas Wright, *Union-street, London*
Mr. Robert Wynne, *Deptford*.

ERRATA.

ERRATA.

Page 38, line 18, for *dear*, read *dearly*.
—— 40, line 3 from the bottom, dele *not*.
—— 43, — 1, — *corration*, — *corporation*.
—— 57, — 12, — *difgraced*, — *difgrace*.
—— 63, — 9, — *perceive*, — *perceived*.
—— 175, at the beginning of line 10, read *Simple*.
—— 198, line 1, for *peirce*, read *peirceth*.
—— 218, — 27, — *as*, — *a*.
—— 219, — 17, — *know*, — *knows*.
—— 239, — 32, — *the* ſtorm.
—— 277, — 6, — *is*, — *are*.

tives, be able to defend them from the just vengeance of the slighted and despised Redeemer.

Should there be any true Christians whose own cold feelings, like *Father Simon*'s will not suffer them to approve of those rapturous joys, and extatic pleasures, which some pilgrims are in this work said to experience; yet, I hope, there are none, or at least very few, who do not desire to enjoy such divine favours and press after them as their privileges. *That* Christian, has but a very slender acquaintance with *Immanuel*, who does not long to know more of his glory, and enjoy more of his love. There are hundreds of religious persons in *Great Britain*, whose conduct in all *secular* affairs evinces them to be possessed of sound understanding; yet, with respect to *religious* things, solemnly declare, that, at times, they have such views of their interest in the favour of God, as to rejoice therein with joy unspeakable and full of glory; and that they frequently have most ravishing communion with the *Father*, and with his son *Christ Jesus*. And why should such persons be censured by their brethren as *Enthusiasts*? Ignorant and irreligious people will, no doubt, so describe them, and affirm that they are righteous over-much; but far be it from professors to adopt such sentiments. On the contrary, let such *cool Religionists* be rather animated by these instances of holy fervor, to seek for the same pleasures; and with them to pray, that they may be filled with all the fulness of God.

Such things as happened in the *Wilderness of Fear*, *Cross*'s *Dungeon*, *Valley of the Shadow of Death*, and *Castle of Scepticism*, with the *Voices from Heaven*, &c. may, notwithstanding the allegorical nature of the work, be considered by some readers as the reveries of *Fanaticism*; or, at least, as flights of *Fancy*: but I believe this narrative will be perused by many, who will allow the propriety of such representations, as

b descriptive

descriptive of what happens to some of the best Christians, in every period of the church. And as to other readers, I shall not be much concerned at their censures; but am very ready to make allowances for prejudice and inexperience: for I have long observed, that every thing of this sort, is deemed fanatical, by some persons, if it is not within the line of their own opinions and experience.

The character of *Fervidus*, both on this and the other side the *River of Death*, may be thought too much strained and exalted. But, as an apology for this, and other parts of the work, I beg that the scriptures referred to, may be well considered; and then, I trust, it will appear that however unworthy the most zealous minister of *Christ* is, of any reward from his master; yet our *Lord* has plainly declared, that there are great honours in reserve, in a future state, for even the *least* of his servants; and, doubtless, there are much greater for such an eminent and faithful ambassador of the *Celestial King*, as is described in the character of that indefatigable servant of *Christ*, *George Fervidus*.

If, in entering on the work, the reader should think, there is too near a resemblance to *Mr. Bunyan's Pilgrim*, to afford him any *new* entertainment; he is desired, not to be discouraged, but to proceed; and he will soon find the scenes vary considerably; new characters will appear, new circumstances and incidents will occur; which it is hoped will afford him the entertainment and satisfaction he seeks for. I must also entreat the serious reader to remember, that it is an *allegorical* work, and should have a a second reading, with candid and close attention, before any part of it is censured. And, after such a perusal I hope the reader will acknowledge, at least in general, that he has not spent his time in vain.

I

I have now only to profess my obligations to the many friendly subscribers to these Memoirs; and principally to my *Reverend Friends* among them. I am conscious of the honour done me, and the confidence reposed in my judgment and candour (for a great part of which, I consider myself much indebted to my worthy correspondent below) and I hope none of my friends will have cause to repent of the encouragement given to this work; but further oblige me, by remembering the writer and his work, when they are nearest to the blessed author of our most holy religion.

The writer of the following letter is well known in the *Religious World*, as the *Author of the Christian's Spiritual Treasury*, and several other useful pieces. He has so far honoured and obliged me, as to examine my Review, correct it for the press, and publicly testify his approbation as follows.

To Mr. WILLIAM SHRUBSOLE.

Dear Sir,

Having been favoured with the perusal of your manuscript, I return it with my hearty thanks for it. Permit me to assure you, I have read it with great pleasure, and hope much profit. In this work, you have been blessed with the happy art of so blending the utile et dulce. *that, I doubt not, but it will prove both entertaining and edifying to your readers. I congratulate the* Christian World, *on the pleasing hopes of seeing soon published,* Christian Memoirs, *or a Review of the present State of Religion, in the form of a New* Pilgrimage to the Heavenly Jerusalem. *You have my sincere wishes for a blessing and success to it. In*
this,

this, and every work of faith, and labour of love, for our dear Lord's glory, and his people's good; may you be kept humble before him, and owned and accepted by Him; in whom I am,

Very dear Sir,

Rotherhithe,
Sept. 24, 1775.

Your most affectionate friend,

and sincere servant,

W. MASON.

NAMES

A

REVIEW

OF THE

PRESENT STATE

OF

RELIGION, &c.

CHAP. I.

Probus *sets out on Pilgrimage.* *He is followed by his friend* Resolute. *They overtake* Friendly. *The manner of their passing the* Slough of Despond.

IN the vast empire of this world there is a large kingdom, which, on account of the mental blindness of its inhabitants, and the sable complexion of a usurper who governs it, is called the kingdom of *Darkland*. The people of this territory are all born in darkness, and are all rebels[1]; for they have withdrawn their obedience and homage from their gracious king of the *Celestial country*, who once reigned over them; and have submitted unto the *Black Tyrant*[2], who is an evil genius, and his mortal enemy: yet notwithstanding this base treatment of their

[1] Ephes. v. 8.   Psalm lxviii. 18.   Rom. v. 10.   [2] Revel. ix. 11.
Ephes. vi. 12.

B   rightful

rightful sovereign, he is continually sending ambassadors unto them, and entreating them to return to their duty.

In the said kingdom of *Darkland* is an extensive province called *Destruction*, which contains several large and populous cities, such as the city of *Destruction* itself, the metropolis; also the cities of *Stupidity*, *Contradiction*, *Resistance*, and others. Some time ago there came into the city of *Stupidity* a celebrated ambassador from the *Celestial King*, named *Evangelist*, and standing on an eminence in the market-place, he began to sing a hymn, which drew a great number of persons about him; he then opened a book, and read therein as follows, " Now then we are ambassadors for *Immanuel*, as tho' his father, your rightful sovereign, did beseech you by us, we pray you in *Immanuel*'s stead, be ye reconciled to your Lord the king ¹." He then proceeded to shew the greatness and goodness of the king, and the wonderful love and exploits of his son the prince *Immanuel*. He also warned those around him of the danger of remaining in their state of rebellion, and earnestly besought them to be reconciled to the king, and flee for refuge into *Immanuel's land*, by way of the *Strait gate* ².

Mr. *Evangelist* was very convincing in his discourse, insomuch that a certain young man of that city, was greatly affected thereby, wept bitterly, and sighed as if his very heart would break. When the preacher had concluded, this young man endeavoured to get near him. *Evangelist* had with pleasure observed the concern he was under, and was desirous to have some conversation with the youth: wherefore they met, walked together out of the city, and discoursed as follows,

Evang. Pray, young man, what is your name?

Prob. Probus, Sir, I am a citizen of this place.

Evang. And what made you weep, while I was preaching?

Prob. I can scarce tell you, Sir. I found I wanted something to make me happy, but I knew not what it was; for I have been brought up in great ignorance of true religion. I never made any enquiry about the salvation of my soul: never bowed my knees in prayer, with any desire to be reconciled to the *Celestial King*; never regarded the prince *Immanuel*; nor ever before heard him preached in the manner you did. When you

¹ 2 Cor. v. 20.   ² Luke xiii. 24.

set forth the glory of the king, and the amazing love of *Immanuel* to such rebels as we are; I was so struck with the view of him, that methought I loved him for doing such wonders for us men. But, when you came to enquire, whether we were really reconciled to him in our hearts by faith, and were actually acquainted with the things you had preached? I was truly convinced, that it must be a great honour and happiness, to know the love of so great and excellent a prince. But, as I knew nothing of this for myself, I wept on account of my ignorance, and sighed and wished to know him to be my friend and my saviour, in the manner described by you.

Evang. May the king be gracious to you, my son. I am rejoiced to find your mind so disposed towards our *Immanuel*. You may be certain that your high thoughts of him, and your earnest desires to be acquainted with him in your heart, proceed from his favour towards you, and shall not be fruitless. But, in order to find peace, it is necessary that you should leave this city, and strive to enter in at the gate, which you may see on an eminence at the farther side of yonder plain: and unto which I direct all those, who are willing to flee from the wrath to come.

Prob. But, Sir, must I go to that gate alone?

Evang. Perhaps you may: yet, if you follow my instructions there is no fear of your succeeding.—Let what will happen unto you, be sure to follow on, and do not dare to return hither again; nay, do not look back, if you do, you are not fit to be a Pilgrim [1].—You will soon arrive at the *Slough of Despond*, over which there are good steps [2], an account of these you may find in this book which I will give you—Turn not aside to the right-hand, or to the left—If you find any good companions, join them—Carefully peruse this volume, and pray to the king for instruction therein. And may he direct you in the way of truth and righteousness.

Prob. Dear Sir, I thank you for your good advice, gracious present, and kind prayers for my welfare, and hope I shall be enabled to profit by them.

So *Probus* parted from *Evangelist*, and setting his face towards the gate, he began to go forward with speed. He had not gone

---

[1] Luke ix. 62.   [2] 2 Peter i. 4.

far before he was overtaken by a young man named *Resolute*, an old companion of his in folly, who came running after him. *Probus* looking at *Resolute*, perceived that his countenance was full of fear, and that his whole body trembled: on which he thus addressed him.

Prob. How now, friend *Resolute!* Whither run you this way? And what is the reason that you, who are naturally so bold and daring, thus tremble and quake?

Res. Ah, *Probus!* All my fortitude is but empty vapour, when opposed by such things as I have lately seen, heard, and felt.

Prob. Pray, my friend, explain yourself. But let us keep on our way, for I am determined to stop for no one.

Res. My dear *Probus*, I desire to be with you. I chearfully follow you: and earnestly long to tell you my case, forasmuch as I expect instruction how to proceed, from your friendly counsel.

Prob. You may command me in what little help I can afford you, if it may be done in the way we go. Wherefore, say on.

Res. You have heard of the frequent earthquakes that have lately shook our city and country. You have seen the fiery canopy, which the other night hung over our rebellious heads. These things portend that we and our country are under the displeasure of the Almighty. And, as to myself, I am convinced that I deserve his wrath. This very day I was informed, that an ambassador from the *Celestial King* had given out, that the world would stand but a short time longer. On this news, all my sins stared me in the face, and I dreaded to appear before the judge: but seeing you hasten away from our city, I ran after you, with a resolution to accompany you wherever you go. Dear *Probus*, will you permit me to join you?

Probus embracing his friend, replied, Thrice welcome, dear *Resolute*, I wanted a companion, and Providence has sent me one to my wish. Know then, my brother, that I am directed by *Evangelist*, who lately preached in our city, to proceed to yonder gate, where I shall hear farther what I am to do. And if you will accompany me, you shall fare as I do. Know also, that whether the world comes to an end soon or not, yet by the

awful

awful confideration of that certain and dreadful event, and other things you mentioned, the king feems to have awakened you to feek him while he is to be found [1]. Wherefore, my friend, be not afraid, let us flee from the worft, hope for the beft, and fet out on Pilgrimage together.

On this *Refolute* became more compofed, and faid,

Ref. I thank you, kind *Probus*, for your good advice, and great readinefs to receive me for a companion. I chearfully forfake my former evil practices, to follow you in the way to the *Celeftial city*.

The two friends went on thus difcourfing in the way, and frequently reading in the book which *Evangelift* gave *Probus*, until they drew near to another young man, who was very fedately walking in the fame path. This perfon they had fome knowledge of. His name was *Friendly*. So they called, Ho, *Friendly*, whither are you bound fo ferioufly ? At this he turned, feemed furprized to fee them, and anfwered,

Frien. I am going, Sirs, to yonder gate. But how is it that you, whofe backs were fo lately turned upon this way, feem now fo eager to walk therein ?

At this queftion, *Probus* and *Refolute* looked at each other, with tears in their eyes. At length faid *Probus*,

Prob. Friendly, your rebuke is very juft. It cuts us to the quick. We acknowledge that our practice has been vile, and if the king had been ftrict to mark what we had done amifs [2], we fhould have perifhed with our city: but he has roufed us from our fatal fecurity, and directed us to yonder gate, that we may further know his mind concerning fuch loft, wretched, and rebellious creatures as we are.

Frien. Bleffed be the king, for working fuch a concern in your minds towards himfelf! It indicates that you will meet with a kind reception at the gate. I wifh I had as good hope of being well accepted there.

Prob. Why, my good Sir, what has inclined you to enter this road, and proceed thus far, if you fear you fhall be rejected? Permit us to travel with you, and let us hear your ftory.

[1] Ifaiah lv. 6.   [2] Pfalm cxxx. 3.

Frien. I am very glad of your company, and will relate my case to you, in a few words. I never was addicted to those vices that appear so notorious in others. I have always been remarkably serious, and a lover of good books. I also loved to hear the ambassadors of the *Celestial King* deliver their message. And tho' I am originally from *Flintshire*, and came young to your city, yet, by insensible degrees I was inclined to go on Pilgrimage. But, as I have not had such strong convictions on me, as you and others have felt, therefore, think I have not so good a testimony, that the king has called me unto himself.

Prob. Dear *Friendly*, I pity you. I am but young in these things. But, if I may hope to speak a word of comfort, it should be from our finding you in the direct road to the gate, and asking you one plain question.

Frien. Dear Sir, what is that?

Prob. Are you at all inclined to return to yonder city?

Frien. Embracing his companion, said, No! no! By the help of the king I will proceed. I know there is nothing but sin and death behind us; but I will now hope that there is life in this way, even for *me*. Wherefore, let us all join hand and heart pressing on to yonder gate.

These three friends went on talking of the *Celestial King*, and reading in *Probus*'s book, until they were suddenly stopped by the *Slough of Despond*, which threw them all into perplexity. At the same time a thick mist arose from the *Slough*, that darkened the bright prospect they before had of the other side, injured their eyes, and damped their spirits. *Friendly* was most affected by these things; after he had looked on each side, and perceived that the *Slough* stretched itself far off and wide, so that to seek its boundaries would be a fruitless task; he cried, " Alas, what an unworthy wretch am I! gladly would I go on in the pilgrim's road, and enter in at the gate;

A genuine Sign of a gracious Heart. but my heart-sins stare me in the face, my exceeding vileness has caused this insurmountable difficulty, not only to me, but to you also." My dear friends, what shall we do now?

Res. O, *Friendly*, be not so dispirited. Surely the king has not called us out of the land of destruction, to suffer us to perish

by

by this *Slough*, which *he only* can bring us over, and which I am perfuaded he will do? What fay you, friend *Probus?*

Prob. I remember that Mr. *Evangelift* cautioned me on my coming hither, to be careful in looking for the fteps over this *Slough*, which are defcribed in this book; but my eyes are fo hurt by this fog, that I fear it will be very difficult to difcover them.

While they were trembling on the brink of the *Slough*, and poring on their book, they perceived a perfon with a fweet afpect, on their right hand, coming towards them, whofe name they afterwards found was Mr. *Revelation*. When he came near, he thus addreffed them.

Revelation. Young men, wherefore do you tremble and look fo fad?

Prob. Sir, we are very defirous of going to the *Strait-gate*, but are ftopped by this filthy bog, and know not how to get over it.

Revel. I perceive you have a book in which the fteps are defcribed, why dont you confult it?

Prob. So we have heard; but, our eyes are fo injured by this pernicious mift, that we are unable to benefit by our book.

Revel. It is my bufinefs and delight to affift in fuch cafes[1].

Then Mr. *Revelation* took the book, and turning to a certain place, he read with a peculiar accent, " This is a faithful faying, and worthy of all acceptation, that *Immanuel* came into the world to fave the chief of rebels[2]—All manner of fin and blafphemy fhall be forgiven unto men[3]." While Mr. *Revelation* was reading thefe and other parts of the book, the fog was fuddenly difperfed, and the fun inftantly fhone out, fo that *Probus* and *Refolute* clearly faw the fteps over the *Slough*; and with very great thankfulnefs to Mr. *Revelation*[4], addreffed themfelves to pafs over. But *Friendly* ftill hefitated. On which, Mr. *Revelation*, with great energy, faid,

Revel. Why do you not follow your brethren? Are you not willing to enter in at the *Strait-gate*[5]?

[1] Matt. xi. 25. [2] 1 Tim. i. 15. [3] Matt. xii. 31. [4] Mat. xvi. 17.
[5] John v. 6.

Frien.

Frien. Willing! O yes, Sir, I am willing with all my foul.

Then faid Mr. *Revelation*, with ftill greater energy,

Revel. Whofoever *will*, let him come freely¹.

Thefe words fo animated *Friendly*, that he entered the *Slough*, found firm footing, and went on exclaiming,

Frien. Bleffed king! Bleffed book! Bleffed Mr. *Revelation!* Bleffed companions! I am willing to come, I rejoice to come, and triumph that there is hope, even for *me!*

Mr. *Revelation* having feen them all fafe over, returned the book, took his leave of them, and they went on finging,

> How fad our ftate by nature is!
> Our fin how deep it ftains!
> And Satan binds our captive minds,
> Faft in his flavifh chains.
>
> But there's a voice of fov'reign grace
> Sounds from the facred word;
> Ho! ye defpairing finners, come
> And truft upon the Lord.
>
> Our fouls obey the heav'nly call,
> And run to this relief,
> We would believe thy promife Lord,
> Oh, help our unbelief!
>
> Stretch out thine arm, victorious king,
> Our reigning fins fubdue.
> Drive the old dragon from his feat,
> With all his hellifh crew.
>
> Poor, guilty, weak and helplefs worms,
> On thy kind arms we fall:
> Be thou our ftrength and righteoufnefs,
> Our Jefus, and our all.
>
> WATTS.

¹ Rev. xxii. 17.

C H A P. II.

The Pilgrims pass by Mount Sinai. *They discourse with Mr.* Fleshly Wisdom. *Resolute attacked by a fiend. They enter in at the* Strait Gate.

THE Pilgrims went on apace, until they came over against *Mount Sinai*, which is a burning mountain [1] a little to the left of the road. It was at that time in a state of eruption. The fire and thick smoke ascended, and the flaming lava came rolling down its side towards our travellers. The earth quaked, and the Pilgrims hearts trembled. One Mr. *Legality*'s house, which stood on the declivity of the hill, was destroyed in their sight [2]: and lo! at the same time, a voice thundered from the mountain, in the following distinct words. "As many as are of the works of the law, are under the curse [3]." This exceedingly terrified the Pilgrims, and caused them to hasten towards the gate [4].

Frien. This is *Mount Sinai*. I have read much about it, but could never have imagined it to be so terrible as I now see it. Many have resorted to this mountain for a blessing, but you hear that only curses issue from it. It is placed near this road on purpose to convince us, that there is no help for us in any thing but *Immanuel*, unto whom we are going, by yonder gate. Let us hasten from this terrifying noise and dreadful danger.

The Pilgrims being advanced a considerable distance from *Mount Sinai*, perceived a well-looking man coming towards them, in a path on the left of the road. This person they found to be Mr. *Fleshly Wisdom* [5]. When he came to them he said,

Fleshly Wis. Your servant, Sirs. I am glad to see you on this rout: and as your countenances appear quite serious and well-disposed, I should be glad to enjoy your good company.

[1] Exodus xx. 18. [2] Rom. vii. 11. [3] Gal. iii. 10. [4] Gal. iii. 24
[5] 2 Cor. i. 12.

Prob.

Prob. We are going, Sir, to yonder gate: if that alfo is your way, you are welcome to our company.

Flefhly Wif. Religion is an excellent employment. My defire is ever to be engaged therein. But, there are many opinions in the world about the ways of religion.

Prob. Yet there is but one true way, I prefume; and that is by the gate unto which we are going?

Flefhly Wif. Some *few* divines infift on what you fay, but by far the *moft* are very different in their fentiments; and affert, that there is no neceffity to be fo attached to the way you are in; and that Mr. *Legality* can do as well for pilgrims as the man at the gate. But I have maturely weighed the arguments brought on either fide, and have reconciled them both, I think, in a juft and rational manner.

Prob. Pray, Sir, what do you mean? We juft now faw the houfe of Mr. *Legality* deftroyed by an eruption of *Mount Sinai*; and if he could not fave himfelf from that calamity, how can he be of any benefit to pilgrims?

Flefhly Wif. As to Mr. *Legality*, I think he is not *able* to do fo much as his admirers pretend that he can: and, as to the man at the gate, he *will* not do what thofe on his fide fay he will: therefore, I direct all whom I am acquainted with to the houfe of Mr. *Reformation*, juft by us, on the right fide of the road. This gentleman wafhes, new clothes, and inftructs pilgrims gratis, and thus prepares them to fpeak with the *Interpreter*. And indeed, it is unreafonable and indecent to appear before fo honourable a perfon in fuch filthy rags, and fo ignorant as many pilgrims really are.

Prob. What fay you, my brethren? I think this gentleman talks very reafonably.

Flefhly Wif. I will engage for your kind reception at that houfe, where you may abide fome time, and when you are properly qualified and difpofed, you may go from thence by a private path into the highway, on the other fide of the *Strait Gate*, near the *Interpreter*'s houfe; and thus avoid the hurt you may otherwife receive from the captain of yonder caftle, who is an implacable enemy to pilgrims.

Ref.

Ref. As to that castle, friend, I hope we are not afraid of the garrison therein; or him who governs them; wherefore, to avoid it, will be no inducement for me to follow your advice; especially as our brother's book says, that we must expect troubles in our way [1].

Frien. Pray, Sir, what may be your name?

Fleshly Wis. I am called in contempt *Fleshly Wisdom*, but my true name is *Human Wisdom*.

Frien. I suspected you by your discourse. Know therefore, Sir, that we will have none of your counsel. You may advise very well in matters of a secular nature, but you are now out of your sphere [2], and should yourself take *Evangelist* for your guide. My brethren, this man, with all his pretended love for religion is an utter stranger to it, and is ever seeking to pervert the right ways of *Immanuel*. Our king receives us just as we are, and does not expect that we can or should be washed, clothed, or taught by any but himself; and whoever pretends to do those things for pilgrims, is an impostor, and an enemy to the *Celestial King*. Your book, *Probus*, says, "that the king justifies the *ungodly* [3]." "That *Immanuel's* blood cleanseth from all *sin* [4]." And, " that he has a robe of righteousness for the naked [5]." Therefore my advice is, that we keep on in our way to the gate.

Prob. Brother *Friendly*, I thank you for your information, and will follow your counsel.

Ref. I did not half like his fawning manner. Wherefore, Sir, pray depart, and seek a better employ than your present wicked one.

Fleshly Wis. I perceive that my good intentions towards you, are frustrated by your conceited minds; therefore I will leave you.

The Pilgrims rejoiced after they had escaped this flatterer, and hastened towards the gate. On the left side of this gate is a strong castle, belonging to the *Black Tyrant*, who keeps a numerous garrison therein, to prevent or molest those who knock for entrance at the *Strait Gate*. As the Pilgrims approached, they

[1] John xvi. 33. [2] 1 Cor. ii. 14. [3] Rom. v. 6. [4] 1 John i. 7. [5] Isaiah lxi. 10.

saw

saw an ugly fiend issue from the castle, and make towards them. On this they ran towards the gate, but *Resolute* being hindmost was attacked by the monster, who, coming up to him, with a dreadful voice, told him to go back, or he would instantly punish him as a deserter.

Res. It is true, I am a deserter from your infernal army, in which I have served too many years, and too faithfully: but, since a better prince than yours has condescended to beat up for volunteers in our country, I am resolved to offer myself to him, and be his servant, if he will but accept me; to know which, I and my friends are making this journey: neither will I go back again let the consequence be as it will.

This bold answer exceedingly enraged the fiend, so that he flew at him like a lion. But *Resolute*, altho' unarmed, yet being naturally bold, and inwardly strengthened by a good cause, made the enemy sensible of his power, by many shrewd blows: but at length *Resolute* received a dreadful fall, and the fiend improving his advantage, fell on him with an intent to tear him in pieces [1].

In the mean time *Probus* and *Friendly* ran hastily to the gate, and being eager to save their friend, they knocked vehemently for entrance. They were speedily heard, and *Goodwill* [2] opened the gate, with an heavenly smile on his countenance. The Pilgrims bowed low at his feet, begged to be admitted, and prayed that he would give assistance to their dear brother *Resolute*.

Goodwill. Enter, my children, the good of this house is before you.

Then *Goodwill* casting his eyes forward, and seeing the wretched plight poor *Resolute* was in; he instantly spake with amazing authority,

Goodwill. Oh thou enemy of all righteousness [3], wilt thou not cease to trouble those who would come in hither? Get

[1] Luke ix. 42.   [2] Deut. xxxiii. 16.   [3] Acts xiii. 10.

thee hence, to thy prison. "Is not this a brand plucked out of the fire¹?"

On this the fiend arose from *Resolute*, and inwardly chafed, returned to his castle. Then *Goodwill* ran towards the fallen Pilgrim², and taking him by the hand, lifted him up, saying, Peace be unto thee, my son. As soon as *Goodwill* had touched *Resolute*, his wounds were healed, and he walked joyfully into the house.

Goodwill. You are all welcome here, I refuse none who knock at this gate. You see in me all the readiness of your king, to receive those who come unto him at his invitation. For he says, "Come unto me, all ye that are weary and heavy laden, and I will give you rest³. He who cometh unto me, I will in no wise cast out⁴."

Then they *all* cried out, What are we that any favour should be shewn by our king to us!

Goodwill. Not for your righteousness are you at all accepted, nor shall your sins prevent farther grace being manifested to you. The king himself inclined you to come to this gate, he drew your hearts out towards *Immanuel*⁵. He now shews you his *Goodwill* towards poor sinners, and you will soon see greater things than these.

Prob. I thank you, Sir, for your inexpressible kindness to us; but we were almost perverted from the way to this gate, by Mr. *Fleshly Wisdom*.

Goodwill. That busy one will be medling to his hurt, and to the damage of all those who follow his counsel. His endeavours in the end, will have the same pernicious effects on the soul, as those of the *Black Tyrant* in the adjacent castle, altho' he thinks far otherwise. For, it will at last be found, that *Fleshly Wisdom* and *Satan*, however contrary at times they may appear to each other, yet are united in one cause, namely, to prevent pilgrims from freely entering this gate of *Immanuel*.

---

¹ Zach. iii. 2.   ² Luke xv. 20.   ³ Matt. xi. 28.   ⁴ John vi. 37.
⁵ John vi. 44.

Ref. Since my conflict with the enemy I think I am better than ever I was in my life!

Goodwill. You will ever find it so, my son. No man ever was, nor ever will be a loser, by his opposition to the *Black Usurper.* He who fighteth the battles of the *Celestial King*, hath good wages, and is sure of victory. " Be thou faithful unto death, and *Immanuel* will give you a crown of life [1]."

Frien. Sir, we would proceed on our journey by your leave, and should be glad of any direction from you.

Goodwill. With all my heart. You have heard of the house of the *Interpreter*. Keep on in this strait path, and you cannot miss it. There, it will be told you what you must do; and I wish you all, great peace, and abounding consolation.

The Pilgrims then took their leave, and went on singing,

> Why were we made to hear thy voice,
>   And enter while there's room:
> When thousands make a wretched choice,
>   And rather die than come?
>
> 'Twas thine own grace that made us fear,
>   That sweetly forc'd us in:
> Else we had never enter'd here,
>   But perish'd in our sin.
>
> Pity the nations, O our God!
>   Constrain the earth to come;
> Send thy victorious word abroad,
>   And bring the strangers home.
>
> We long to see thy churches full,
>   That all the chosen race
> May with one voice, and heart and soul,
>   Sing thy redeeming grace.
>
>   WATTS.

[1] Rev. ii. 10.

CHAP. III.

The Pilgrims arrive at the house of the Interpreter. *An account of what they saw there.*

AFTER the Pilgrims had finished their song, they went on discoursing with great satisfaction of the dangers they had escaped, the favours they had already received, and the reason they had to hope, that they should experience every blessing and comfort flowing from the blood of prince *Immanuel,* even the forgiveness of all their sins, according to the riches of his grace [1]. They were in warm expectation of what they should see and hear at the house of the *Interpreter,* when it appeared in sight. Being arrived at the door, they knocked, the porter opened to them, and asked who they were, and what they would have?

Prob. We are poor lost sinners, and are desirous of knowing more fully how we are to be saved: being recommended hither by Mr. *Goodwill.*

Porter. Whosoever will, let him come in freely [2].

So he opened the door, and conducted them to his master [3]; who ordered food and drink to be set before them; and when they had refreshed themselves, he enquired what had induced them to go on pilgrimage, and what they had seen in the way? To which they answered as above. Then he shewed them all the rarities of the house, at the same time telling them that it was his office to instruct their minds in those important truths which most deeply concerned them; that they might know how to behave in their future progress.

Now besides the many curiosities of this house, which others have mentioned, there was a spacious gallery of pictures, that

[3] Eph. i. 7. [4] Rev. xxii. 17. [5] Job xxxiii. 23.

afforded

afforded great pleasure and instruction to these young men. The first piece presented a woman whose countenance was smiling; pleasure sparkled in her eyes, while she seemed to speak with earnestness unto two reverend persons who stood near her.

Frien. What may this picture represent to us, Sir?

Interpreter. That piece, my son, is the work of that most accurate painter, and beloved physician, *St. Luke*[1]. That woman is the sincere convert *Lydia*, whose heart *Immanuel* opened at *Philippi*[2]. You may perceive the sweet effect the word had on her heart, by the pleasure in her aspect. Here was no thunder or terror; all was calm and gentle, yet was it not less efficacious. Her whole heart was engaged to hear of, and opened to receive *Immanuel*; and she, is here represented as praying the ambassadors of our king to come into her house, and abide with her. Those persons therefore who receive *Immanuel* into their hearts, love his faithful servants, and obey his word and ordinances; tho' they may not, like others, be able to tell of great terrors of conscience, dreadful shakings over the pit, and powerful applications of particular parts of the word of our king; yet, by this example of *Lydia*, they ought to take courage, and trust in the mercy of *Immanuel*.

At this *Friendly* looked on his brethren, with tears of joy, and said,

Frien. Thou, O *Celestial King*, maketh me glad through thy word. Surely there is yet hope in *Israel* concerning unworthy me!

Interpreter. Our king speaks often in the soft still voice of his spirit, and not always in the tempest, thunder, and earthquake of terrible convictions[3].

From this, they turned to another piece, which was wholly different from the former. It represented the effects of a dreadful earthquake in the night; a prison with its foundations shaken[4]; two men, of the same aspect as those in the other picture, stood just without the prison; and another in great dis-

[1] Col. iv. 14.   [2] Acts xvi. 14, 15.   [3] 1 Kings xix. 11, 12.   [4] Acts xvi. 26.

tress

ſtreſs was fallen down before them, and ſeemed to ſpeak in the moſt earneſt concern unto them.

Ref. This appears to be a ſcene of great trouble. Pray, Sir, oblige us with an explanation of it.

Interpret. This is the priſon of *Philippi*, into the inner part of which thoſe two perſons, ambaſſadors of the *Celeſtial King*, were thruſt by *that* man on the ground, who ſeems to tremble in every limb. He had alſo ſorely whipped them, made them faſt in a moſt uneaſy poſture, and exerciſed great barbarity towards them. But, at midnight, while they ſang praiſes to their king (who would not ſuffer ſuch precious birds to be ſo vilely confined); he ſhook the priſon, burſt the doors, and broke their chains; at the ſame time, he pierced the harder heart of the jailor, whom you perceive all aſtoniſhment, and inquiring for ſalvation of the very men, whom he had juſt before mortally hated and cruelly puniſhed. Thus does our king deal with perſecuting ſinners, ſuch as *Manaſſah*[1], *Saul*, and this jailor: and all this is to humble their proud hearts, that they may be ſaved by grace alone. Our king wounds in order to heal.

Ref. Dear Sir, you may inform others who ſee this picture, that this jailor is a figure of *Will Reſolute*; I deſpiſed good men, I loved bad men and wicked practices, but the king has terrified me with apprehenſions of death, judgment, and hell, ſo as to make me tremble like this ſinner, and cry out, What muſt I do to be ſaved?

Interpret. And like theſe miniſters of our king, I ſay unto you, Believe in the prince *Immanuel*, and you ſhall be ſaved, and ſhall ſoon have it manifeſted unto you.

Ref. Lord, I believe! Help thou my unbelief[2]!

Interpret. The next is a truly evangelical piece. It is the Prodigal's return to his father[3]. It was drawn by the inimitable hand of our prince *Immanuel*, and glows with the warmth of divine love, and the genuine effects of the king's grace on the

---

[1] 2 Chron. xxxiii. 10 to 13.—Acts ix. 4.   [2] Mark ix. 24.   [3] Luke xv.

heart of a rebel. Mark the speaking features of the son, looking at his injured father with the utmost affection and confusion! Behold the amazing tenderness of the father! How he hangs on his neck, and kisses the ragged foundling! This reception works so powerfully on the penitent, that he can hardly support himself under it. So, some sinners are more affected with *Immanuel*'s love in dying for his enemies, than with any fears of the vengeance of our king. This is a good evidence of a gracious work on the soul.

Prob. Ah, Sir, you have spoke my very heart, which has been ready to break in viewing a crucified Saviour; when, reflections on the torments of *Hell* have made no impression on me.

Interpret. All these things worketh that one and the self-same Spirit, dividing graces as well as gifts to every man severally as it [1] pleaseth him; and in them all, he glorifies *Immanuel*, and him only.

Ref. This next scene seems to be a martial one. Here are two armies in battle array, and the space between them is filled with two principal figures, which appear very different from each other in several respects. Pray, Sir, who do they represent?

Interpret. That is a representation of the 17th chapter of the first book of Samuel. The enormous figure between the armies, is the impious *Goliath*; and that ruddy boy is the pious *David*, who, in height, was little more than half the stature of his enemy, and who could hardly have carried his spear. Here you see this young *Israelite* in the spirit of *that* verse, which says, that *David ran to meet the Philistine*. Neither the monstrous stature, brazen armour, ponderous shield, nor terrible menaces of the giant, made any impression of fear on *David*'s mind. The reason of this was, his stedfast faith in the God of *Israel*. Tho', but a youth in stature and years, he was a giant, a *Methuselah* in faith. Read his manner of reasoning, admire it, and bear it ever on your minds. " The *Lord* who delivered me

[1] 1 Cor. xii. 11.

out of the paw of the lion, and out of the paw of the bear, will also deliver me out of the hand of this Philistine; for who is this uncircumcised Philistine, that he should defy the armies of the living God?" *David* saw *Goliath* marked as an enemy unto God, therefore despised all his parade, pride and power. So, my children, let your practice be. In no wise fear your enemies, however strong and crafty they may be; for they are the enemies of your *Lord*. Like *David*, set your faces as a flint. Like this zealous youth, run forward to oppose the foe. And, like him, despise all human schemes of defence, all untried and doubtful methods of attack; but, go to battle in the name of that God who has often delivered you, and has promised ever to be with you, and to make you more than conquerors[1]—*Probus*, I perceive that your attention is drawn towards a softer subject.

Prob. I believe I can guess the history of this picture, in which is a fair but disordered female, sitting on a couch, and a young man fleeing from her with the utmost precipitation.

Interpret. That excellent piece was drawn by *Moses* the Great, from a matter of fact[2], that forms a part of one of the most instructing and affecting stories that ever was written. You see the beauty of that woman: she is the worthless wife of *Potiphar*. Let not your eyes dwell on her charms; but, like that young fugitive, look thro' her fair form, to the base and deformed soul that animated it. You see *Joseph* looks not on the dangerous flame of her eyes, but averts his face. You observe, he will not endure the pernicious magic of her arms, but breaks away, and is fleeing from the unequal conflict, where, but to tarry, is to fall. The reason of this conduct, is also founded on his faith. *Joseph* saw in this room, however retired, not only his beauteous mistress, but his awful and glorious God, in whose sight the action unto which he was solicited was an attrocious crime; therefore he exclaimed, with astonishment at her infidelity, "How can I do this great wickedness, and sin against God!" My dear sons, go, and do likewise. You admired the prowess of *David*, in the last picture; but, *Joseph* shewed far greater courage. It is better far, to engage an armed *Goliath*, than to be

[1] Rom. viii. 37.   [2] Gen. xxxix.

exposed

exposed to the snares of a fair wanton. In this case, to flee, is to conquer. Flee youthful lusts[1]. Turn away your eyes from beholding vanity[2]. Suffer not your minds to dwell on any impure objects. Set the *Lord* always before you[3]; and tho' for the present you may suffer by your virtuous conduct, as did *Joseph*; yet, *God* will be with you in trouble, as he was with that amiable youth; and as *he* was raised to be next unto *Pharoah*, so shall every virtuous conqueror sit down with *Jesus* on his throne[4].

Frien. Sir, your lecture is most seasonable unto us young men, and demands our warmest thanks. If I am not mistaken, this next picture will point us, to the means by which we may be furnished for this warfare, and for every good work.

Interpret. You are right indeed, *Friendly*. That amiable young man is king *Josiah*, in the 26th year of his age[5]. He is reading the book of the law, which the high-priest found in the temple. Observe, how solemn is his aspect. How the tears pour from his eyes. And how his whole frame seems to tremble under a sense of his own and his people's sins. You see also the eye of *Heaven* from above, fixed upon the royal penitent: all this is expressive of that solemn declaration of *God*. " To this man will I look, who is poor and of a contrite spirit, and who trembles at my word.[6]" Here, my sons, is a pattern for you to follow thro' all your pilgrimage. Pray that your hearts may be tender, as was that of this pious king. Lay *God*'s word before you; by that only can young men be strong, and overcome the evil one[7]. Read the law of our *King* with a deep sense of your own and others sins; and cry to him, by faith in *Immanuel*, for mercy for yourself and them : in doing this, you may ever be assured of the attention of your heavenly father.—One only scene remains now for you to see.

Prob. Surely this gracious person, whose countenance is so full of benevolence, is intended to signify the *Lord* of pilgrims?

[1] 2 Tim. ii. 22.   [2] Psalm cxix. 37.   [3] Psalm xvi. 8.   [4] Rev. iii. 21.
[5] 2 Kings xxii. 1, 3. & xxiii. 3.   [6] Isaiah lxvi. 2.   [7] 1 John ii. 14.

Interpret. It is so. And in it, you may see something of those words of the evangelist, viz. *And Jesus beholding him, loved him*[1]. You see, he is looking with divine pity and tenderness after that youth, who has turned his back on him and heaven, and is retiring in great confusion and sorrow. Mistaken youth, how little did he know of his own heart! What a wretch is he, who in such a choice hesitates at all! But how unspeakably despicable are *his* sentiments, who loveth this perishing world more than *Immanuel!* Take heed, therefore, and beware of covetousness. Let the words of *Jesus* ever ring in your ears. " It is[2] easier for a camel to go through the eye of a needle, than for a rich man to enter into the kingdom of Heaven." Every one is grasping after those things, as if riches were easy to manage: but, *God* knows that they are not, and therefore has most wisely ordered, that very few of those he loves shall be tried that way. " Love not the world, nor the things that are in the world; if any man love the world, the love of the father is not in him[3]."

In the morning the Pilgrims being desirous to depart, the *Interpreter* dismissed them, at the same time exhorting them, to think frequently on what he had shewn them: and promised that they should very soon, see greater things than these. So they departed with thankfulness to the *Interpreter*, joyfully singing.

> Let all the heathen writers join,
> To form one perfect book;
> Great *God*, if once compar'd with thine,
> How mean their writings look!
>
> Thy word is everlasting truth,
> How pure is every page!
> That holy book shall guide our youth,
> And well support our age.
> WATTS.

[1] Mark x. 21.   [2] Mark x. 25.   [3] 1 John ii. 15.

CHAP. IV.

The Pilgrims arrive at the Cross. Deist, Arius, Socinus, *and* Lord Search, *appear. Discourse between them.* Prince Paraclete *appears to the Pilgrims. They depart; overtake, and discourse with father* Simon *and his wife.*

SOON after the Pilgrims had left the *Interpreter*'s house, they entered the narrow way that was fenced on each side with the walls of salvation.

Prob. I cannot but admire the materials and workmanship of these excellent walls on each side of us. The foundations seem to be laid with the most durable and beautiful stones, and the contexture is inimitably fine. Surely the nature and wisdom of the contrivance must be divine!

Frien. Dear *Probus*, The whole is the labour of *Heaven*. The design was formed in the counsels of our king from everlasting, and the materials and construction are the work of the great *Immanuel*, as anointed by *Prince Paraclete* the eternal Spirit. O how perfectly safe are those men, to whom salvation is appointed for walls and Bulwarks[1]!

Ref. Safe indeed! And why may not we hope to be thus secured? I am by far the greatest sinner amongst us, but here is an inscription on this wall which testifies, that it was built to save the CHIEF of sinners[2]; and you may perceive certain memorandums here and there, of persons, of the most vile character, who have received the benefit you speak of. Wherefore let us hope the best, and humbly wait for that consolation, which our friends have given us reason to expect, from our gracious king;

[1] Isaiah xxvi. 1.   [2] 1 Tim. i. 15.

who hath himself, by his counsel and oath, ratified it; that those who flee for refuge to *Immanuel*, shall have strong consolation[1]. Are not we such refugees?

Just as *Resolute* said these words, they beheld at a distance before them an high cross, and *him* who was nailed on it. The distant sight of him gave them all fresh spirits, and greater expectations: so they hastened towards it. When they arrived at the foot of the cross, they stopped, and looked awhile on him whom they had pierced[2]. Then they sat down under his shadow, with their faces towards the illustrious sufferer, and each mourned apart with the most unfeigned sorrow.

Res. O *Immanuel!* who am I, or what is my father's house, that thou shouldest bring me hitherto[3]! Lord, I am not worthy of the least of thy mercies; and much less of one drop of thy precious blood, which thou didst pour out for *me!* Is this bloody scene transacted for *me*, a brand of hell! Dost thou thus, Oh, dear Redeemer, dost thou thus bear *my* sins in thy body on the tree[4]? Then,

" Furnish me, Lord, with heav'nly arms,
" From grace's magazine;
" And I'll proclaim eternal war,
" With every darling sin." WATTS.

Frien. Thou hast overcome me, Oh *Immanuel!* My doubts and fears are dissipated. I marvel, that thou didst so long bear with my perverseness! And hast now crowned thy love to me, by this glorious manifestation! Oh that my head were waters, and mine eyes fountains of tears[5], that they might dissolve in love and tenderness to thee, my bleeding Saviour. Like the once darkened sun,

" So let me hide *my blushing face*,
" While thy dear cross appears,
" Dissolve my heart in thankfulness;
" And melt mine eyes to tears!" WATTS.

Prob. Was ever any sorrow like unto thy sorrow, Oh thou wonderful sufferer! Was ever any sins like my sins, who am

[1] Heb. vi. 18. [2] Zech. xii. 10, &c. [3] 2 Sam. vii. 18. [4] 1 Pet. ii. 24.
[5] Jerem. ix. 1.

the vileſt of men! I ſee, I feel, O *Immanuel*, that thou doſt fully and freely forgive me; but, I cannot forgive myſelf. Oh, *Lamb of God*, break my heart, while I meditate on thy love in dying for me!

"See from his head, his hands and feet,
"Sorrow and love flow mingled down!
"Did e'er ſuch love and ſorrow meet,
"Or thorns compoſe ſo rich a crown!

"Were the whole realm of nature mine,
"That were a preſent far too ſmall,
"Love ſo amazing, ſo divine;
"Demands my ſoul, my life, my all!" WATTS.

Then a loud voice came from the croſs, ſaying, "Look unto me, and be ye ſaved [1]; For I, even I only, am *Jehovah*, and beſides me there is no Saviour[2]." This opened afreſh the ſprings of grief, ſo that they were all ſwallowed up in "Godly ſorrow, which worketh repentance unto ſalvation.[3]"

While the Pilgrims were thus exerciſed, they were diſturbed by the ſound of feet and voices, coming from the way oppoſite to that in which they came: and looking thither, they ſaw three men drawing near the croſs, whoſe names they afterwards underſtood to be *Deiſt*, *Arius*, and *Socinus*. When theſe perſons perceived the ſtate of mind that the Pilgrims were in, and heard their lamentations; they ſet up a loud laugh, and declared, that they were beſide themſelves. Then looking up to the croſs, *Arius* ſaid,

Arius. This ſufferer was an excellent perſon!

Juſt as he uttered theſe words, up came a reſpectable perſonage from the left-hand croſs-way, whoſe name was *Lord Search*, a noble *Berean* [4]; he, looking up with a ſerene countenance, turned to *Arius*, and ſaid,

Search. An excellent perſon indeed! There is not in the univerſe a perſon more wonderful, for this is the incarnate *God Jehovah*.

[1] Iſaiah xlv. 22.   [2] Iſaiah xliii. 2.   [3] 2 Cor. vii. 10.   [4] Acts xvii. 11.

Arius.

Arius. I cannot say so: nor is there any necessity arising from scripture, for giving him such a divine title. It is sufficient, that we acknowledge him to be a *God*, and superior to angels. But it is irrational to consider a suffering person as the supreme Being.

Search. You appear, Sir, to be in a very dangerous error. The scriptures plainly ascribe divine names and perfections unto him. Besides, the circumstances we are in, require, that our Saviour should be Almighty: but, if he was not *God* equal with the Father, he could not make an atonement for our sins.

Socinus. Atonement! I hope no man of sense, as you, Sir, appear to be, will insist on that absurd opinion, and thus unite with such enthusiasts as set there; who are quite mad with that wild notion.

Search. As to my understanding, it is none of the best: but, the scriptures fully establish this blessed truth. What you deem absurd, I see to be quite consistent, and perfectly orthodox.

Socinus. Orthodox! For shame, Sir, drop such antiquated words and tenets. This person was a wise teacher of morality, a bright example of piety, and a glorious martyr for the truth of his doctrine. This was the whole design of his mission, and is quite sufficient to save us, if we are not wanting to ourselves.

Search. If this is all, I cannot see why *Socrates* may not save us as well as *Immanuel*. In short, Sir, I find old words and ways are best. I can by no means like your unscriptural notions in religion, nor approve of that dogmatical pride assumed by your party; by which you lay an exclusive claim to reason, and brand with opprobrious names such as dissent from you. The agony of *Immanuel* in the garden, will for ever stand in opposition to your opinions. For, suppose it not to be caused by the sins of men, then laid upon him[1], the sufferer will appear very far from being an example of intrepidity. Nor were things much better on the cross; for, many of his disciples have endured as cruel deaths, with apparently greater courage and heroism.

[1] Isaiah. liii. 6.

Your notion, therefore, of *Immanuel*'s death being only as a witness unto the truth, or an example unto his followers; is destroyed by plain matters of fact.—But if it be considered as a sacrifice for our sins, as it really was; then all the offerings, and bloody rites of the Old Testament appear proper and significant: and the horror and agonies of *Immanuel* in the garden are well accounted for; as are also, his dolorous cries on the cross. Did you, Sir, know what a hell the guilt of sin creates in the conscience, you would eagerly seek for some one to remove it, and gladly embrace the glad tidings of the gospel, which asserts, " that this person gave his life a ransom for many[1], and his soul a sacrifice for sin[2]."

Drift. I find you will not agree in your opinions. And indeed this notion of *Christ* had better never been known in the world, for it has been the source of infinite mischiefs. If such a person did ever exist in the world, he never pretended to say, nor ever did, what is related of him. If I had *my* will, I would overthrow this cross, and leave this high road unencumbered with all such superstitions.

Search. I do not take upon me, Sir, to defend the sallies of fanatical minds; however, I look upon your party to be blinded by the grossest prejudices. That there really was such a person in the world, cannot reasonably be denied; and that he taught and did as is written of him, is equally certain; as hath been abundantly proved against you: but I have not time at present to enter further into the argument with you.

So saying, *Lord Search* blessed him, who hung on the cross, and departed in the road to the right of the highway. Afterwards the other three went off in the road to the left of the cross, disputing very warmly on the above subject.

While the aforesaid persons were in dispute, the Pilgrims sat contemplating the great Redeemer in his labour of love for them: and when they heard him thus treated by the disputants, they were amazed, and heartily blessed the king, for giving them such powerful internal arguments, in their own hearts,

[1] Matt. xx. 28.   [2] Isaiah liii. 10.

of the truth and sufficiency of the Christian religion. To confirm them yet more therein, behold a voice the second time came from the cross, saying, "Sons, your sins are forgiven you, go in peace[1]." With this, came a power which they had not felt before, which overthrew every doubt that remained in their minds; answered all their objections, "and filled them with all joy and peace in believing[2]." Then suddenly a light shone round them, and *Prince Paraclete*, from the celestial court, appeared, who commanded them to strip themselves, and clothed them with change of raiment; saying,

Prince. Oh, men greatly beloved! Behold, I bring you the garments of salvation, and robes of righteousness[3], which are the manufactory of the *Celestial City*. Your glorious Saviour wrought them by his life and death. No other beings, however excellent, are permitted to wear them; put them on therefore, and angels may envy you such honour.

Then he sealed them in their foreheads[4], gave each of them a white stone, with a new name in it[5], and vanished away. The Pilgrims were now in an extacy of pleasure. Each appeared to the other as better than himself; and all were happy. Then, after bowing down at the foot of the cross, they departed, singing,

"Oh the sweet wonders of that cross,
"Where *God* the Saviour lov'd and dy'd!
"Her noblest life my spirit draws,
"From his dear wounds and bleeding side."

WATTS.

Frien. My brethren, I never thought that such pleasures were in reserve for such a wretch as I am: But now I feel such love to *Immanuel*, and delight in his ways, that I am ready to say with the spouse, "Yea, he is altogether lovely! And he is my beloved, and my friend[6]!"

Ref. I wonder not now at the faith and courage of the blessed martyrs, which I have read so much of: methinks I could em-

[1] Luke vii. 48, 50.   [2] Rom. xv. 13.   [3] Isaiah lxi. 10.   [4] Eph. i. 13.
[5] Rev. ii. 17.   [6] Cant. v. 16.

brace

brace a stake, for blessed *Immanuel*; sing on the dreadful wheel, or triumph on the tormenting rack: *Immanuel* is dearer unto me than life, and more precious to me than all the most desirable things!

Prob. I am glad to find your souls thus happy. I rejoice with you, and find every thought, brought sweetly into captivity to the obedience of *Immanuel*[1]. Let us sing,

" Dearest of all the names above,
" My Jesus and my God,
" Who can resist thy heavenly love,
" Or trifle with thy blood."

" Sweet Jesus, when thy face appears,
" My hope, my joy begins,
" Thy name forbids my slavish fears,
" Thy grace removes my sins." WATTS.

As the Pilgrims went on thus rejoicing, they overtook an elderly man and woman, whom *Probus* thought he knew to be father *Simon* and his wife. As the young men passed by, the old persons considered them very attentively.

Ref. Well, Father, what think you of us, after your scrutiny?

Simon. Think, why by your garments, and the matter of your songs, I find you are Pilgrims; but by your pace, noise, and tumultuous behaviour before you come up with us, I took you to be a knot of drunken topers.

Ref. Father, we have seen and heard such things as make our hearts glad.

Simon. Others, I suppose, have seen as much, and yet do not break the rules of decorum. I fear that you will give the world reason for what they say of pilgrims; namely, that they are mad men and enthusiasts. I have been on the road a great while, but I cannot say that I ever saw such extravagances before.

[1] 2 Cor. x. 5.

Ref.

Ref. Have *you* been on this road a great while, and got no further? Why *we* entered it but very lately, and have overtaken you. We think that we have not ran as we ought to have done, surely then, Father, you must have strangely loitered?

Simon. Ye are hot-headed young men, with strong passions, and e'er long, will probably run as fast back again.

Prob. I think, Sir, if you loved pilgrims, you would rejoice to see them alive, and lively in the king's highway; and would encourage them to go on, instead of filling their minds with needless fears about their present tempers, or future declensions. Are not our expressions of joy within the bounds of scripture? Are our passions forbid to meddle with sacred things? Or, are not the servants of our prince represented as being filled with the Spirit; the fruits of which are love, joy, peace, &c.[1]? I fear that you are cold-hearted yourself, and are pleading an excuse for your own faults, rather than the cause of true religion. Is not your name *Simon?*

Simon. Yes; and this is my sober spouse. We are well known in the way of pilgrims. We have been at the cross, as well as you, but we took care to guard against all intemperate sallies of religious zeal, as much as we would against the grosser intoxications of the flesh.

Prob. You are the person I took you to be. You are known among pilgrims for taxing your creditors bills. There is a true report got abroad of you, that when you had reduced a bill so low as to fifty pence, yet then it was found that you could not pay one farthing[2]; but, was obliged to submit to the mercy of your creditor: and what is worse, when he freely forgave you all the debt, you loved him but little, and found fault with him for forgiving others; whereas, you should have loved him much, for not throwing you into a jail, and been glad to see his grace extended to others. We tax not our Lord's bills. We acknowledge the debt of ten thousand talents; and since our king has freely forgiven us all, we are endeavouring by our songs and services, to express a joyful sense of our obligations.

[1] Gal. v. 22, 23.   [2] Luke vii. 42.

Simon. Aye, aye, I well know ye all. There is the fwearing, carding, fighting *Refolute:* and you, *Probus*, who ufed to make the tavern ring with obfcene fongs. Shall I allow myfelf to have been as bad as you? No, no; and I much fufpect, that this flafh of religion among you will foon go out in fmoke.

Frien. Father *Simon*, I have heard you with trembling. You cannot impeach *my* character of any grofs fins, yet I am fully convinced, that my nature is as vile as any man's, and has in it the feeds of every iniquity; which at times I have found fpringing up, and only wanted opportunity, courage, or fome other means, to have produced the moft profligate fruits. This leads me to confider my obligations to my Saviour to be as great as any perfon's in the world, and makes me thus zealous in my returns of love.

Wife. You all feem to be very fenfible perfons. I wonder you cannot walk orderly in the way, as we do; and not ufe fuch geftures as become ftage players rather than pilgrims. I perceive there is a village juft before us; we fhall be finely hooted and ftared at, if you continue your noife and anticks.

Ref. You feem to be well matched for keeping each other from religious furfeits; but your cooling lectures will have little influence on me. For if this is to be vile[1], I intend to be more vile; and, if poffible, fhame and roufe fuch as you from your criminal lethargy. We are penitent fpendthrifts, juft returned unto our dear father's houfe: we have juft had a precious meal on the fatted calf, and we truft that this is but the beginning of our mirth: and, O thou fnarling elder brother, remember that our father fays, " It is *meet* we fhould fing and make merry, fince we who were dead, are alive again; we who were loft, are found[2]."

Simon. Adieu, you go too faft for us. I dread to follow you thro' yonder village, and heartily wifh that we had paffed it before you.

[1] 2 Sam. vi. 22.   [2] Luke xv. 32.

CHAP. V.

The Pilgrims enter the village named Carelefs. *What paffed there. They are driven from thence, and joined by Mr.* Sincere.

THE happy Pilgrims went on apace in the king's highway, until they came into a village, which is built on the left fide of the road.. The name of it is *Carelefs*; it is inhabited by the children of *Simple*, *Sloth*, and *Prefumption*; for tho' themfelves were hanged for their crimes, yet they left behind them a numerous iffue, which increafed very faft, had now built this village, and trod in their father's fteps. As the Pilgrims went by, they obferved that fome were at cards, others afleep, and fome were burning books, which appeared like bibles. This fight filled the Pilgrims with indignation: and, being warm with love to their king, full of the fire of youth, and zealous to make all men fee and act like themfelves; they turned a little out of the way, to expoftulate with them.

Prob. What mean ye, [1] O fleepers? Arife, and call upon God, leaft you perifh in your fins.

On this the fleepers arofe, and ftared about them; and many others ran towards the Pilgrims, to hear what they had to fay.

Sleepers. Wherefore, Sirs, do you thus difturb us?

Prob. Becaufe ye are fleeping on the brink of deftruction.

Sleep. We are fpending our time as did our fathers, who lived a quiet and peaceable life, and died like lambs.

Prob. According to the beft accounts, your fathers were hanged; and if you fleep on thus, you will follow the generation of your fathers, and will never fee light[2].

[1] Jonah. i. 6.   [2] Pfalm xlv. 19.

Carelefs.

Carders. Gentlemen, you are very severe on our neighbours, who are an honest and well-meaning people.

Frien. I cannot think that you will condemn *their* sloth in the most important matters; because ye yourselves are equally guilty.

Card. What, in playing a harmless game at cards?

Frien. You can never prove it to be an harmless practice, to squander thus your precious time; if there was no other evil in it.

Card. All men stand in need of some recreation.

Frien. As did your fathers in the wilderness, who sat down to eat and drink, and rose up to [1] play before their idol *God:* so I perceive you have done, and if you persist in such crimes, you will reap their punishment.

Card. We believe there is no danger but what arises in *your* gloomy minds.

Frien. Ye are simple ones indeed; and will continue in your simplicity.

Presumption. I perceive, Sir, that you take most of your discourse from this book which I am destroying. I am sure it has ever perplexed mens minds, and spoiled good company: I wish I could burn every copy of it.

Ref. If you could do that, you must slay your conscience too, or you would not have perfect peace.

Presump. Conscience! that is only the prejudice of education, which, thanks to reason, I have nearly overcome.

Ref. I have read of a king who once employed [2] himself in such an impious work as you have been about; and he received such a reward as you are likely to have.

Presump. Who was he, I pray; and how was he rewarded?

Ref. His name was *Jehoiakim*, a king of *Judah.* He died like a dog, and had the burial of an ass[3]; and was a means of

[1] Exod. xxxii. vi.   [2] Jerem. xxxvi. 23.   [3] Jerem. xxii. 19.

increasing

increasing that divine revelation which he endeavoured to destroy[1]. Beware, therefore, thou despiser of God's word[2], lest thou perish without mercy.

While this dispute was carrying on; there was one [3] *Balaam*, a very crafty man, and a religious renegado, who got together several careless daughters of the village, brought them half naked, and dancing in a wanton manner, before the young Pilgrims: who, remembering the picture of *Joseph*, and advice of the *Interpreter*; immediately hastened into the road, and ran out of the village, much wondering at the ignorance and prophaneness of the people.

Altho' it seemed at first as if the Pilgrims had done no good in that village; yet it appeared afterwards, that the people could neither sleep, play, or blaspheme so cordially as they did before; and several of the card-players were observed to be much in reflection.

As for the Pilgrims, they went on chearfully until they came to the foot of the hill *Difficulty*; at which they made no hesitation, but all three went to the spring to refresh themselves, before they went up the ascent. Here they sat down, and drank plentifully from the word of life[4]. While they were thus employed, they perceived a man running towards them, from the road on the right side of the hill, called *Danger*; as he drew near, they saw that his clothes were those of a pilgrim, but sadly disordered and defiled; his visage was pale and dejected, and he trembled exceedingly. When he came to the road, he took no notice of them; but turned, and began to ascend the hill as fast as he could. On this *Probus* said,

Prob. Ho, Friend, will you not take company with you?

Sincere. I have been so deceived by company, that I am afraid of every man I meet.

Prob. There is great reason for circumspection, no doubt, in the choice of our company: but, praised be our king, his true pilgrims are not now so scarce, that a man should walk alone: come, make trial of us.

[1] Jerem. xxxvi. 32. [2] Acts xiii. 41. [3] Revel. ii. 14. [4] Rev. xxi. 6.

Sincere. There is another reason for my declining your offer, and that is, you see that I am in no condition to keep you company.

Prob. But where do you think to make yourself better? Is not that done by uniting with pilgrims, and making use of the means of grace? Now, here are three who invite you; and, here is a spring of water to wash and refresh you. Once more, I entreat you to come among us.

On this he came, and *Resolute* with *Friendly* took him to the spring, where he began to wash himself, and having drank of it: behold, every spot soon disappeared from his robe! which so revived him, that his aspect became gay and serene; and he exclaimed,

Sincere. My brethren, I bless *Immanuel* that I met with you. Oh the virtues of this spring! What a happy change is effected on me, a vile sinner, who deserved for ever to have been deprived of such pleasures!

Prob. You see that all men are not deceivers. I knew the virtue of this water of life by sweet experience; therefore was desirous of prevailing on you to join us. This spring, my friend, arises from the *River of Life*[1], which I hope we shall see by and by. The spring retains all the precious qualities of that river, when it is clear, as you now see it.

Sincere. I am sure that its streams make my heart glad, and my garments to shine: so that I who just now was ready to faint, am disposed to sing. Assist me therefore, my friends, to praise the Lord for this great favour.

" *Jesus*, my *God*, thy blood alone,
" Hath power sufficient to atone:
" Thy blood can make me white as snow,
" No Jewish types can cleanse me so."   WATTS.

After the song, they all set forward like giants to ascend the hill; but, notwithstanding their youth and inward vigour, the steepness of the ascent soon retarded their pace, and made them pant for breath: at length they reached the arbour that was built

[1] Psalm xlvi. 4.

for the refreshment of Pilgrims, and being now weary, they sat down to rest themselves, and difcourfe a little.

Prob. I congratulate you on our arrival thus far. I hope this difficulty, inftead of weakening, has rather confirmed your refolutions in favour of a pilgrim's life. Our mafter has told us, that we muft have tribulation in our way; but withal, he bids us to be of good chear[1], becaufe he has travelled this road himfelf, has removed the greater part of the obftacles, and has erected feveral arbours and houfes of entertainment, for all who fhould come after him: one of which, we at this time enjoy the benefit of.

Ref. I believe that I may fpeak for my brethren, and fay, that we are fully refolved, by our king's help, to go up the remaining part of this hill, enduring unto the end: and we defire to adore our Lord *Immanuel,* for thus providing for our refreshment, and leaving us fuch an example that we fhould follow his fteps[2].

Prob. I congratulate you all on this pious refolution; and join with you in praifing our *King,* who has thus far helped us; but, that we may avoid the error that *Chriftian* fell into, in this place; let us converfe on our experience, to keep us awake: and if our brother, who has lately joined us, will give us an account of our king's dealings with him, I imagine that he would greatly oblige us.

Sincere. That I am bound to do on various accounts, and therefore fhall chearfully comply with your requeft.

[1] John xvi. 33.   [2] 1 Pet. ii. 21.

CHAP. VI.

Sincere relates his story, which includes the fearful examples of two false Pilgrims, one named Soft, *the other* Tamper. *The Pilgrims arrive at the* City of Eſtabliſhment.

Sincere. MY name is *Sincere.* I was even from a child inclined to go on pilgrimage; tho' my parents dwelt in the *City of Destruction*, and were nearly related to that *Obstinate* who endeavoured to ſtop *Christian* when he left our city. I was very fond of the bible, which I found in an obſcure part of the houſe, as I was hunting for books; and as ſoon as I was capable of travelling, I ſet out for the gate at the head of this way, and paſſed the *Slough of Despond* with little trouble, by the acquaintance which I had formed with my bible. As I paſſed by *Mount Sinai*, which at that time flamed greatly, I was joined by a young man from a road on the mountain ſide of the way, who wept bitterly: when I aſked him the cauſe of his ſorrow, he ſaid, "My name is [1]*Soft.* I am a native of the town of *Stupidity.* I had indulged myſelf in all the vices to which youth are inclined; but a man named *Fervidus* has lately viſited the town, and preached in the Market-place, denouncing the curſe of *Jehovah* on all who lived as I had done. This alarmed me, I made the beſt of my way from ſuch a wicked place, and I beſeech you to let me go with you." This youth was very fond of prayer, and would entreat me to pray with him; at which ſeaſons he would weep very plentifully, and ſeem extremely penitent. By and by we were met by Mr. *Fleshly Wisdom*; but, I was enabled to diſcover his evil deſign, and to eſcape him. However, I found afterwards, that his doctrines had made an impreſſion on my companion; for he wept leſs, and was often talking in favour of Mr. *Reformation*, and his ſafe way of letting

[1] Mala. ii. 13.

pilgrims into the road. I set before him the danger of quitting the *King*'s highway; yet he grew so confident of his own opinion, that at length he gave me the slip, and went his own way. I kept on, entered the gate, and arrived at the house of the *Interpreter*; where I continued a long time, and was like one of the family. At length I set out again, and proceeded to the village named *Careless*. As I passed by, looking into an house, I saw my former companion fast asleep, with many others in the same condition. On this I went in, and endeavoured to rouse him; but he only yawned a little, gave me a few idle and incoherent answers, and then fell fast asleep again; so I left him. In another house, I saw several at cards; and when I reproved them, one of the company left off, and joined in the propriety of what I said, told me he thought of going on pilgrimage himself, and discoursed so warmly and fluently of the doctrines of pilgrims, that I was much taken with him. When I urged him to set out, he said, that his affairs obliged him to tarry two or three days, after which he would set out with me, if I would wait so long for him. I complied, under the specious hope of winning one soul; but, by various pretences, he detained me at the village above a fortnight: and, by his smooth tongue, I was led into certain compliances among them, instead of reproving them, as was my duty to have done. However, Mr. *Tamper*[1], (which I afterwards found was his name) at last set out with me, we arrived at the foot of this hill. When he saw the steepness of the ascent, he began to survey the roads that turn to the right and left, and proposed to turn to the right, with so many plausible arguments, drawn from his own knowledge of the country, the pleasantness of the right-hand way, when compared with the direct road, and his certain assurance of its meeting again with the road on the other side of the hill; that I began to consult my own ease, and incline to him. I told him *that* road had a bad name among pilgrims. He replied, "This path is truly bad to some weak men: but, I hope you know better, than to be frightened at such vulgar bugbears. We know, that we have knowledge[2], and if we are *Immanuel*'s sheep, suppose we do wander a little, he will certainly bring us back again

[1] Rom. iii. 8.   [2] 1 Cor. viii. 1.

to his fold; wherefore, let us take the fair and easy path." While I stood hesitating, he gave me a pull, and I followed him into the path called *Danger*. There we went on pleasantly for some time; at length we found ourselves far advanced into a wilderness, the day declined on us, the heavens lowered, and threatened us with a dreadful storm. I now repented my turning aside, and trembled for the consequences. The night came on exceeding dark, the wilderness was shaken with a tempest, it thundered and lightened so, as I had never known before: and, to make my case more alarming, a voice was heard in a dreadful cadence, saying, [1] "*Tamper, receive the just reward of thy presumption,*" and instantly my wretched companion was struck dead by my side. Then, every flash was succeeded by a stroke of guilt in my conscience; and every clap of thunder was re-echoed with the severest reproaches on my conduct. A torrent of rain fell, the road became deep and slippery, and there, had I fallen for ever, had not the *Lord* in mercy prevented me.

Prob. Alas, poor man, how dear you payed for your wandering!

Sincere. Not half so severely as I had merited, for sinning against such rich grace, such repeated tokens of *Immanuel*'s favour.

Frien. But what did you, in this straight, and how was you delivered?

Sincere. I was made to see that my turning aside did now reprove me[2], that my own folly had brought me into this trouble; and also to receive some comfort from my being made sensible of it.

Ref. Comfort! from whence could you derive comfort in such circumstances?

Sincere. It was a comfort arising from hope in the word of our *King*, and from experience of his favour. I remembered the word which says, " He brings his erring people into a wilderness, that he may speak comfortably unto them[3]." I found myself in a wilderness, was heartily ashamed of my folly, and

[1] Rom. iii. 8.   [2] Jerem. ii. 19.   [3] Hosea. ii. 14.

therefore

therefore concluded, that the *King* was about to restore my soul. This was confirmed to me, by having experienced his favour in being preserved when the wretched *Tamper* was cut off. Accordingly, I kneeled down in that dark, miry, and dismal situation; confessed, with much contrition of heart, my great backslidings, wrestled for forgiveness, and earnestly sought direction from our *King*, that I might recover the true path.

Frien. In what manner was you answered, and restored?

Sincere. The storm soon blew over; the day dawned upon me; and lo! A hand reached a small phial, and a soft voice said, " Take, and use this *Backslider's Cordial*, and turn again by the way in which thou camest hither[1]:" I opened the phial and took a little, which enlightened my eyes, and strengthened my heart wonderfully; so, that I distinguished the path, and with willing feet hastened towards the foot of the hill, where you saw me arrive as you sat by the spring.

Prob. Brother, I thank you for this instructing narrative; and hope we shall all learn thereby, both the devices of the *Black Tyrant*, and the mercies of our *King*. But what do you think of young *Soft?* There seemed the signs of a work of grace in his heart.

Sincere. I have frequently reflected on his case, and compared it with my own heart, and the experience of others. The result of my inquiries is, that *Soft*, and others like him, are convinced only of the perverseness of *their practice*, but do not see the depravity of *their nature*. For where the corruption of nature is discovered, there ever seems to be a real work of grace, and no where else. I well remember, that in all the tears and complaints of young *Soft*, he expressed only a sorrow for the evil consequence of his *transgressions*, the sense of which wore off, as he made use of religious exercises.

Prob. He is a dreadful example, of the fatal effects which follow, on listening to the schemes of *Fleshly Wisdom* in such matters.

[1] Jerem. xxv. 5.

Frien. And so is the fate of *Tamper*, which manifests the vengeance of Heaven against such abuse the precious doctrines of grace.

Sincere. I shall never forget him. May our *King* preserve us from such crimes.

The Pilgrims being sufficiently refreshed, arose, and set forward up the remaining part of the hill, which they ascended with great ease, after their agreeable discourse in the arbour.

Prob. My brethren, I must take notice, that this hill, now we are on its summit, does not appear so steep as it did when we drew near its foot; nor is the ascent so difficult as some represent it to be.

Sincere. By nature our eyes are carnal, and make false representations of heavenly things, much to their disadvantage: besides, the *Black Tyrant* is ever ready to assist the deception, that he may pervert us from the good ways of our *King*.

Ref. I find it best to suspect all the ideas that are any way connected with my own ease, honour, or interest. I think *St. Paul* put flesh and blood quite out of his council [1]; and did not suffer them to have any vote in his determinations. They are certainly very corrupt counsellors; and, by *Immanuel*'s grace, I am resolved to treat them as did that excellent apostle: But see, my friend, yonder glittering building on a distant-hill before us; pray what is it?

Sincere. That is the famous house *Beautiful*, which is pleasant for situation: It is an exact model of the *City of God*, which is built on *Mount Zion* [2]; and which I hope we shall one day see. That house you see, is set on a hill; so that it neither can, nor should be hid.

Friendly. On this side of the house in a vale I perceive a large city, and our road seems to run through it.

Sincere. It does so; and, that is the *City of Establishment*, with its large suburbs; where we will rest ourselves a little. I have heard that there is good entertainment for pilgrims, in that city.

[1] Gal. i. 16.   [2] Heb. xii. 22.

In

In a short time they arrived at the city, which was very populous; but the Pilgrims passed the streets quietly, they being only a little gazed at. When they came towards the middle of the city, they saw an elderly man at the door of a corner house, who kept his eyes on them until they came up to him; when saluting them very kindly, he desired them to come into his house and refresh themselves. The Pilgrims thanked him, and went in: he desired them to be seated, and ordered his servants to bring in suitable refreshments.

CHAP. VII.

The Pilgrims entertained by Mr. Candidus. *He relates his story, and his reasons for receiving them. An account of the people of the city, and of the celebrated Mr.* George Fervidus.

THE Pilgrims were delighted with the agreeable manner of their host, and with every thing they saw in his house. When they had refreshed themselves, *Probus* said,

Prob. Kind host, will you permit me to ask you a question or two?

Candidus. With all my heart, sir.

Prob. Be so kind then to inform us, to whom it is that we are obliged for this kindness, and your reasons for giving us such a reception.

Cand. My name is *Candidus*[1]. I am the son of *Moderation*, by his wife *Experience*. I am now as you see, in years, and have spent all my days in this city, where I have seen various changes. From a child I have been blessed with the knowledge of the scriptures[2], and was never desirous of joining in the diversions unto which youth are inclined; but spent my leisure time in religious exercises, and in acquiring useful learning.

[1] 1 Cor. xiii. 7.   [2] 2 Tim. iii. 15.

My

My dear mother was very fond of me, and would come to my bedside, when she thought I was asleep, and kiss my face and breast, bless the *King* for giving her a pious child, and earnestly pray for my future welfare. When I grew up, I united myself with religious persons, and took great delight in social religion. The *Lord* blessed me in business in the world. I was in flourishing circumstances when my parents died; and they departed full of heavenly peace, joy, and gratitude to *Immanuel*; who had given them the pleasure of seeing me treading in the path, that would certainly bring us together again, in a state of eternal felicity. After many years, my circumstances being easy, and the world growing troublesome to me, I left my business to my children; and now spend my time entirely, in using hospitality towards those who love my dear *Lord*, of whatever denomination they may be: besides them, I have a few dear old friends in this street, who visit me; among whom is Master *Metaphor*, an old and lively disciple, and whom it is likely you may see presently. These meet here, and we sometimes enter so deeply into discourse on *Immanuel*, and the joys above; that if the *King of Terrors* was to enter the room, we should struggle among ourselves who should first receive his mortal stroke.

Sincere. I have heard much of you on the road, and guessed that you was the person, by the manner of your receiving me and my friends.

Cand. What fame says of a person is but of little account, unless he has a friend within him, bearing a testimony, that what he does for pilgrims, flows from a love to their master.

Frien. True, sir: and even then, you are sensible it will be of no avail in certain cases.

Cand. My mother taught me, that I can do nothing to render my person accepted before our *King*; for I am to look to my Lord *Immanuel* for *that:* after which, all my works of faith, and labours of love are remembered as the fruits of his grace. In this faith I entertain Pilgrims, not to merit the *celestial world* thereby, but to obtain in the pleasures of their conversation, a foretaste of its joys.

Prob.

Prob. Ah, friend *Candidus*, I perceive that you are a covetous man, and very artful in your way. If I underſtand your intention, you have opened your doors to us with a view of obtaining a viſit from our maſter, or of having ſome converſation in the celeſtial world.

Cand. That indeed is my deſign; and I have had ſuch frequent bleſſings in ſo doing, that I am now almoſt certain of ſucceſs.

Frien. You have our *Lord*'s word in your favour. " He that receiveth you," ſaid he, " receiveth me [1]." If we therefore can prove ourſelves to be true Pilgrims, you certainly have our dear maſter himſelf in our company.

Cand. I had a ſhrewd gueſs of you, as ſoon as I ſaw you: and I think there is ſomething even in the mien of real diſciples, which often puts me in mind of that ancient prophecy, namely, " [2] All that ſee them ſhall know them, that they are the ſeed which the *Lord* hath bleſſed."

Ref. Permit me to aſk you, Sir, how matters go on in this city, which is large, and we hear not under very good diſcipline; ſo that I ſhould think perſons of your ſtamp muſt live unquietly?

Cand. It is true, diſcipline is much relaxed among us; which gives great grief to many of its beſt citizens. But on mature conſideration, we may obſerve, that in ſuch cities as this, it would be very difficult to enforce a diſcipline becoming the laws and character of the city. It is my opinion, that religious people ſhould be thankful, that things are ſo well as they are. I live at the corner of *Church-ſtreet*, or as ſome have nick-named it, *Methodiſt-lane*; and am very civilly treated in general; tho' ſome of the baſer ſort [3] frequently diſturb the inhabitants of this ſtreet in their devotions. But the bulk of the people are too much ſet on the gain and vanities of this world, to trouble themſelves with us, not even thoſe who make a pretence to religion, and pride themſelves in being members of this corporation.

[1] Mat. x. 40.   [2] Iſaiah lxi. 9.   [3] Acts xvii. 5.

Ref.

Ref. I have heard that most of the inhabitants of this city are so fond of their privileges, that they think a person cannot go to heaven without being made free of it.

Cand. In every town in *Christendom* there are people, who, not caring to trouble themselves in seeking the *Celestial Kingdom*; are willing to believe their own place enjoyeth such exclusive privileges, as will entitle *them only* to that inheritance. This opinion they embrace, not only because it feeds their bigotry, but also indulges their idleness in such matters; thus it is with many of this city. Religion is the most indifferent thing in the world unto them. In religious affairs, they will implicitly swallow the most absurd doctrine from a *regular* divine, and strictly attend his preaching, however profligate and irregular his behaviour; tho' in forming worldly bargains, they are exceedingly cautious of the smallest imposition: therefore, with persons truly acquainted with christianity, it matters very little what such people think or do, provided their bigotry does not disturb those who know better than themselves.

Ref. Very true; and yet it becomes us to use every likely method to convince them, of the great danger of living in such a state.

Cand. Every method has been, and is still employed to rouse them from this security. This street, and almost every common adjacent to this city, has rung with warnings of their danger, and the most earnest invitations to a contrary practice; and many have thro' grace, taken the alarm; nay, this whole street near us, is inhabited by many who were as arrant bigots as any the city. It happened as follows. A few years since, one *George Fervidus*, a young ecclesiastic of this city, and chaplain to the noble *Lady Liberal*, (of whom you will hear more by and by) was stirred up by Providence, to bear a testimony against the corruptions, which had crept into the principles and manners of the citizens. This stripling was indefatigable in his zeal, and preached boldly thro' every part of the town and country, in fields and on commons. This street which appears so new, did at that time consist of old and dark houses, and was called *Armenian Row*. But, as the land was held by the tenure of

church

church-lease, and was reformation-ground; the friends of *Fervidus* took the greater part of the street into their hands, and pulled down the old houses, which were built on a loose sand, that was brought into the city from *Freewill Forest*, when Dr. *Laud*, the arch-prelate, new modelled it. The new proprietors removed the sand, and laid the foundations of the new edifices on the rock, which is the original foundation of our city. The materials with which these houses are built, were taken from a wood and quarry [1], which are common for the freemen of this city, tho' very few of late years had made use of them. These dwellings are light and warm, and have so good an appearance, that they are an ornament to the city. *Fervidus* also erected two large buildings in this street, for public worship; each of which will contain several thousands of persons; and which are greatly crowded, especially when he is in town; but he is now abroad, labouring to persuade men to become Pilgrims. These places are supplied by many eminent ambassadors of our *King*, who preach there by rotation. Among these are, The thundering *Mr. Chichester*, the correct and majestic *Mr. Bethesda*, the honourable and amiable *Barnabas of Talgarth*, the soft and humble *Mr. Wooburn*, the alarming *Capt. Nauticus*, the experienced *Capt. Miles*, the smart and popular *Juvenal Allchurch*, the sweet *Leeds*, venerable *Halifax*, veteran *Brooks*, and many others.

Prob. This is good news, Sir, I should be glad to see these places.

Cand. In the morning, *God* willing, I will shew you the city and its celebrated suburbs.

[1] Articles and Homilies.

CHAP.

CHAP. VIII.

The Pilgrims discourse with Father Metaphor. *The beauty of family religion. The use of gifts among religious persons.*

JUST as *Candidus* had given his guests the above promise, his old friend *Metaphor* entered the room.

Cand. Here is my worthy brother *Metaphor*: come, be seated, I am glad to see you this evening. Here are some young men who are travelling the good old way, and will be pleased with your company.

Metaphor. Brethren, I am glad to see you. I imagine that you young men are all *Solomons*, and are building the first temple: ye hear no noise, no enemy stirs, every stone is fitted [1] ready to your hands, and ye have nothing to do but to build.

On this, the Pilgrims looked on each other, and smiled: then *Probus* thus addressed the venerable speaker.

Prob. Sir, we are young men who are very desirous of shewing our love to our *Lord*, by pressing on towards *Sion*.

Metaph. That is what I mean. *Solomon* now reigns in you. Ye are just married to *Immanuel*, and are not to go to [2] war as yet: but, remember, that *Solomon*'s temple had little light in it: and its porch was four times as high as the temple [3]: that is, it was higher in appearance than in reality: so you will find by and by, that you have not so much knowledge, nor holiness, as you may now think you have. This temple will be overthrown by *Nebuchadnezzer* king of confusion; and you must build again with enemies all around you [4]: a *Tobiah*, and a *Sanballat* will trouble you, so that you must have a trowel in one hand, and a sword in the other: but, be not discouraged, for the [5] glory of the latter temple, shall be superior to that of the first.

[1] 1 Kings vi. 7. [2] Deut. xxiv. 5. [3] 2 Chron. iii. 4. [4] Nehem. ii. 10.
[5] Haggai ii. 9.

Res. I know not what enemies we may meet with; but I trust that we shall be more than conquerors over all, thro' *Immanuel*, who hath loved us[1].

Metaph. Yes, yes; I hope so too: but, I suppose that[2] *Adonibezek* is now a prisoner among you, if not dead; and perhaps *you* was the man who took him prisoner.

Resolute stared at him, and said, really, father, I know not what you mean.

Metaph. Perhaps not, and yet I speak the truth. *Adonibezek* means the thunder of *Jehovah*, or the law of our *King*. This law in our first convictions, cuts off our thumbs and great toes[3]; that is, maims us so, that we find ourselves unable to do any thing pleasing to the *King*. He keeps us in this wretched state, until the *Prince Paraclete* enables us to conquer him, and take him prisoner in *our* turn; that is, *Immanuel* delivers us from its power as a covenant of works. Then the soul brings *Adonibezek* to *Jerusalem* (which means, the sense of gospel peace) as did the *Children of Israel* of old; and there he dies; for, I suppose, you also, now find *that* dead by which you was held[4].

Prob. Sir, I find what you say to be true, tho' you deliver your sentiments in such a manner, as is not easily to be understood by young men.

Metaph. I have, my friends, made our *Lord*'s word my study, and compared my own heart therewith. I am delivered from the *Egyptian bondage*. I have passed the *Red Sea*. I have been at *Mount Sinai*, and wandered long in the wilderness. I have passed *Jordan*, entered into *Immanuel* as my true rest, and now dwell on *Jordan*'s banks as the *River of Death*; and trust I shall go over dry-shod into my everlasting *Canaan* above.

Candidus sat silent, enjoying this conversation between his old friend and his guests. It now being late, father *Metaphor* took his leave, and *Candidus* rung a bell; on which all his family entered the room: he then read a few verses from his bible, very sensibly explained them, and exhorted all present to the most sincere and fervent service of a covenant *God*. After

---

[1] Rom. viii. 37.   [2] Judges i. 6.   [3] Judge. i. 7.   [4] Rom. vii. 6.

this they all kneeled down, and *Candidus* poured out a moſt earneſt prayer to the *King*, for a bleſſing on himſelf, his family, and gueſts. He bleſſed the *Lord* for all the favours of the day, and commended himſelf and houſe to the divine protection for the enſuing night. After this, they all retired to reſt. In the morning, *Candidus* having again bleſſed the *King* for the mercies of the night, and beſought his preſence and help for the preſent day, they ſat down to breakfaſt, and the following diſcourſe enſued.

Prob. There is a certain beauty, as well as pleaſure, in holineſs. How amiable does the family of our hoſt appear, thus walking in the paths of true godlineſs!

Cand. What you have ſeen in my houſe is only a faint imitation of what was formerly the glory of this city. But alas! our gold is become dim; family religion is ſhamefully neglected by moſt perſons; and in the few houſes where it is ſtill kept up, it is evidently carried on in ſuch a formal way, and incumbered with ſo many cares and diverſions, that its beauty is deſtroyed.

Ref. What, are there any in this famous city who live as I once did? For twenty years, I never bowed my knees to our *King*, but I went to bed and roſe up again like a brute beaſt.

Cand. I have too much reaſon to believe, that there are hundreds of ſuch families: and what is worſe, they will laugh at thoſe who keep up theſe duties of our religion; altho' the bible ſays plainly, "[1] I will pour out my fury upon the Heathen who know me not, and upon the families that call not on my name."

Ref. How then are ſuch perſons better than thoſe of the City of *Deſtruction?*

Cand. They are much worſe than them: for it will be more tolerable for thoſe of *Stupidity* and *Deſtruction*, in the day of judgment[2], than for theſe members of this highly favoured corporation.

[1] Jer. x. 25.   [2] Matt. xi. 22.

Frien.

Frien. But the inhabitants of your city are very tenacious of praying by a book; yet, I perceive that you make no use of such a directory.

Cand. Our *King* has blessed me, with a sense of my wants, and the gift of expressing them by words, both for myself and others. Every one hath not the latter, who is favoured with the former blessing. I believe many good Christians cannot use free prayer in their families; and some, not in their closets. I would have every one strive to acquire that gift; and I know, that use and exercise, by *Jehovah*'s blessing, will do wonders this way. Every man is to pray in such a method as will best suit his capacity; always endeavouring to improve himself therein. But as to the ignorant and vain world, it is of no moment to me or to them how they pray: as I said before, it avails nothing what they think or do in religious matters—Gifts are not grace. They are given to some, for general good. Where much is given, of such is the more required[1]. Were this rule well attended to, it would quench that fiery zeal used for the attainment of gifts, prevent the envy of such as do not possess them, and humble the pride of those who have them: for, who is there among *Immanuel*'s servants, that can or dare say, "He has improved his talents as he ought or might have done."

Sincere. Ah, *Candidus*, you have indeed given me a breakfast. From considering what you have said, I must mingle my drink with weeping at the remembrance of my ingratitude to my dear *Lord*, and my unprofitableness in his service.

Sincere then related to *Candidus* his memoirs, as above.

Cand. I commend your tears, and bless the *King* for giving you a heart to remember your ways, and be ashamed of them. But come, firs, let us rejoice that we are brought safe hitherto.

  Here we fix our *Ebenezer*,
   Hither by thine help we're come,
  And we trust by thy good pleasure,
   Safely to arrive at home:

[1] Luke xii. 48.

Jesus sought us out when strangers,
Wandring from the fold of *God*,
And to rescue us from danger,
Interpos'd his precious blood."

WHITEFIELD's HYMNS.

CHAP. IX.

Candidus *shews the Pilgrims the city and suburbs. A view of* Presbyterian, Independent, Quaker, *and* Baptist *Streets, and* Arminian Row. *An account of* Dr. Voluminous, *and* Mr. John Duplex.

BREAKFAST being over, *Candidus* took his guests out to see the city. He shewed them *Fervidus*'s two places of worship, which they admired. He shewed them the walls and gates of the city, which were neglected and out of repair. On this occasion said,

Cand. Many of the clergy of this city are for taking down these well-constructed, ancient walls and gates, and laying the city open. These reformers are now assembled at the *City of Vanity*, where you will hear more of them, and their scheme. —We are now in the *High-street* of the city, which, like most of the rest, is in a dirty condition. It was formerly named *Orthodox-street*, and therein is the great temple; but it is now called *Arminian-street*, and is the residence of the principal officers of the city. Before its name was changed, it was remarkably clean, airy, and healthy; but, since the high-priest *Laud* presided here, it has suffered much in these respects, as well as changed its name. For tho' the inhabitants talk much of cleanliness, yet you see how little reason they have to boast. Take notice also how the street is darkened, and the circulation of the air obstructed, by the number of signs and sign-posts therein;

almost

almost every house having one, on which is pompously set forth the abilities and good deeds of the inhabitant, each one thinking himself better than his neighbour[1]. Behold what a majestic temple is this! But there is too much reason to say of this, and other such structures, "The glory is departed from them[2]:" because there is not that attention given to the fundamental constitution of our city, as there was, when our *Rulers* made the temples resound, with the glad tidings of salvation, thro' the crucified *Immanuel*. Whereas now, many are too indolent to compose their discourses, and too careful of themselves, to raise their voices, so as to be heard by the people. This great and honourable work is chiefly done by a few despised *Lecturers* and *Curates*.

Prob. That's a pity, for I suppose the revenues are large.

Cand. They are noble, Sir, yet very little is done for them. Some few of our prelates and beneficed clergy, have stepped forth against the growing power of the *Giant Infidelity* (of whom you will know more by and by) and have acquitted themselves with great honour; and this is all that can be said in their favour: but I should be much wanting in respect to our city, if I mentioned not some of those shining lights[3] which at present illuminate her horizon. Among them is the reverend *Dunstan*, who eminently lives and walks by faith; with his *Foster* son, a levite of great abilities. Mr. *Lock*, and his *Portrait Painter*, are very successful in the city. Here is also a singular *Wen*, which, the more it grows, the more it adorns and supports the health of this body corporate. Yonder high house, in that obscure place, is the habitation of the keen, orthodox, and formidable *Augustus Hembury*; who chuses to live in *Pepper-Alley*, but we hope he will soon remove to *St. James's-street*[4]. Here is also the eloquent *Andrew Marden*. To whom, I will only add at present, the venerable *Everton* of *Christ's Church*, who, the other day, met an old hag, disguised for some vile purposes, and with apostolic zeal, boldly tore off her mask; then, with keen and just satyr, exposed the sorceress to the contempt of every considerate by-stander.

[1] Luke xviii. 11, 12. [2] 1 Sam. iv. 21. [3] Matt. v. 14. [4] Jam. iii. 17.

Prob. We are now out of the city gate. Pray, Sir, what large ſtreet is this?

Cand. This is *Preſbyterian-ſtreet*, and a member of a large, populous, and reſpectable city, called *Preſbyterian city*, which is ſituated in the north, and maintains its excellent laws and diſcipline much better than doth our city. The fundamental conſtitutions of this ſtreet are the ſame as thoſe of our city. They differ only in things reſpecting government and ceremonies: for the inhabitants of this ſtreet uſe no prayer-books in their worſhip—You ſee the buildings are high and grand, but, like ours, the ſtreet is not very clean. Many great and excellent men in the pilgrim-world have lived in this ſtreet, which has ever been conſidered as a friend to civil and religious liberty. The inhabitants have ſuffered much from the hands of oppreſſors, eſpecially on *Bartholomew-day* 1662, and for twenty-ſix years after; when our city rulers revoked the free charters of this and the neighbouring ſtreets, and diſtreſſed the people many ways: of theſe evils this ſtreet experienced the greateſt ſhare. Many eminent men, who are firm friends to *Immanuel*'s cauſe, and formidable enemies of the *Giant Infidelity*, ſtill flouriſh in this ſtreet; but too many of the houſes are blacked and defiled, both within and without, by the ſmoke of two founderies, which have been lately conſtructed, out of two large meetings, in the principal part of the ſtreet—One of them is ſuperintended by *Dr. Tinkle*¹, maſter of the art of preaching, and is called the *Arian Foundery*. The other is the *Socinian Foundery*, where *Dr. Knowall*² preſides. He firſt abſurdly gave out, "that our *Immanuel* was only a man, and that his ſufferings were of no atoning uſe to any." He has lately declared, that we have no ſouls. It is expected, he will next aſſert, that there is no *God*; and remove from this ſtreet to the caſtle of *Scepticiſm*, to be deputy-governor there, under the *Giant Infidelity*. In theſe forges images are conſtantly made to vend in the ſtreet, and in our city, where they are eagerly caught up. The black ſmoke ever riſing from theſe founderies, is a nuiſance to the whole neighbourhood, and is complained of by ſome, but would not

¹ 1 Cor. xiii. 1.   ² 1 Cor. viii. 1, 2.

have been endured by any in former days, when such founders would have been cast out of the street. By this trade also, they forfeit the protection of our city laws, yet times are so changed for the worse, that our rulers rather favour than frown on them: and in short, from the behaviour of those founders and their patrons, it may be said of them. " They have loved idols, and after them they will go¹."

Prob. I should think, that the horrible destruction of the *Eastern Empire*, by the *Turks*, and the present wretched state of the *Greek* churches, all which evils came upon them on account of their love for *Arian images*; would deter any other people from such idolatry. But Heresy, as well as every sin of every sort, is very stupifying.

Cand. This next is *Independent-street*. It was begun in the days of the *Common-wealth*. You see it now makes a good figure. It is said to be built on the best plan in the world, even from the original pattern dictated by *Immanuel*. I wish the inhabitants would abound in love, towards those who differ in opinion from them; for they are a very respectable body, and send out many on pilgrimage. The street is in excellent order, altho' there are scarcely two houses in it alike. It is well paved, very clean, open and airy. There is a *Brewer* lives in yonder high house, who makes as good ale as any in this country. It is very sound, and salutary for pilgrims. I have a *Kinsman* who dwells at the farther end of the street, who is very useful in our father's house, and for some time was a companion of *Fervidus*. At the hither end is the house of *Mr Deptford*, the *venerable lecturer on Mr. Bunyan's Progress*, and warm patron of ejaculatory prayer. I heard him once tell a sweet story, on *Isaiah* xlv. 8.

Frien. The next street appears very different from the last. It is pretty commodious, but very plain and unornamented. Every house is of one height, and all the doors, windows, &c. are in one uniform fashion; but I think the sashes are very small.

¹ Jer. ii. 25.

Cand.

Cand. This is *Quaker's-street*, began by *George Fox* in the laſt century. Theſe people are peculiarly fond of candle-light, and very little concerned about their windows. Nay, at noon day, in their aſſemblies, they will neither preach or pray ſimply by day-light, but will return without doing either, if they are not indulged with a candle lighted up in their meetings. The voice of ſinging, or the ſound of any inſtrument of muſic, is not heard among them. Swearing, in all its forms, is an abomination unto them. They make no uſe of water, wine, or bread in their aſſemblies, but reſolve all outward ceremonies into inward light and myſtery; and yet with reſpect to their diſcourſe and dreſs, no perſons are more rigidly plain. They are excellent oeconomiſts, ſincere and juſt in their dealings, very careful of their poor, war and ſtrife they abhor, nor can a lawyer live in this ſtreet.

Frien. Are there any pilgrims among them?

Cand. They evidently live in the neglect of the poſitive commands of our *Lord*; but you know, "He will have mercy and not ſacrifice[1]." Yet it becomes all his ſubjects to be fully perſuaded in their own minds[2], about the legality of their proceedings. I have known ſeveral excellent pilgrims who lived in this ſtreet; but theſe pilgrims did not approve of many things in principles and practice, that were adopted by the vulgar and bigotted. In general, there is much wood, hay, and ſtubble among them[3]; but many of them love our maſter, and make him their alone foundation.

Ref. The next ſtreet is very oddly conſtructed, for I can ſee no way of acceſs to it but by croſſing the water, for here is a large pond quite acroſs the ſtreet. Is there no other way to it?

Cand. That is *Baptiſt-ſtreet*, the original of which is very doubtful, both as to the time and perſons. There is another ſuch pond at the farther-end of it. The ſtreet and ponds are in better condition, now than ever they were: for *Dr. Voluminous*, a late very eminent man of this ſtreet, cleanſed and put them into that order you now ſee them. The ſtreet is

[1] Matt. ix. 13.   [2] Rom. xiv. 5.   [3] 1 Cor. iii. 12.

rather

rather contracted, and the houses confined. Many of them also have such large sashes, and small stoves, that, for want of more fire, the rooms are cold and aguish: but others are more warm, and I have visited therein with great pleasure. About the middle of the street is a set of people, who distinguish themselves, by keeping two days of rest from secular affairs, every week. And at the farther end there is another class of inhabitants, called *Universalists*, who are remarkable for being short-sighted. These have no veneration for the discoveries of *Dr. Voluminous*. That part of the street has a communication with *Arminian-Row*, which you will see presently. *Dr. Voluminous* cut the ponds close to the houses on each side the street, and directed, that every inhabitant, on his or her first coming, should wade thro' the pond to their new dwelling. But there is a private avenue for visitors.

Ref. I think the *Doctor* was an odd man, or he would not have been so singular in his institution.

Cand. He had much to say in support of these things. He affirmed, that the primitive Christian corporations, had each of them such a laver before its gates, that none but adult persons were admitted into the number of their members, and that all other bodies who use a bason only, and admit infants among them, have departed from the original pattern.

Ref. Tho' I love zeal in religious matters, yet I would curb it, especially about circumstantials; for I cannot bear to quarrel with those whom I see to be followers of *Immanuel*. We shall sit down together in the *Celestial city*, however we treat each other here.

Cand. There is a back way to some assemblies, by which candid men have, and do receive to communion with them, any other pious persons, who care not to wade thro' the water; but this is not approved of by many among them. Good *Mr. Bunyan*, to whom pilgrims are so much obliged for his works, lived in this street, and was one of the moderate men; but he was censured by his neighbours, for his candour.

Frien. I love the street and people for *Mr. Bunyan*'s sake; but, by no means can like their unkind behaviour to other real pilgrims.

Cand. There are several curiosities in this street. There is a most commodious *Booth*, which is much resorted unto. And a *Martin* that abides, and sings excellently of redeeming love, all the year. I heard him once sing most charmingly about the water of life, *Rev.* xxii. 17. Here is also *Immanuel*'s *Pine-Apple*, which is a *Medley* of sweets, and furnishes a constant feast of fat things. It grows near the great *Pool*, in the north-west. *Northampton-house* in this street is a noble building. Dont you see yonder cupola, erected on an high house in this street? That was the habitation of the great *Doctor Voluminous*, who used to spend much time in that observatory. It is said, that he had glasses by which he discovered amazing things. That he not only could see the book in which are written the names of all the elect, but also plainly discern them as justified, and united to *Immanuel*, from eternity. So that the vile sinner who was wallowing in iniquity; in the perspective of *Voluminous*, appeared to be really justified, and united to our holy *Immanuel*.

Sincere. These are deep paradoxes indeed! I am sure my head would be dizzy with such prospects. What do you think of them, Sir?

Cand. Altho' I have a great veneration for the *Doctor*'s judgment, yet I think he might as well affirm, that they were glorified from eternity, and so make short work of it. Our bible says, that all who believe are justified[1]: and that all who are in *Immanuel* are new creatures[2]. This is very satisfactory to me. Altho' I believe the doctrine of election, and experience it to be very full of comfort to my soul; yet, I believe that election makes no real change in its object, before it is called by sovereign grace. If I am a new creature, I am *more* than elected, for I am happy in *Immanuel*; but I was miserable before, for I was dead in sin; which is a *real evil*, whatever may be affirmed to the contrary.

[1] Acts xiii. 39.   [2] 2 Cor. v. 17.

The Pilgrims having seen the suburbs, *Candidus* took them to his house by a different way, and entered *Methodist-lane* or *Church-street* (which was long, and lay north and south), at the northern extremity: when they came into the street, he said,

Cand. This is the most obscure part of our street, it is wholly inhabited by the friends of Mr. *John Duplex*, of whom probably you have heard. He set out in the same work with *Fervidus*, but did not think it expedient to make such a thorough reform in this street, as *Fervidus* did; for you may perceive that many of the old buildings are suffered to remain, which disgraced this quarter of the street. Nay, the old name is so far adopted by these people, that they have ordered *Arminian-Row* to be engraved in the corner of the street, and the old houses are chiefly supported by props, cut down from *Baxter's-heath*, which you will see by and by: in short, *Duplex's* reformation is not worthy the name. He has often been told of these improprieties, and sometimes he seems inclined to pull all the old houses down; but, he is too wavering to effect so good a work. I hope he will do it before he dies; for he is in many respects a useful man, and has been the means of sending many on pilgrimage.

C H A P. X.

A strange matter of fact. The Pilgrims depart. Probus *and* Friendly *are decoyed by* Mr. Fear *into* Nicodemus's-lane. Sincere *and* Resolute *arrive at the house* Beautiful.

THE Pilgrims being arrived at their quarters, were entertained several days by *Candidus*. On the evening before their departure, they desired to know what they were indebted to him.

Cand.

Cand. I am commanded not to be unmindful to entertain strangers[1]. The *Lord* has blessed me with ability to do it, therefore you are all welcome to what you have had; for I never, in these cases forget that excellent saying of our dear *Lord*, "It is more blessed to give, than to receive[2]." I only beg that I may have your prayers.

Sincere. Your great generosity, Sir, reminds me of what I heard concerning you, while I lived at the house of the *Interpreter*; which I am glad I thought on before we went away; because the fact was so remarkable, that I would have it from your own mouth.

Cand. I guess what you mean. The story has some way got abroad, which I did not intend; but I am fully persuaded that there was something extraordinary in the case.

Prob. Pray, Sir, favour us with a relation of it.

Cand. I was reading one evening by candle-light, in this very parlour, which is near the door; when I heard a tap at the outer door. The maid went to it, and saw a person who asked, if strangers were not entertained at this house? The maid brought the question to me. I took the candle, and went to the door; where I was amazed to see a young man, whose face shone so bright as to illuminate the street, and render my candle quite useless. I said, Sir, won't you come in? He said, "*We* have other business in town, but you may be sure *we* shall not forget your house." He turned and went away. I came back, and found the lustre of his presence had so filled the parlour, that I could have read by it a quarter of an hour; it went gradually away. About two months after, a young man whom I had never seen before, came hither, and lodged with us, whose face was exactly like that we had seen at the door. This man was a pious soul, he sickened and died in my house; and I cannot but look on the appearance at the door, as an intimation of his future happiness. This was the fact, you, or others may think of it as you please[3].

[1] Heb. xiii. 2.   [2] Acts xx. 35.
[3] This happened at a city in *Kent*.

Prob.

Prob. This is a singular story indeed, and is well calculated to encourage you in your hospitable behaviour.

In the morning, the Pilgrims addressed themselves to their journey. Their kind host told them, the house *Beautiful* was but a few miles distant, where they would be welcome, and might see many curious things. They then thanked him for all his favours towards them, and took their leave. When they were got out of the city, they went on singing,

" Happy the heart where graces reign,
" Where love inspires the breast;
" Love is the brightest of the train,
" And strengthens all the rest.

" Before we quite forsake our clay,
" Or leave this dark abode,
" The wings of love bear us away,
" To see our smiling *God*."   WATTS.

Thus they proceeded until they came to a turning on the left side of the way, at which stood a well-looking man, whose name they afterwards knew to be *Mr. Fear*. As they approached him, he addressed them thus,

Fear. Good morning to you, gentlemen. I perceive you are going to yonder house, but are not aware of the danger that awaits you in that road; for, just on the other side of yonder copse, sits old *Prejudice*, who is a bitter enemy to pilgrims, and makes it his daily employ to set his dogs at them; which often worry and tear them in a shocking manner, while he sits and laughs at their misery: wherefore, I advise you to stop, and consider what you do.

Ref. But is not this the direct road to the house *Beautiful?*

Fear. Yes, it is the direct way. But the *Lord* of that house seeing the mischief done to pilgrims by that inveterate foe; has opened this lane, as a secure by-way to the said house, and has placed me here to direct pilgrims to make use of it. This is called *Nicodemus's-lane*[1]; being so named from that eminent man who

[1] John iii. 2.

first

first used it. But while pilgrims were impressed with primitive zeal, and cared for no prudential means of safety, this lane was disused, and became quite obscure: when that fervour expired, I was sent to open it, for the benefit of any who would make use of it.

Prob. My brethren, I perceive that yonder old fellow is peeping at us from behind the copse, and he will surely attack us; but as here is such a convenient opening to elude these dangers, and which was used by so great a man, without being reproved for it by our *Lord*; let us turn in here, and go the back way to the house.

Sincere. Stop a little. Pray, Sir, is not your name *Mr Fear?*

Fear. Yes, Sir. And they are called *blessed* who put themselves under my protection and direction at all times.

Sincere. It is indeed written, "Blessed is the man that feareth always[1]." But *that Fear* is no relation of yours, for he is a true man; but you are a thief, and steal away the hearts of pilgrims from their *Lord*.

Prob. O, my brother, do not use a stranger so, for he has been very kind to us. I am inclined to follow his advice, and hope that I shall be at the house as soon as you.

Fear. Our *Lord* commands, "That if we are persecuted in one city[2], we should flee unto another;" which is the same as to say, If you cannot go on peaceably in one way, make use of any other.

Sincere. Brother *Probus*, I see you are for separating from us; but you will certainly repent this procedure.

Frien. I also will accompany him, for I like not the dogs, and think the texts of scripture, which Mr. *Fear* has quoted, are to the purpose, and will justify our proceedings.

Ref. I look on Mr. *Fear* as a very corrupt commentator on the Scripture. I wish you well, brethren, but I will be companion to friend *Sincere*, and by the grace of *Immanuel*, I will serve him without fear all the days of my life[3].

[1] Prov. xxviii. 14.   [2] Matt. x. 23.   [3] Luke i. 74, 75.

Thus

Thus were the Pilgrims separated from each other; and *Resolute* and *Sincere* went up the eminence towards the house *Beautiful*. When they came to the copse, old *Prejudice* appeared with his dogs. He was a hideous figure, and trembled with malice at the Pilgrims. *Resolute* and *Sincere* walked close on the other side of the road. The old man endeavoured to set on his dogs, but they seemed quite full and idle, and paid no regard either to the Pilgrims or their master; who, when he saw they had escaped his power, was almost frantic with rage, and ready to kill his dogs; but they shewed themselves surly towards him, so that he did not dare to chastise them. Then sang the Pilgrims,

  " A thousand savage beasts of prey,
  " Around this forest roam,
  " But *Judah*'s *lion* guards the way,
  " And guides the travellers home."

They went on singing until they came to the house *Beautiful*, when the porter, who was standing at the door, thus addressed them.

Watchful. Gentlemen, whither are you bound in this chearful mood?

Res. We are bound to *Mount Zion*, and sing, because our *Lord* has thus far made our journey prosperous. Pray, have you any room in your house for us? I perceive that you have much company, and if we shall encumber you, we will go farther, as it is yet high day.

Watchful. Go farther! No, no; we want such joyous souls as you seem to be: my mistresses will kindly receive you. Come in therefore, ye blessed of the *Lord*, and partake of all this house can afford.

So the two pilgrims entered, and were graciously received by *Prudence*, *Piety*, and *Charity*, who still keep the house, and, it is imagined, will never die. These questioned the Pilgrims, before the company, concerning their journey, and the views they had in making it; to all which having given satisfactory answers; they were joyfully welcomed by all present, who desired fired them to fit and affift in finging a hymn on their arrival.

"Who can defcribe the joys that rife,
"Thro' all the courts of *Paradife*,
"To fee a Prodigal return,
"To fee an heir of glory born?

With joy the Father doth approve,
"The fruit of His eternal love:
"The Son with joy looks down and fees,
"The purchafe of his agonies.

"The Spirit takes delight to view,
"The holy foul he form'd anew;
"And faints and angels join to fing,
"The growing empire of their king. WATTS.

Sincere and *Refolute* were much pleafed with the company, and the kind reception they met with; for they were as friendly to each other, as if they had been many years acquainted. But the Pilgrims greatly defired to know, how it happened that fo many perfons were affembled together at this houfe. An opportunity foon offered, for informing themfelves in thefe particulars; but the evening coming on, it was propofed to fing, and prepare to part. So they fung,

"Who on earth can conceive, how happy we live,
"In the city of *God* our great *King?*
"What a concert of praife, when our *Jefus*'s grace
"The whole heavenly company fing?
WHITEFIELD.

After this they all kneeled down, and one of them very warmly recommended the whole company to the grace of the *King*, in *Immanuel*. He prayed for all pilgrims, for the profperity and fpiritual peace of the *City of Eftablifhment*, and its fuburbs: for all who laboured to win fouls, of all denominations; and for the greater abounding of candour and charity among all Chriftians.

They then arofe, gave our Pilgrims the right-hand of *Fellowfhip*, and departed towards the *City of Eftablifhment*.

·C H A P.

CHAP. XI.

The utility of candour and communion among religious people of different denominations. The manner how Probus and Friendly were restored.

WHEN the company was gone, *Resolute* looked eagerly after them, to observe how the dogs would behave towards them; and was surprised to see that they regarded not the beasts, nor the beasts them. Old *Prejudice* indeed gnashed his teeth at them as they passed, and wished the house on fire, and all its inhabitants burning therein. The matrons of the house seeing the Pilgrims attention drawn towards the departed company, thus addressed them.

Prudence. I perceive you were very attentive to those people while here, and to their behaviour on the road.

Res. We were, and would gladly be informed whence they came, and who they are?

Prud. They are inhabitants of the city and suburbs which you passed by.

Res. What! Do those different sects unite together in such matters?

Piety. Some of them do. Oh, Sirs, these are golden days to what we have seen. This house is now become the resort of warm-hearted unprejudiced souls, both of the *City of Establishment*, and its suburbs. Here they often assemble, as you have seen, and laying aside their peculiarities, unite in sweet discourse on the beauties of *Immanuel*, the riches of his grace, the glory of his salvation, and the experience of it on their own hearts. It would do your souls good to be here, when *Fervidus* and other ministers of the city and different streets, meet here,

and

and unite in devotion. They come here alſo to ſee the armory, and the many curioſities of our houſe and garden; for tho' each of theſe ſects has its curioſities, yet they are neither ſo rich, or uſeful as ours; which is an accurate model of all that is to be ſeen, in the *City of God*, whither you will arrive in *good* time. Nor can any perſon of the city or ſtreets know what may be ſeen of theſe things, unleſs they will viſit this houſe.

Sincere. There are then, certain in thoſe places who do not viſit you?

Piety. Yes, too many, and ſuch as we muſt believe to be pilgrims too, who not only refuſe to enter theſe doors; but, are very ſevere againſt ſuch as do. They urge, that it is a breaking down all neceſſary diſtinctions, and laying things in common which ought to be kept ſeparate: that it is an unſcriptural candour, and ſuch a relaxed diſcipline as ſhould not be tolerated.

Sincere. I fear, that ſuch perſons have too much of the bigoted pride of the ruler of the ſynagogue, who rebuked the man with the withered hand[1], and others, for coming to be healed on the ſabbath-day. Such perſons may have great gifts, but are little acquainted with *St. Paul*'s more excellent way[2]. It ſeems plain to me, that our holy religion, with reſpect to rites ceremonies, and church-government, is a law of great liberty; and leaves Chriſtians at large in ſuch things, to follow the dictates of reaſon, governed by the word of our *King*. For if there had been a deſign to bring all Chriſtians into one uniform method of divine worſhip; theſe things would have been as accurately deſcribed in the New Teſtament, and guarded with proper ſanctions, as were the rituals of the Moſaic ſervice. But it is evident they are not ſo; and it is plain that our *King* hath and does bleſs perſons of different practices in theſe matters; which conſiderations ſhould inculcate in all, that precious grace of LOVE, which is the bond of Perfectneſs[3].

Charity. Our *King* is love; and it becomes all his children to walk in love towards each other; and it is moſt for their happineſs ſo to do. It rejoices me greatly to ſee this ſpirit prevail a-

---

[1] Luke xiii. 14. [2] 1 Cor. xii. 31. [3] Coll. iii. 14.

mong

mong good people. This house was never so pleasant to me as it now is. I think myself in the *Celestial city*, when I behold persons of the adjacent city and its suburbs, of different denominations, unite here to sing, pray, hear, and discourse together about the best things, without one word of contention. O, may this temper more generally prevail, and *Immanuel*'s ministers see eye to eye [1], while he makes his *Zion* the praise of the whole earth!

Ref. To this I give my hearty amen. But I would fain be informed, why was it that the dogs took no notice of those who went from hence?

Prud. The dogs know those persons; for they have passed and repassed so often, and frequently have thrown them a crust, or shewed kindness to them some other way; that they now give them no molestation, nor will regard the spiteful endeavours of old *Prejudice* to set them on. They had received some scraps from our visitors in the forenoon, which was the reason that they were so easy about you. And, indeed, the fears that arise in the minds of pilgrims are their worst enemies. A bold and resolute practice of their duty, never will injure them; for, " when a man's ways please the *Lord*, he maketh even his enemies to be at peace with him [2]."

Ref. That I know to be true by experience. But this brings to my mind what happened to two of our friends this day, when we came within sight of the dogs.

Resolute then informed the good women of the house how his brethren were decoyed away by *Mr. Fear*.

Piety. Ah! were they so prevailed on, by that enemy of our *Lord*? He has hurt many good pilgrims. I have heard of the virtues of those two men, and have no doubt of their being honest pilgrims; but am sorry they were so deceived by *Fear*, and blinded to their best interest.

Charity. But why did you not inform us of this before? that some proper means might have been taken to bring these stragglers home. Surely it becomes all true pilgrims, to restore such in the spirit of meekness; ever remembering, that themselves may stand in need of the same compassion [3].

[1] Isaiah lii. 8.   [2] Prov. xvi. 7.   [3] Gal. vi. 1.

Sincere

Sincere. My brother *Resolute* and I remonstrated against their separation, yet they would not hear. And I thought to have made it the first thing I would mention at this house; but the company we found here made me forget it until now.

Charity. These are affairs of moment, and ought not to be deferred; however, I am glad we are now informed, and will take measures accordingly.

Res. It is now late, and I fear they will not return to-night. If any persons are sent in search of them in the morning, I beg to be of the party; for I earnestly long to have them with us again.

Charity. As to their coming in of themselves, there is a thousand to one against them. Fear has drawn them into some of his pernicious snares, and will there detain them until we give assistance.

She then called the marshal of the house, whose name was *Spiritual Man*, a trusty officer; and said unto him,

Charity. Mr. Spiritual Man, early to-morrow morning, take *Meekness* and *Considerself*, your assistants[1], proceed to the *Wilderness of Fear*, in search of two Pilgrims decoyed thither; and bring them with all imaginable tenderness unto this house. These their brethren will accompany you.

Spiritual Man. I shall gladly and punctually obey you, God willing.

Early in the morning the party set out on their search. Mr. *Spiritual Man* was their guide, who declared, with tears in his eyes, that he was too well acquainted with that part of the country: having been drawn away when young by the same deceiver. And, said he, I have no doubt of finding the Pilgrims in some pit or snare. They went on talking until they entered the wilderness, which, from the house of Mr. *Fear*, is called by his name. They had not advanced far, when they heard at a distance a mournful sound. As they drew nearer, it seemed to arise out of the ground, and they found it to be the voice of a man in great distress; for they heard him distinctly

[1] Gal. vi. 1.

say

fay, "Ah, woe to us, poor Pilgrims! We are now made fully sensible that the fear of man bringeth a snare[1]. Had we listened to the advice of our dear friends, we had now been happy with them at the house *Beautiful*, and not thus ensnared by our enemy, thrown into a dreadful pit, and left to perish in our own divisings."

Ref. Oh, my friends! that is the voice of my dear brother *Probus:* let us hasten to deliver them from their misery.

So they made speed to the place from whence the voice proceeded; and found it to be a deep pit, in which lay *Probus* and *Friendly*, breast high in filthy water, in a very uneasy posture, and utterly unable to help themselves. When the two prisoners saw their friends and the company above, they were ready to sink under the water with shame and remorse.

Prob. Oh, my beloved friends, the sight of you gives me both pleasure and pain. You see what a situation we have procured for ourselves, and how dreadfully we are overtaken in a fault[2].

They both burst into tears.

Spiritual Man. Brethren, be not swallowed up with overmuch sorrow. We are sent by our SHEPHERD to seek you, and to restore you to liberty and joy. Take these strong cords of love[3], and place them under your arms: they have drawn many a pilgrim out of far worse circumstances than those you are in.

Then *Probus* and *Friendly* had a tender strife, about which of them should be first drawn out; for *Probus* insisted that he would be the last out, as he was first in fault. The cords therefore being fixed to *Friendly*; *Meekness* and *Considerself* with great care drew him up, and afterwards *Probus* also; and gave them a salute of congratulation, as did all who were present.

Just at this time, Mr. *Fear* appeared at a distance, and cried out,

Fear. Hold! hold! what mean you to take my prey from me, and thus deliver my lawful captives?

But *Resolute* took the staff out of the hand of *Spiritual Man*, and ran towards him; the villain seeing that weapon in the

[1] Prov. xxix. 25.   [2] Gal. vi. 1   [3] Hosea xi. 4.

hand of *Resolute*, made his escape with great precipitation; and *Resolute* returned smiling at the haste with which he retreated.

Ref. I wish he had waited for me, I would have avenged on him the injury he has done to my dear brethren.

He then embraced them, with a pearly drop shining in each eye.

Spiritual Man. Ah, *Resolute*, that enemy of pilgrims is a coward, and never will stand any contest with one who has this staff of *Perfect love* in his hand.

Ref. I marvelled greatly at his hasty flight; but knew not the cause. Seeing this staff has such admirable virtues, I should be very glad to have that, or one like it.

Spiritual Man. This you cannot have, because it is a badge of my office in the house, and was purchased at a great price.

Ref. Pray, what may such a weapon be worth?

Spiritual Man. That is a hard question indeed! I never knew any one who could answer it. This I have heard, that if the richest man in the world were to offer all his substance for one of them, he and his wealth would be despised[1].

Ref. Where do they grow? and how are they to be obtained?

Spiritual Man. That you will hear more about by and by; for the present let us hasten home with our friends, who doubtless want both food and rest.

Ref. I ask pardon for pursuing this subject so unseasonably; but the virtues of that weapon so charmed me, that I forgot my duty to my dear brethren. Come, my *Probus*, lean on me as you walk. I wish I could carry you both. I thank our *King*, I had last night a good supper, and a refreshing night's rest, therefore am strong, willing to bear your infirmities, and not to please my own flesh[2].

Prob. Thank you, thank you, kind *Resolute*. I know your friendly heart will bear any burden of mine, but I hope I shall

[1] Cant. viii. 7. [2] Rem. xv. 1.

do

do with your arm only. Come, *Friendly*, make the fame ufe of brother *Sincere*.—So they proceeded leaning on each other[1].

Sincere. My brethren, I have a cordial in my pocket, which is a folution of *Peter*'s pills, and is called *Backflider's cordial:* it was given me juft before I joined you. I found it raifed my fpirits, and enabled me to run fafter into the path of duty.

Then he gave each of the Pilgrims a little, which fo ftrengthened them, that they walked apace towards the houfe finging,

" O may the righteous when I ftray,
" Smite and reprove my wand'ring way!
" Their gentle words, like ointment fhed,
" Shall never bruife, but cheer my head.

" When I behold them prefs'd with grief,
" I'll cry to Heaven for their relief;
" And by my warm petitions prove
" How much I prize their faithful love.

WATTS.

C H A P. XII.

How Probus *and* Friendly *were received at the houfe* Beautiful. *A walk in the garden.* Mr. Spiritual Man *begins a remarkable Story.*

CHARITY was eagerly expecting the return of her party. She ordered the porter to look out for them, had provided a repaft fuitable to the circumftances of the family, and was herfelf with the porter when they came in fight. As they approached, fhe ran and welcomed them back; and, with a fmile of great delight, congratulated the two Pilgrims on their deli-

[1] Gal. vi. 2.

verance; while they inwardly groaned, under a fenfe of their utter unworthinefs of fuch a gracious reception.

Being all come in, *Piety* folemnly bleffed the provifion, and they all fat down to eat. Each had his portion, but *Charity* had provided a peculiarly precious mefs for *Probus* and *Friendly*. It was compofed of thofe exceeding great and precious delicacies, which *St. Peter* fpeaks fo rapturoufly about [1]; and which render thofe who feed on them both chearful, ftrong, and free from grofs humours. The Pilgrims foon felt the happy effects of this diet; for they began to look very tenderly towards each other, and faid,

Prob. I am amazed, that fuch a wretch as I am fhould find a place within thefe holy walls! Why was I not left to expire with famine! Why did not the pit fhut her mouth upon me! O, I am loft in wonder and praife!

Friend. Why is it that fuch a vile mifcreant, was not left to languifh under the power of *Fear*, all my days! And then to have my portion with the fearful and [2] unbelieving, in everlafting mifery! O my brethren, and ye virgins of this houfe, I am not fit to fit with you; I am afhamed and confounded at my own moft deteftable ingratitude! O how does grace reign!

Piety. I am glad to find that our folicitude for your recovery has fo happily fucceeded, and that our provifion is fo well-digefted by you. Pray be comforted. We are all debtors to the fame rich grace of our *Lord*. All pilgrims are more or lefs *Runaways* from him. The eleven apoftles of our dear *Lord* were typical of their fucceffors in the pilgrim life, for they all forfook him and fled: but he recalled them by his grace, and received them again in love. So let us receive each other, and unite in celebrating the high praifes of him, whofe love is like himfelf, unchangeable and everlafting.

" O Lord, how great's the favour?
" That we, fuch finners poor,
" Should, thro' thy blood's fweet favour,
" Approach thy mercy's door;

[1] 2 Pet. i. 4. [2] Rev. xxi. 8.

" And

" And find an open paſſage
" Unto the throne of grace,
" And hear the welcome meſſage,
" That bids us go in peace.   WHITEFIELD.

After this refreſhment, *Probus* and *Friendly* defired a little reſt, as they had none the preceeding night. *Charity* conducted them into the *Chamber of Invitation*; over the door of which was wrote in golden letters, " Come unto me all ye that labour, and are heavy laden, and I will give you reſt [1]." It was a ſpacious room, and had every convenience in it for thoſe who were invited. At the upper-end was a ſtriking picture of *Immanuel*, ſo contrived, that it ſeemed to ſpeak and act from life. The walls were adorned with rich tapeſtry, in which were wrought many wonderful cures effected on perſons who had ſlept in that chamber; ſuch as *David*, *Heman*, and *Hezekiah*, with many others; who were repreſented as finding inſtant relief in this place. The pilgrims repoſed themſelves on the downy bed of *Promiſe*, which was made purpoſely for them by *Immanuel*'s own hands [2]; and ſoon fell aſleep. Where we will leave them awhile, and return to the other company. They were now walking in the garden; which is one of the wonders of the world: For here grows the *Balm of Gilead* [3]; the vine, of which *Jehovah* is the huſband-man [4]; the fig-tree, whoſe fruit cured *Hezekiah* [5]. Here alſo is the *Tree of Life*, and the famous *Apple Tree*, whoſe ſhadow and fruit is ſo celebrated by *Solomon* [6]. Here is the *Roſe of Sharon*, and the *Lilly of the Vallies* [7]. Here grow alſo the Myrrh and Spikenard, Camphire and Pomegranates, with all the ſpices of the merchants [8]; and a thouſand other rarities, which engroſſed the attention of *Reſolute* and *Sincere*, who were ready to ſwoon away in this wilderneſs of ſweets.

Sincere. Happy are ye, O inhabitants of this houſe! How goodly your tents, O *Prudence* and *Piety*, and thy garden, O *Charity!* Who is like unto you, ye true *Iſraelites*; a people ſaved and bleſſed by the *Lord!* Who enjoy the privilege of walking daily in this garden, and conſtantly taſting theſe fruits.

[1] Matt. xi. 28. [2] Heb. vi. 13. [3] Jer. viii. 22. [4] Iſaiah v. 7.
[5] Iſaiah xxxviii. 21. [6] Cant. ii. 3. [7] Cant. ii. 1. [8] Cant. iv. 13, 14.

Spiritual Man. When we confider our unworthy felves, we may well be amazed at this profufion of bleflings: but when we reflect on the price that was paid for this fpot, and the dignity of *Him* who laboured to cultivate it; our wonder then ceafes: for it was bought with the precious blood of our *King*'s only fon; and every thing in it was planted by his heavenly father. It is alfo watered every moment, and watched night and day, by the gracious *Prince Paraclete*[1].

Ref. Here is a fingular tree, which has feats round it, methinks I would fit down under its fpreading fhadow, as the fun advances to his meridian.

Piety. This is the [2] apple-tree, fo famous among pilgrims in all ages, for hundreds of years paft, it being fpoken of by King *Solomon.* Come, let us all partake of the offered benefit.

So they fat down under the tree, whofe fpreading branches, laden with precious fruit, bent down and courted their acceptance. They plucked and found them fweet unto their tafte. Alfo the very feat communicated eafe; and at the fame time a refrefhing breeze, having fwept over the beds of fpices, brought a moft delicious fragrancy to their fenfes, fo that the whole company was overcome with the odour. *Sincere* and *Refolute* not being accuftomed to fuch delights, fwooned, fell back againft the tree, and there lay in a moft pleafing trance.

Piety. What a fatisfaction it is to fee young men thus delighted with the beft things! We have here a double pleafure, for we enjoy the fame happinefs as thofe pilgrims, and alfo the delight of feeing the grace of *Immanuel* operate on their tender minds. Let them enjoy this rapture while they may; I forefee that much trouble will attend their future progrefs; and our *King* is thus preparing them for future trying fcenes.

The virgins arofe, and retired into the houfe, leaving the Pilgrims afleep under the apple-tree. When dinner was ready, it was thought neceffary to call them; for they were all fo fweetly repofed, that otherwife they would have flept all day. So *Prudence* rung for *Probus* and *Friendly*, who foon roufed and came down: fhe then ran into the garden to

[1] Ifaiah xxvii. 3. [2] Cant. ii. 3.

the

the other two, whose pleasant countenances as they lay, manifested the tranquility of their minds. They started at her voice, arose immediately, and followed her.

The dinner was made up chiefly of fat things full of marrow, and of wines on the lees well refined[1]. The Pilgrims eat and drank abundantly, and were again transported at their rich entertainment.

Ref. Well, brethren, of all the houses I have been in, I never saw the like of this; and I fear we shall never find such another.

Spiritual Man. This house, indeed, well deserves the name it bears: but do not think you have seen all that our *Immanuel* has to shew you, for you will see greater things than these.

Prob. Now you are speaking of sights, I have heard that there are many curiosities in this house. We should be very glad to see them.

Spiritual Man. There are, and after dinner you shall see them.

Ref. Before we see your curiosities, pray, Sir, satisfy my inquiry, in respect to your staff, which was so terrifying to Mr. Fear: for, I long to hear your story, and to know how you obtained that excellent weapon. I would encounter some trouble to obtain such a favour.

Spiritual Man. If I mistake not, my young friend, your resolution will be sharply tried; but trust in the *Lord* for ever, he will never leave you, nor forsake you. But I fear my story will appear rather tedious.

Prob. Dear Sir, pray make no abridgments, nor any farther apology.

Spiritual Man. My original name was *Alien*. I was born in the *City of Resistance*, the capital of *Flintshire*, many leagues north of the *City of Destruction*; and there abode till I was grown up to manhood. I was frequently troubled in the night with an apparition, that called itself *Eternity*; which used to tell me, our city would be destroyed for ever, and a final

[1] Isaiah xxv. 6.

end put to all the affairs in which I was employed. This much frightened me, and caused me to shrink in my bed, and wish for the morning; that I might go to work, and lose these reflections: but the apparition would return at night, and read its dismaying lecture to me. This was done so often, that I began to be serious, to reflect on my future state, and inquire about the salvation of my soul.

About that time, our city was visited by certain preachers in connection with *Fervidus*, who confirmed all that the apparition had said, warned me to seek for a refuge from the approaching storm, described the way to the *Strait Gate*, and told me the certainty of a welcome reception there. They also dispersed many books in the town, which contained directions for such as would go on pilgrimage. One of these books I obtained, and, being naturally reserved, kept all that I felt to myself; but was determined to set out in search of the great things, that I had heard and read concerning the *City of God*.

Accordingly, I left our city, and our shire, and came on apace, incessantly reading in my book; until I came to the *Slough of Despond*, which I got well over, by the help of my guide. When I had advanced a little way from the *Slough*; I was accosted by two persons, whom I afterwards found to be Messrs. *Suspicion* and *Folly*. These gave me joy on my easy passage over the *Slough*; but hinted withal, that those pilgrims who were most bemired in that place, or were much terrified at *Mount Sinai*, generally were the most steady, happy, and highly favoured in their future progress. " But you," said *Suspicion*, " who have fared so well at the *Slough*, and passed this mountain while it is quiet and pleasant, must not expect such testimonies of our *Lord's* favour as others." In short, they made out that I ought to question whether I was a pilgrim. I began to listen to them, and to be of their opinion. Mr. *Folly* observing this, advised me, as it was a fine day, and no sign of an eruption; that I would visit *Mount Sinai*, and make some discoveries on its summit.

I foolishly turned aside, went with them quite to the top of the mountain, and looked into the horrid crater, or

dreadful

dreadful furnace of flaming sulphur. While I, with my foolish counsellors, stood looking, Lo, the mountain suddenly trembled, which was succeeded by the most terrible thunders; and a shower of stones and cinders was thrown from the volcano, which fell thick around us. *Folly* was slain by my side. *Suspicion* fled away like lightening. Immediately I perceived rising from the flaming *Tophet*, a terrible person, who, with a flaming sword in his hand, made towards me; at the same instant a voice cried, "Escape for thy life; strive to enter in at the *Strait Gate*[1]." On this I turned towards the *Gate*, and ran swiftly down the hill[2]; the hideous form following me. I made towards the road, and soon got into it: then a man named *Fleshly Wisdom* endeavoured to detain me; but I threw him down in my hurry, and ran over him, while he cried aloud after me, "An enthusiast! a madman!"

I pressed on to the *Gate*, expecting every moment to feel the flaming sword in my heart, and ready to faint with fear and fatigue. When I drew near the *Gate*, the enemy fired thick at me from the castle, and one of the arrows sticking in my path, I tripped against it, and being too weak to recover myself, I fell with my whole weight against the *Gate*[3], which flying open, I fell prostrate on the threshold of the *Gate*, and fainted away.

Ref. That was a hard push indeed, you may be said to take the kingdom by violence[4]. Pray, how was you received by the man?

Spiritual Man. When I recovered, I found myself in the arms of Mr. *Goodwill*, who, as soon as I opened my eyes, bid me be of good cheer. I began to look about for the person with the dreadful sword, and to apologize for my rudeness in bursting open the *Gate*. But he graciously smiled, and said, "He knew I was at hand, and had set the *Gate* a jar, that I might the more easily enter." Then turning to the avenger who had pursued me, he told him, "that he might return from whence he came, and inform those who sent him, that *He* would be [6] *surety for me*."

[1] Gen. xix. 17.—Luke xiii. 24.   [2] Heb. vi. 18.   [3] Luke xviii. 39.
[4] Matt. xi. 12.   [5] Gal. iii. 13.

On which the avenger smoothed his frowning aspect, put up his sword, and, bowing respectfully, retired. Mr. *Goodwill* changed my name to *Hopeful*.

C H A P. XIII.

Mr. Spiritual Man *finishes his Narrative. The Pilgrims view the curiosities of the house, and depart.*

Spiritual Man. WHEN I came to the *Cross*, I had a glorious discovery of what Mr. *Goodwill* hinted at, namely, That he would be surety for me. For I saw clearly how my sins were laid on the *Crucified one*, and how the curse was removed, by his being made a curse for me. From thence I came on to the *City of Establishment*, where I was decoyed into the house of Mr. *Shame*, who lives in *Sneaker's-Alley*. There I abode a long time, and was so bewitched by that enemy of pilgrims, that I would not be seen where pilgrims resorted, unless by night; and then avoided all converse with them: but altho' my conscience daily reproached my conduct; yet I strictly attended *Temple* service in *Arminian-street*, against my better knowledge.

Here I lived very low, for Mr. *Shame* kept a wretched table I grew lean, hagged, and low-spirited. One evening as we sat by the fire, we were alarmed with a surprizing loud rap at the door; on which I arose, and went to know the occasion. When I had opened the door, I saw a glorious form before me, which immediately turned, and walked away, saying, with a solemn accent, "Whosoever is ashamed of me, before this wicked generation, of him will I be ashamed, when I come in the glory of my father, and his holy angels¹." At this I gave a

¹ Luke ix. 26.

shriek,

shriek, and swooned away. When I came to myself, I told Mr. *Shame*, that I would stay no longer with him, but was determined to depart in the morning.

The next day, Mr. *Shame* kindly offered to go a little way with me, which I had not the courage to refuse. We came together as far as *Nicodemus's-lane:* Mr. *Fear* was attending there: *Shame* and he being near a kin, were very social; and I was easily persuaded to go with Mr. *Fear*. He conducted me into the wilderness from whence we lately brought our friends, and led me to his habitation, which is a large house in a wood, and in continual alarm from thieves and wild beasts. Here I was put into the custody of *Mrs. Torment*, who is the cruel sister of Mr. *Fear*, and keeps his house¹. Now I perceived that I was a prisoner at large; for all my motions were watched; and altho' I did not like my situation, yet I had no heart to attempt an escape. Mrs. *Torment* took pleasure at my misery: for she shewed me a room hung round with various representations of the torments of the *Pit*, which she said I had merited, and probably would suffer. She terrified me with horrid views of death; and at the same time put a yoke on my neck, which I could not get off all the while I abode in that house².

Here I had no rest day or night; I could hardly eat or drink, and was worn to a skeleton. I was sensible of my miserable situation, but I had wilfully submitted to the power of these enemies, and therefore was left to their mercy. Now I was dejected almost to despair, and here I had ended my days, had not the *Keeper of Israel* made a way for me to escape.

Ref. I long to know by what means you was delivered.

Spiritual Man. It was as follows. The person who then bore the office in this house which I now enjoy, was named Mr. *Newman*, and was preferred by our *Lord* to a more honourable employ. When the order for his dismission came hither, it was commanded, "that Mr. *Newman* should take his marshal's staff with a posse, and proceed to the house of *Fear* in the wilderness; and, in the *King*'s name, demand one *Hopeful*, who

¹ 1 John iv. 18.   ² Heb. ii. 15.

was detained there, bring him to the houfe *Beautiful*, and appoint him marfhal in the ftead of Mr. *Newman*; by the name of *Spiritual Man*."

Accordingly, the marfhal arrived at *Fear*'s houfe: and ftanding at the door, he called aloud, [1] " *Hopeful*, the mafter calleth thee!" At this I ftarted, and faid, fomebody calls me, and I believe fome good news is at hand. But Mr. *Fear* faid, the call was not directed unto me. However, Mr. *Newman* came in, faying yet louder, " Fear not *Hopeful*, I am with thee, be not difmayed, for I am thy God[2]. I am *Immanuel*, who came to deliver them, who thro' the fear of death are fubject to bondage[3]. And then fhewing his ftaff, *Fear* and his fifter fled by a back door; my yoke fell from my neck, and an amazing inexpreffible change for the better was inftantly wrought upon me, and in me. Mr. *Newman* then conducted me to this houfe, and prefented me to my good miftreffes.

In thefe bleffed quarters I foon recovered my flefh and ftrength[4]. But when I was informed of my promotion, I was exceedingly confounded, and ftrongly remonftrated againft fuch a feeming impropriety, that I, who had been fo fhamefully duped and foiled by the enemy, fhould be chofen to an office of fuch truft. But it was anfwered, that " It was their *Lord*'s pleafure; who very frequently chofe weak things to confound the mighty, and things that are not, to bring to nought things that are[5]." So I was obliged to fubmit; and am fo happy as to find, that I, who was fo timorous as to think that I muft be new created to be otherwife; yet, by *Immanuel*'s grace, and the virtue of this ftaff, I now am ftrong, and triumph over my former enemies.

Frien. Sir, I am particularly thankful for your narrative; you have in many things laid open my vile nature, and cowardly practice. I remember when I was fo foolifhly employed, not only to go out of my way to feek for terrors, as you did to *Mount Sinai*; but I even prayed the *Lord* to fend them; and have been anfwered to my great trouble. My *folly*, indeed, is flain, and all my *fufpicions* of that fort, are now fled away.

[1] John xi. 28. [2] Ifaiah xli. 10. [3] Heb. ii. 15. [4] Pfalm xcii. 14.
[5] 1 Cor. i. 27, 28.

They then arose, and were taken to see the curiosities of the house, which had in miniature almost every thing that is to be seen at the *City of God*. First, they went into the cellars, and saw the vast stores of delicious meats, wines and fruits, which were all like the widow's barrel of meal, and cruise of oil, which never waited, tho' they had been in use several thousand years. From thence they went to the banqueting-house and galleries, taken notice of by King *Solomon*[1]. Next they visited the wardrobe, and saw the garments of wrought gold[2]. In the treasury were unsearchable riches[3]; and at the opening of the doors, the diamonds, pearls, gems, &c. poured on them such a blaze of glory that the Pilgrims could not behold: but passed on to the library; which consisted only of sixty-six volumes; but they were amazing compositions. They contained a concise history of that house, and a narrative of the life and atchievements of *Immanuel*. The things they treat of, are of so copious a nature, that the whole world could not contain the books that might be written on them[4]. From thence they went to the armory, and saw all that was shewn to *Christian* in that place.

The chambers of this house were noble and exceeding pleasant. That of *Invitation* has been already mentioned; from thence they ascended to the *Chamber of Peace*; above which is that of *Joy*. These were each of the same dimensions as the *Chamber of Invitation*. That of *Joy* had noble sashes looking full south; so that the sun sometimes shines into it with unspeakable glory, as it did when *St. Peter* was there[5]. Over this chamber is the famous observatory; from whence may be seen the *Delectable Mountains*, and even the gates of the *Celestial City*. Up thither they took the Pilgrims; and, the horizon being clear, they had a charming view of those things; so that the Pilgrims cried out in rapture, Surely, to depart, and be with *Immanuel*, is better than groveling in this wilderness[6]!

Prudence. These enjoyments are certainly very desirable; and your passage unto their full fruition may be very afflicting; but a great part of your duty and happiness as pilgrims, con-

---

[1] Cant. ii. 4. [2] Psalm xlv. 13. [3] Ephes. iii. 3. [4] John xxi. 25.
[5] 1 Pet. i. 8. [6] Phil. i. 23.

fifts in fubmitting, without referve, unto the will of our *Celeftial King*; and to be willing either to ftay in this world, or to depart, as it pleafeth him.

Piety. That, my fons, is the fum of your duty; attend to it, and be happy: for, be you well affured of the truth of that precious promife, "All things fhall work together for good to you[1]."

They defcended from the obfervatory, and fpent the evening in difcourfing on the wonderful things they had feen. When the Pilgrims were inclined to fleep, they were lodged in the *Chamber of Peace*; the walls of which were adorned with paintings, that fet forth the amazing deeds of the *Prince of Peace*. The foftnefs of the bed furpaffed all underftanding; for it was the contrivance of the *King* himfelf[2]. An unufual pleafure was felt when the Pilgrims reclined thereon, which induced them to break forth into this fong of praife.

" Lord, how fecure and bleft are they,
" Who feel the joys of pardon'd fin!
" Should ftorms of wrath fhake earth and fky,
" Their fouls have heav'n and peace within."

WATTS.

When they ceafed, they were fweetly lulled by the echo of their fong, which reverberated from the roof and fides of the chamber, untill they fell afleep. In the morning they awoke like giants refrefhed with wine. Thus they continued a few days, enjoying all that the houfe could afford, and receiving various leffons of inftruction. When they defired to depart, they were prefented with fome of the beft provifions; and each was clothed with the garment of *Humility*[3]: which *Piety* faid, if they took proper care of, would in moft cafes fupply the want of armour; and be much lefs encumbering to them in their journey. Being thus furnifhed, they took their leave with many expreffions of gratitude, for the numerous favours they had received.

[1] Rom. viii. 28.   [2] Phil. iv. 7.   [3] 1 Pet. v. 5.

CHAP. XIV.

The Pilgrims insulted in going down Immanuel's Path. Resolute *and* Probus *drawn aside.* Sincere *and* Friendly, *at the* Bridge *of* Trial, *decoyed by Mr.* Trim *up* Demas's *stairs, and fall into* Cross's *dungeon.*

FOR some time the Pilgrims proceeded in a fine, pleasant, open country: at length they came to a large road, which turned off to the left; this road seemed much beaten by carriages and horses; but the direct way began from thence to grow narrow, and appeared to be not much frequented. At the turning of the road stood a high post, with an index pointing to the left, and an inscription as follows; *The new road thro' the Vallies.* The Pilgrims stood a little while to reflect, but *that* direction occurring to their minds, by which they were advised, to seek for the *good old way* [1]; they kept strait forward; and soon found themselves on the brow of a steep hill, down which was a path into the *Valley of Humiliation*, which is called *Immanuel's Path* [2].

The Pilgrims were grossly treated as they went down this descent, by a great number of the baser sort, of both sexes, and of all ages. They were inhabitants of the *City of Depravity* [3], which was a little to the left, and through which the new road lay. The Pilgrims bore with their scoffs and insults for some time, with great patience and temper; which made the mob yet more outrageous; so that, to their cruel mockings, they added spitting, and throwing dirt on them. At length the Pilgrims began to be chaffed. *Resolute* on the right-hand, and *Probus* on the left, remonstrated against their unreasonable abuse

[1] Jer. vi. 16.   [2] Phil. ii. 2.   [3] 1 Pet. iv. 4.

G

and ill-treatment, but they only became the more insolent: and one, more audacious than the rest, gave *Resolute* a severe blow on the face; which so irritated him, that he stepped aside to chastise the offender; but he being nimble, escaped into the adjacent wood, and *Resolute* foolishly pursued the fugitive, leaving his brethren to proceed without him.

On the other side, the enemy fell on *Probus* with their tongues, and one especially, whom he knew, abused him in so gross a manner, that, desiring his brethren to excuse him a little, he hastened to the adjacent town, with a resolution to bring the offender to justice. Thus were *Sincere* and *Friendly* left to pursue their journey by themselves. They soon got clear of their enemies, for they left *Sincere* and his brother, in order to observe the proceedings of *Resolute* and *Probus*.

When these two Pilgrims, *Sincere* and *Friendly*, had advanced into the *Valley of Humiliation*, they were amazed at each other; for the sun shone so powerfully on them, that every spot of dirt which had stuck to them, fell off; and in its place appeared a beautiful mark, adorning their garments of humility. At the same time, their hearts were filled with joy and exceeding gladness; because all manner of evil had been spoken against them falsely, for *Immanuel*'s *sake*[1]. Therefore they went on singing,

" Bless'd are the suff'rers who partake,
" Of pain and shame, for *Jesu*'s sake;
" Their hearts shall triumph in the *Lord*,
" Glory and joy are their reward." WATTS.

After singing, they kneeled down and blessed the *King*, who had enabled them to endure cruel mockings for *Immanuel*'s sake: they also recommended their dear brethren to his protection; and prayed that *Jehovah* would have mercy on their enemies, persecutors and slanderers, and turn their hearts. Now, they sweetly experienced, what *St. Peter*[2] says, the pilgrims of his time enjoyed.

[1] Mat. v. 11.   [2] 1 Pet. iii. 14.

Thus

Thus they went on with much pleasure, until they had proceeded a few miles in the valley; having high hills on each side. At length they were overtaken by a smart young man, who came from a road on the left of the highway, whose name was *Trim*[1]; but the Pilgrims neither knew him, nor inquired his name. Being come near, he saluted them, and asked very kindly whither they were bound?

Sincere. We are going to *Mount Zion*, the *City of the living God*.

Trim. I am very glad of that, for I am going to the same place, and shall be happy in your company.

Sincere. But how is it, that you have not kept in the highway?

Trim. I heard of the insolent mob, that obstructs the road at the descent of the hill; so I took a small compass to avoid them.

Sincere. They were very troublesome to us; but, it is dangerous turning out of the road, on any such pretence.

Trim. I am perfectly acquainted with all the cross-roads in this country, having made geography my study from a boy: unless a person has such skill, I acknowledge it is dangerous, and sinful to turn aside; but, to me, and any one thus endowed; all things of this sort are lawful. I know, by my skill in this science, that we are not far from a most disagreeable part of our journey, which is called *St. Paul's Arch*, because he mentions his passing thro' it[2]. But geography, like other sciences, has been much improved since the Apostle's time: and, if my art does not deceive me, I shall find out a way, by which we may easily overcome that obstacle.

Then lifting up his eyes, he pointed, saying, Yonder is the impediment I speak of. It was an enormous bridge of hewn stone, built quite across the valley, and raised nearly to the height of the hills on each side. It is called the *Bridge of Trial*, has a balustrade on each side, and over it is a spacious

[1] Mat. xvi. 25, & John xii. 41, 43. [2] 1 Cor. iv. 13.

highway, where carriages may commodiously pass each other. This road is called, The *Way of the world*; and was made on purpose to accommodate those, who do not care to go down into the *Valley of Humiliation*. It is a prodigious thoroughfare; for the turnpike road, from the *City of Depravity* to that of *Sensuality*, lays over this bridge. The water and filth collected on the bridge, are drained off, by various channels, into one common sewer; which empties itself into the *Valley of Humiliation*, directly over a single small arch that is turned under the bridge, and is the only passage for pilgrims thro' this valley. The sewer was venting itself very plentifully when our Pilgrims came to it; the arch also was low, and must be passed on the knees—After looking at it for some time, said,

Sincere. Oh, what a vile project was this, to interrupt the *King*'s highway!

Frien. I can scarcely bear this intolerable stench, but must retire a little, and wait until the sewer has vented itself of its filth.

Trim. That will exercise your patience indeed! rather be advised by me; put yourselves under my direction, and I will engage to conduct you safe to the other side. We are not to rush blindly into trouble, but are commanded to be [1] wise as serpents, and to try all things and ways[2]. As for me, I am not ignorant of the *Black Tyrant*'s devices, and hope I shall find some method that is provided to elude this vile passage.

So saying, he turned to the left, and the Pilgrims followed him. He led them on by the side of the bridge, 'till they began to ascend the hill; at length he discovered a stair-case up the bridge, at which he exclaimed,

Trim. Ah! my knowledge has not deceived me. I judged it could not be our duty to defile our garments, and stoop to that mire, in these times of universal christianity; accordingly, behold a way of escape. I have heard of this flight of steps, they will lead us to the top; and there is another flight on the

[1] Mat. x. 16. [2] 1 Thess. v. 21.

oppofite

opposite side, which will convey us down again. You see the steps are well worn, let us embrace this kind offer.

So up he ran, and the Pilgrims went after him, until they were near the top: when, behold, a trap door opened under them, and they fell into a dungeon at the bottom of the bridge! *Trim* escaped the trap, but the door closed on the Pilgrims, and they were left to reflect on their folly.

CHAP. XV.

What passed in Cross's *Dungeon.* Probus *and* Resolute *deliver their brethren. They all pass* St. Paul's Arch, *and arrive at the* Lamb Inn.

AFTER lying astonished a little while, the Pilgrims roused, and said,

Sincere. Ah, brother, where are we now?

Frien. I was suspicious of that deceiver; but his smooth tongue and the filthy condition of our way, perverted my judgment.

Sincere. So they also did mine; and we are now justly punished for our folly. But let us examine our situation, and endeavour to get out of it.

They then arose, and looked about them; when, by the light of a small iron grate window thro' the wall of the bridge; they discovered near them, a most hideous form, with a key in its hand. This figure made them tremble; especially when, with a ghastly smile, it thus addressed them.

Cross. Pilgrims, fear not my forbidding aspect and appearance. My name is *Cross*. By my father's side, I am of an ancient and honourable family. I am a friend to true pilgrims; all of whom I have at times had in my dungeon, or in other places

under

under my difcipline [1]; but I never did them any real injury. It is often for want of acquaintance with me that many go aftray; as one of the moft eminent among you has [2] acknowledged. *St. Paul* was my friend; nay, he [3] gloried in my company. Look round my grotto; it is not, indeed [4], joyous to refide in; yet here are no damps that will injure the health of *your fouls*; for the air is much better here, than it is at the top of the bridge; and will have happy effects on you, after your deliverance.

At the laft word, *Sincere* took courage, and faid,

Sincere. Deliverance, Sir! Is there hope of that? When will it happen? Who is to bring it about?

Crofs. Be not fo affrighted. You muft learn to be more familiar with me; you will then find me a fkilful advifer in many cafes incident to pilgrims. Deliverance you certainly will have: for this confinement is a fure fign of your being children of our *King*. I [5] never had a baftard in this dungeon. I was ordered to take you into cuftody; for what reafon you will know hereafter; but how long you are to be here, or how you are to be releafed, I know not. This is the key of the prifon, but no mortal can unlock the door; fo make yourfelves as eafy as poffible, and pray to the *King* for help. This place has been famous for praying pilgrims; I have feen and heard fuch tranfactions of this fort in my cave; that I have thought our *Lord* had put his beft birds in this cage, on purpofe that he might hear them mournfully fing, and powerfully pray.

Frien. What, does our *Lord* deign to regard us while in this difmal place?

Crofs. I fuppofe you think yourfelves to be in trouble; and if fo, your *Lord* has not only promifed you fhall have his notice; but alfo that *he himfelf* will be with you [6]. I had a fine lady once within thefe walls, who was a type of you Pilgrims; fhe could by no means be reconciled to her fituation, but wept and took on moft bitterly; on which our *Lord* came, and looking at her thro' the window, called her his love and his dove.

[1] 1 Tim. iii. 12. [2] Pfalm cxix. 67. [3] Gal. vi. 14. [4] Heb. xii. 11.
[5] Heb. xii. 8. [6] Pfalm xci. 15.

Tho'

Tho' her eyes were full of tears, her features marred with grief, and her voice tremulous and broken; yet, I well remember his speaking to her in the following tender words, namely, " O my dove, that art in the secret places of the stairs; let me hear thy voice, let me see thy face; for sweet is thy voice, and thy countenance comely¹." So after he had confined her for a small moment, he ordered her to be released, and embraced her in his arms of everlasting love².

This speech of Mr. *Cross* soothed the anguish of their hearts. He added,

Cross. Come, be a little chearful. Have you not brought something to eat from the house *Beautiful?* My dungeon does not afford much to satisfy present hunger, tho' it generally brings those to an appetite who are confined here, leads them to rummage their pockets, and draw forth many a precious morsel, which would otherwise have grown mouldy.

Frien. We have plenty of good victuals about us, which we had forgot.

On examining their store, they found some precious fare, and good old wine, on which pilgrims live; and with which they were much refreshed; nay, *Sincere* declared, that he had not fed so heartily, since he came from the wilderness at the hill *Difficulty.*

Cross. I told you that the air of my grotto was healthy. It has done my heart good oftentimes to see how some pilgrims have eat in this place: and that not of delicate food neither: no, no, this is a good situation for getting rid of a squeamish appetite. Here, scraps, crumbs, and small things will go down, without being despised, or any repining: some, indeed, have been sullen for a time, but in the end I bring every one to his submission. *Jonah* was the most wayward that I ever had to deal with; but I put him into a fish's belly, and made him glad to obey his master's orders³.

Frien. We thank you for your information in these particulars. But why is it that you appear with such a rueful aspect?

¹ Cant. ii. 14.   ² Isaiah liv. 8.   ³ Jonah iii. 3.

Cross. I am, indeed, frightful only in appearance; for in reality, I am not so; but it is impossible that I should be agreeable to any obstinate offenders, because, in such cases, I am a minister of justice.

Frien. We had two brethren, who parted from us at the descent of the hill into this valley: we hope they are well, and should be glad to be again united to them.

Cross. Then pray, pray Sirs. Heaven's eyes and ears are ever open to pilgrims who are under my custody[1].

On this the Pilgrims kneeled down, confessed their transgressions with brokenness of heart, and their sins with many tears; they besought the *Lord* to forgive them; they thanked him for bringing them into that place; earnestly prayed for their brethren, and that *he* would bring them together in his holy way once more.

Cross. This will do, my friends. I have an intimation that your deliverance is near. I had the same when *David* was under my discipline. He prayed against *Ahithophel*[2], and his prayer was instant destruction to that politician. It is a fearful thing for any person to have the prayers of pilgrims in my cave against him.

When he had done speaking, they heard the voices of persons without; on which the Pilgrims cried aloud for help. They were heard by those without; who made up to the grate from whence the sound came. But who can describe the joy and wonder of the Pilgrims, when, thro' the grate, they saw their dear brethren *Probus* and *Resolute*. They immediately made themselves and their situation known, and begged them to find some way to effect their deliverance.

Res. That, you may be certain, we will endeavour to do. But where did you enter into that horrid place?

Sincere. Don't you perceive the flight of steps that ascends the bridge? near the top is a trap door, thro' which we fell in hither.

[1] Psalm xxxiv. 17.   [2] 2 Sam. xv. 31. & xvii. 23.

Ref. We will go in search of the door.

Then *Resolute* and his brother went up the steps; carefully surveying every part, left they should share the same fate as their brethren. At length they discovered the door, and endeavoured to open it, but all in vain.

Cross. My children, you must pray earnestly to our *King*, or you cannot get forth from this place.

On this, the Pilgrims within and without, cried to their *King* for help.

Cross. Prayer will open Heaven[1], and much more my dungeon. Go forth, therefore, ye prisoners of hope, and sin no more, left a worse thing befal you[2].

Mr. *Cross* was then permitted to unlock the door, and he helped them to get out. The Pilgrims returned thanks, and embraced each other with exceeding great joy.

Frien. Blessed be the *King*, that we are once more at liberty and in the company of our brethren; but let us hasten from this dangerous place, left we meet with some further trouble.

Prob. What, is this a dangerous place?

Frien. I think our late situation proves it to be so.

Prob. Why, we were in this place before we saw you?

Frien. And probably had shared our fate, if our good *Lord* had not opened your ears to hear our cry; which was a blessing both to us and you.

Then *Friendly* told them how he and his brother had been deceived by Mr. *Trim*, and fell into the dungeon.

Prob. How wonderful are the ways of *Jehovah!* How unworthy are we of the blessings which he every day showers down upon us!

Frien. I think our garments appear much soiled and torn, for the short time we have worn them.

[1] Jam. v. 18.   [2] John v. 14.

Prob.

Prob. O brother, I find it very difficult to keep the garment of humility clean. I am sure mine is so shamefully foul, that I cannot endure myself.

Ref. Ah, fool that I am, mine is not only foul, but torn in many places.

Sincere. When I fell into the trap, I rent my robe terribly, and was almost deprived of the whole.

Thus, they mutually reproached themselves, until they came again unto the arch, and into the high road.

Sincere. Hither we came with the flatterer, but our proud stomachs were too high to suffer that indignity which the blessed *Paul* submitted to, when he wrote the words which I see are engraven over the arch: namely, "We are made as the filth of the world, and as the off-scouring of all things[1]."

Sincere then paused a little, burst into tears, and lifting up his streaming eyes to *Heaven*, he exclaimed,

Sincere. Dear *Lord*, forgive my pride and vanity, and assist me to take up thy cross and follow thee, as thy true disciple; that I may honour thee, and set an example for the imitation and encouragement of my dear brethren.

So saying, he chearfully bowed down to pass the filthy sewer, crying to his brethren.

Sincere. Strait is the gate that leadeth to everlasting life. Follow me, good *Friendly*, I have been a means to lead you wrong, now let us all go forth out of the camp with *Immanuel*, bearing his reproach[2].

This example and exhortation animated them all; so that they followed him into the arch, tho' a number of gay, vain persons were looking over the balustrade, and scoffing at them[3]. But, to encourage the Pilgrims, a voice came from *Heaven*, saying, "And ye shall be hated of all men for my name's sake, yet not a hair of your heads shall perish[4]."

[1] 1 Cor. iv. 13. [2] Heb. xiii. 13. [3] 1 Cor. iv. 9. [4] Luke xxi. 17, 18.

When they had passed this severe trial, they were surprized at the strange effect the filth had on their garments; for every spot was vanished, and every rent made whole, and they appeared more pure than when they first put them on.

Sincere. Ah, my brethren, now we have learned, that *Jehovah's* ways are far above our ways; and that before honour is humility[1]. Our carnal minds were for evading this filthy passage, as an insufferable degradation of our character; but we now find, that there is infinitely more pleasure and real advantage, in submitting to obloquy and scorn for *Immanuel*, than there is to be found in conforming to the world.

Prob. While I am amazed at the lustre of our garments, I am filled with inexpressible joy in my own soul! This brings to my mind that true saying which is written, " But, and if ye are persecuted for righteousness sake, happy are ye; for the spirit of glory and of *Jehovah* resteth on you[2]." Therefore let us sing,

" *Jesus*, the despis'd and mean,
" Our master let us own,
" He the sacrifice for sin,
" The *Saviour* He alone:
" Let us take and bear his Cross,
" Despis'd disciples let us be;
" Mock'd and slighted as he was
" For you, my friends, and me."   MADAN.

The day now began to decline, and the Pilgrims were desirous to put up for the night, that they might refresh themselves before they entered the *Valley of the Shadow of Death*, which was not very far off. Perceiving a house at a distance in the way, they hastened towards it, in hopes of finding a place of entertainment; and to their great joy, they found it to be the *Sign of the Lamb*, with an inscription signifying, that there was good entertainment for true pilgrims, by *Gideon*, a converted *Jew*, or true *Israelite*. So they went in.

[1] Prov. xv. 33.   [2] 1 Pet. iv. 14.

C H A P.

CHAP. XVI.

The adventures of Gideon, *a converted* Jew, *and master of the* Lamb Inn.

THE Pilgrims being entered the *Lamb Inn*, were shewn into a handsome parlour, and desired to sit down. Having inquired for the master of the inn, he waited upon them.

Sincere. Sir, from what we saw on your sign at the door, we have entered your house, and before we take any refreshment, beg leave to ask you, what you mean by that sign and inscription?

Gideon. By the Lamb, I mean him whom our fathers crucified at *Jerusalem*, whom I believe to be the *Lamb of God*, that taketh away the sin of the world[1]: and who, I trust, has taken away my sins.

Sincere. And who do you mean by true pilgrims?

Gideon. I mean all who love the lamb. I am, Sirs, a converted Jew. I am not converted to any particular set of notions, or any sect of Christians, but unto the *King of Saints* himself. And all who love and serve him, and are travelling to *Zion*, are most heartily welcome to my house: nor do I desire to see any others within these walls: but, as it is a public Inn, notwithstanding my scheme to prevent it, some will obtrude themselves on me.

Sincere. This, Sir, is such a house as we desired. Pray let us have what provision your Inn will afford.

[1] John i. 29.

Gideon immediately rung his bell, and ordered the servants to prepare a good supper: but, at the Pilgrims desire, he sat down, and entered into conversation with his guests.

Prob. Pray, Sir, where was you born?

Gideon. My great ancestor was a *Syrian* ready to perish [1] in idolatry, when *Jehovah* called him to become a Pilgrim. As to myself, I was born in the *City of* [2] *Contradiction*, which is inhabited wholly by Jews, who are different from all other people in the world. This city was once called *Jehovah Shammah*, because the *Lord* dwelt in it [3]. But the inhabitants rose in rebellion, and killed their lawful Prince. On this account, the city is disfranchised, the walls dismantled, the palace deserted, all their former glory is departed, and a frowning black cloud always covers it; so that no place in the world is so punished; yet the inhabitants are under no concern about it.

Prob. And how came you to be of a different disposition?

Gideon. By the free, sovereign, distinguishing grace of our *King*, no doubt: for all my countrymen have a vail on their minds, and a stone in their hearts, which our fathers cruelly imprecated from *Heaven* on their posterity: for when they murdered their Prince, they cried, "Let his blood be on us, and on our children [4]."

Sincere. That was a dreadful prayer, I tremble at your repeating it.

Gideon. This imprecation lieth heavy on them to this day. However, there is a sense in which they are still said to be beloved of the *Lord*, that is, for their pious ancestors sakes [5]. On this account, they are preserved a distinct people; and tho' their city is absolutely defenceless [6], without a king, prince, temple, sacrifice, or priest; yet Providence has, for seventeen hundred years past, preserved them from being swallowed up and lost among the nations.

Ref. And what do you think will become of them at last?

---

[1] Deut. xxvi. 5. [2] 1 Thess. ii. 15. [3] Ezek. xlviii. 35.
[4] Mat. xxvii. 25. [5] Rom. xi. 28. [6] Hosea iii. 4.

Gideon.

Gideon. I believe they will have the horrid cloud removed from their city; the [1] vail and stone will be taken away; they shall look on the Prince whom their fathers murdered, and repent; that the *King* will then pardon their sins, again visit them, and honour the city with his presence.

Ref. Are there no endeavours used by christians, to bring about these things?

Gideon. Many excellent books have been addressed to them, and dispersed in the city; and some persons have preached to them; but in general, they have hitherto shewn an obstinate refusal to acknowledge their crimes. The labours of these pious men, however, were not intirely in vain; for it was by their means, I, among others, was made acquainted with my perverseness.

Prob. Pray, what was it that made the first impression on you?

Gideon. There is one *Fervidus*, a notable ambassador of our *King*, whose zeal for his master leads him to visit almost every place. This man came into the great square of our city, and preached from the following words. " Turn ye, turn ye, for why will ye die, O house of *Israel* [2]?" I believe *that* text was never better handled since the Prophet wrote it, than it was at that time. He shewed, how the whole city was deeply concerned in it: that we had all revolted from the *King*, and rejected and killed the *Prince of Life*. For a proof of this, he appealed to the ruined walls, temple and palace, and to the desolate state of the city; which he declared never would have happened, but for such atrocious crimes. He added, that still the golden sceptre of mercy was extended towards us; that his master commanded his servants, to [3] begin their preaching in our city, and would gladly receive us again to his favour. In short, he wooed, he besought us, he wept over us; then threatened, and warned us to turn unto *Jehovah*; and was like a tender parent amidst a number of perverse children. I was struck at this sermon, and began to consider my ways. I searched the scriptures on my knees, and *Jehovah* was pleased

[1] Rom. xi. 26. & 2 Cor. iii. 25.   [2] Ezek. xxxiii. 11.   [3] Luke xxiv. 47.

to rend the vail, and remove the stone from my heart. I then sought the company of *Fervidus*, who received me with joy, and promised to go with me to the *Strait Gate*, at the head of this way.

Ref. But did not your relations and friends endeavour to prevent you?

Gideon. My parents were dead, I was left in good circumstances, and had no dependence on any of them. They of the city, indeed, made a great stir about my conversion; but I left the place, after giving them proper warning of their obstinacy and danger.

Frien. And Pray, did you succeed in your journey, and what induced you to settle in this part of the road?

Gideon. It was a great advantage to have *Fervidus* with me, in my journey to the *Gate*; for, he assisted me at the *Slough*, and preserved me from turning aside at *Mount Sinai*; unto which, I found a strong propensity. *Fervidus* told me, he knew many of my countrymen had suffered much, from their attachment to that mountain[1]; and therefore it was, that he had accompanied me. Many fiends appeared at the castle, to obstruct our entrance in at the gate: but *Fervidus*, who had often been that way, laughed at all their puny malice; and holding up his broad shield[2], easily preserved himself and me from the arrows. He then spoke some words to the enemy, that made them and their castle tremble to its foundation. After this, he knocked at the *Gate* in his peculiarly bold manner, and it was instantly opened. *Goodwill* embraced *Fervidus*, and thanked him for his care of a true *Israelite*, as he was pleased to term me. He also said, that he longed for the time, in which the whole Jewish nation should come in a body, pull down the adjacent castle, and seek to enter *that Gate*[3]. *Fervidus* left me at the *Interpreter's* house. From thence I came on by myself. At the *Cross*, I had a glorious revelation of the *Crucified one*, as the power, and the wisdom of *Jehovah*[4].

[1] John ix. 28, 29.   [2] Ephef. vi. 16.   [3] Rom. xi. 26.   [4] 1 Cor. i. 24.

I attentively confidered the road as I came along, and compared the remains of antiquity with the ancient hiftory of our nation; and have feen many houfes and monuments that were erected or inhabited by my pious anceftors, moft of which are now in ruins. When I came into the valley; I found it very delightful; and as I knew that our great lawgiver had an eminent houfe therein¹, I fearched diligently for the fpot where it had ftood, and at length found it by its ruins. I cleared away the rubbifh, and found the foundation as good as when *Mofes* began to build; fo I determined to fettle here. Accordingly, I built this houfe thereon, and being well to pafs in the world, and delighting in good company; I made my houfe an Inn, on purpofe to allure good pilgrims hither. To fhew alfo that I am not afhamed of my mafter, I made choice of the fign of the LAMB.

Gideon having finifhed his ftory, the Pilgrims arofe and embraced him, wifhing him abundant health and happinefs of foul in that place, from the prefence of the LAMB.

Gideon. I thank you for your good wifhes, and fhould be glad to know fo much of *your* hiftory as you may think ufeful to relate, for it is my great pleafure to hear, and remark the various dealings of our wonder-working *Lord* with his people. I perceive by your garments that you have been at the houfe *Beautiful*; and by their luftre, I know you have paffed *St. Paul's Arch*.

On this, the Pilgrims beheld each other with crimfon blufhes.

Gideon. What, do you blufh! by that I fear you are not without guilt; however, be not afhamed to confefs your faults one to another. I have had many fuch criminals under this roof, who have proved afterwards great men in the pilgrim world.

Ref. God forbid, that I fhould be afhamed to fpeak of his grace to my foul. My confufion arifes from a keen fenfe of mif-improvement of his grace.

¹ Numb. xii. 3.

Gideon. Both grace, and the improvement of grace, are from the *Lord.* He does not give us a portion of grace at first, and then leave us to improve it by ourselves; like an artist setting his machines in motion. Perhaps you did not sufficiently attend to this; therefore your *Lord* was obliged to put you to a school, where your pride might be humbled, by learning that most difficult lesson: " Without me ye can do nothing[1]."

Res. Really, Sir, I believe there is much truth in what you say; for I never saw myself so incapable of doing any thing, as I now do.

Gideon. Let me hear therefore, if you please, in what manner the *Lord* instructed you.

CHAP. XVII.

Probus *and* Resolute *relate their adventures while separated.* Gideon *makes proper remarks, and gives suitable reproofs. They depart.*

Res. AS we came down the hill, into this valley, we found the road on each side beset with a multitude of persecutors, of various complexions, who incessantly plied us with ridicule and dirt. We bore with them for some time: we then reasoned with them; but they grew rather more insolent. At length, one more spiteful than the rest, gave me a smart blow in the face, which threw me into a passion; and I pursued the offender into the wood on the right side of the road; but he led me a long chace, thro' briars and thorns, and at last escaped me. While eager in this pursuit, I was more hooted at and pelted than before. At length my heat abated, I gave over the chace, and returned to the road again, vexed and ashamed of my foolish conduct. When my mind became serene, I felt my

[1] John xv. 5.

H   heart

heart smite me, with thefe words, " Beloved, avenge not yourfelves, but rather give place to wrath; for it is written, vengeance is mine, I will repay, faith the *Lord*¹". I found alfo, that
my beautiful garment was fadly torn and foiled by this excur-
fion; and that I had loft my company: fo I went on very
much chagrined and penfive, until I perceived my brother
Probus, coming juft behind me.

Gideon. This affair fhould teach you, that your warm, natural
temper is not that grace of courage, which *St. Peter* exhorts us
to add to our faith²; and that perfons of fuch fanguine complexions, frequently are guilty of intemperate fallies of paffion,
and fhamefully foiled by the enemy. The perfons who affaulted
you, are the children of thofe who mocked at our *Lord*, when
he came down that hill: from whence it is called *Immanuel's
Path*; and thofe fcoffers dwell in the neighbouring *City of Depravity*. True courage confifts principally in bearing injuries
for our *Lord*'s fake; and, in fuppreffing that irritable paffion
within us. In this fenfe, *Solomon* declares, that, " He who
ruleth himfelf, is better than he who taketh a city³." This is
a hard leffon to our proud nature, and even *St. Paul*, after being
many years in the fchool of *Immanuel*, feems to be wanting in
it: for, when the high-prieft commanded him to be fmitten on
the mouth; the Apoftle loft his temper, and ⁴ reviled the ruler
of *God*'s people. Our divine mafter did not act fo, but calmly
appealed to the bar of equity. " If," faid he, " I have fpoken
evil, bear witnefs of the evil; but if not, why fmiteft thou
me⁵?" Here, O *Refolute*, is your pattern and mine: therefore, all thro' your Pilgrimage, confider him who fuffered fuch
contradiction of finners againft himfelf, that your mind⁶ may
not faint, nor be petulent in the time of trial.

While *Gideon* thus exhorted *Refolute*, he reclined his head
on the table, and fighed as if his heart would break.

Gideon. I know, my fon, that bringing near unto you fuch
an amazing pattern of meeknefs, as *Immanuel* is, will try you:
but, be comforted, he knows whereof we are made, he remem-

¹ Rom. xii. 19.   ² 2 Pet. i. 5.   ³ Prov. xvi. 32.   ⁴ Acts xxiii. 3.
⁵ John xviii. 23.   ⁶ Heb. xii. 3.

bers

bers that we are but dust[1]. At the same time he chastises his erring children, he pities them like a tender and indulgent parent.

But this only caused *Resolute* to weep more.

Prob. I would my heart were as soft as is that of my brother *Resolute*, for surely, I have equal cause to reproach myself. I was also incensed at the behaviour of the mob; and one of them, whom I knew, happening to revile me in terms which were actionable; I stepped to the city, and procured a warrant to carry the offender before a Justice of the Peace. But the Justice favoured my enemy. I could procure no witness of the abuse; therefore, instead of obtaining any satisfaction, I was obliged to quit the house, amidst a torrent of ridicule; some plucking my garments, others spitting upon me, and the Justice threatning me for detaining the criminal. When I was clear of the city, I was soon convinced of my unscriptural proceedings; for I ought not to have gone[2] to law before infidels; but rather suffered wrong, even from a brother, and much more an enemy, from whom I could expect no other. I got back into the road, hastened to overtake my brethren, and, it was with great pleasure that I perceived *Resolute*, at a small distance before me.

Gideon. Your case is indeed somewhat similar to your friend's, and I trust will prove a warning to *you* also in future; and convince you, how contrary our natural tempers are to our *Lord*'s word. You ought to have known, no justice is to be expected in the *City of Depravity*, for persons of your character. I have known far greater instances of oppression, in religious matters, done by that corrupt officer of justice; whose name is *Alexander*, a genuine son of the famous [3] copper-smith of *Ephesus*. I am not against a person's using the laws of his country in his own defence, as a religious man; but then, his case must be clear, and his evidence strong, or he may be certain of a rebuff: for, it is too true, that iniquity has invaded the place of judgment[4]. So that, in general, it is better to put up with affronts of this nature, than to pursue the offender by law; and especially if it

[1] Psalm ciii.14.   [2] 1Cor. vi. 6,7.   [3] 2 Tim. iv. 14.   [4] Eccles. iii. 16.

affects our own perfons only, and does not injure the caufe of religious liberty in general; which fhould be defended at all hazards.

Prob. I found this affair fhamefully tarnifhed my garment; and *that* filled me with great confufion.

Gideon. Whatever fullieth this garment, fhould indeed be matter of concern to pilgrims; for it was worn by our *Lord*; therefore fhould be kept clean by us; nor muft we think to be happy, when it is defiled.

Prob. I am truly afhamed and humbled at my fhort comings. Efpecially when I think on what followed. When *Refolute* and I came together, we faid little to each other, from a confcioufnefs of guilt; only expreffed concern for the lofs of our company. We came on apace, hoping to overtake them, when behold, we were ftopped by the monftrous bridge, that is built acrofs the valley.

Gideon. That is the *Bridge of Trial*, but fhould never ftop pilgrims, as there is a paffage thro' it in the direct road, and an intimation thereon, that fo great a man as *St. Paul* went under it. The prize we Pilgrims prefs towards, is of fuch infinite value, that only to hefitate at any trial in our way thereto, is, in fome meafure criminal. *St. Paul* did not permit this *Bridge* to ftop him; but, on the contrary, tho' the *Arch* was then moft filthy, yet he entered it heroically, and paffed under it meekly, faying, " I take pleafure in perfecutions and afflictions, that come unto me for the Gofpel's fake[1]."

At this, *Sincere* and *Friendly* beheld each other in much confufion.

Prob. Such noble examples may juftly make me doubt of my being a true Pilgrim; for I not only hefitated, but caufed my brother *Refolute* to do the fame. Our late foil did not awaken us, as it fhould have done, to a fenfe of our duty; but we began to confider, how it was poffible for us to elude that filthy paffage: and, accordingly, we turned to the left, in fearch of a more agreeable way.

[1] 2 Cor. xii. 10.

Gideon.

Gideon. You consulted with flesh and blood more than with your bibles, and, by so doing, exposed yourselves to great danger.

Sincere. But it was well for me, and my brother *Friendly*, that they thus turned aside; for by this, they became instrumental in delivering us, from our confinement in *Cross*'s dungeon.

He then related to the company how they were decoyed by *Mr. Trim.*

Gideon. Ah, were ye so far off your guard, as to be thus decoyed! The name of that deceiver is *Trim.* The stairs you followed him up, are called *Demas*'s steps; because that unhappy man, having parted from *St. Paul*, when the Apostle went thro' the *Arch*; he ascended that stair-case, [1] mixed with the people on the bridge, and was no more seen in the pilgrim road. Your falling into *Mr. Cross*'s dungeon, was a blessing to you; but the escape of *Mr. Trim*, was a curse unto him: for he now conforms to the vain world on the bridge, and looks with contempt on the pilgrims in the valley; as you would have done, if our *King* had permitted you to follow him. *Mr. Cross* is a grim looking person, but he is a stanch friend to pilgrims; for he has done them far more good in *his* way, than I have in mine.

Your being delivered by means of your friend's errors, does by no means excuse their folly in turning aside, but only proves, that our great master can serve the purposes of his amazing grace towards us, even by the devices of the *Tyrant*, or our own folly. Be humbled, therefore, under a deep sense of your transgressions, and rejoice for your deliverance with trembling.

While *Gideon* spake thus, the Pilgrims covered their faces, and with silent tears, and heaving breasts, expressed great remorse for their folly; and a lively sense of *Jehovah*'s goodness towards them.

Gideon. I see the *Lord* has blessed you, by enabling you to pass the *Arch*, which is manifest from the lustre of your garments. I think myself honoured and happy in having your

[1] 2 Tim. iv. 10.

company. My *Lord* has condefcended to chaſtife you, as a teſtimony of his love. Let not, therefore, the precious balm of reproof feem grievous unto you[1], my brethren: for in this, as well as in every other refpect, I am only expreſſing my affection for you.

All. Thank you, thank you, good *Gideon*, may the *Lord* reward you, for this labour of love towards us vile and unworthy Pilgrims.

Gideon. Now let my dear friends be comforted. Come, here is a fupper that is prepared for the rebellious[2], therefore none of us can pretend he is excluded from this table of the *Lord*. Eat, therefore, O my friends, and drink abundantly, ye beloved of my maſter.

So faying, he arofe, bleſſed the table, and adored *Jehovah* for his bounty towards his ſinful creatures. They then all eat and were filled.

Sincere. I think this valley produceth as good food as ever I taſted.

Gideon. Much may be afcribed to the appetite with which people come to the table. Yours have been lately whet up by a feries of trials, which operate in favour of my feaſt: yet, I muſt fay, that the proviſion is as good here, as you will find in any part of your journey. *Mofes* was a man of a delicate taſte in thefe things; and he would not have built here, if the air and foil had not been peculiarly good. *St. Peter* alfo was one, who had his fenfes exercifed to difcern good and evil[3]; and he teſtifies, that this is a fruitful valley, for our *King* gives more and more grace to all thofe who dwell therein[4]. We *Jews*, you know, are remarkable for our lucrative ingenuity; and I declare, that I never in my life was fo thriving as fince I have kept this Inn. My hand has been fo liberally opened towards pilgrims, that my neighbours on the adjacent hills, fay, I ſhall be ruined; and this they have ſtupidly afferted for thefe thirty years. But, from my own experience, I muſt declare, that it

[1] Pfalm cxli. 5.   [2] Pfalm lxviii. 18.   [3] Heb. v. 14.   [4] 1 Pet. v. 5.

feems

seems impossible for me to become a bankrupt. I can afford to give out of my abundance, and might lessen my principal stock; this I endeavour to do; but when I come, at the years end, to settle my accounts, I have always found my stock increased. So true is that paradox of the wise man, namely, "There is that scattereth, and yet increaseth[1]."

By this time it grew late, and the Pilgrims were desirous of going to rest; *Gideon* directed the chamberlain, to shew them into the *Chamber of Security*. It was decorated with inscriptions wrote in golden characters, expressing the various solemn obligations, which their *Lord* had laid himself under, to protect *his* servants. One of these was peculiarly magnificent, and wrought very curiously into the hangings of their bed. This attested, that altho' their *King* was eternal, and the high and lofty one; yet he was ever with the *humble*, to secure and comfort them[2] In this bed the pilgrims lost all their fears and cares, awoke in the morning, renewed in strength, and eager to press onward in their journey; to which their host consented, after they had taken a slight repast.

As they were at breakfast, a well-looking person came in; on which, *Gideon* arose and saluted him, by the name of *Mr. Cross*. This made the Pilgrims take the more notice of him; but they were much surprized when *Gideon* thus addressed them.

Gideon. My friends, this is *Mr. Cross*, to whom you, and many others of us Pilgrims, are so much obliged. He is often at my house; and the more I know of him the better I like him.

Sincere. Sir, I heartily thank you, in behalf of myself and brother, for all the favours you shewed us while with you. I now consider *that* Providence as a most rich mercy to us. But I think your person is much altered for the better.

Cross. I told you, when you were with me, that I could not but be terrible to you in that situation; but you now see me in

---

[1] Prov. xi. 24.   [2] Isaiah lvii. 15.

another character, and I hope you will ever look on me as your friend.

Prob. Now, good *Mr. Gideon*, let us have your bill, and we will depart.

Gideon. That I by no means can do; for all my bills of this sort I send to my master, and he answers them at the year's end, as I told you. I am a *Jew* in this respect also, for your cash would not satisfy me. I expect more than you can give me; wherefore put up your money; I am amply repaid by your good company.

Prob. You are very kind indeed, such a disposition does you honour.

Gideon. I do assure you, it is not in my nature to be generous: much may be imputed to the situation of my house, and more to the grace of our *King:* wherefore, return *him* thanks, and pray for me.

Cross. You are soon to enter the *Valley of the Shadow of Death*, which is dreadful to some pilgrims, while to others it is nothing terrifying. There is no saying what will happen to you there. You have the day before you. Take heed to yourselves.

Gideon. May [1] *Jehovah* turn the shadow of death into the morning of light, unto you. So they embraced each other, and the Pilgrims went on singing.

" Blest are the humble souls that see,
" Their emptiness and poverty;
" Treasures of grace to them are given,
" And crowns of joy laid up in Heav'n.

WATTS.

[1] Amos v. 8.

CHAP.

CHAP. XVIII.

The Pilgrims in the Valley of the Shadow of Death. *A total eclipse of the sun, and a storm. They are separated.* Probus *at* Deist-Hall. *His dialogue with* 'Squire Humus.

THE Pilgrims went thro' the remaining part of the valley very happily, their tempers became assimilated unto it, and their souls found *that* rest which *Immanuel* gives to them who are meek and lowly in heart[1]. The conversation of good *Gideon* had been very useful to them: and, as they drew near the *Valley of the Shadow of Death*, they began to encourage each other, with the many promises which their *Lord* had given Pilgrims; that he would never leave them, nor forsake them: they remembered *Jehovah*'s many and great mercies already experienced, and received comfort and strength[2].

The two ranges of hills, one on each side the *Valley of Humiliation*, inclined nearer and nearer to each other; that on the south-side, rose high and steep, so as to intercept the light of the sun, some part of the day. These hills formed the sides of the *Valley of the Shadow of Death*, which ran several miles between them. It was deep and gloomy, full of dark caverns, pits and snares; the haunt of fiends and spectres, most horridly waste and wild. Thro' the midst of this valley lies the road to *Mount Zion*.

The Pilgrims knew there was no other right way, so did not attempt to shun it; but, putting the best face on it they were able, they boldly entered the valley, and advanced apace, hoping to get thro' it while the sun shone. But on a sudden, the heavens grew black as sackcloth, and every thing around

[1] Mat. xi. 29.   [2] Psalm cxix. 52.

presaged

presaged a dreadful storm at hand. At the same time happened a total eclipse of the sun, which, with the black clouds, covered the valley with midnight darkness. Great was the terror of these poor souls, when they found themselves thus overtaken. The tempest came on; attended with awful thunder and lightning; and all nature seemed to groan with horrible pangs. Now they remembered the case of poor *Christian*, and trembled with apprehensions of some fatal accident.

At this time, one of the Pilgrims looking behind him, thought he saw a number of dreadful forms coming fast after them: and he crying out, they all looked round, and seeing the formidable troop, their souls were at once bereft of all courage. Imagining the fiends were just at their heels, they began to run; but the darkness of the valley, and the terror of their minds, so confounded them, that they took different roads. *Friendly* and *Sincere* hit on the right path; but *Resolute* ran to the left, and *Probus* to the right hand: thus were these brethren again separated from each other.

Probus had not ran far, when he perceived a light just before him; he made up to it, and found a large house, situated on the right, upon the declivity of the hill. There stood a person at the door, who welcomed him to the place, and invited him in. So *Probus*, being in a great fright, went into the house.

Prob. Little did I think of finding such a building, in this forlorn part of the creation. Pray, Sir, what may be your name, and the name of this house?

Prejudice. Compose yourself a little, Sir, for I perceive you have been terrified with the dreams which possess weak minds, when they frequent these parts. My name is *Prejudice* junior. I am the son of that venerable person who keeps the dogs, near the house *Beautiful*; and who is so staunch an enemy to superstition. This is *Deist-Hall*; it was first built by one *Herbert*, about an hundred and fifty years ago; but it has since been repaired and decorated by several lords and gentlemen, who made it their favourite residence. It is now occupied by 'Squire *Humus*, a very ingenious gentleman. So that this is not so despicable a situation as you imagine; for the persons I have mentioned

tioned, were men of high taste, and found reason; and chose this place before any other.

Probus, finding where he was, silently prayed *Immanuel* to assist him, and make a way for his escape;—he then replied,

Prob. I have heard somewhat of this *Hall*, but never could think it was so miserably situated. I perceive that its occupiers love darkness rather than light; for they not only have built here in the *Shadow of Death*, but also the sashes of their house are so small, that at mid-day the rooms must be dark. Pray, do you serve *Mr. Humus*, and is he at home?

Prej. He is now on a visit to the neighbouring *City of Sensuality*, on the adjacent hills; and to which there is, from this *Hall*, a very commodious coach-road. There are two large avenues or gates to this building; one is called *Revelation-Gate*, of which I am keeper; the other is called *Pagan-Gate*, and is kept by *Mr. Creaulity*. My master keeps a lady, whose name is *Misrepresentation*. This lady he is very fond of, and she has the sole management of him and this house. His favourite footman's name is *Sceptic*.

Prob. I would just look into the house, if you please, while this bad weather continues.

Prej. Sir, you are very welcome.

So he conducted him into a spacious hall, that was hung round with a great number of pictures of philosophers, both ancient and modern; but chiefly of the atheistic and deistic sort. Among them *Probus* saw *Epicurus*, *Lucretius*, *Julian*, *Spinoza*, *Hobbs*, *Shaftsbury*, *Collins*, *Tindal* and *Bolingbroke*. While he was viewing these, *Mr. Humus* arrived, and was pleased to find a young man so curious in examining the pictures.

Humus. Well, Master Door-keeper, who have we got here?

Prej. This is a young man, Sir, who calls himself a pilgrim: he fled hither from the storm, but seemed most frightened by the fear of apparitions, with which, weak minds imagine this valley is haunted.

Humus.

Humus. Weak minds indeed! The present darkness is only an eclipse of the sun; and in truth, Sir, there is not a more pleasant spot in our country, than this whereon I have fixed my residence.

Prob. Pardon me, Sir, if I think you have a very odd taste; for, I look on the valley which I have just passed thro', as greatly preferable unto this.

Humus. What, the *Valley of Humiliation!* A most mean and sordid place indeed! It should be called the *Valley of Infatuation.* It is fit only for low life souls to walk and dwell in. No man of spirit will ever own that he has walked thro' it.

Prob. No, Sir! not when *Moses, David,* and *Immanuel* himself walked thro' it?

Humus. These, Sir, are persons of no credit with me. I consider them only as enthusiasts and impostors.

Prob. Impostors! Where will you then find persons of truth and ingenuity?

Humus There, Sir, in the excellent pictures before you. There are the oracles of reason. The lights of the world. The noble assertors of the independency of the human mind.

Prob. From what acquaintance I have with them, I think they rather perplex, than inform the mind. They lead their disciples from the truth; nor, can they give a sincere inquirer any good ground for a future hope.

Humus. Hope, Sir! By *that* word, I suppose you are pursuing that *Ignis Fatuus* called everlasting happiness. Read *Shaftsbury,* and blush at your folly.

Prob. If it is folly, it was put into us by the author of our nature: and I believe, that *you,* Sir, found it no small difficulty to conquer it, if it is *yet* mastered.

Humus. I must confess, that these prejudices of my education hung about me for along time, and still visit me: but reason, and the company I visit in the neighbouring city, have nearly compleated my victory over them.

Prob.

Prob. I am surprised that any gentlemen should chuse to live here!

Humus. I declare that it is a *Paradise* to me. Here I retire into the original light of nature, unsullied with the glare and false day of tradition, or what is termed revelation; which has imposed on the world for so many hundred years. Here I sit and sigh for the return of those golden days, of paganism and philosophy, when reason had *fair play*.

Prob. And what did reason do with *fair play*, as you term it, but fill the world with superstition and idolatry? Thank Heaven, you cannot now retire into the pure light of nature; you cannot return to original heathenism: for the Christian day hath penetrated *that* gloom with millions of glorious rays; so that you are indebted to revelation, even for that light by which you oppose it.

Humus. I indebted to revelation! I scorn the thought: and desire that you will either retract your words, or depart my house.

Prob. Your house, Sir, is less agreeable to me than the tempest, from which I fled hither for refuge.

Humus. Ah, tempests, fiends and apparitions, are the goblins which your class is ever dreaming of; but we, who dwell here, laugh at all such chimeras.

Prob. I understand that your house has a commodious communication with the *City of Sensuality*; it is no wonder, therefore, that you are unmolested by such things; for the *Black Tyrant* has no interest to serve by disturbing you.

Humus. Black Tyrant! That is another of your whims. There is no such being.

Prob. Excuse me, Sir, for I must look on such persons as you to be striking instances, both of the being and craft of such an evil spirit. For when the *Usurper* had greater power in the world, he made his votaries to believe and teach, that he was a *God:* but, since he has been confined by the glorious light of Christianity, he endeavours to persuade men, that there is no Devil, nor future punishment: and thus does infinite mischief in the world.

Humus. We let our thoughts rove freely, not regarding consequences.

Prob. Ye boast of liberty, but are notoriously the slaves of *Sensuality*[1] and prejudice. Ye blindly give credit to the most palpable falshoods, and will not believe the most self-evident truths. Having embraced a system of universal scepticism, ye are given over to a reprobate mind: for who, but such as are infatuated, would reside in such obscurity as this? Surely, ye are those who stumble at noon day as in the night, and are in solitary places as dead men[2]. Ye rebel against the light, even while the Gospel shines with meridian lustre, and thousands all around you are rising to a resurrection of heavenly life and glory.

Humus. Young man, depart my house, and infect not these rooms with the pestilential breath of fanaticism.

Prob. I will not long trouble you: but will observe, that ye pretend to be friends to toleration, yet are ready to cast me out of doors. Whatever you, or your party may pretend, you have no right to any indulgence from church or state: since, your principles tend to loose the bands of society, poison its cordials, and ruin its polity; without offering any equivalent for such an horrible violation of order, such an infamous piracy on the sons of men.

Humus. You grow warm, and are a modern zealot I perceive.

Prob. It is time to rouse, when a snatch is made at the downy pillow, both of present repose, and future happiness, by a gang of cruel desperadoes; who usurp the authority of reason, and claim the highest pretensions to wisdom; for no other purpose than to unhinge the whole system of religion, both natural and revealed. Could I believe you in the right, I should sit down and weep out my eyes; whereas ye can dance and sport on the edge of the dreadful gulph of *Annihilation*. Vain pretenders to

[1] 2 Pet. ii. 19.   [2] Isaiah lix. 10.

wha:

what is *beautiful*, *fit*, and *proper**, when your conduct and fyftem are chaotical and prepofterous in the utmoft extreme.

Humus. How can we alter the decrees of *Fate?* It is therefore beft to put a good face on it; and eat and drink for tomorrow we die.

Prob. If none but yourfelves were injured by fuch principles, it would be hardly worth while to difturb fuch groveling minds, but let you feed on, in the vile trough of fenfuality. Yet, for the fake of your fervants here, who may not be fo far funk into the depths of the *Black Tyrant*; permit me to afk you, how men came firft to entertain any hope of a future ftate?

Humus. It was originally a romantic idea, that fprung up in the human mind; and has been induftrioufly propagated from generation to generation, until people thought it a reality.

Prob. Induftrioufly propagated, indeed! Nor can it be rooted out of our nature. It came firft from a divine revelation, and would never have occurred to the mind of man, if it had not been true. *Jehovah, the bleffed one*, has no pleafure in the mifery of his creatures: but, if a future ftate be only a *romantic idea*, the moft ingenious tyrant could have invented no fcheme to render man fo perfectly miferable, as that of giving him a power to *conceive* of eternal happinefs, and, at the fame time, depriving him of any *hope of enjoying* it. According to *your* view of things, every creature in the world is more happy than the rational being. Man is exalted both in reafon and wretchednefs. He is a blot in *Jehovah's* work. A real *Magormifabib*, or terror to himfelf [1]: whereas, grant him to be, what he undoubtedly is; an immortal being, tho' fallen; he then ftands on a noble preheminence; and altho' fubject to a thoufand evils, yet he appears grand in ruins, and magnificent even in mifery. Our *King* alfo, is feen to be wife, and juft, and good in all; while you and your party appear to be difturbers of the public peace.

Humus. It is impoffible for us to difturb or injure fociety fo much as your religion has done.

* Words often ufed by *Lord Shaftfbury* and his admirers.
[1] Jer. xx. 3, 4.

Prob

Prob. When your atheiftical and philofophical anceftors had prejudiced the world, by their impious fpeculations; it was impoffible that true religion could recover its juft influence, but by great oppofition. Nor can a true religion unite with a falfe one; this is one proof of its divinity. The many gods who were worfhipped in the golden days, unto which you defire to bring us back, were all falfe gods; and tho' in fome things diverfe from each other, yet they all ferved the intereft of the *Black Tyrant*; who cultivated a general toleration among polytheifts, becaufe it fupported his throne of darknefs. But, the true religion will have no communion with error and idolatry.

Humus. So, I find you are for the fecular arm to make converts to your religion.

Prob. By no means. I only defire that proper diftinctions fhould be made. Such pernicious opinions as combat the interefts of fociety, fhould not be fuffered to come abroad, to infect the world with a difeafe, that tends to metamorphofe focial creatures into favage beafts. I confider your fceptical tribe in no better light, than as men, in whom, according to your own principles, there is neither honour, juftice, or humanity; therefore you appear far more mifchievous to fociety, than fo many of the moft favage animals let loofe in a large and populous city.

Humus. This cannot be endured in my own houfe. *Prejudice*, lay hold of him, and lead him out of doors.—There would be no need of compulfion, if your religion were divine; for it would then fupport itfelf.

Prob. That it is divine has been proved a thoufand times, and various ways, by the moft convincing evidence, againft the gentlemen, whofe pictures difgrace thefe walls; and yet you, and your brethren plod on in the old beaten track of calumny and mifreprefentation, without attending at all to the force of the arguments urged againft you. But you continue to retail fcraps of infidelity from one to another, with the utmoft credulity and effrontery. And, in fhort, you are arrived at the extreme of that implicit faith, which ye are fo zealous in exclaiming againft. From which moft dangerous fituation, I pray *Jehovah* to convert you.

Then

Then *Probus* turned, departed from the house, and soon recovered the high road: when lo, there came a most horrible smoke from *Deist-Hall*, which so darkened the way, that he knew not where to set his foot; on which, *Probus* cried, "*-Lord, open thou mine eyes, that I may see the wonders of thy law*[1]." Immediately the smoke vanished, and, the storm being over, the sun began to appear. The Pilgrim taking courage, hastened on his way, and being rejoiced that his *King* had strengthened him to escape from *Deist-Hall*, he went on singing,

" Should all the forms which men devise,
" Assault my faith with treach'rous art;
" I'd call them vanity and lies,
" And bind the gospel to my heart.

WATTS.

CHAP. XIX.

Probus meets the Black Tyrant, *and defies him. He is joined by* Resolute. *They find their Brethren at the* Prodigal Inn. Sincere *and* Resolute *relate their surprizing adventures.*

*P*ROBUS had not sung long, before he was met by a person, with a very gloomy aspect; who asked him, why he disturbed the solemnity of that valley with such a noise? This was the *Prince of Darkness* himself, but *Probus* knew him not.

Prob. I am in the king's highway. I love the *King*, and am singing his worthy praise.

Tyrant. There is a time to mourn, as well as a time to sing[2].

Prob. This is *my* time to sing. My heart is merry, and as *St.*[3] *James* directs, I am singing psalms.

[1] Psalm cxix. 18.   [2] Eccl. iii. 4.   [3] Jam. v. 13.

Tyrant. This valley belongs to me; and I will not be thus disturbed.

Prob. If you were a friend of our *King*, you would help me to praise him.

Tyrant. I know of no king here but myself; wherefore, I command you, on your peril, to be silent.

Prob. *Tyrant*, you have now discovered yourself, and I defy you! I will go on in the strength of the *Lord my King*[1]. The joy of the *Lord* is my strength[2]. You, and your rebellious associates refused to praise him in the *Celestial City*, therefore, you are confined in such dreary glooms as this; and we *redeemed men* are going to supply your places in our *King*'s courts. Remember, O enemy of *Jehovah* and men, that "*Immanuel* passed by the nature of angels, and took on him the seed of *Abraham*[3]."

Probus then sang aloud.

" Down headlong from their native skies,
" The rebel-angels fell,
" And thunder-bolts of flaming wrath,
" Pursu'd them deep to *Hell*.

" Down from the top of earthly bliss,
" Rebellious man was hurl'd,
" And *Jesus* stoop'd beneath the grave,
" To reach a sinking world." WATTS.

At this the *Tyrant* knit his brows, bit his lips, and seemed ready to attack the Pilgrim; but was curbed by an invisible power; he therefore passed by him, and went on in great fury[4]; while *Probus* made the valley ring with singing of distinguishing love.

Having finished his song, he thought he heard a voice at a distance, calling to him; he therefore halooed aloud, and was immediately answered again. Perceiving the voice to draw nearer to him; he continued hallooing, 'till he saw his friend *Resolute* running into the way, with his countenance aghast, and

[1] Psalm lxxi. 16. [2] Nehem. viii. 10. [3] Heb. ii. 16. [4] Jam. iv. 7.

all

all in great confusion. He ran and embraced *Probus*, blessing the *King* for restoring him to his companion.

Prob. I am very glad to see you, my dear *Resolute*; but why are you so terrified? This is truly a dreadful place, yet *Immanuel* is with us. Remember the pictures at the *Interpreter*'s house.

Ref. A *dreadful place* indeed! Never did I hear, or see the like. I am hurried almost out of my wits. I was afraid that I should never have recovered the path again; but our *King* was better to me than I deserved, and made your singing a means to guide me into the right way. I cannot now tell you what terrible things I have seen: let us hasten out of this valley, and obtain some place to rest in, before the night overtakes us; I shall then be composed, and we may find our brethren.

They walked on apace, and, at length, reached the end of the valley, from which they went up with great joy. The country now opened to their view, the evening was fine, and all nature seemed to welcome them from that baleful region. Having gained an eminence, they saw, at a small distance before them, a large house, and, as they drew near, were pleased in finding it a place of entertainment for pilgrims, it being the sign of the *Returning Prodigal*. Here they entered, and, to their unspeakable pleasure, found within, their dear brethren *Friendly* and *Sincere*, whom they cordially embraced.

Prob. Blessed be our *King*, for bringing us all together once more, after seeing such dreadful things in the *Valley of the Shadow of Death!* But into whose house are we now come?

Frien. This is the *Prodigal Inn*, it is kept by *Mr. Experience*, a tried friend to pilgrims. He has given us a very kind reception, and is gone to order a supper for us and you, whom we hoped to see soon; and we bless *Immanuel*, that we are not disappointed of our hope. Here comes our host. This, brethren, is *Mr. Experience*.

Experience. And these are your expected friends. You are welcome, Sirs, to the best I have. I imagine that you are fatigued

tigued and hungry; have therefore ordered, both for your refreshment and repose.

Prob. Thank you, good Sir, and the sooner it appears I think it the better.

Experience then rang, and in a little time the servants brought in the supper. It was well-chosen, and excellently dressed; for *Mr. Experience* was famous for these things, among pilgrims. The appetites of his guests were keen, and they played well their parts.

Exper. My friends, I am well pleased to find that you like my fare.

Prob. Excellent, excellent, Sir! you keep a rich table; and I am as hungry as was *Mary*, when she sat at the feet of our dear master[1].

Exper. I wish your food was as good as that she was regaled with.

Prob. *That*, we know cannot be: but you had it as fresh as possible, and have dressed it according to the directions he has left for his servants.

Exper. I ever keep his directions hung up in my kitchen: and, when I carve, I have rules to divide the joints[2] aright, and to dispose of them as will best suit my guests.

Thus they ate and drank, till they had satiated their weary souls, and filled their hungry souls with good things[3]. As the servants were removing the cloth, they sang as follows:

 " Bless'd *Jesus*, what delicious fare!
 " How sweet thy entertainments are!
 " Never did angels taste above,
 " Redeeming grace and dying love."   WATTS.

They then drew round the fire, and entered into conversation.

Exper. Permit me, Sirs, to inform you, it is a rule of this house, that every person entertained here, must inform me

[1] Luke x. 39.   [2] 2 Tim. ii. 15.   [3] Jer. xxxi. 25. & Psalm cvii. 8.

of his setting out on Pilgrimage, and of the principal events that have befallen him in his way. By this means, many false pilgrims have been detected; and many real ones have been honoured and encouraged.

Prob. Sir, I will answer for my brethren, that we approve of this regulation, and are ready to comply therewith.

So *Probus* began, and related his own story. The others followed him, as far as their separation in the *Valley of the Shadow of Death*, as has been related. The rest follows.

Sincere. We proceeded together until one of us looking back, saw a company of ghastly forms coming after us. He crying out, induced us all to look, which we had no sooner done, than we were filled with great fear; and thinking them just at our heels, we all wildly ran forward in the dark, but, *Friendly* and *I* soon found we were by ourselves. We kept on as fast as we could, tho' our path was rough and difficult; the darkness also continued, and the tempest roared in the trees and caverns of the valley. Hearing voices behind us, we turned, and beheld the same terrible troop very near us. Our path was now so difficult that we could not go fast, so were obliged to endure their approach. They accordingly came up, and surrounded us; but never did I before behold such terrifying objects, such fearful aspects! for every thing that was horrible seemed to meet in their look and form. We shut our eyes, and kept on slowly; but then our ears were filled with most horrid yells and blasphemies; and when we dared to look forward, we were sure to see some object of a terrifying or obscene nature. Sometimes they would stand just before us, then we endeavoured to avoid them. Sometimes they would form a chain quite across the road; but, on our advancing resolutely ᵗ they always broke and gave way; which reminded us of the picture of *David*, at the *Interpreter's* house. At this time, we were silent thro' fear, but inwardly cried to the *Lord*, for a way to escape. At length, observing that the fiends had no power to stop us, we both cried out together. " Tho' I walk thro'

ᵗ 1 Pet. v. 9.

the valley and shadow of death, I will fear no evil for thou art with me!" When lo, a voice came from *Heaven*, saying, " For this purpofe was the Son of *God* manifefted, that he might deftroy the works of the *Devil*[2]." On this all the frightful fpectres made a precipitate retreat from us, howling in a doleful manner, fo that the whole valley feemed to fhake. The weather inftantly cleared up, we foon came to the end of the valley, and to this houfe, without further annoyance.

Ref. I find none of you was fo befet as I was: nor is the valley worthy of its name from what any of you faw and heard. Soon after we began to run from the fiends, I found myfelf alone in a by-path, as I judged, to the left of the road. But I feared to go back, left the enemy fhould meet me alone. And as my path feemed to incline forward, I kept on, in hopes of finding an avenue on my right, by which I might again recover the highway. The tempeft, thunder and lightning, ftill continued. As I went on, I perceived an opening on my left hand, a little before me, from whence feemed to proceed a faint light, and a variety of ftrange noifes. When I came oppofite unto it, I beheld the moft petrifying fight. It was the ftate of the damned, the mouth of the infernal pit; into which I faw many dragged, and from which came the moft heart-rending and difmal cries. I turned my eyes from it, ftopped my ears, and was haftening by, when a moft dreadful monfter feized me: I ftruggled, and broke from him, bidding him be gone, for I was the *Lord*'s fervant. He told me, that he knew *I was*, but for my many and great fins, *Immanuel* had given me to him, as he did *Judas* the traitor. Thefe words were like a magic wand touching me, for I loft my ftrength inftantly, and could refift no longer, fo as to difengage myfelf. He then dragged me, ftruggling and crying for help, towards the horrible pit[3]; unto which I drew near very faft, and thought I muft foon unite in the doleful groans that arofe from that *Tophet*. As I was hurried along, and catching at every thing that might retard my progrefs; I perceived feveral low trees acrofs the road where he dragged me, and I found that the

[1] Pfalm xxiii. 4.   [2] 1 John iii. 8.   [3] Pfalm xl. 2.

fiend

fiend endeavoured to convey me, where I could least reach them. However, as I drew near, I inwardly sighed out, *Lord help me*[1]. And, making a desperate struggle, I reached a friendly branch of one of the trees, that seemed to bend itself towards me. When the monster found I had got hold of it, he raged with hellish fury, and dragged as if he would tear my arm from my body. But I twisted the pliant branch round my hand, and was determined to lose an arm, or break the twig: but, thanks to our *Lord*, both held against all his violence. When the *Tyrant* had wasted his infernal strength, he let me alone; saying, go your way. But I kept my hold, and would not venture from the tree. He then threw something in my eyes, which so wrought on my mind, that I conceived myself to be in the jaws of *Tophet*, and dropping into the pit, out of the reach of mercy[2]. How I kept my hold of the tree, our *Lord* only knows; but so I did, until this terror dispersed, and my spirits recovered sufficient composure, so as to reflect on my situation, and consider how to extricate myself from that horrid place. I looked attentively on the trees, and it occurred to me, that they were certainly planted by a divine hand: but I was much surprized at the toughness of their nature; especially, when I observed, that several branches had been slipped off; yet from all such I saw young shoots were springing. Thus ruminating, I was led to hope these were trees of life; from which, if I could obtain a branch, I might easily escape from the power of the enemy. Therefore, lifting up my heart to our *King*, I besought him to hear me from the jaws of *perdition*[3], and grant me both direction and assistance. I then tried to break off the branch that was round my hand, and found that it slipped very easily from the stock; which, when the fiend perceived, he endeavoured to seize me; but I brandished my wand, saying, " The *Lord* is my light, and my salvation, whom then shall I fear[4]?" At this, he cast on me a look of ineffable malice and envy, and retired. I made the best of my way from that horrid scene; but, just before I heard *Probus* sing, I was met by a party

[1] Mat. xv. 25.　[2] Jonah ii. 2.　[3] Psalm cxvi. 3, 4.　[4] Psalm xxvii. 1.

of the enemy, who were dragging three men towards the pit, with dismal yells of triumph. As I passed by them, I thought I had seen the prisoners before: but the fiends fixed their eyes on my wand, and took no further notice of me. Just then I heard *Probus*'s voice, and, hastening towards it, I was so happy as to find the singer to be my dear friend and fellow Pilgrim; with whom I soon after arrived at this house.

CHAP. XX.

The sentiments of Mr. Experience, *on what had happened to the Pilgrims in the dark valley. A dialogue on the excellency of faith.*

WHEN the Pilgrims had thus told each their story, their host said,

Exper. You are all heartily welcome to my house; for I perceive you are true pilgrims, and not strangers, either to the afflictions or consolations of *Jehovah*'s *Israel*. You have found the words of my brother *Cross* true, namely, that the *Valley of the Shadow of Death* is a place of danger. The enemy raised that storm on purpose to frighten and separate you. He has also made several roads there, to bewilder and distress Pilgrims. The fiends you saw, are ever in the valley, for they haunt it day and night to do mischief, but, they only affright: they can do no hurt to real pilgrims, who keep in the way, as *Friendly* and *Sincere* found. They have a power to present blasphemous, impure, and terrifying ideas to our minds: but, if pilgrims keep on resolutely, calling upon their *King*, as you did, he never fails to make a way for their escape.

Sincere.

Sincere. They were truly horrible; and their power in operation and reprefentation is furprifingly exact, and very diftreffing.

Exper. In like circumftances, I have found my mind fo wrought on by hellifh fuggeftions, and the *Black Tyrant* fo very affiduous and powerful; that I have been ready, almoft, to confider him as an almighty and omnifcient being. But our corrupt nature is fuch a party in his favour, that he appears to us, to be ftronger and wifer than he really is. However, he certainly was a being of vaft confequence, before his fall; fince, notwithftanding his dreadful defeat, he ftill retains fuch amazing powers.

Sincere. I marvel that the Almighty fhould fuffer him to poffefs them!

Exper. Known to *Jehovah* are all his works from the foundation of the world[1]. He has wife defigns in permitting this fpirit thus to oppofe *Him*, and diftrefs his fheep. The *Tyrant* knows he is not always to do thus: he believes that our *King* is almighty, and will punifh him for his crimes; nay, he trembles at his fate[2], and yet continues to aggravate the doom.

Sincere. This fhews the dreadful hardening nature of fin, which will always keep him a Devil, and render him incapable of repentance, or of loving our *King*. The *Black Tyrant* cannot *love*, which is the quinteffence of his mifery. But what think you of *Probus* being at *Deift-Hall?*

Exper. Probus's cafe is not fingular, tho' it is not very common among pilgrims. I was in much the fame fituation, many years ago; and would advife him, to take heed to himfelf; for I fear he will not always fucceed fo well with thofe enemies, whom he may again, probably, meet with in his travels. That *Hall* is a rendezvous for thefe *Janizaries* of the *Black Tyrant*. *That* is their college, from whence have iffued all thefe volumes of blafphemy and flander, againft the author of chriftianity and his people, which have difgraced our country. But, however they

[1] Acts xv. 18.   [2] James ii. 19.

may

may talk about virtue, and the law of nature; yet, they hold a criminal connection with the *City of Senfuality*. In fhort, they are the fcoffers, who are prophefied of, as to come in the laft days, walking after their lufts, and faying, " Where is the promife of his coming'?" Our *King* has raifed up many great men, both in the *City of Eftablifoment*, and its fuburbs, to anfwer their cavils; fo that the evidence for the truth of our religion, ftill fhines with a luftre nearly equal to its primitive glory.

Prob. Sir, I thank you for your information, and hope I fhall profit by your fiiendly warning to me: but I am very defirous to hear, what you will fay to our brother *Refolute*'s ftrange adventure.

Exper. Refolute's remark was juft, " That to *him*, only, the valley appeared in its moft awful terrors." He came in a path that has been trodden by many of our *Father*'s dear children; and has feen what he can never forget. The wolf fcattered *You*, but, he was permitted to catch and ufe violence with *Him* [2]: his *Lord* was pleafed, for fome valuable end, to have him fifted as wheat. I have feen the fame dreadful fight, and heard feveral relate nearly the fame ftory. Our *Lord* fuffered himfelf to be diftreffed with a fenfe of the wrath of his *Father*, and views of the punifhments of the damned. It was when he vifited thofe dreary regions, that he fpilled fome of his precious blood, acrofs the mouth of the pit; from which fprung up thofe trees of life, which are of the fame qualities with thofe in the *Paradife* of our *King*. Thefe trees preferve every true pilgrim who is dragged thither. When falfe pilgrims are carried near them, they catch at them, but having no true faith, the trees elude their attempts; yet they bend towards real pilgrims: nor can all the power of the enemy drag them from their hold. And yet *Refolute* found little trouble to feparate the branch from the ftock. This fhews us, that faith has much more power with *Jehovah*, than the enemy can have over a true pilgrim: for that which is impoffible to the *Tyrant*, namely, to pull one

[1] 2 Pet. iii. 3, 4. [2] John x. 12.

branch

branch from these trees, is easy to be accomplished by faith. All things are possible to him that believeth [1].

Ref. Why, I never could have thought I had so great faith.

Exper. I lay no stress on the *measure* of your faith; that was but small, as appears from your great fears while in the valley. But it is of the *nature* of your faith that I speak. One grain of true faith is as sure a pledge of everlasting life, as the greatest measure. Because, *Jehovah*'s promises are not made to a believer as *strong, wise, rich,* or *happy*; but, simply to him as a chosen *believer in Immanuel*. A little faith, or a weak faith, takes as effectual hold of our *Lord*, as a great or a strong faith. *Immanuel*, with respect to *relation*, is the same to both, tho', in *manifestation* there may be, and is, a mighty difference. Thus, in its *measure*, faith may be weak, tho' its *nature* is immortal and divine. So that you, who was so strong that the *Tyrant* could not tear you from the tree; may, in another trial, feel yourself like a bruised reed [2]: yet here is no change in the *essence* of your faith, but in its *measure* only.

Ref. What! is there nothing due, Sir, to our improving or not improving the grace of our *King*?

Exper. Nothing at all, my friend, in the light you seem to intend.

Ref. How is it then, that many of our *Lord*'s children are commended or reproved for their weakness or strength of faith?

Exper. Immanuel makes us white, and then calls us fair! If he commends the faith of any persons, you may be certain it is of those who have a mean opinion of themselves. This was the case, both with the Centurion, and Woman of *Canaan*; in whose thoroughly humbled souls the tree of faith produced such fruit, that it seemed to surprise its great author. " O woman," said he to the latter, " great is thy faith, be it unto thee even as thou wilt [3]." But, where self-confidence possesses the mind, there is but little faith; and *that* faith has more need of *Immanuel*'s

[1] Mark ix. 23.　[2] Psalm xxxi. 6. 7.　[3] Mat. xv. 28.

prayers,

prayers, that it fail not[1], than of his commendation: as was the case with *St. Peter*.

Ref. Wherefore is faith of so much account with our *King*?

Exper. Because it is the effect of his exceeding mighty power, in the soul of a pilgrim[2]; therefore it is called precious faith[3]: and because *Immanuel* is of so much account to those who believe; for to all such he is precious[4]. *Immanuel* is so much all in all to a true pilgrim, that he is content to be swallowed up in him. So says *St. Paul.* " I live, yet not I, but *Immanuel* liveth in me[5]."

Ref. What shall I do with this wand that I brought away with me?

Exper. Let me look at it.

Resolute gave it him, and he, having carefully examined it, returned it, saying,

Exper. This is a genuine branch of the tree of life. Look here, Sirs.

He then shewed them what was wrote upon it, which they had not observed before. They were these words, namely, " I give unto them eternal life, and they shall never perish; neither shall any pluck them out of my hand[6]."

Ref. Why, Sir, that was the very promise which supported me, in the dreadful conflict with my enemy.

Exper. So I imagined. Every branch of those trees has some such sweet sentence on it. I will shew you mine.

Mr. Experience fetched it, having shewed them the following sentence thereon. " Because I live, ye shall live also[7]." Then looking on *Resolute*, while he returned his wand, he said,

Exper. Keep this as the apple of your eye. With this in your hand, you may go down into the belly of *Hell*, and to the bottoms of the mountains, like *Jonah*[8]. You may walk in a fiery

---

[1] Luke xxii. 32.   [2] Eph. i. 19.   [3] 2 Pet. i. 1.   [4] 1 Pet. ii. 7.
[5] Gal. ii. 20.   [6] John x. 28.   [7] John xiv. 19.   [8] Jonah ii. 2. 6.

furnace, or repose yourself in a lion's den unhurt, as did *Daniel* and his brethren[1]. You may go on the lion and the adder; the young lion and dragon you may trample under your feet[2]. It was this that brought you from the mouth of the pit: this preserved you from the infernals, who were dragging *Deist*, *Arius*, and *Socinus*, three notorious apostates, to their den: from whom every twig of those trees will withdraw its aid, and leave them to perish in their unbelief. I heard, this morning, that they were apprehended. They have done much mischief on the road, and will now receive their reward.

Ref. I thought I knew the criminals, and now remember they were the same persons whom we saw at the cross.

Exper. They were the same. Their end is dreadful. Let us praise our *Lord* that we are not in the unhappy number. So they sung.

" Arise our souls, our joyful powers,
" And triumph in our *God*,
" Awake our voice, and loud proclaim
" His glorious grace abroad.

" He snatch'd us from the dreadful pit,
" The gates of gaping *Hell*,
" And fix'd our standing more secure,
" Than 'twas before we fell. WATTS.

Ref. Well, this is better than being in the mouth of destruction.

Exper. My son, your *Lord* saw *that* to be needful for you. He does nothing in vain, but orders all things according to the counsel of his own will[3]; that is, he disposeth our lives according to a deep, wise, and gracious design.

Ref. I believe so, good host, and that our *King*'s design was gracious to us, in placing you here, to advise and comfort us. Now, in the name of my brethren, I have two words to say to you. First, we are much obliged to you, for the kindness you have already shewn us. And secondly, we beg you

[1] Dan. iii. 26. & vi. 22.   [2] Psalm xci. 13.   [3] Eph. i. 11.

to favour us with some account of your Pilgrimage; from hearing of which, we promise ourselves much pleasure and improvement.

Exper. Ye are welcome, my friends, to every thing in which I can serve you; and I beg you would look to *Immanuel*, for a blessing upon us, while I declare his wonders to my soul.

C H A P. XXI.

Mr. Experience *relates his own affecting story.* Clericus, *a clergyman of the* City of Establishment, *arrives at the Inn in a chariot.*

MR. *Experience*, having thus bespoke their attention, proceeded as follows:

Exper. I was born in the *City of Establishment*, of religious parents, who early presented me to our *Lord*, and daily recommended me to him in prayer, before I was of age to know good or evil. As soon as my capacity would admit, I was instructed in the holy scriptures, and, was constantly found in all the public and family duties of religion; in which I often heard my father wrestle with *Jehovah*, for his grace to take possession of my soul. But as I grew up, my father's religious character, and exemplary piety, became offensive and irksome to me; which he soon perceived; therefore, hoping that another person would have more authority over me, he put me apprentice to a religious friend of his, in the city. With him I lived some time; but, gave up myself to the sinful fashions and diversions of the prophane world. My master and father often exhorted me to the contrary, to which were added rebukes and stripes; but all in vain; for, neither the anger of my master, nor the tears of my father, moved me. At length, one day, after I had been chastised by my master, I left the city, and running from our

King and my parents, I leaped over the wall, where *Formality* and *Hypocrisy* once entered the road, and made speed to the *City of Destruction*. There I continued for a season; but could not be so perfectly easy as I wished, and as I perceived the greatest part of my vicious companions were: for I never could make game of religious people, ridicule sacred things, nor forget the prayers and tears of my parents. My whole desire was, to have nothing to do with religion [1]; and, that religion should have nothing to do with me.

Thus I lived; or rather breathed, for some time. At length the famous *Mr George Fervidus* visited that city, and raised such an uproar, that the whole town was moved; he engrossed the chief conversation, and his fame would suffer no persons quietly to enjoy their diversions and pleasures: because, he constantly and vehemently affirmed, that the city would be destroyed by our *King* [2], and all who were found there, would go into *Tophet*. At the same time happened several shocks of an earthquake, which so corresponded with *Fervidus*'s words, that many believed him to be a man of *God*. You know it was usual with him to preach in the adjacent fields, and I, hearing much of him, was resolved to go and hear what he had to say. When I came there, I was sorry to see a priest of the *City of Establishment* so scandalize his cloth, as to preach in the fields; for I had a great regard for religious characters. *Fervidus* took the following text. "I will arise and go to my father, and will say unto him, Father, I have sinned against heaven, and in thy sight, and am no more worthy to be called thy son [3]." This startled me; but when he came to set before us the circumstances of the poor runaway; I concluded, that there must have been a combination between him and my father, to preach such a sermon, at that very time and place; tho' I had never informed my father where I was. Under this discourse I was pricked to the heart [4]; and my disobedience, ingratitude, and impiety appeared so hateful to me, that I could no more go into wicked company, but kept by myself. When the time came for his preaching again, I attended; and heard him from that precious

[1] Job xxi. 14. [2] 2 Pet. iii. 7. [3] Luke xv. 18, 19. [4] Acts ii. 37.

text

text in *Isaiah*, "He shall feed his flock like a shepherd: he shall gather the lambs with his arm, and carry them in his bosom, and gently lead those that are with young¹." This sermon broke my hard heart. *Fervidus* shewed, in a striking manner, how *Jehovah*'s sheep wander from him, and how the good shepherd, by various means of grace, gathers them to his fold.

I began now seriously to think of returning, both to my heavenly and earthly father. I read and prayed incessantly; and, at this time, I found my religious education to be of great service: for I had a theory of sound doctrine in my mind, which was very useful to me. Accordingly, I sat out for the *Strait Gate*, at the head of the road; my gracious education helped me at the *Slough of Despond*, against the wiles of Mr. *Fleshly Wisdom*, and enabled me also to be useful to others, whom he was endeavouring to deceive. The *Tyrant*, indeed, fired dreadfully at me from his castle, while I was knocking at the *Gate*; but my dear father's manner of praying, and frequent discourses of his devices, occurred to me, and made me knock the louder. Mr. *Goodwill* received me with peculiar pleasure. He blessed me, and bid me hasten on my way, to wipe the tears from the eyes of my dear parent, and to comfort his heart. The *Interpreter* shewed me all his rarities, and quickly dispatched me to return home. At the *Cross* I almost lost my eyes; and quite lost my heart. Never shall I forget the sweet wonders which I saw there; and that perfect assurance of pardon for all my sins, which I was then favoured with.

I went on my way rejoicing, until I came quite to the top of the hill *Difficulty*, and, with great pleasure, beheld the abode of my father, whom I ardently longed to see; but thought it proper to make myself known first to my master. He rejoiced to see me, and freely forgave all the injury I had done him; but he could not rest, until he had made my father acquainted with this happy event. He hastened therefore to him, and in a gradual manner, let him know how gracious the *Lord* had dealt with me. On which, the dear man exclaimed, "*Joseph*, my son, is yet alive; I will run and see him²!" He forgot his infirmities, and ran to bless his eyes with a sight of his prodigal son. I

¹ Isaiah xl. 11.   ² Gen. xlv. 28.

never, never shall forget the tender look he cast on me, when he entered the room; and shall ever feel the ardent embrace with which he saluted me: he then threw himself into an arm chair, in a speechless rapture; and sat feasting his eyes on my person, and his ears with the humble confession of my faults, and intreaties for absolution. When he was able to speak, it was in the same affecting language which was used by the Prodigal's father, namely, " Bring hither the ring, the shoes, the best robe, the fatted calf, and let us be merry; for this my son was dead, but is alive again, was lost, and is found[1]."

Sincere. O my friend, it was, no doubt, the greatest happiness that our *King* could give him in this world!

Exper. It is impossible for any one, but such a father, to know what the venerable man felt at this time. Like *Hezekiah*, it seemed as if his sun had gone ten degrees backward[2]; for he appeared many years younger than he was. O that every disobedient son and daughter would consider, what pangs of sorrow their behaviour occasions their godly parents; and what a celestial pleasure their return to our *King* and their duty, must afford those, to whom, under *Jehovah*, they are indebted for their being.

Sincere. But you did not tarry long with them?

Exper. I continued there long enough to shew, that the change on me was a real work of grace: so that when Providence called me away, my parents chearfully gave me up, saying, " Go, dear son, in the name and work of the *Lord*. If we see you no more in this world, we know you will ever be preserved in the fear of *Jehovah*, and that we shall meet you in the general assemb'y and church of the first-born, who are written in the *Celestial City*[3]."

Ref. You, doubtless, have had a variety of adventures since?

Exper. I have. Some of which I will mention. When I came into the *Valley of the Shadow of Death*, there arose a dark thick fog, so that at the place where many ways meet, it was very difficult to discover the true path. I happened to take

[1] Luke xv. 22, 23, 24.   [2] Isaiah xxxviii. 8.   [3] Heb. xii. 23.

that wherein *Probus* ran, which brought me to *Deist-Hall*; but I did not escape so honourably as he. For, being naturally curious, *Mr. Tindal*, who then kept the house, took advantage of my disposition, and engaged me so long among his curiosities, such as pictures, &c. that evening came on unperceived by me; I was then prevailed on to take a supper with him, and tarry all night. But either the supper or sleeping in the house, or perhaps both of them, so wrought on me, that, in the morning, I was very indifferent about going on pilgrimage; and chose rather to accept of an invitation to visit the *City of Sensuality*. Accordingly, I went to that city, and there tarried awhile, indulging my vicious inclinations; and, indeed, I had perished there, if I had been treated as I deserved. But the *Lord*, who had created me anew in *Immanuel*,[1] would not suffer his work, to be ruined and spoiled by the *Black Usurper*.

Prob. Your situation was very dangerous; no human arm could save you.

Exper. No, *Jehovah* only could deliver me; and, adored be his name, he made bare his [2] arm for my salvation. About midnight I was alarmed by a terrible noise in my chamber; on looking round, I saw a most dreadful figure standing by my bed-side, armed with a drawn sword, which, in an angry tone, said, "What do you in this city?" I was speechless. The wickedness and ingratitude of my conduct so reproached me, that the bed shook, with the agitation and horror which seized me. The apparition then shaking his sword over me, said, "My name is *Boanerges*[3]. Arise, and depart, for this is not your rest[4]. Get hence immediately; for, if you linger, and oblige me to visit you again, woe, woe be unto you." So saying, he disappeared. I instantly arose, and dreading his return, more than any thing I could meet in the *Shadow of Death*; I left the city, and came speedily down the hill, having only the light of the stars to direct me. I passed by *Deist-Hall*; severely reflecting on myself for lingering there. When I came to the cross roads; thro' haste, darkness, and inattention, I took the path that *Resolute* pursued, and was met by the *Prince of*

[1] Phil. i. 6.   [2] Isaiah lii. 1.   [3] Mark iii. 17.   [4] Micah. ii. 10.

Darkness;

Darkness. He reproached me as a runaway, and said, I might as well return again to the city, for our *King* would never receive me; whereas, if I persisted, he had power to destroy me. On my absolutely refusing to return; he seized me, and treated me nearly in the same manner as he did *Resolute:* and I was saved by the tree of life, as he was. When I escaped from the valley to this house, I was well received by *Mr. Patience*[1], who kept it at that time, it being the *Sign of the Martyr.* With him I lived some years, until he was preferred by our *Lord*; who was pleased to appoint me to succeed him. On which, I changed my sign to that of the *Prodigal*; as it best suited my own history.

Just as *Mr. Experience* had finished his narrative; a servant entered, and told him, there was a chariot at the door, with a gentleman in it, who desired to speak with the master of the Inn. So the host went out, and the gentleman said,

Clericus. My name is *Clericus,* of the *City of Establishment.* It is rather late, and I do not choose to travel by night; can you entertain me until morning?

Exper. That, Sir, must be as *you* please. I seldom have any carriages stop at my house, therefore am not very well provided; but if you alight, I will entertain you as well as my house can afford.

Cler. I like your plainness, and will tarry with you until morning.

He then alighted, and came into the room where the Pilgrims sat; who arose, and saluted him. Soon after came the landlord, and asked, if he chose to have a private room?

Cler. No, no, landlord; bring me something to eat, and I will sit here, and enjoy your conversation.

[1] Rom. v. 3, 4.

CHAP. XXII.

A dialogue between Clericus *and* Mr. Experience, *in which is some account of* Mr. Shandy *and* Dr. Diotrephes.

AFTER *Clericus* had refreshed himself, the landlord thus addressed him.

Exper. It is my invariable custom, Sir, to inquire of all who are entertained at my house, their reasons for travelling this road. And I hope that you will not be offended at my putting this question to you?

Cler. Not in the least, landlord. I am a clergyman of the *City of Establishment*, of no mean family. I am of an inquisitive turn of mind, and having heard much of the curiosities, and wonderful things, which are to be heard and seen in this road, I set out, on purpose to examine it with my own eyes; and find, as I suspected, that persons have been much imposed on, by those who are called pilgrims.

Exper. I much approve, Sir, of your resolution to examine[1] things yourself, before you passed your judgment. Many will not take that trouble. But, I must say, that tho' I have kept this Inn many years, and have entertained several hundreds of pilgrims; yet, in general, I have found them to be without guile[2]. Some few, indeed, there are, who dishonour their profession. But pray, Sir, wherein do you think they impose on persons?

Cler. In the frightful account they give of the difficulty of going down into the *Valley of Humiliation*, and travelling through it. The dangers, horrors, and terrors of the *Valley of the Shadow of Death*, and many such things.

[1] 1 Thess. v. 21.   [2] John i. 47.

Exper.

Exper. They do, indeed, tell strange stories of those vallies; and pray, Sir, what have *you* to say about these things?

Cler. Say, why I came by those places this day, and found it as good, safe, and pleasant travelling, as I could desire.

Exper. You must pardon me, Sir, for differing from you. I, indeed, believe that *you* have been imposed on, but not by those who are called pilgrims.

Cler. By whom then, I pray?

Exper. The plain truth, Sir, is this. The before-mentioned vallies have for many years had a very bad name in the *City of Establishment*, which has brought them much out of repute. This induced a certain[1] *Lord of the Manor*, contiguous to those vallies, and, who is an enemy to the *King*'s royal highway therein; to propagate a bad report of that road, to open others thro' his own manor, and give them the same names as the old one. But in doing this, he has consulted more the present ease, than future welfare, of pilgrims; having acted contrary to the *King*'s command. This enemy has proceeded so artfully, and has got his new road so well recommended to the great men of the *City of Establishment*, and its suburbs; that not many [2] wise, not many mighty, or noble among them, will frequent the royal, safe, and *good old way*[3].

This new road turns off to the left, passes thro' the *City of Depravity*, and runs along the side of the hill that is on the left of the *Valley of Humiliation*, until it reaches the *Bridge of Trial*; over which it crosses the valley; and then runs on the side of the hill to the right of the vallies. It leaves *Deist-Hall* a little on the left; and, passing thro' the *City of Sensuality*, enters the highway near *Whimsy-Hill*, about three miles from my house. This, Sir, I imagine to be the road you came.

Cler. By your description, I believe it is the very same: but I found it in excellent order[4], for I had not one jolt in my carriage.

Exper. The other road, Sir, is very troublesome for carriages. I believe there never was a chariot seen in either of the

[1] 2Cor. iv. 4. [2] 1Cor. i. 26. [3] Isaiah xxxv. 8, 9, 10. [4] Prov. xiv. 12.

vallies. Not that no persons who use carriages have been that way; for, to my certain knowledge, there have been several; but they found it very difficult to descend into the vallies with them, so quitted them, went thro' on foot, and found it much the safest way. There was one *Jehu* who came in his chariot to the declivity of the hill[1]; but finding it very steep, he would neither descend in it, nor dismount; but turned off to the left, and was never seen in the highway any more.

Cler. You seem, landlord, not to be a friend to improvements.

Exper. Yes, Sir, I am: but I do not think that the new road has the least title to that denomination.

Cler. Why? you confess that it is a better road than the old one. You live by trade; and as the new road unites with the highway before it reaches your house, you enjoy all the benefit arising from it.

Exper. I do allow, as to present case, the new way is the best; but I am taught, that, "Not those things which men approve, are right; but those which *Jehovah* approves[2]." I am well assured, that the old way was trodden by *Immanuel*, and therefore no other ever will, or can be safe for pilgrims.

Cler. Landlord, you appear to be quite positive, and very contracted in your opinions: too much, I think, for a man of your profession.

Exper. Ah, Sir! I have lost a great deal since the new way has been opened.

Cler. Lost! why, you own there have been more pilgrims since; how do you mean then by saying that you are a loser?

Exper. There certainly have been more travellers; yet there have not been many more pilgrims than before. Those new-road gentry come hither, eat and drink, and when they depart, have no good money to pay me: for my master, with whom I annually reckon, will take no money brought by such as use the new road; and this makes me a loser: however, when a few

[1] 2 Kings x. 15. 31.   [2] Luke xvi. 15.

real

real pilgrims come, they pay me so well for their entertainment, and my matter is so indulgent to me, that I am glad to continue in the house.

Cler. According to *your* account, host, you will lose money by *me*.

Exper. Yes, Sir; and so I do by all who travel in carriages; therefore I do not provide for such, and appeared indifferent about it when you called. But, it does not become me to turn away any who chuse to continue.

Cler. Pray, what is your name, and what sign do you keep?

Exper. My name is *Experience*, and I keep the *Returned Prodigal*.

Cler. Ah! the darkness deceived me. I took it for the *Weather-Cock*, that is kept by the famous and facetious *Mr. Shandy*.

Exper. You are egregiously mistaken, indeed, Sir. That Inn is some miles from hence, on the left side of the road, near the *City of Vanity*, to which it belongs. If you had gone thither, he is now so full of company, that you could hardly have got a bed.

Cler. But I should have had some good merry companions, no doubt.

Exper. The noise of mirth is there; but some of those who have been at the house, when they were most gay and jovial, afterwards owned, their hearts were sorrowful [1] at that very season. Indeed, Sir, that house is no credit to those who use it; and least of all, those of your profession. The matter is a scandal to all clergymen, yet he is permitted to hold his preferments in the *City of Establishment*. He keeps that Inn, which was ever a house of ill-fame; but since *his* being there, his wit and learning have been prostituted as panders for debauchery. The manners of our day are so depraved, that many persons of rank and fortune, of both sexes, are not ashamed to put up there, and keep company with *Mr. Shandy*; tho' he has

[1] Prov. xiv. 13.

proclaimed

proclaimed his principles by many licentious advertisements of his opinions: and even on his sign-post, there are stars, dashes, and certain impure hieroglyphics, which, in a well-regulated city, would have subjected the author to severe fines, if not to corporal punishment.

Cler. Landlord, you are very bold, thus to censure the prevailing taste of this enlightened age. Why, Sir, *Mr. Shandy*'s advertisements contain a luxury of sentiment; and are greedily swallowed by fashionable people, both of the clergy and laity. I have heard that one of our prelates always carried them in his pockets. And another, in a private letter to the author, encouraged him in his licentiousness.

Exper. Such behaviour in prelates, when your city was in its purity, would have endangered their lawn sleeves, and justly to—I hope I never shall fear, in a prudent manner, to censure public vice. But when the pest appears in the habit of a clergyman, with the high claims of *taste, sentiment, fine feelings**, and other delusive blandishments, so as to deceive many; it is time to espouse the cause of injured virtue and religion, at any hazard

Cler. You are one of the precise ones, I find, as your name and sign intimate. I am a clergyman of the *City of Establishment*, but have no good opinion of such very singular people, as are ever finding fault with others.

Exper. Sir, I believe you are a clergyman; and am sorry for what you say.

Cler. Sorry for what? That I am a clergyman; or, that I have no opinion of *you* ?

Exper. Both, Sir. I have a great regard for your city, would have all its clergy of the best sort; and I am certain, that there are not better men in the world, than some of them.

Cler. But you seem to have no good opinion of *me*.

Exper. As a pilgrim, or clergyman, Sir, I cannot say I have. For, no man ought to desert the *King*'s highway to [1] please himself, and much less should a clergyman.

*Words much in use by *Mr. Shandy*, and his disciples.   [1] Rom. xv. 1.

Cler.

Cler. I tell you, landlord, the times are altered. This is an age of improvements. You must not think to palm the puritanical opinions and practice of the last century, upon the enlightened and free-thinking spirits of the present æra

Exper. I am too sensible that the times are altered, but it is for the worse. Arts and sciences may be improving, but I fear, that religion is losing the ground, which it had lately gained among us.

Cler. Your very name and sign would drive half my brethren from your house; but I love novelties, so chose to have a little confabulation with you.

Exper. Had you not loved novelties, you would have kept in the good old way. My name and sign, Sir, are venerable among true pilgrims, and to such only I endeavour to recommend myself.

Cler. I suppose, by your name, that you have much to say of inward motions, impulses, and revelations. You, and your brethren, who go thro' the vallies your own way; dream of goblins, demons, and voices, which I consider as only the workings of your over-heated imaginations.—Come, host, let me have a pipe, and a bottle of your best. I like to talk with you, because you are cool: tho' by your own account, I shall eat and drink for nothing.

Exper. Sir, you shall have any thing my house will afford; for, if I lose money by *you*, here are four true pilgrims, arrived this day, who will amply repay me any loss I may sustain by you.

Cler. O ho! have I happened upon a knot of you ? Well, I hope you will not look on me as a *reprobate*; for I declare, that I have no ill will to any of you.—I think, *Mr. Experience*, you was born in our city ?

Exper. Yes, Sir, I am the son of *John Orthodox*, a native of that city.

Cler. Yes, yes, he has been dead some time, and his family is gone to decay.

Exper.

Exper. That is too true. They were once the principal people in the city.

Cler. They were so. But, I imagine, that the corporation will be better managed by the *Arminii*; which is a learned, rising, and flourishing family.

Exper. Are not you, Sir, of that house?

Cler. I have that honour, Sir; and my friends and relations fill the principal offices of the city.

Exper. There never was a good harmony between our families. However, I do not see why we should quarrel about things which our *King* only can reconcile.

Cler. How do you mean, landlord?

Exper. Why, Sir, it is my opinion, that no man will unite cordially with our family, until *Jehovah* inclines his heart thereunto.

Cler. That, Sir, is saying great things in your own favour.

Exper. It is speaking according to the scriptures[1].

Cler. I think not; and how are we to determine in such cases? In short, host, there is so much to be said, pro and con, on these things, that I think it best not to be positive or dogmatical in any matter.

Exper. If I understand your meaning, it is this. "There are some differences among religious people: therefore it is best to be indifferent about religion." But you would not so act in worldly matters. You are probably a man of real property; suppose the title to your estate were disputable, would you be easy and indifferent about it?

Cler. That is a case in which we can obtain a clear decision.

Exper. Not more so than in the affair of religion. The difference lies not in the obscurity and uncertainty of religion; but in our indisposition to set about seeking it. Present things strike our carnal minds; but future things, of a religious nature, make little impression on them.

[1] Mat. xi. 25.

Cler.

Cler. Really, host, that is a home thrust; I find it too true. But you must acknowledge, that so many various opinions do hurt the cause of religion.

Exper. They are no other than might have been expected from the vast importance of the subject, and the just right which every man hath, in such matters, to think for himself. There cannot be a more serious inquiry, nor are our intellects ever more properly employed, than in the business of religion.

Cler. But when truth is so very difficult to obtain, it is very discouraging.

Exper. Wisdom's ways, doctor, are all plain to them who *will understand*[1]. A wayfaring man, tho' a fool, shall not err therein, says *Prince Paraclete*[2]. Do you understand me, Sir?

Cler. No, indeed, landlord: for who is there that seeks and would not find?

Exper. All those who seek amiss, may be termed of that sort. "Ye ask, and receive not," saith an Apostle, "because ye ask amiss[3]."

Cler. And what do you think is seeking or asking amiss?

Exper. The Apostle defines it for us. "Ye ask," says he, "that ye may consume it on your lusts." From whence it is plain, that whosoever searches for truth, to gratify his curiosity, or nourish his pride, by obtaining matter for carnal reasoning, and vain disputing; such a person seeks and asks amiss; and shall not find the truth in the love of it. He is not solicitous to *do* the will of our *Lord*, therefore shall not be rightly informed of the doctrine that is according to truth[4].

Cler. But, after all, how can any person be certain, whether he is rightly informed in these things?

Exper. We have an unction from *Prince Paraclete*, and know all things[5].

Cler. Ah! my good host; you must, as I said, come to inward feelings, experiences, &c. But such testimonies will not

---

[1] Prov. viii. 9. [2] Isaiah xxxv. 8. [3] Jam. iv. 3. [4] John vii. 17.
[5] John ii. 20.

do

do in thefe days.—A diftinguifhed ruler in our city, and of our family, hath fhewn the fallacy and weaknefs of fuch pretenfions, in a book, entitled, *The Rule of Grace*. Wherein he afferts, that *Prince Paraclete*, who wrote the bible[1], and of whofe company and affiftance, you pilgrims pretend fo much to; did not tarry in this world long, after he had finifhed that book: but went back to the *Celeftial City*, and carried away with him, all his cordials, oils, and falves[2], together with his commentaries and notes on his own works: fo that we muft not expect thofe indulgences; which the primitive pilgrims were favoured with. Nay, my learned kinfman attempts to prove, that there is no need of them; fince *Mr. Natural Man*[3], who was then very blind and impotent, is now fo well recovered, as to do very well for us, with the help of *Prince Paraclete's* writings.

Exper. I have heard of that writer. I think his name is *Diotrephes*[4]. He made a pretty fuccefsful expedition againft the *Giant Infidelity*, under the command of *Mofes the Great*. But being a ftranger to himfelf, he was puffed up[5] with his good fortune, and thought himfelf mafter of the whole fcience of divinity. Full of fuch notions, he removed from the *City of Eftablifhment*, unto the *City of Vanity*, by the way in which you came. I faw him roll by in his coach, and exprefs his difguft at us, as he paffed my houfe. However, he did not fail to call on *Mr. Shandy*, whofe tutor, fome fay, he was. From thence he went and took apartments in *Cold-Bath-Fields*, in the faid city; and there he wrote the book you mention. In that work he treats the famous *Meffrs. Duplex* and *Fervidus*, and all the inhabitants of *Church-Street*, in your city, with great feverity; denominating them, the enthufiafts of our age. But, I think, he has been fuitably anfwered.

Cler. There is one *Andrew Marden*, who immediately replied to my relation; and proved fufficiently, that if thofe prelates, who reformed the *City of Eftablifhment* from the grofs innovations of *Pope Peter*, are to be credited by us; the *Prince Paraclete*, at that time, had neither left the city, nor carried away any of his drugs or notes. From thence he infers, that if the *Prince*'s

[1] 2 Pet. i. 21.   [2] Rev. iii. 18.   [3] 1 Cor. ii. 14.   [4] 3 John 9.
[5] 1 Tim. iii. 6.

presence and aid, were found absolutely necessary, and graciously afforded, fifteen hundred years after the bible was finished; they surely, at present, are equally necessary, and may chearfully be expected, by all those who seek them. He also further establishes his point, by shewing, that *Mr. Natural Man*, instead of being less purblind and impotent, as *Diotrephes* had asserted, grows worse and worse[1]. Therefore the *Prince*'s aid is more wanted. *Marden* confirms his sentiments, by shewing, the divine *Prince* had prophesied in his writings, that there always would be the greatest need of his presence and assistance in the city[2]; and that he never would absolutely withdraw from it[3]. In short, I must confess that, *Marden* has the better of the argument, tho' I cannot adopt his sentiments.

Exper. I think *Mr. Marden*, tho' too much for *Diotrephes* with his pen, yet, in other things, respecting temporal power, was too weak to stand against him.

Cler. He was so. *Marden*, when he wrote against *Diotrephes*, dwelt in that prelate's rents, in the *City of Establishment*. But his work was so stinging to his landlord, that he never was satisfied, till he had drove him from his district. At length, the friendly *Dr. Seek* took him under his protection, and made a comfortable provision for him, on his own estate.

Exper. Thus you see, Sir, that it is with us, as it was with *Immanuel* himself; who, when treating on this very subject, with a great doctor of the *Jewish Church*, said, "We speak that which we know; and testify that which we have seen, and ye receive not our witness[4]." So we Pilgrims constantly assert, that the presence and aid of the *Prince* are with us, and we confirm our assertions with a series of strict piety, in all relations of life; yet ye will not give credit to our testimony. And are *you Clericus*, a teacher in our *Israel*, and knowest not these things?

Cler. If I were to discourse of such things in my pulpit, I should give great offence to my best parishioners.

[1] 2 Tim. iii. 13.   [2] John vii. 38, 39. & xv. 5.   [3] Isaiah lix. 21.
[4] John iii. 11.

Exper.

[142]

Exper. That is, becaufe you have fo long departed from the religion which glows in your prayer-book, and which, I dare fay, has led you to think it enthufiaftical in fome parts of it.

Cler. That's true, landlord. I muft own, I have often wifhed, that the antiquated terms of *Queen Befs* were changed for modern ones. Such as, *Tied and bound with the chain of our fins; and being one with Chrift, and dwelling in Chrift, and Chrift in us,* &c. Which are terms I could never underftand. But I confider them as an oriental way of fpeaking, adopted by our reformers. So I hobble over them as well as I can, and heartily defire a reformation of the prayer-book.

Exper. Hobble over them indeed! The good men who compiled our prayers, were truly orientals: they dwelt near the fun, in a warm climate, and a latitude which you *cool divines*, never were in. I would advife you to feek for a reformation of *yourfelves*, and then you will think the prayers want none, in *that* refpect. I often pity you clergymen, who know nothing of the power of religion. Some parts of your duty muft certainly be a burden to you.

Cler. In truth, landlord, fometimes I had rather go to plough than to preach.

Exper. And, unlefs *Immanuel* changes your heart, it had been much better for you to have wrought in the meaneft occupation, than to have thruft yourfelf into the miniftry. Such divine offices it is moft awful to trifle with. You muft certainly render, to our *Lord*, an account of your ftewardfhip: and what can you fay for yourfelf? Permit me to afk; Do you think you have been inftrumental in converting one foul?

Cler. Converted to what? All my parifhioners are Chriftians. I believe there is not a Deift, nor a Jew, among us.

Exper. I fear that you need not go out of your parifh in fearch of Infidels. But I find you are an abfolute ftranger to your duty, as a minifter of *Immanuel*.

Cler. I am as diligent in my duty as any man in the city. I perceive we fhall not agree; my pipe is out, fo I will bid you a good night. You are welcome to *your* oddities, and muft permit me to enjoy *mine*. Gentlemen, I wifh you a good night.

CHAP.

C H A P. XXIII.

Clericus *departs. The Pilgrims take their leave of* Mr. Experience. Probus, *going in search of* Clericus, *is taken prisoner by the Giant* Infidelity.

AFTER *Clericus* was withdrawn, said the landlord.

Exper. You see, my friends, what persons I have sometimes to deal with. However, very few of this sort will call here, for they choose to pass by, and put up at the *Weather-Cock*. This gentleman is a free, good tempered soul, and has more to boast of, than many of his brethren.

Prob. I like his temper, tho' I detest his principles. I bless my *Lord*, that I did not ride in a chariot, as it might have hindered me from going down into the pleasant *Valley of Humiliation*.

Ref. Ah, *Probus*, let us pity and pray for such as this gentleman; for they cannot open their own eyes, tho' they might, and should, decline entering into such sacred employments; since they can have no liking to any thing in them, but their salaries. It is *Jehovah's* work to convert sinners; and, if this gentleman were converted, he would make an excellent minister of *Immanuel*. Let us pray for him.

It being late, they went to prayer, and did not forget *Clericus*. The Pilgrims were then conducted into the noble *Chamber of Hope*, which was fitted up by the hand of *Mr. Experience*[1], and was the same that *Jeremiah, St. Paul,* and other great men, had reposed in. Here they sweetly slept, and arose in the morning much refreshed. They had not been long down stairs before *Clericus* appeared, and ordered his carriage to be got ready.

[1] Rom. v. 4.

Exper.

Exper. Good morning to you, Sir; I hope you flept well?

Cler. Thank you, landlord. I find you have a good bed in your houfe; but the decorations of the room are very peculiar. My chamber, I perceived, was denominated, *Novice Chamber*[1], and was hung round with fcripture pieces, chiefly of a melancholy nature. But I confidered it all as the way of the houfe I was in; fo flept very foundly, tho' I was furrounded with reprefentations of death, judgment, heaven and hell: with many other fuch whimfical fcenes.

Exper. We deal much in fcripture, and make all we do, fome way look to affairs of an eternal nature; becaufe we know that thofe things muft foon be experienced by us.

Cler. That is true, Landlord; but they tend to four our difpofitions, and caft a gloom over all the enjoyments of life.

Exper. I think otherwife, Sir. What fay you to *my* temper and conduct?

Cler. Why, to be plain with you, hoft, I like your free manner very well. The lines of your face are neither mopifh nor auftere. I find there are exceptions to our general opinion of your party; and, for *your* fake, I fhall think more liberally in future.

Exper. And, as to pleafure, Sir, whenever our *Lord* fhall incline your heart to feek him in truth, you will be afhamed of your prefent falfe tafte of happinefs; and acknowledge, that you never enjoyed any real pleafure until then.

Cler. It muft be the *Lord* indeed; for he only can work fuch a change in me; fince, at prefent, I find no kind of inclination to your monaftic rules. So, landlord, farewell.

Exper. The *Lord* blefs you, Sir, and bring you to another way of thinking.

Clericus being gone, *Experience* and the pilgrims went to breakfaft: after which he took them up into an elevated obfervatory, directly over the *Chamber of Hope*. In this place, they found themfelves freed from many depreffions, which are inci-

[1] 1 Tim. iii. 6.

dent to those who dwell below. Their lungs played freely, their spirits flowed lively, and they looked round on various objects with great delight. They now saw the *Delectable Mountains* very plainly; and, tho' the road to them seemed to have many difficulties in it; yet the green and delectable appearance of the mountains so attracted their souls, that they were willing to encounter whatever trials might lie in their way; under a strong confidence, that he, who had hitherto helped them, would never leave nor forsake them.

The Pilgrims now prepared to set out; and *Mr. Experience* said,

Exper. My brethren, the next place you will put up at, is the *Pilgrim Inn*, in the *City of Vanity*, kept by *Mr. Standfast*, for the use of pilgrims. Remember my love to him. As to you, friend *Resolute*, take care of your wand. Remember whence you had it. You may still be roughly handled, but the *Lord*, who hath so eminently appeared for your aid, will still deliver you. *Probus*, add to your knowledge, temperance[1]. And, finally, be ye all faithful unto death[2], and your *Lord* will give you crowns of glory.

He then embraced them, and the Pilgrims thanking him for all favours, went on their way rejoicing.

    " Our journey is a thorny maze,
    " But we march upward still,
    " Forget the troubles of the ways,
    " And reach at *Zion's Hill*.

    " Our souls will tread the desert thro',
    " With undiverted feet,
    " And faith, and flaming zeal subdue,
    " The terrors that we meet." WATTS.

The Pilgrims walked great part of the day with pleasure; discoursing on the wonderful things they had seen and heard on the road. At length they saw at a distance, a carriage waiting near a stile, which led into a field on the right-side of the road. When they drew near it, they found a way-post erected at

[1] 2 Pet. i. 6.   [2] Rev. ii. 10.

the stile, on the top of which was an inscription, signifying, that the stile led into the pleasant *Field of Speculation*; thro' which, lay a beautiful and easy path to another stile, that issued again into the high road, at the farther end of the field. This inscription was signed by several, whose names were famous among pilgrims.

When the Pilgrims had observed the chariot, they knew it belonged to *Clericus* who had slept at the *Prodigal*, the night before. The servant told them, "That his master, on reading the inscription, had gone over the stile, and ordered him to wait his return; but, he had been so long gone, that he was uneasy about him." On this, *Probus* looked over the stile, and seeing a plain path, with a great variety of beautiful flowers; was inclined to take that road.

Ref. Pray, brother, do not part from us; let us keep the common path, and not endanger ourselves by venturing into new ways.

Prob. This is not a new way. You see it has been used by many great men. It is well trodden, and soon issues again into the highway. I will take this rout, and if I find *Clericus*, I will bring him to the other end of this field. So, Mr. Coachman, I would have you drive to the farther stile, and wait there till we come.

Probus went over the stile, and proceeded by himself in the *Field of Speculation*, leaving his brethren to go on in the highway. He had not walked far before he became so delighted with the fragrancy and beauty of the flowers, that he could not confine himself to the path; but thinking those flowers which were farthest from him, appeared most lovely, he went to examine them; and was so charmed with the new objects which every step presented to him; and stopped so often to consider their peculiarities; that the day declined, and night drew her sable mantle over him, before he was aware of it. The evening, however, proved very fine, and the moon arising, he made no haste to attain the stile: but eagerly rambled among these beauties, 'till, being quite ravished with their

sweets,

sweets, he laid down, and spent the night in a rapture of intellectual pleasure.

Here he lay, lulled with the sweet melody of the birds, 'till the sun had risen high above the horizon. When he awaked, he began to think of *Clericus*, and his brethren; being resolved to look well after that good-natured son of *Levi*, and get him into the way with him. In this resolution, he strayed farther and farther to the right; until he perceived the southern boundary of the field; which he approached, and found it to be a high, thorny hedge; but not so thick as to prevent his eyes from penetrating into the next field. Thro' the thicket *Probus* attentively looked, and thought he discovered many flowers far more beautiful than any he had yet seen. He then said to himself. " This is a new discovery: if I can but find a way into the next field, I shall bring from thence some curious productions of nature, that were never yet seen by the learned." He accordingly explored the hedge very carefully, 'till he reached the eastern end of it, where he found an avenue, with a stile; and over it, written in capitals, the following admonition. *Secret things belong unto God*[1].

The Pilgrim, infatuated with the flowery prospect, and the delusive hope of making some useful discovery, did not sufficiently weigh the admonition; but rashly ventured over the stile, and eagerly pressed on to gratify his intemperate mind. In this field, the name of which was *Free-thinking*, he found many things to engage his attention; but none that fully satisfied him. He wandered from one thing to another, 'till the sun went down; but *Probus* was so absorbed in his inquiries, that neither food nor company were desirable. Thus intoxicated, he again fell asleep, amidst a flattering variety of exquisite flowers; the glowing images of which, so employed his imagination, and their fragrance so soothed his senses; that he lay entranced until high day; when, behold, he was roused by a huge *Giant*, of a most fearful aspect! who, with a terrible voice, demanded who he was, and what he did there?

Prob. I am a Pilgrim, in my way to *Mount Zion*.

[1] Deut. xxix. 29.

Giant. You may be a pilgrim, but this is not the way to any such place as you dream about, and this you shall soon be convinced of.

On this, the *Giant* commanded *Probus* to arise: so he arose, and stood trembling before the monster; who, with a grinning aspect, told him, that he was *his* property, as he had found him upon his ground; therefore he must go with him. He then seized the Pilgrim, threw him on his broad shoulders, and stalked with him over the *Field of Free-thinking*, towards a castle, which was situated in a thick wood adjacent to the field.

C H A P. XXIV.

Probus's dreadful adventures in the Castle *of Scepticism. He finds* Clericus *there. They escape; arrive at the* City of Vanity, *and find the brethren.*

THE *Giant* carried *Probus* into the castle, the outward court of which, was filled with people of various ages, who were engaged in several diversions, and appeared quite unconcerned with every thing that passed. The *Giant* conveyed him to a gloomy dungeon, and setting him down, thus addressed him.

Giant. My name is *Infidelity*. You are now in the strong *Castle of Scepticism,* from whence, you can have no hope of ever escaping; wherefore content yourself, renounce all the chimerical hopes you have entertained as a pilgrim, give up yourself to me, and you shall fare as well, and be as happy, as those whom you saw diverting themselves in the court of the castle. Many of whom were once, as full of fanatical expectations of future happiness, as you; and had gone farther in the pilgrim road, than you have done.

Probus

Probus looked melancholy, but made no reply. The *Giant* therefore left him. When he was gone, the unhappy Pilgrim began to reflect on his foolish conduct; and now the admonition over the stile, into the *Field of Free-thinking*, came to his mind, and pierced his very soul. So he threw himself on the ground, and with many tears besought the *Lord* to pardon him, for desiring to be wife above what He had thought proper to reveal; and to deliver him from the dreadful place, into which his vain and sinful curiosity had brought him.

Probus then arose, and examined the dungeon in which he was, but found no probable way of escape. It was gloomy and horrid beyond description, and had such a pernicious effect on his spirits, that he sat down on the ground in the deepest dejection of mind. The *Giant* brought him food from the adjacent field; but he found *that* food rather increased his misery; he therefore declined to eat any more of it. On which, said the *Giant*,

Giant. You may as well eat and drink while you can, for you must soon die and perish, and that will be the end of you: for as to *Mount Zion*, *Heaven*, and eternal happiness, there are no such things in existence.

These words were more terrible than daggers to the soul of *Probus*, who was now bereft of all the strength and reason which he exercised at *Deist-Hall*; and had neither wisdom nor power to answer the *Giant*. He only told the monster, that by his *King*'s help he would never submit to him. And then sat stupidly silent, and swallowed up in sorrow. The *Giant*, enraged at his obstinacy, took him by the arm, and, with a dreadful, menacing look, said, "Come with me." He led the trembling captive, thro' many dark and dismal apartments; at length he opened a door, and told him, *that* was the *Dungeon of Annihilation*, into which he *must* go. *Probus* drew back with all his might, but the monster forced him in, and bolted the door upon him.

This was the most dismal dungeon in the castle. Nothing was to be seen, heard, or conceived therein, but absolute confusion

confusion, horrible discord, and gloomy despair. As soon as the door closed on the wretched *Probus*, it appeared to him as if *Jehovah* was angry with all his works both in heaven and earth, and was determined to destroy every created being, and reign alone, happy in his own GREAT SELF. As to the Pilgrim hope, it was represented to *Probus*, not only as a delusion; but, as a weak and silly ebullition of the human imagination, blown up by the pride of man. The thunders, earthquakes, and general eruption of nature, which were to bring on the universal destruction of every existence, seemed begun; and *Probus*, overwhelmed with grief and despair, threw himself on the floor, and exclaimed, ALL IS LOST.—Farewell, ye pleasing scenes, that once so animated my heart! Farewell, ye reflections of supreme delight, which once caused me to hope, that I should enjoy a happy, happy eternity, with the glorious, the dear author of my being; towards whom I stretched my eager arms of love. But he is TOO GREAT to regard so contemptible a worm; and I *must* perish in the general ruin! O what a change is here! Ah, my dear *Immanuel*, is thy sweet name only an empty sound! Is thy glorious religion, which appears so honourable to *Jehovah*, so agreeable to reason, and so suitable to sinful man; is it all a delusion! A thing of nought!—What, no *Mount Zion!* no future happiness! —Must my bright day be thus *horribly* overcast!—Shall my sun thus hopeless go down *for ever!*—Is there no hope for me? no, not even in my *Lord!*—God forbid! My frame shudders with an instinctive opposition to such horrid suggestions!—They *must not*, they *cannot* be true!—

On this, a voice came, saying, "Fear not *Probus*, I am alpha and omega, the beginning and the end, the first and the last. And I will give to him that is athirst, of the fountain of the water of life freely[1]." Immediately the door flew open, and the Pilgrim arose, hastened from the dungeon, and following a gleam of light, he ascended a stair-case unto the top of the castle, from whence he had a prospect of the adjacent country. He soon perceived, with pleasure, that there were several com-

[1] Rev. xxi. 6.

panies

panies of soldiers drawing towards the castle, and bringing with them every requisite for an attack on the fortress. They soon cleared the ground, intrenched themselves, raised their batteries, and began to fire upon it most furiously. Two of the chief leaders in this enterprize, were known by the Pilgrim: they were Captains *Leland* and *Doddridge*, who were commanded by the brave *General Revelation*, whom *Probus* rejoiced to see again; it being the same person, who had helped him at the *Slough of Despond*. Their batteries shook the castle to its foundations. The *Giant* was not idle. He had procured several from the adjacent *Cities of Vanity* and *Sensuality*, to assist him in defending his castle; and among these auxilaries, *Probus* discovered *Mr. Humus*, of *Deist-Hall*, who was peculiarly alert in supporting this enemy to truth, the *Giant Infidelity*. *Probus*, seeing the conflict, fell down on his knees, and cried mightily to his *King* for deliverance; earnestly beseeching him, to bless the arms of the besiegers, to the overthrow of the *Giant*, and the destruction of his *strong hold of Scepticism*.

After this prayer, *Probus* thought he heard a groaning at some distance from him, and advancing towards it, he found it to proceed from a man whose legs were fast in the stocks, and his body in a very uneasy situation. *Probus* immediately knew him to be *Clericus*, and asked him, how he came there?

Cler. Pray, Friend (if you are such) assist to deliver me from this misery.

Prob. I am a prisoner myself, how then can I help you?

Cler. You are more at large than I am, therefore, pray try to succour me.

Prob. I will do my utmost for you, as the *Lord* hath raised me from the dungeon, and conducted me unto you.

He then loosed his legs, and set him at liberty; which, when *Clericus* experienced, he looked eagerly at his deliverer, and said, in surprize,

Cler. Whom do I see so opportunely helping me! Were you not lately at the *Prodigal Inn*, the house of *Mr. Experience?*

Prob.

Prob. Yes, Sir, and saw you there also.

Cler. I thought I knew you. I now find that there really is more in religion than I imagined. I have suffered a very great trial.

Prob. I hope this adventure will be of use to us both: but, let us endeavour to escape from this horrid place, that we may talk of these matters with greater freedom.

Cler. I will unite with you most heartily.

While the contest was carrying on below; the prisoners searched every place for a way to escape, but all in vain; for they found the walls too high, and every part of them impenetrable.

Cler. I have heard much of this *Giant* aforetime, but could not think that he was so formidable; for I judged it to be an easy thing to elude all his power, and escape his stratagems.

Prob. I, who ought to have known better, had too great an opinion of my own abilities; but am now fully convinced, that his power is truly alarming. However, let us endeavour to escape hence, under the fire of *Captains Leland* and *Doadridge*, whose cannon seem to do most execution against the castle.

So they drew near to the part that was attacked by those skilful engineers; and at length a breach was made in the wall of the castle, to which the prisoners hastened; but the *Giant* perceiving their attempt, pursued them. At that instant a voice came from *Heaven*, saying, "I have prayed for you, that your faith fail not[1]." With this voice, came a rushing mighty wind, which filled the prisoners with courage; but fell like a flash of lightning on the *Giant*, blasted his strength, and prevented his further pursuit. However, he fired after them, and wounded *Probus* in the left arm; but the prisoners jumped thro' the breach, and ran into the field towards the stile; nor stopped 'till they had reached the highway. There they prostrated themselves on the ground, and returned hearty thanks to the *King*, for delivering them from the mighty power of the terrible *Giant Infidelity*.

[1] Luke xxii. 32.

The

The faithful servant of *Clericus* was attending with his chariot. So he took *Probus* up with him, and ordered his man to drive into the *Town of Vanity*, a few miles distant. As they went on, they passed the *Weather-cock Inn*, where *Clericus* had intended to stop, and which was now crouded with company, who made the air ring with their music and dancing. As the carriage went by, *Mr Shandy*, the master, came out, and with many bows and scrapes, invited them to stop, and partake of their mirth: but *Clericus* cried out,

Cler. Drive on, drive on; I now see the folly and danger of visiting such houses; and, by *Immanuel's* grace, will in future avoid them.

Probus rejoiced to see the resolution of *Clericus*, and besought him to put up at the *Pilgrim Inn*, in *Grace-church-Street*, kept by *Mr. Standfast*. So he ordered his servant to drive to that part of the city. When the chariot stopped at the inn, the citizens were amazed at the novelty, and the master and servants came forth, not a little surprized at the adventure: but they received the new guests with great respect, and conducted them into their best room, where they found the three brethren. But who can describe the joy and astonishment of the Pilgrims, when they not only saw again their wandering brother; but also saw him return with *Clericus*, and in his chariot.

Ref. Ah, friend *Probus*, you have had a long ramble. I was fearful that some dreadful disaster had happened to you, and was about to go in search after you; but am very glad to see you returned in safety, and long to hear your adventures.

Prob. My dear brethren, strange and dreadful things have happened unto me. But, good landlord, let us have something to refresh us, before we say any thing more on that subject.

Mr. Standfast hastened to provide for them, according to their circumstances. After which, they entered into discourse, and *Probus* related all that had passed since his departure from them; which narrative drew tears of sympathy from every one present.

CHAP.

CHAP. XXV.

Clericus relates his story. Mr. Standfast's sentiments on infidelity. Story of Colonel Sceptic. Clericus becomes a pilgrim.

AFTER *Probus* had related his adventures; *Clericus* said,

Clcr. I am amazed at the good providence of the *Lord* in thus sending *Probus*, as a prisoner, to relieve me from my bonds. I am naturally inquisitive; and after my converfation with *Mr. Experience*, I became *more* fo; efpecially about religious matters. When I came to the *Field of Speculation*, it exceedingly delighted me; I went over the ftile, and amufed myfelf fome time with the gay produce of that rich foil. I rambled on to the arch which *Probus* mentioned, but took no notice of the admonition that was written over it; for I boldly preffed on into the *Field of Free-thinking*, until I faw the monftrous *Giant* approaching me. I trembled at the fight of him, and would have retired; but he inftantly feized, bound, and conveyed me to his caftle. When we arrived there, he would fain have perfuaded me to renounce all religious hopes, and unite with the company in the court of the caftle. But I fhewed great reluctance to that propofition. So he took me to the top of the fortrefs, placed me in the painful fituation in which *Probus* found me, and would certainly have deftroyed me, had not the *Lord* fent a friend to deliver me. I now clearly fee a divine hand thro' this whole affair. For while I was in the ftocks, my mind was forely diftreffed, and I cried bitterly in the anguifh of my foul, befeeching the *Lord* to grant me falvation, and to bring my foul out of prifon. The *Lord* heard me, and has done more for me than I afked; for he has delivered

me

me by one of his dear servants; and brought me into the company of such as fear his holy name, and rejoice in his great salvation.

Standfast. The ways of *Jehovah* are above, out of our sight. He works, and none can let, or stay his hand. *Probus* erred, by wandering beyond the bounds which *Jehovah* has placed to our speculative powers; and it is a mercy that he is recovered. The human mind was made, indeed, to enjoy noble discoveries of knowledge and happiness; but since the fall of man, these prospects are fled. *Immanuel*, however, has recovered for his people, all that was lost in ADAM, and a rich accession both of knowledge, holiness and joy. But these are not to be fully enjoyed in this world; we are to wait for them, until we are clothed with our house which is from the *Celestial City*. Some curious souls, even among pilgrims, are not content to wait: but are eager to pry into these hidden things; and our *King* has so far indulged their propensities, as to permit them the enjoyment of the *Field of Speculation*; but has cautioned them from proceeding too far, by the admonition which *Probus* mentioned. It is too evident, that all do not take the warning, therefore fall into the hands of the monster *Infidelity*, who is of the race of *evil Genii*, and whose power extends over the *Field of Free-thinking*, which surrounds his castle. Thro' that field there is an highway to the *City of Sensuality*, and *Deist-Hall*. And another more private way to the *Weather-cock*.

Prob. Wherefore is it that some are so prone to err in this respect?

Standfast. Our souls being confined in this dark prison of the body, eagerly exert their native powers; which being depraved, are far more desirous of making curious inquiries, than they are of obeying the known commands of our *King*. Many good pilgrims, instead of being thankful for, and contented with, the discoveries which divine wisdom has condescended to make; rashly pass the bounds of moderation, wander into the labyrinths of unbridled thought, and fall a prey to the worst enemy of pilgrims, that horrid monster *Infidelity*. You have abundant reason, my friends, to bless the *King* for your escape. It

is

is not very common for persons to be thus favoured. You saw how many there were in the court of the castle. They, poor wretches, have given up their hope in a future state, for the vile pleasures of this momentary life. Many brave captains are continually attacking this castle, and the *Giant*; yet he still remains a most formidable foe to the way, and the souls, of pilgrims And, what is very astonishing, he has the address to persuade some, even among mankind, to assist him in his diabolical designs; and these, in general, are persons of no small learning and human abilities.

Cler. How is it, good Sir, that such men as most exert their faculties, are in the greatest danger of falling into this enemy's hands?

Standf. You may as well ask, Sir, why it happens, that persons who are in perfect health, and in affluent circumstances, are most in danger of sensual intemperance? The faculties of our souls, and the food convenient for them, may be abused, as well as our corporal appetites and provisions. A sick, or a poor man, cannot be so intemperate, as a healthy and rich man; because he has not the means. Nor can a weak or illiterate person, abuse the gifts of the mind, like a man of strong intellects. Our nature is fallen. Our *King* has thought proper to set bounds to our inquiries, beyond which, he has commanded us not to venture; but in many cases to take his word implicitly, and rather believe, love, and obey, than speculate. The proud carnal heart will by no means submit to this rule. The plain common pilgrim acquiesces in it. and neither has leisure nor inclination to seek further: he believes, loves, obeys, and is happy. On the contrary, the more refined pilgrim, not being sufficiently humble or thankful for what he knows; perplexes himself with curious inquiries, how such and such things can be; and thus subjects himself to the designs of his enemies, because he will not submit to the plain instructions of the *Lord*'s most holy word.

Cler. While I was in the castle, I often reflected, that it was a thousand pities we had not more evidence for divine things.

Standf.

Standf. Many good pilgrims have indulged such wishes to the great hurt of their faith; and many, who were only professors of the pilgrim religion, to their eternal ruin. Man, while in a state of innocence, lived by sight, more than by faith. He conversed with his maker, face to face; and, perhaps, was frequently visited by celestial beings. But man, tho' so highly favoured, proved disobedient; therefore, although in infinite mercy, our *King* has redeemed us by his own son; yet he has not thought proper to restore us, in this world, to that vision of himself and celestial beings, which our progenitor enjoyed; but has determined, that while we abide here, [1] we shall walk by faith. We may rest assured, that, on the whole, this is best for us. For, our *King* does nothing of this nature, purely to declare his sovereignty over his subjects; but wil make even this trial of our obedience conducive to our glory, and future happiness. I confess that this dark situation is not joyous, but oftentimes very afflicting to *Jehovah*'s children, to be at such a distance from, and to remain so ignorant of, their divine father, and celestial things. And this vehement passion for divine knowledge, has been frequently made use of by their enemy, to distress and afflict them. But, when we reflect how unworthy we are, of what we know and enjoy of our dear *Lord*, his love, grace, and ways; it will lead us; thankfully to submit, to all his wise dispensations, and patiently to wait for greater revelations.

Cler. Pray, do you know of any remarkable instance of a person being reclaimed, who had fought on the side of the *Giant Infidelity?*

Standf. Yes, Sir, a singular instance* of this sort happened very lately in this city. It was as follows: One *Colonel Sceptic*, was a brave officer in our national army; but at the same time, was warm in behalf of the *Giant Infidelity*; and would often stand forth in defence of the *Castle of Scepticism.* A few years ago, a battle was fought near this city, between the contending nations; in that battle the Colonel was mortally wounded, and brought as

---
[1] 2 Cor. v. 7.
* This fact happened at *Frankfort* in the year 1759.

such into the city. The colonel's servant was a friend of ours, a good soul, and would not cease importuning his master, 'till he had prevailed on him to send for an eminent divine, who was then at my house. Accordingly, he went to him; the servant having previously informed him of his master's principles, and of his being given over by his surgeons; the Divine entered his chamber, and thus addressed him.

Divine. I am told, Sir, that your life is nearly at an end; I presume, therefore, without any more ceremony, to ask you one plain question. Is the state of your soul such, that you can entertain a solid hope of salvation?

Sceptic. Yes, Sir.

Divine. On what do you ground your hope?

Sceptic. I never committed any wilful sin. I have indeed been liable to frailties, but I trust in *Jehovah*'s mercy, and the merits of his son, that he will have mercy upon me.

These words, *The merits of his son*, he uttered very slowly.

Divine. I am apt to believe, you are not tainted with the grossest vices; but I fear, that you a little too presumptuously boast of never having committed wilful sin. If you would be saved, you must acknowledge your being utterly corrupted by sin, and consequently deserving of the curse of *Jehovah*, and eternal perdition. I beg leave to ask, Do you believe that *Jehovah* has a son? That his son assumed our nature, in order to save us? And, that in the execution of this office, he has given ample [1] satisfaction to divine justice for us, and recovered our title to the *Celestial world?*

Sceptic. I cannot now avoid a more minute description of the state of my soul. Let me tell you, doctor, I have some knowledge of philosophy, by which I chose for myself, a way of salvation. I have always endeavoured to live a sober life to the utmost of my power, not doubting, but that the being of all beings would then graciously accept me. In this way I stood in no need of *Immanuel*, and therefore did not believe in him. But, if I take the scriptures to be a divine revelation, this way

[1] 2 Cor. v. 21.

of mine, I perceive, cannot be right: for then I muſt believe in *Immanuel*, and thro' him come to *Jehovah*.

Divine. You ſay, Sir, *if* you take the ſcriptures for a divine revelation?

The Colonel then fetched a deep ſigh, and ſaid,

Sceptic. O *Jehovah*, thou wilt make me ſay *if*, becauſe I *muſt* after all ſuſpect, that the ſcriptures are thy word!

Divine. There are grounds and reaſons enough to demonſtrate the divine origin of the pilgrim religion, as I could ſhew from its moſt eſſential principles, were not the period of your life ſo ſhort. But we need not now, that diffuſive method. Faith, being the gift of *Jehovah*, a poor ſinner tottering on the brink of eternity, has not time to inquire about grounds and reaſons. Rather, Sir, betake yourſelf to earneſt prayer for faith; which, if you do, I doubt not but our *King* will give it you.

No ſooner had he ſpoken theſe words, than the Colonel, pulling off his cap, and lifting up his hands and eyes, cried out,

Sceptic. O Almighty *Jehovah*, I am a poor curſed ſinner, worthy of *Tophet*. But *Lord Immanuel*, eternal *Son of Jehovah*, thou died for ſinners. It is thro' thee alone I can be ſaved. O give me faith, ſtrengthen that faith, and break effectually my vile connections with the *Giant Infidelity*.

Being extremely weak, he was obliged to ſtop. A little after, he aſked,

Sceptic. Is faith ſufficient for ſalvation?

Divine. Yes, Sir, if it be a living faith.

Sceptic. Methinks it is ſo already. I perceive it will be more ſo by and by. Let us pray for it.

The Divine ſeeing him to be very weak, to give him ſome reſt, retired into another room. But he ſoon ſent for him. When he came, he found him praying, and *Immanuel* was all he prayed for. The Divine reminded him of ſome

[1] Eph. ii. 8.

ſcriptures

scriptures which treated of faith in *Immanuel*, and he was much delighted with them. Indeed he was quite swallowed up with the grace of our *Lord*, and would hear of nothing but *Immanuel*, and him crucified[1]: he cried out, I do not know how it is with me, for I never in all my life felt such a change! I have power to love *Immanuel* whom I opposed, and to believe in him whom I so long rejected! O my *Immanuel*, how merciful art thou to me.

The Divine and Colonel were filled with joy, as partakers of the same grace of our *Lord*, and that in such a manner, as if they had been acquainted together for many years. Many officers of the army were continually coming to see the Colonel. To whom he talked freely of *Immanuel*. And wondered, without ceasing, at his having found *Immanuel!*

The next day the Divine visited him, and said,

Divine. Has your view of *Immanuel*, and his salvation, been at all altered or obscured since yesterday?

Sceptic. I have no doubt, not even a remote one. It is just the same with me, as if I had always believed, and never doubted; so gracious is the *Lord* to me a sinner, and a soldier of the monstrous *Giant Infidelity!*

On the second day, the Colonel was unwearied in prayer, and towards evening, expired, while the Divine was giving him a word of comfort. We heard, afterwards, that his mother was a good lady, had prayed earnestly eleven years for his conversion, and received the news with the greatest joy.

This story was peculiarly acceptable to *Clericus* and *Probus*: especially the latter; who was so much affected with the narrative, as to make him quite inattentive to the pain in his arm.

Cler. I now see that I am a great debtor to the goodness of the *Lord*, and begin to be solicitous to unite myself with you; for I am convinced that you are right, and will obtain peace at the last. Will you, Sirs, admit me into the number of pilgrims?

[1] 1 Cor. ii. 2.

Standf.

Standf. We make no exceptions; whosoever will, may come, and partake of every privilege freely[1]. I would only ask you, What are your sentiments of yourself, and of our *Lord Immanuel?*

Cler. As to myself, I find, that I am a most vile offender, and justly condemned by the holy law of the *King.* And, as to *Immanuel*, I believe him to be the *Son of Jehovah*, and son of man, in one mediator; and the only person who can save me.

Standf. You are a wealthy man, and preferred in the *City of Establishment*; you must expect to be persecuted and slandered by the world, and many of your brethren. Can you suffer the loss of reputation and preferment for *Immanuel?*

Cler. Sir, when I was in the *Castle of Scepticism*, I did, in some measure, learn the great worth of religion. Since that time, I have endeavoured to count the cost of professing it. And shall be enabled, I hope, if called to it, to sacrifice all that I have in the world, to keep my conscience void of offence.

Standf. Sir, I rejoice to hear your resolution, and beg that you would begin your Pilgrimage, by being our chaplain this evening.

They all devoutly kneeling, *Clericus* wrestled mightily in prayer, and intercession; and comforts were poured down upon them by their *King.* When he had done, they gave him the right-hand of *Fellowship*, and all retired to rest.

[1] Rev. xxii. 17.

CHAP. XXVI.

Mr. Standfast's account of himself. Folly of Mr. Lindsey Woolsey, the Reviewers, and Dr. Flippant. Alderman Industry obtains the great church, from Dr. Fleece, for Clericus to preach in.

THE Pilgrims were lodged in the *Chamber of Resolution.* In the morning their host said,

Standf. Good morning to you, Sirs. I hope your lodgings were agreeable. All my guests use that chamber: and some of the best men, in passing this city, have slept in that, and another over it, named *Patience.* An inspired writer once said, that pilgrims had need to lodge there[1]."

He then shewed them a book, containing some of the names and great actions of men who had slept there.

After they had refreshed themselves, *Resolute* said to the landlord,

Res. Kind host, I like your name, and imagine your behaviour has corresponded thereunto: therefore I should be glad to know so much of your history, as you may think profitable to relate.

Standf. By the grace of our *King*, I am what I am[2]. And I bless his name for so keeping my feet, that I have never deserted his holy path. My original name was *Fearless.* My father lived in the *Town of Civility*, which is situated on the north, or

---

[1] Heb. x. 36.   [2] 1 Cor. xv. 10.

pleasantest

pleafantelt fide of *Mount Sinai*. All the inhabitants of that town are fo amazingly deaf, that they never hear the awful thunders of that volcano. And, as the eruptions never run on that fide, they are under no terror; nor will they believe that there is any danger to be expected from thence. As I was rambling about one evening, I drew near to the mouth of the volcano; when, fuddenly, my ears were opened[1], and the moft terrible thunders fhocked me; to which was added, an audible voice, faying, " As many as are of the works of the law, are under the curfe[2]." On this, I ran home, and informed my father what I had heard. But he told me, my brains were turned; for he had lived on the mountain from his childhood, and never had heard any fuch things.

Yet the words which I had heard, fo rang in my ears, that I could get no reft in my mind; and therefore refolved, as I was near manhood, to leave the town, and feek a better fituation. I fled into the open country, and inclined infenfibly to the road which leads to the *Strait Gate*, to which I faw many go, knock, and enter. On this, I joined fome who were going that way; and inquired why they reforted thither? They told me, to obtain mercy for their fouls, and pardon for their fins. This, fo fuited my cafe, that I was determined to knock for admittance. Accordingly, I went, and met with a moft gracious reception. When I came to the *Crofs*, all my terrors were removed, by looking on that glorious fufferer. There, *Prince Paraclete* appeared, and gave me a wand, which he called *Shemiah; changed my name to Standfaft; and, fuch joy poffeffed my foul, that I came finging[3] thro' the *Village of Carelefs*, which fet the people in an uproar of contempt and laughter.

* *The name of the Lord.*

I abode fome time in the *City of Eftablifhment*, where I became acquainted with the celebrated *Mr Fervidus*, who mightily ftrengthened me in *Immanuel*. When he faw my wand, he told me to keep it carefully. That he poffeffed one of them, and that I need fear no enemy while I had it, and walked in the

[1] Ifaiah xxxv. 5.   [2] Gal. iii. 10.   [3] Acts viii. 39.

right way; for, said he, "My wand has been to me every thing I could want. If I wanted wisdom, power, holiness, joy, &c. The wand would furnish me with them, by attending to it." He also said, that, "*David* had one of them, of which he made great and successful use [1]."

When I came down *Immanuel's Path*, into the *Valley of Humiliation*, I was sorely beset by the mob; but, I girt my garment of *humility* close round me, looked to my wand for patience, and went thro' them with great compofure. Yea, I at length began to rejoice that I was counted worthy to suffer shame for [2] *Immanuel's* fake. The enemies seeing that, were exasperated above measure: and loaded me with dirt, curses, and many blows. However, I bore it all with patience; 'till, at length, they, being weary of persecuting, left me to go on my way peaceably. When they had left me, I fell down on my face to adore and bless our *Lord*, for enabling me thus to endure; and heartily prayed for my persecutors [3]. Arising, I was amazed to see before me, a most glorious person, who soon convinced me he was my beloved *Lord*. He blessed me, bid me fear nothing, and disappeared [4]. Soon after this, I was overtaken by a young man, who earnestly desired to walk with me. He said, he was one who had persecuted me as I came down the hill; but, perceiving my great patience, and meekness of behaviour, he was struck to the heart; and had no peace in his mind until he determined to set out after me. He begged my pardon for the treatment given me [5]; and hoped I would not reject him. This man proved afterwards an excellent pilgrim; his name was *Confideration*.

I passed *St. Paul's Arch* with a glowing heart, tho' covered over with filth. In the *Valley of the Shadow of Death*, *Tophet* seemed to be moved at my coming. Every step I took discovered new terrors. Here my wand was both wisdom and fortitude to me. The *Prince of Darkness*, as usual, raised a gloom, and in it, haunted me with horrid and filthy spectres,

[1] Psalm cxviii. 10, 11, 12.   [2] Acts v. 41.   [3] Mat. v. 44.
[4] John xiv. 21.   [5] Rom. xii. 21.

terrible noises, and blasphemous speeches: but, all in vain: for my mind was kept so calm and strong, that when the *Tyrant* himself appeared, I defied him. I shewed him my wand, told him his power was so limitted that he could not hurt *me*, a poor man in human flesh. And, that his time to do mischief was short; and, very soon, I should sit as his judge, see him dragged to the bar, condemned, and punished, with all his wicked associates[1]. At this, he raved with infernal madness; and the fiends compassed me about like bees[2]; but, with the wand, I soon made my way thro' them; nor were they permitted to touch me; so I came safe from the valley to the house of *Mr. Experience*. He told me, he had heard an unusual commotion in the valley, and thought some courageous pilgrims were coming thro' it. When I came hither, I found an order from court, for me to continue here, master of this *Inn*, in the stead of *Mr. Love*, who was preferred.

Just as *Mr. Standfast* had finished his story, they heard a great noise in the street; and looking out to see what it could be, they saw it was occasioned by a large body of men, dressed in black. In the midst of them were four men in party-coloured clothes, bearing on their shoulders a chair, in which sat a man dressed like a clergyman of the *City of Establishment*. Around this person, the men in black, and a number of the citizens, kept huzzaing in a very loud and extravagant manner. When this black and tumultuous rabble came before the *Pilgrim Inn*, they became still more frantic; and, as they passed, they all roared out, as with one voice, " Right reason and liberty for ever. Away with the enthusiasts!"

Cler. What can all this mean ? for I perceive that most of these men, as well as the person in the chair, are clergymen of the *City of Establishment*.

Standf. They are, Sir, of that honourable order. The name of him in the chair is *Lindsey Woolsey*. The four men who bear him are called *Monthly and Critical Reviewers*. They are the

[1] Cor. vi. 3.   [2] Psalm cxviii. 12.

common Criers of this *City of Vanity and Falshood*; and are *hired* thus to carry about the streets, this singular ecclesiastic. You, doubtless, have heard of him: he seems to be honest, but is very weak, and extremely ignorant of what is his duty as a clergyman. He has lately given up his benefice in the *City of Establishment*, because he judged the constitution of the city so corrupt, that he could not in conscience any longer conform thereunto. He has taken a large house in this city, near the *Turk's Head Tavern*, in *High-Street*, kept by Mr. *Apostate*. Unto this tavern, all these disaffected sons of *Levi* are now convened, to draw up a petition for certain alterations, which, in their wonderful wisdom, they think necessary to be made, in the laws and fortifications of the *City of Establishment*. On Mr. *Lindsey Woolley's* leaving his benefice, and retiring hither, his party were mad with joy, and illuminated their apartments for three days: what extravagant expressions of triumph they will manifest, if any others of their party shew themselves so *far honest*, I cannot say: but, at present, they appear as foolishly fond of *this* their idol, as were the stupid *Egyptians* when they had found their *horned God, Apis*.

Cler. I heard there was some scheme in agitation, before I set out in this journey, and was to have been consulted in it.

Standf. Nothing, Sir, can be more wild than is their plan. The sum of it is, a request, "That those of the *City of Establishment* will, in complaisance to them, pull down their ancient and venerable walls and gates, and entirely alter the laws and plan of their institution, as a body corporate." One vain reason urged by them, in support of their ridiculous request, is, "That they will believe nothing asserted by *Jehovah* or men, unless they are able to comprehend it." Another reason is, "That it is unlawful and unreasonable for any city in *Christendom* to have walls and gates." These gentlemen are, in general, very fond of *Arian* and *Socinian Images*, but inveterate enemies to pilgrims; therefore it was that they made the outcry against enthusiasm, as they passed my house. In short, I consider them all as united in the interest of the neighbouring *Giant Infidelity*.

Cler.

Cle. I am ashamed for them, and shall think it no disgrace to be despised and slandered by such a set of men.

Rel. This tumultuous cavalcade reminds me of what we saw, as we came thro' this city. It was a great concourse of persons, chiefly of the genteel sort, round a very elegant mountebank stage, in a grand square. On the stage was a person of noble mien, with a star on his breast; and with him a youth, whom he was addressing with great volubility of speech.

Serif. The person you mean, is a quac of the first magnitude. He is of the noble family of *Stars-ay*; but, very lately, has descended to figure in the character you saw, by the name of *Dr. Flippant.* His business on the stage is, to recommend and dispose of his medical catholicon; to instruct his natural son, the youth you saw with him; and to vend copies of such instructions. Sometime, the hoary pedagogue will ape the silly tricks of a *Buffoon.* His catholicon is a nostrum, by which he promises to deliver any patient from the irksome, and embarrassing disorders of sincerity and a tender conscience: so that the *religies* of his patient, shall fit so perfectly easy on him, that neither the person himself, nor those about him, will be at all affected thereby. His instructions to his son, principally consist in, shewing the neatest method of paring his nails; the genteelest manner of using his knife, fork, and handkerchief, and disposing of his hands and feet; with the most polite way of being vicious; and so managing every muscle and feature of his aspect, that no one shall discover the corrupt disposition of his mind. In short, the whole theory and practice of this illustrious empiric contain a general assemblage, and artful distillation, from all the gaudy flowers of wit, politeness, frolic, gaity, folly, insincerity and dissipation, which are produced in this great *City of Vanity.* The singularity of this phænomenon, like a powerful vortex, attracts unto it, all the light and gay people from every quarter; who laugh at the doctor's tricks, and purchase his nostrums, and volumes of documents, with great avidity, without any apprehension of their most pernicious effects.

Cler. The report of *Dr. Flippant* had reached the *City of Establishment*, before I left it; and some of my brethren condemned him, as an enemy to morality; while others extravagantly applauded his practice. One of them has even set up the doctor's image on a *Trustle*, for the use of boarding-schools. I now pity those weak and vain people, who do not perceive the futility and immorality of his instructions. Are there any churches in this place, which are used by the citizens of our city? I should like to give them a sermon, while I continue in town.

Standf. Yes, Sir, there are several: and I believe we can procure you the pulpit in the largest of them. Tho', I fear, you will not be permitted to preach more than once; for I imagine you will be too plain with them.

Cler. Let us leave that to our master. Procure the church, and I will preach as often as *He* shall permit.

Mr. Standfast had a staunch friend in the town, *Mr. Alderman Industry*, a person of some influence; to whom he repaired, and told him who he had at his house, and what was his intention. The alderman readily adopted the scheme, and said, he had no doubt of success; because, he was on good terms with *Dr Fleece*, the rector. Accordingly, *Mr. Industry*, uniting with himself some other men of consequence, applied to the doctor; informing him, that a friend of theirs, a clergyman of the *City of Establishment*, was arrived in his chariot at *Mr. Standfast*'s house, and was desirous, if he pleased, of giving them a sermon in the evening.

The rector did not like the clergyman's being at such an Inn; nor did he approve of his zeal in desiring to preach on a weekday; these things appeared to him irregular and fanatical; but, as he was unwilling to disoblige the gentlemen, he thought proper to grant him the pulpit. It was soon noised abroad, that a clergyman, who arrived in his chariot, would preach in the evening at the great church.

Accordingly, the church was crouded, and *Clericus*, preached, taking for his text the following words. " Except ye repent, ye ye shall all likewise perish¹." It was a thundering sermon, for it came warm from his own heart, which had recently felt the great danger of perishing in sin. The audience, both high and low, learned and ignorant, were in much agitation, while *Clericus* shewed the utter insufficiency of all external religion to appease an angry *Jehovah*, or to save one sinner from perishing. And proved, that a zeal for this and that sect, was no part of true repentance, nor of any avail for salvation. He set forth the folly of those citizens, who patronized the disaffected clergy, with respect to *Mr. Lindsey Woolsey*; and proved *that* party to be avowed enemies to the gospel of the grace of *Jehovah*. He sharply rebuked the general practice of the city, severely censured the great and gay for their attachment to *Dr. Flippant*, and his nostrums; and declared, that the whole corporation would perish, like those on whom the tower in *Siloam* fell²; unless they repented. He shewed what was gospel repentance; and thundered out the curses of *Jehovah*'s law against the impenitent. His eyes darted lightning, and his voice was like a two edged sword; insomuch that all were amazed at him. When he came to lay before them the grace of the gospel, he recommended *Immanuel*, as the friend of sinners, and the saviour of the lost, with all the soft arts of persuasion. And he happily saw the powerful effects of his words, for the hearts of many were pricked³, the tears ran from their eyes, nor could they conceal the strong emotion of their souls.

Clericus finished, and returned to the inn: many of the principal citizens branded him for a *methodist*; while others, of various distinctions, came and inquired of him, what they should do to be saved? So that *Clericus* and his friends had enough to do to discourse with them, and direct them in the way of salvation, thro' the grace of the *crucified one*.

Alderman Industry was in raptures with *Clericus*, and bestirred himself so well, that he procured the pulpit for him the next evening; but, when *Dr. Fleece* perceived, that the people were so affected by *Clericus*'s discourses; he was offended, declared

¹ Luke xiii. 3.   ² Luke xiii. 4.   ³ Acts ii. 37.

that

that the inhabitants would all run mad, and, being advised by some of his brethren of the *Turk's Head Tavern*; he absolutely refused *Clericus* any further use of it. And, to gratify some of the great men of the city, *Criers* were sent about the town, to traduce him as a *methodist*. *Clericus* finding this, received the new converts at his lodgings, formed them into a religious society, advised them to meet often, to read the scripture, and pray together; and by all means to withdraw themselves from the dreadful errors, and vain, sinful diversions of the city.

C H A P. XXVII.

The dreadful death of Lord Profligate. *The Pilgrims obliged to leave the* City of Vanity. *They meet with* Mr. Simple, *who describes the* Town of Avarice. *They arrive at the* Pharisee Inn, *in the* City of Formality.

THE evening after *Clericus* had preached, he was waited on by a gentleman, who begged him to attend a young man named *Profligate*, a person of high rank, great fortune, and much esteemed in the city; but who was then at the point of death. *Clericus* followed the gentleman. When he came into the room, there were present, his physician, and an intimate friend of the patient, whom he loved, and had ruined. As soon as the dying man saw *Clericus*, he said,

Profligate. Sir, you and the physician are come too late; I have neither life nor hope. You both aim at miracles: you would raise the dead.

Cler.

Cler. Heaven, Sir, is exceedingly merciful.

Profl. Yes, or I could not have been thus guilty! What has not the almighty done to bless and to save me? But I have been too strong for omnipotence, I have plucked down ruin on my own soul!

Cler. Remember, Sir, the great and blessed Redeemer of lost men.

Profl. Hold! hold! there you wound me. That is the rock on which I have split. I have denied his name—I have assisted the *Giant Infidelity.*

He lay silent a little while, until the clock struck, and then, with vehemence, cried out,

Profl. Oh time! time! it is fit that thou should'st thus strike thy murderer to the heart—How art thou fled for ever! A month! Oh for a single week! I ask not for years; tho' an age were too little for the much I have to do.

Cler. Jehovah, indeed, is most worthy of our hearty and diligent services, and the *Celestial World* will amply repay all our toils, for it is a most blessed place.

Profl. So much the worse for me! 'tis lost! 'tis lost! That word unto me is the severest part of my torment! Ah, fatal *Case of Scepticism.*

Cler. Let us go to prayer, Sir, and seek a blessing from our *Lord.*

Profl. Pray you that can. I never prayed. I cannot pray—nor, need I, for the *Lord* is already on my side. He closes with my conscience. His severest strokes but second my own.

His friend burst into tears, and *Clericus* could not refrain. When the dying man perceived it, he gave his friend a most affectionate look, and said,

Profl.

Profl. Keep thofe tears for thyfelf. I have undone thee—Doſt thou weep for *me*? That is cruel. What can pain me more?

His friend being too much affected, would have left him: but he faid,

Profl. No, ſtop. Thou ſtill may'ſt hope, therefore hear me. How madly have I acted and talked! How madly haſt thou liſtened and believed! But look on my prefent ſtate as a full anſwer to thee, and to myſelf. This body is all weakneſs and pain: but my foul, as if ſtung up by torment to greater ſtrength and ſpirit, is full powerful to reafon, full mighty to fuffer: and *that* which thus triumphs within the jaws of mortality, is, doubtleſs, immortal—And, as for a deity, nothing leſs than an Almighty Being could inflict the pains and terrors which I feel. Oh, flee from *infidelity!*

Clericus was about to congratulate this involuntary and ſuffering confeffor, on his aſſerting the two prime articles of our faith, which were extorted from him by the wreck of nature; when he very briſkly interrupted him.

Profl. No, no, let me fpeak on; I have not long to fpeak— My dear, and much injured friend, my foul, like my body, lies in ruins, in the fcattered fragments of broken thought. Remorſe for the paſt, throws my thoughts on the future: worfe dread of the future, ſtrikes them back on the paſt. I turn, and turn, but find no ray of hope. Did'ſt thou feel half the mountain that is on me, thou would'ſt ſtruggle with the martyr for his ſtake, and blefs *Heaven* for the flames. *That* is not an everlaſting flame! *That* is not an unquenchable fire!

Clericus, and thofe with him, were aſtoniſhed at the force of his reafoning, and the keenneſs of his remorfe. He was about to adminiſter fome confolation to the fufferer, when, with an eye of diſtraction, and a face of defpair, he cried out,

Profl. My principles have poifoned my friend! My extravagance hath begarred my boy! My unkindneſs hath murdered

dered my wife! And is there another *Hell?* Oh, thou blafphemed, yet moſt indulgent *Lord Almighty. Tophet* itſelf, will be a refuge, if it hides me from thy frown!

Soon after uttering the above words, his underſtanding failed, his terrified imagination cauſed him to utter horrors not to be repeated; and before the ſun aroſe, the gay, young, noble, ingenious, accompliſhed, but moſt wretched *Profligate* expired*.

Clericus returned to his friends much affected with the awful ſcene; yet thereby greatly confirmed in his belief of the Being of *Jehovah*, and in the truth of the pilgrim religion. When he related the melancholy ſtory unto his brethren; they were all, but eſpecially *Probus*, ſtrengthened thereby, in their reſolutions of proceeding ſtedfaſtly in the courſe of their Pilgrimage. *Probus* had again foun' his arm pain him, but the caſe of *Lord Profligate* was like a precious balm thereunto. After *Mr. Standfaſt* had well conſidered the wound, he ſhook his head, and ſaid,

Standf. Brother *Probus*, you muſt cry mightily to our *King* for faith, for I perceive that nothing elſe will cure your arm. Take this for your conſolation, your wound is not mortal; but it may be very troubleſome to you; do therefore as I have directed. And when you arrive at the *City of God*, you muſt repair to *St. Thomas's Hoſpital*; for, if a cure is to be obtained, you will find it there, from *Dr. Evidence* the phyſician.

The next day, the *City of Vanity* began to be in commotion. For, ſeveral perſons who were the principals for ſports, plays, and various diverſions, were among thoſe who adhered to *Clericus*; and now refuſed to act in ſuch ſcenes[1]. This enraged the gentry ſo much, that they ſtirred up the mob againſt *Clericus* and his friends; a great multitude united, and came to the *Pilgrim Inn*, with an intention to pull it down. When *Mr. Standfaſt* went out to expoſtulate with them, they inſiſted that *Clericus*

---

* This is taken from *Dr. Young's Centaur*, and was, I am informed, the caſe of one of our noblemen.   [1] Acts xix. 18, 19.

should depart the city, or they would demolish his house. *Mr. Standfast*, perceiving their enmity to be so violent, and knowing, that if he complained to *Mr. Sneer*, the mayor, he should obtain no redress; thought it best to promise, that *Clericus* should depart the next morning. With this, the mob were appeased, and dispersed themselves.

The next day the Pilgrims prepared to depart; but *Clericus* found time to give the new converts a few useful instructions, how to conduct themselves in their present situation; one of which was, often to resort to the *Pilgrim Inn*, and commune with *Mr. Standfast*. Then they all embraced *Mr. Standfast*, and took an affectionate leave of the serious citizens. *Clericus* stept into his chariot, and took *Probus* with him, promising his brethren to stop and provide for them at the next town. In the mean while, many of the inhabitants were assembled to see them depart; and when they were going, they could not help saying, " How loving and affectionate are these Pilgrims to one another."

Sincere, *Friendly*, and *Resolute* went on very comfortably, until they were come over-against the hill *Lucre*: but there had been a great change in that place, since *Christian* passed by. For the children of *Gehazi*, *Judas*, *Demas*, &c. were so greatly multiplied, that they had built a large town round the hill *Lucre*, which they claimed as their inheritance. In this hill they spent all their time and strength; for they had digged vast cavities therein on every side, in searching for silver and gold. Many had been buried alive by the earth falling in upon them; for, being blinded by avarice, they worked foolishly[1], and neglected to use the necessary precautions to secure themselves.

As the Pilgrims passed by this town, they saw a man coming from thence, in a path that entered the highway a small distance before them. The man seemed very thoughtful, and being come up to the Pilgrims, they entered into discourse with him, concerning the manners of the place he had just left.

[1] 1 Tim. vi. 9.

Sincere.

Sincere. Good morning to you, Sir; I perceive that you came from yonder town. Permit me to aſk, if you are an inhabitant of it?

Simple. The name of the town is *Avarice:* but I do not dwell there. My name is Mr. *Simple,* of *Reputation-Street,* in the *Ci y of Formality,* which is a few miles before us, and thither I am going.

Sincere. Pray, *Mr. Simple,* what news is there ſtirring in the town you have left?

News, Sir! Alas! they have no time to *think,* and much leſs to inquire about news. The whole t wn is in a continual hurry of buſineſs.

Sincere. But buſineſs naturally leads to inquiries after intelligence.

Simple. Every perſon, Sir, in that town hath his eyes and heart centering in himſelf[1]; no does any perſon care a ruſh what becomes ot his next door neighbour. There is neither friendſhip, charity, nor religion among them. If you enter into diſcouiſe with any of them, they will be ſure to turn it upon the profits of the hill, which is in the middle of the town. And their ſpirits will fluctuate, be high or low, juſt according as they have had good or bad fortune in the mines. The people, in general, have a downward look, are very ſuſpicious of, and envious againſt, each other.

Sincere. I can ſee no ſign of a place of worſhip in the town: have they any religion?

Simple. There is no church, nor any place for public worſhip, in the town, tho' it is large and populous. N r is there any regard paid to the *Lord's* day; but the miners work, and trade is carried on then, juſt the ſame as on other days. The reaſons they aſſign for ſuch conduct, are, "That they have no time to be religious: and that the inſtitution of the Sabbath was founded in idleneſs[2]."

[1] Iſaiah v. 8.   [2] Exod. v. 17.

Sincere.

Sincere. Do not those persons die like other people? One would imagine they were exempted from death, or they would not live so inconsiderately.

Simple. They seem to be infatuated: and what is remarkable, there are few of them who die a natural death. Many are buried alive under the hill. Hundreds of them are taken with a strange dizziness, that makes them rush headlong into a lake, at a small distance from the town, called the *Lake of Perdition*[1]. Others are seized with a delirium, in which they imagine that they and their families shall come to poverty[2]; therefore they will not afford themselves the common necessaries of life, but actually perish of want, while their houses are full of every kind of subsistance.

Sincere. Did you never perceive any traces of religion among them?

Simple. They make no public profession of any. But, by what I have observed, they are idolators[3]; for they pay a kind of religious regard to the hill *Lucre.* They affirm, that it is the life and support of the town[4], and therefore ought to have all their veneration.

Sincere. Are you, Sir, a native of that city?

Simple. Yes, I was born there, and lived amongst them many years; but being weary of their irreligious proceedings, I left it, and went with my family and settled in the *City of Formality.*

Sincere. Did you ever hear of any attempt made to reform the *Town of Avarice?*

Simple. Yes, Sir, an effort of this sort was made some years since, by one *Mr. Fervidus,* of whom you probably have heard; I lived there at that time.

Sincere. And pray, what success had that eminent servant of *Immanuel?*

Simple. Hardly any. When he first came, he preached near the hill *Lucre,* and told them plainly, that they worshipped that

---

[1] 1 Tim. vi. 9.   [2] Eccles. vi. 2.   [3] Ephes. v. 5.   [4] Job xxi. 24. & Psalm lii. 7.

hill,

hill, which would certainly prove their eternal ruin, if they did not repent. He proved what he said, by the miserable fate of many of their forefathers. He denounced many woes against them, and declared, that it was easier for a camel to go thro' the eye of a needle, than for any of them to go to the *Celestial City*[1]. However, he said, *Jehovah* was able to save them; which he proved by the examples of several eminently religious men, who had formerly lived in that town; but, on their conversion, had left it, and settled elsewhere. In short, he was very alarming, and several of the people were affected with his sermon. But the impressions soon wore off, and the love of the hill *Lucre* so captivated them again, that no one but myself removed from the town. I was so sensible of the truth of what *Fervidus* said, that I could not sleep at peace while I continued among them: I therefore collected together my substance, and removed from the town; but still do some business there, which often calls me among them.

Frien. And how do you like the behaviour of the citizens, among whom you now reside?

Simple. No one can say any thing against a people, who are so famous for their regularity in all the offices of religion.

Frien. Are all the inhabitants of your city of one persuasion?

Simple. No, Sir, but they are all very friendly to each other.

Frien. What denominations are there among them?

Simple. The principal part, are of the *City of Establishment*; but, there are great numbers of every sect in its suburbs.

Frien. And you say, they all agree together very well?

Simple. They will on no account frequent each others places of worship; but they visit each other, and unite together in going to the public places of diversion. In short, we are very neighbourly. I never knew a more social people.

Rep. Then you have public places of diversion in your city?

[1] Mat. xix, 24.

Simple. Yes, Sir, there are theatres, affembly-rooms, &c. all, very elegant.

Ref. And yet you fay, They are a very religious people?

Simple. God forbid, Sir, that recreations fhould deftroy religion, or religion fhould put an end to all recreation! which is fo falutary to human nature.

Ref. Are there no perfons among you, who refufe to join in fuch diverfions, and fpeak againft them?

Simple. None refident amongft us, I believe. But, as *this* road runs thro' the city, there frequently arrive, travellers who diflike fuch diverfions, and who will neither go to any of them, nor continue long in the city.

Ref. Did not *Fervidus* preach among you?

Simple. Yes, and handled the citizens very roughly, even as plainly as he did the people of the *Town of Avarice*. I thought he was too fevere. He made few converts among them, and thofe who joined him, foon afterwards left the city.

Ref. Which is the beft Inn for entertainment in that city?

Simple. It is near my houfe. It is a noble Inn, and is known by the *Sign of the Pharifee*, in *Reputation-Street*, kept by *Mr. Conceit*.

Ref. And how do the citizens receive you?

Simple. I have a good character among them. And, as I removed from a wicked place, for confcience fake, I am much careffed; and, I thank *God*, I am very happy both in body and mind.

Ref. Do you frequent theatres and affemblies?

Simple. I am not fond of fuch things, but find it neceffary to attend them at times, in order to cultivate good fellowfhip, and carry on bufinefs.

Ref. And do you not find fuch diverfions to be hinderances to religion?

Simple. Not at all, Sir. We always take care to prevent *that*, by keeping our days of recreation at a proper diftance from our

religious

religious seasons. For instance, We never have any of those diversions on a Saturday night, nor in the whole week before Sacrament Sundays; because they would interrupt our *Week's Preparation*. We are very punctual in these particulars, I assure you.

They now drew near the city, which was large and populous; and principally inhabited by the children of *Formality* and *Hypocrisy*. Which two families had intermarried. And altho' they were of different sects; yet were now become one incorporated body, and dwelt together in great cordiality. The highway to *Zion* runs thro' this city. The Pilgrims entered *Reputation-Street*, and, as they drew near to the *Pharisee Inn*, they perceived *Clericus* and *Probus* in a window of the house, which commanded the street. So they thanked *Mr. Simple* for his kindness, begged him to call on them in the evening, and went in to their friends; to whom they related the discourse they had with *Simple*; and then called for supper, which their friends had ordered against their arrival.

CHAP. XXVIII.

A dialogue between the Pilgrims and Messrs. Simple, Formal, and Merit, shewing the emptiness of all external religion, and the danger of trusting therein. They depart from the City of Formality.

WHEN the supper was brought, they found that it was dressed in the best manner; but the quality of the food was very dry and insipid.

Cler. Landlord, are these the best dishes your city affords?

Conceit. Sir, I imagined you were persons of taste, and therefore have provided for you, such things as I knew to be in greatest

greateſt repute with our gentry. This is *Reputation-Street*, which is famous for its good manners and proviſions.

Cler. I know of nothing againſt your *manners*; but if they are no better than your *fare*, your ſtreet and city will be of no reputation with us. See, Sir, here is no gravy, and but very poor ſauce.

Conceit. Gravy, Sir! we never ſuffer any in our food; it is an obſolete cuſtom. And, as to ſauce, we are very ſparing. You have more than would be found at any nobleman's table in the city, and far richer in quality.

Cler. You are dry fouls indeed! Surely you have no ſpirit among you?

Conceit Our citizens, Sir, are remarkable for the coolneſs of their difpoſitions.

Cler. I believe, my friends, that this place will not agree with us. Pray, *Mr. Conceit*, are there any religious people in this city?

Conceit. Religious people, Sir! Why, you are now at the head-quarters of religion. This city is devout, thro' all and every ſtreet thereof.

Cler. I am glad to hear that. But do any perſons frequent your houſe, who are remarkable for their piety.

Conceit. Yes, Sir, I expect *Meſſrs. Formal* and *Merit* in, every minute. They ſeldom fail me—Here they come, I perceive.

Theſe were two of the principal characters of the city; who much frequented the *Phariſee Inn*, and were very fond of the company of *Mr. Conceit*; who knew how to humour them extremely well. *Mr. Formal* was a fat man, and came in with a ſolemn confequential ſtep. *Mr. Merit* was lively, and rather loquacious. They were both in years. *Mr. Simple* came juſt after them.

Cler. Your ſervant, gentlemen. Pray, be ſeated. We are ſtrangers in this city; but tarrying the night, we are deſirous of ſpending the evening profitably; therefore are glad of your company.

Formal.

Formal. I am very glad to find you are so well disposed, and I hope we shall discourse to our mutual satisfaction.

Chr. To be most profitable, I have started the subject of religion; having asked our host, if there are any religious persons among you?

Merit. By that question it appears that ye are strangers here, indeed: for we are so happy in this city, as to be all religious. We all are born such.

Prob. I must beg leave to object to *that*, as a new opinion. It was a saying among the christian fathers, "That men are not *born* Christians, but *made* such."

Merit. That was true when the world was heathen, but will not hold so now.

Prob. I imagine it is true now; for I dare say, you think that no one is a Christian 'till he is baptized, and received into the church.

Merit. True. *That* was a slip of my tongue. I meant that we are all religious from our infancy, which is a great matter you know.

Prob. It is a blessing to be born of christian parents; but that does not make us truly religious.

Formal. You are to know, Sir, that our city is remarkable for strictness in all the offices of religion. It is common to see persons at their devotion in our streets[1]; and to hear them pray very long in their houses. On Sundays, our city is like one great temple. Here are no shops half open; no cheating, nor evading the laws of *God*, and our country; but every one who is able, constantly attends some place of worship.

Prob. All this is very commendable. I hear there are many sects among you. Have you any of those who are called Pilgrims?

Formal. We have many denominations in the city, but we live in great harmony with each other; and as to those named Pilgrims, we have none abiding with us, nor do we wish for

[1] Mat. vi. 5.

them

them. I took you for such, by your deportment, but I hope you are of a different way of thinking.

Cler. Wherein do such persons differ from you?

Formal. They affirm, that there is no religion in this city. Which is a notorious falsity. They talk much also of *Immanuel*'s dwelling in their hearts; of communion with *Jehovah*; of hearing his voice; tasting his grace; knowing their sins are forgiven; that their names are written in the *Celestial City*; and many other such strange things.

Cler. I freely own that we are all of their opinion in these matters.

Formal. How can these things be? We are eminent for religion, have been so for many years, and yet know nothing at all about them.

Cler. And so was I, Sir, and yet I now find them to be sweet realities. But, permit me to ask you, how you became religious at first?

Formal. It is my natural choice, and what I was ever inclined to.

Cler. Do you not sometimes find it very difficult to be devout?

Formal. Never, never, Sir. I thank *God*, I go always to church with a good heart.

Ref. That is just such a heart as I once had; but I have since found it to be a very bad one.

Formal. Some persons have a strange knack of calling themselves wretched sinners, and vile creatures, and thus undervaluing themselves; but I could never think them sincere in so doing.

Frien. I am afraid, Sir, that such suspicions proceed from not knowing yourself better, and being unacquainted with the grace of *Immanuel*. Pray, did you ever shed a tear on account of your sins?

Formal.

Formal. I beg to be excused, Sir, you are not *my* confessor. I am not the person you may wish me to be. I fear that you are a *Papist.* I am a true *Protestant.* I neither mortify nor whip my body; nor am I any friend to monkish confessions, or austerities.

Frien. Your bulky appearance, Sir, is a sufficient voucher for you in the latter case. But if your sins never troubled and distressed your conscience, I cannot think that you have any love in your heart to our saviour: because you do not believe in him, who is set forth, as the saviour of the lost, the miserable, and the desperate. No one knows the preciousness of a saviour, 'till he sees and feels the exceeding sinfulness of sin.

Prob. I am of my friend's sentiments: for, altho' I love to see persons walk blameless, in all divine ordinances; yet I must insist upon it, that *they* are but the outside of religion, and may be found where there is not a grain of true piety. Real religion begins in the soul, by believing with the heart in *Immanuel* unto righteousness[1].

Merit. O, Sir, I find you are a pilgrim, by your insisting so much on *Immanuel,* for righteousness. This is trusting for merit on an *opinion* only, a thing that exists only in your brain, and cannot be seen by any man; whereas, *we* keep strictly to all the forms of godliness; and thus possess and rejoice in a righteousness, that is seen and approved of by all men. Which, likewise, we thank *God* for[2], and have the greatest reason to believe he is pleased with; but, however that may be, we depend on a *merciful God* for the event at last.

Prob. Your dependence is a delusion; for how can you depend on the *Lord* for mercy, while you reject the word of his grace, which has plainly revealed the way of his shewing mercy to the miserable?

Merit. I cannot think there is no virtue in attending the ordinances of religion. Why, Sir, I have laboured and sweat in those duties for thirty years, both on sundays and week days.

[1] Rom. x. 10.   [2] Luke xviii. 11.

Conceit. That I can bear witness to. *Mr. Merit*, gentlemen, is reputed to be as rich in good works as any one in this city. I have heard it remarked as he passed the street. "There goes the mirror of modern piety. If there were no clock in the city, you might know the hour of prayer by *Father Merit*. O that we may be as well off as he, when we die."

Merit. Fye, fye, landlord, this is too much—Tho', I must confess, that it is my constant practice, to render my conduct acceptable both to *God* and man.

Prob. However decent, and well-proportioned, Sir, the superstructure of your religious edifice may appear to you, or to others; give me leave to tell you, there is too much reason to believe, it is built on the sand. *Immanuel* is not laid for the foundation, therefore in a day of trial it will fall, and bury you under the ruins[r].

Merit. Here you return again to your former cant about *Immanuel, Immanuel.* I tell you, I do believe in him, and hope to be saved at last by him, as much as you do. But we must first save ourselves from this wicked world[2]. You are all for one side only, and dangerously reject the other. I put both together, therefore must be safest of the two; because I have all that both *Immanuel* and myself can do: whereas, you have only your faith in *Immanuel* to depend upon.

Cler. Amazing ignorance and pride! Excuse my freedom, Sir, but, really, I tremble to hear you talk in such a manner. Yet, when I reflect on my own blindness and arrogance in these things, so little time ago; I ought rather to pity and pray for you, than to be angry.

Formal. You take greatly upon you, indeed, young gentleman, thus to censure grey hairs, and a person who is much respected by many of your cloth, in this city: who consider him as the standard of orthodoxy, as to his judgment; and his practice as a living comment on that excellent book, *The whole Duty of Man.*

[r] Mat. vii. 26, 27. [2] Acts ii. 40.

Cler.

Chr. Sir, I ask pardon for any thing I have said, that but infinuates a contempt of *Mr. Merit*'s perſon, or moral character. It is his offenſive deſire to be an aſſiſtant with *Immanuel*, in the great buſineſs of ſalvation, that diſguſts me. This exorbitant eſteem of his own devotion, muſt be changed. Theſe ſtrong holds of human pride, muſt be pulled down. Theſe towering imaginations of his own ſufficiency, muſt be levelled; and theſe rebellious thoughts which will not ſubmit to *Immanuel*'s righteouſneſs, muſt be brought into a happy captivity to the obedience of our *Lord*[1]; or, neither he, you, or any other perſon, who indulges them, can be ſaved.

Formal. You are very uncharitable in your ſentiments; and diſcourſe exactly like ſeveral pilgrims whom I have occaſionally met at this houſe: and who were ſo unſocial as to condemn the innocent diverſions of the inhabitants of this city.

Frien. If the inhabitants were truly religious, they would neither have time, nor inclination for ſuch vanities.

Formal. Surely, religion can be no enemy to harmleſs mirth?

Frien. No, Sir, but we differ vaſtly in our ideas of harmleſs mirth. Religion is the alone ſource of true mirth; but the utter deſtruction of falſe joy and ſinful pleaſure.

Merit Our citizens have found the happy method of reconciling true religion with the innocent diverſions of life; this has made our city ſo very eminent. It has alſo a moſt wholeſome air to breath in, both for body and mind. In ſhort, it has every convenience and advantage to recommend it. A perſon who reſides here, is neither affected by the reveries of enthuſiaſm, nor by the terrors of a guilty conſcience.

Sincere. You ſeem to mean that you have found a way to ſerve *Jehovah* and Mammon; but our *Lord* tells us, that no man can do ſo[2].

Formal. We do not ſerve the world or pleaſure; but we make our buſineſs and diverſions ſubmit to religion.

[1] 2 Cor. x. 4, 5.   [2] Luke xvi. 13.

Sincere.

Sincere. Vain recreations and the *form* of religion will easily unite together: but the power of religion in the heart, would soon set aside balls, assemblies, plays, &c.

Merit. You are very severe, and put religion into so plain a dress, that no body would ever fall in love with it.

Ref. Pray, Sir, do you talk of religion in your assemblies?

Merit. O, Sir, I am surprized at your question! *That*, would destroy all good company.

Ref. All such assemblies, you should have said: therefore, it is evident, that the power of religion would ruin all your vain associations.

Formal. There are some people who would be ever at their devotions: but, "Every thing is beautiful in its season[1]." I like to be found in my pew on sundays and saint's days very well.

Ref. Are you never uneasy, even when you have discharged those duties?

Formal. No, Sir, then all is well; my conscience speaks peace, and I am satisfied.

Ref. Do you never find your mind wandering from the *Lord* while you are at church, and your heart very dead and cold in your devotion?

Formal. No, Sir, not I, truly. I hope my attention is as close as any person's. I always follow our minister in the prayers, and am sure to be heard in the responses.

Ref. Permit me to relate a fact that happened the other day. Two brothers who were real pilgrims, were complaining to each other of the treachery and deceit of their hearts, in respect to wandering thoughts in religious duties. They were overheard by a brother workman, who was a weaver. He interrupted them, saying, "I always suspected that ye were two hypocrites, and now I have heard it confessed by your own mouths. *My* heart is better than yours, for I never find it so wandering as yours are." On this, one of the two, put a piece of money into the hand of the accuser, saying, "Call that money your

[1] Eccles. iii. 11.

own,

own, if, when you next go to church, you can afterwards honestly tell me, that you had not a wandering thought at your devotion." After the person had been to church, he came and faithfully returned the money, declaring, "that he was no sooner in the church, but he began to consider how many looms might be set up therein."—I will leave you to make the application.

Simple. This may be the case with many *low people*, who have not the piety nor abilities of these my worthy citizens: for their minds are so well furnished with divine things, that they have no need to wander for a subject of meditation. Why, do you know, gentlemen, that *Messrs. Formal* and *Merit* have all the book of *Week*'s *Preparation* in their memories? So that they are at all times prepared for the most solemn duties of religion.

Formal. Ah, neighbour *Simple*, it has cost me many a weary hour to make that acquisition; but, I thank *God*, I now reap the benefit of it.

Merit. And yet you find that *our* piety is nothing set by, in these gentlemen's account. Altho' we are judged to be as devout as any men in the whole world.

Cler. Not such as commend themselves are approved[1], but whom the *Lord* commendeth; they, shall never be condemned. In short, Sirs, ye *must* be born again, or ye cannot see the kingdom of *Jehovah*; neither its grace here, nor its glory hereafter[2].

Merit. That text means baptism without doubt.

Cler. It means a great deal more; even nothing less than a new creation of the soul, wrought by the *Prince Paraclete*; without which neither you nor I can enter into the kingdom of our *Lord*.

Merit. You are so mystical, dogmatical, and censorious, that we shall never agree together: so, gentlemen, a good night to you all.

Formal. Sirs, I wish you a good night, and a great deal more charity.

[1] 2 Cor. x. 18.   [2] John iii. 3.

Simple.

Simple. I cannot think that all the trouble I have been at to be religious, amounts to nothing. Gentlemen, a good night to you.

Cler. I wish you all the power of religion; and then you will have a good night indeed.

Conceit. Dear Sir, what hard thoughts you entertain of the best of our citizens! If *Meſſrs. Formal, Merit,* and *Simple* are not in a safe state, what will become of me?

Cler. Why, friend, you may read your fate in *Luke* xviii. 14. You shall be abased, and your end will be condemnation, unless you pull down your sign, and set up that of a pilgrim.

Conceit. That would by no means do. This is a reputable Inn; and if I were to change my sign, I should lose all my customers. Besides, I have no heart to do such things.

Cler. Thou hast now spoken the truth from your heart. Come, it is late, shew us our chamber, and we will retire.

Conceit. You shall have my best and largest chamber, where are beds sufficient for you all.

So he shewed them into the *Chamber of Vanity*; which was very large, and gaudily furnished. The walls were covered with wretched drawings of persons, engaged in all the punctilios of religious ceremonies, awfully turning their backs on HIM, who is the way, the truth, and the life. The room was quite cold, and the beds very indifferent; so that the Pilgrims passed a very uncomfortable night therein. They arose early in the morning, determined to leave the city as soon as they could[1].

Accordingly, they called for the reckoning, and found they had a very large bill to pay; the landlord observing, very archly, that it was the custom of their city, not to have any thing, or sell any thing, *without money, or without price*[2]. The pilgrims paid him, and hastened out of the place.

[1] 2 Tim. iii. 5.　　[2] Isaiah lv. 1.

CHAP.

CHAP. XXX.

The Pilgrims purſued and overtaken by Dr. Lex *a lawyer, and* Captain Militus *of the army, brethren of* Clericus *Dialogue between them and* Clericus. *The awful caſe of* Mr. Serious, *a pilgrim. His death and burial.*

THE morning was fine, and the Pilgrims went forward a great pace. Probus was with Clericus, who drove on before, in order to provide accommodations for their friends. The other three came forward, diſcourſing on the miſerable ſtate of the city they had juſt left. They had not proceeded many miles, before they were overtaken by two gentlemen on horſeback; who aſked, "If they knew of a gentleman, named *Clericus*, who was travelling on that road in a chariot?" The Pilgrims informed them, that he was a few miles before. On which, they ſet ſpurs to their horſes, and ſoon came in ſight of the carriage. Clericus looking out, exclaimed,

Cler. Oh, *Probus*, here are my two brothers, *Dr. Lex* and *Capt. Militus*. Come to invite me back, I ſuppoſe. Pray for me, while I diſcourſe with them.—Brethren, how do ye? I am glad to ſee you in this road.

Lex. I am alſo glad to ſee you; but we have had much trouble in finding you. We thought you were only on a ſhort viſit to the *Weather-cock:* when, behold, we heard that you had turned pilgrim! But, I hope, this is only one of your little whims, that you have now finiſhed your ramble, and will return home with us to our friends and relations, who long to ſee you.

Cler.

Cler. I must confess, that it was my intention, when I set out, to visit *Mr. Shandy*; but, mistaking the way, I turned into the *Field of Speculation*, and was taken prisoner by the *Giant Infidelity*; who, I feared, would have killed me; but the *Lord*, in great mercy, sent me *this* precious friend, now with me; who was the happy means of saving my soul, and for which I shall ever highly respect him.

Lex. Speculation! Giant! killed and saved! Why, brother, I fear that your brain is injured, or you would never talk at this rate. That friend, as you term him, has certainly bewitched you, as we were informed he had done: but, come, leave him to his vagaries, and return with us.

Cler. You may think of me as you please; but I am very certain, that I never was so much in my senses as at present[1]. Am I not of age to chuse for myself?

Lex. Yes. But I hope you are not above receiving good counsel?

Cler. By no means, but I will hear of no advice, unless it be decently offered.

Lex. I beseech you to consider your own character, and the happiness of your family and friends.

Cler. I have already given these things a very mature consideration.

Lex. For whom then do you forsake your relations, and your rich and learned friends? For this fanatic with you, and those other mean creatures who are behind, and who, I suppose, are a part of your company?

Cler. Pray, brother, learn to form your estimate of men, otherwise than from outward appearances. A mean coat may cover a noble soul: a mechanic tool has been found in the hand of a *Son of God*.

Lex. I perceive your intention; but you must not draw these things into your imitation.

[1] Luke xv. 17.

Cler.

Cler. Nor will I when you can render a sufficient reason to the contrary; which I am certain you will never do—What can you advance in support of your idle notions of distinction? What are you better than those persons whom you so much despise? The sum of your boasted preheminence consists, in your eating and drinking more costly provisions, living in grander houses, sleeping in finer apartments, and on softer beds than they; ye also dress in richer apparel, and are more intelligent in the ways of men, and labour less than they. But can you boast that you have better appetites, sweeter sleep, firmer health, or that you are more sincere and honest than they? By no means: for in all these things the peasants and mechanics have much the advantage of you. A truly discerning person, therefore, will ridicule your vain pretensions to an importance, which consists only, in a criminal or pernicious corporal indulgence in dress, food, and idleness; while your minds are inflated with an insincere and fantastical politeness. But, with respect to any sentiments worthy of rational and immortal beings, ye are most inexcusably base and negligent. While ye continue in such sentiments, all you can urge in support of your wretched cause, will appear to me in the same contemptible light, as the sophistical declamation so much in use among *you gentlemen* of the long robe. For, I declare, that I have heard more real wisdom drop from the lips of these plain men, in the short time I have been with them, than ever I heard from you and all our former friends.

Lex. O *Clericus*, how art thou fallen! As for these men, they had much better mind their business; and, for you, pray return to your relations and friends, where Providence has placed you.

Cler. Providence makes not that invidious distinction of persons, which you do.

Militus. Brother, say not so; for it never was designed that all men should be upon a level.

Cler. Do not mistake me, *Militus*. I do not mean, that *Jehovah* intendeth that all men should be on a level. I mean, that

there

there should neither be *envy* on one side, nor *contempt* on the other. I am very sure, that the gentleman has more need of the husbandman and mechanic, than they have of the gentleman. In *civil* life, therefore, it is proper to behave with regard and good nature, to the *inferior classes* of people, as you love to term them; but, in *religious* affairs, all distinctions are vain and impertinent.

Militus. Then I shall have very little to do with religious things.

Cler. That will be found a crime in you; and arises from a false judgment of things. Far greater men than you, have though and acted in a different manner.

Militus. How preposterous would it be for me to be seen conversing on such things, with any of my subalterns, or common soldiers!

Cler. It is far less so, than for you, or others, called Christians, to be heard to swear, or seen disguised in liquor, which is so common among you. But all this notion of the incongruity of discoursing with such persons, proceeds only from an error in your education, and from vicious custom. *Cornelius* a *Roman* captain[1], and *Colonel Gardiner* a *British* officer, were taught better.

Militus. The discourse of such people could never be agreeable or profitable unto me.

Cler. You don't know *that*: however, if you knew more of religion, your discourse might be very useful to your men, which would be an eternal honour to you. *King David* calls for *all* who feared *Jehovah*, (without exception) to come and hear what the *Lord* had done for his soul[2]. He did not call for his learned and noble officers of state: no, he knew that such in general, (as they now are) were totally ignorant of such things. Nor did he prescribe *any* rank in civil life, if they did but fear *Jehovah*, they were welcome to *David*, whether they were rich or poor; and he professes himself to be their companion[3].

[1] Acts x. 7.   [2] Psalm lxvi. 16.   [3] Psalm cxix. 63.

Militus.

Militus. I can never think it my duty to follow such examples.

Cler. Neither ever will you, while you take the vain customs of men for your rule, in opposition to the word of our *King.* Our holy religion observes no deference to the civil circumstances of men. Custom, indeed, has introduced fine pews, and chief places in our churches; but originally it was not so. There is still but one table for the communicants; and, if you will not go to it with a common soldier, you are not a worthy communicant, nor are you fit to attend it at all.

Militus. I must acknowledge, that I seldom have gone to the table, without observing the want of distinction there: and, I think, there should be some method thought on for that purpose.

Cler. No, Brother. This, and the levelling nature of the holy scriptures, form a noble testimony for the divinity of our holy religion, and the vast worth of our immortal souls; to compare with which, all the distinctions of the present life are merely trifling and insignificant. Under a lively sense of these things, *St. Paul* thus writes, "Art thou called being *a slave?* Care not for it; but, if thou can'st be free, choose it rather[1]." Here is a case put, which is the *lowest* condition in life, and yet the Apostle, from a view of the vanity of the present state, and the superiority of soul matters; appears quite indifferent about extricating one's self from it.—There will come a time, Captain, in which you will be placed among common soldiers; therefore, I would advise you to think seriously about it.

Militus. In the grave, I suppose, you mean? Yes, yes, *there,* we must all meet.

Cler. I do not mean in the grave; because the rich, by funeral pomp, and magnificent monuments, have a method of supporting these distinctions after they are dead: but I had in view that awful day, in which, *St. John* informs us, that "kings, mighty men, and great captains, will be herded together, with every slave, and every common freeman[2]." But, in the account

---

[1] 1 Cor. vii. 21. [2] Rev. vi. 15, 16.

he gives us of this motley affembly, fo mortifying to the haughtinefs of great men; he does not tell us, that thefe kings and captains affumed any fupercilious airs towards the *low people*. No, the fcenes of a future ftate had entirely difperfed the falfe mediums, which deceived them while on earth; and the dreadful appearance of their judge, (the promife of whofe coming they had made the fubject of fcorn and ridicule [1]) now fo terrified thefe fons of pride, that they chofe rather to be crufhed under the mountains, with flaves, than to wait the execution of divine indignation upon them.

Lex. O, brother, let us leave thofe dreadful fcenes, which will come foon enough; and let us act in our places, and all will be well.

Cler. I am in my place. I am a minifter of *Immanuel*. My mafter has bid me feed his fheep[2]. He admitted both the rich and poor into his company and favour, and wafhed the feet of poor fifhermen. I intend to follow his example to the utmoft of my power. And, I befeech you, brethren, to take the bible, and not the corrupt maxims of the world, for your directory. What are all the fciences when compared to foul matters? What are all the refearches of the royal and antiquarian focieties, to the important objects which ingrofs the hearts, and exercife the tongues, of thofe defpifed men, called Pilgrims?

Lex. I fear you are incurable, and that we muft return without you; for what man in his fenfes, would prefer a conventicle of enthufiafts, to the venerable circle of the royal fociety!

Cler. I do not fay, that the difcoveries of the royal, and other focieties of arts and fciences, are ufelefs; or, that thofe learned men who compofe them, as individuals, do totally difregard foul matters. But I do infift on it, that *Religion* fupporteth and exalteth a nation, or an individual [3]: confequently, thofe perfons who have moft true religion, are of greateft ufe and honour to a nation; and are the moft worthy and honourable, as individuals. And where will you find any men who have more reli-

[1] 2 Pet. iii. 3,4.   [2] John xxi. 16.   [3] Prov. xiv. 34.

gion

gion than pilgrims? From hence it follows, that an aſſembly of ſuch perſons, however illiterate and mean, yet is more wiſe and honourable in itſelf, and more uſeful to a nation, than any other aſſembly of perſons can be. A man may be eminent in arts and learning, and yet be unacquainted with, yea, an enemy to true religion; therefore, he is in his ſins, and may periſh with all his knowledge. It is highly probable, that the *Fiends of Darkneſs* are greater adepts in every art and ſcience, than any man will ever be, in the preſent ſtate. How abſurd then is it to purſue *ſuch* ſtudies, and neglect religion! Or to eſteem learned men, merely as ſuch, beyond thoſe who are truly religious, but who happen to be poor and unlearned! Remember the words of the laboriouſly learned, but dying *Grotius*. Reflecting on the inutility of a great part of his ſtudies, he cried out, "I have thrown away life, in doing nothing with a great deal of pains!"

Lex. I am ſorry to ſee you thus loſt to the world, and to your relations: I muſt leave you, but hope you will ſoon think otherwiſe.

Cler. I pray, that you both may be made ſenſible, that a friend of the world is an enemy to the *Lord*[1]. And that very ſoon, *Jehovah* will return, and diſcern between the righteous and the wicked; between thoſe who have ſerved him truly, and thoſe who have not[2]. I heartily appeal to that deciſion, and chearfully wait the iſſue. Farewell.

Clericus's brothers returned without ſucceſs, amazed at his obſtinacy, and the perverſeneſs of his ſentiments. *Clericus*, and his friends, went on their way rejoicing, that the *King* had ſo enabled him, to reſiſt this temptation of returning again to the vanities of the world. The Pilgrims on foot were now come up, and they went gently on together. When lo! They perceived a man to iſſue from a wood, on the left ſide of the road; who appeared in great diſcompoſure; and ran with all his might into the highway; into which he came, juſt before the carriage. But, taking no notice of them, he threw himſelf on the ground, and kiſſed it, while a flood of tears guſhed from

[1] Jam. iv. 4.   [2] Mal. iii. 18.

his eyes; then with a heaving breaft, and ftrong emotion, he cried out,

Serious. Bleffed, bleffed be the *Lord*, who has permitted me, a vile backflider, once more to recover this road to life! Bleffed way! Bleffed pilgrims, who walk therein! O wretched *Serious*! how ungratefully, how abominably, haft thou tranfgreffed againft thy *Immanuel*, and thy brethren! Then lifting his ftreaming eyes to *Heaven*, he faid, And wilt thou, wilt thou, O offended *Lord*, yet receive fuch a rebel to favour! Can thy blood, O Saviour, cleanfe fuch deep ftains as mine? Will the provoked, grieved *Prince Paraclete*, ever any more witnefs in this polluted breaft? Ah! how is it, that the ground does not open and fwallow up fo vile a traitor! Why is it, that the pit of *Tophet* does not receive me, and fhut its horrid mouth upon me for ever!

Clericus and *Probus*, on feeing the man in fuch agitation, had alighted, and advanced towards him.

Sincere. Good *Lord*, whom do I fee thus miferable! Whom do I hear fpeaking fuch bitter things againft himfelf! Is it my friend *Serious*?

Serious then fixed his eyes eagerly on *Sincere*, ran to him, throwing his arms round his neck, and laying his head on his bofom, exclaimed,

Serious. Forgive me, forgive me, dear *Sincere*, can'ft thou forgive me? And, all ye dear Pilgrims, can ye pardon me, a poor miferable Pilgrim; if I dare ufe that holy name? Can'ft thou, friend *Sincere*, receive fuch an apoftate wretch to thy bofom again?

Sincere. Be compofed, dear brother: we know not your crime; and if it be ever fo heinous, as the *Lord* hath thus humbled you, foftened your heart, caufed you to deteft it, and turn to him; furely, he will alfo put away your fin, thou fhalt not die[2].

Serious. I hope he will, dear *Sincere*. But how can I look you, and my holy brethren, in the face? I, who have brought

[1] Ezek. xvi. 63.   [2] 2 Sam. xii. 13.

fuch

such a reproach on the pilgrims life! Oh, I cannot forgive myself. Oh, wretched *Serious!*

Sincere. Be comforted, brother. Come, sit down, and open your heart freely to us, that we may unite to bear your burden [1].

Serious. Thank you, my dear friends. But how shall I relate my henious crime!—You know that I was going on pilgrimage with my dear wife. It pleased our *King* to afflict her with much bodily sickness: and when we had advanced thus far, she was so ill, that we were obliged to put up at the adjacent village; there she continued ill some time. In an unguarded hour, I committed folly with a single woman who nursed her; the effect of which appeared soon after my wife's death; which threw me into the greatest perplexity and terror, not knowing how to hide my shame. In this distress I wandered into yonder wood; where a horrid gloom came over me, and a voice more terrible than thunder, said, "Thou shalt not commit adultery [2]." Immediately a legion of terrors took place in my mind; and a thousand horrid spectres attended my every step. I cried for help, but could see no way to escape. At length I discovered a gleam of light at a distance, I ran towards it, calling aloud on the *Lord* for mercy; when, lo, a voice, soft and yet clear; spake unto me, saying, "*Serious*, all manner of sin shall be forgiven unto men [3]." This made me run faster towards the light; and, blessed be my *Lord*, I at length issued from the wilderness, and have again recovered the highway. But whither shall I fly from my own tormenting reflections! How have I fallen [4]! How have I scandalized the good ways of *Immanuel!* I will go down weeping to my grave, my soul refuseth comfort!

He then fell to the earth in a deep swoon—When *Serious* recovered, he looked very wild, and exclaimed,

Serious. Oh, Religion, Religion, how have I wounded thee!

Sincere. My brother, as the *Lord* has given you a broken heart, and contrite spirit, he will also pardon your sin.

[1] Gal. vi. 2.   [2] Exod. xx. 14.   [3] Mat. xii. 31.   [4] 2 Sam. xii. 14.

Serious. I know it is pardoned; and the sense of that, pierces my heart thro' and thro'[1]. O precious Saviour! Ah vile, most vile *Serious!* Do not frown on me, dear *Sincere!* Do, smile on me—Can you forgive me, my brethren?—Oh, my heart will break!——

Sincere. I beseech you to reflect on the infinite virtue of *Immanuel's* blood to pardon all sin, and do not despair.

Serious. I do not despair.—My Saviour has washed my soul. I abhor myself.—I hate my crime.—I cannot survive the stabs of my own reflections.—I go hence.—My heart breaks.—My sins are forgiven.—I go to *Immanuel.*—Brethren, take warning by me.—Oh, Religion, how have I injured thee, by giving such occasion of triumph to thine enemies!

So saying, he fell into *Sincere's* arms, and with a deep groan expired.—Then all the Pilgrims lifted up their voices, and wept over their departed brother.—After they had vented their grief, they prepared for his funeral, which was at the adjacent village; and almost all the people of the place attended at his burial: for he was greatly respected among them, and unblamable in his conduct, before his terrible fall. *Clericus* made an oration over him, at the grave, from the following words, *Rom.*vi.23. " For the wages of sin is death." From hence he took occasion to shew the malignant nature of sin, and its dreadful consequences; not only with respect to ungodly men, but also to true pilgrims, who wander into bye paths. He declared, that altho' the *Lord* doth pardon the sins of his people; yet he often makes them monuments of his displeasure against sin, in the places where they reside. This he proved from the example of *David.* For altho' the *Lord* forgave his horrid crimes, yet he suffered not the sword of his vengeance to depart from his house. So also with respect to the *Corinthian Church*, which had profaned *Immanuel's* feasts[2]. Many of them were punished with sickness and death; altho' we may reasonably hope that their souls were saved. This, *Clericus* said, was the case of *Serious*, their departed brother; whose sin, the *Lord* had pardoned, and sealed the pardon by the witness of *Prince Paraclete* in his heart;

---

[1] Jer. xxxi. 19.   [2] 1 Cor. xi. 30.

yet

yet, inasmuch as he had given great occasion to the enemies of religion to blaspheme; the *Lord* was pleased to punish him with a corporal death, as a warning to other pilgrims. *Clericus* then addressed the people of the village, and remarked to them, that if sin was so hateful to *Jehovah*, as to be thus punished in pilgrims; what must be the miserable end of such, as neither knew nor cared any thing about the salvation of the *Son of God?* Kiss *this Son*, therefore, said he, lest he be angry, and ye perish from the way; if his wrath be kindled but a little. Blessed are all they that put their trust in him[1].

This discourse seemed to fall with great weight on all that heard it, both Pilgrims, and the people of the village. Many tears were shed, and great lamentation was made over the grave of *Mr. Serious*, the once upright, and after penitent Pilgrim.

C H A P. XXX.

The Pilgrims pass by the Town of Illumination. *They arrive at the* House of Meditation, *near the* River of Life. *Mr. Meditation gives an account of himself. A dialogue concerning the* Town of Illumination.

AFTER the burial of *Mr. Serious*, the Pilgrims went on their way with fear and trembling; and began to discourse on the mysteries of grace and Providence, from the striking instance of their departed brother. *Sincere* observed, that he had known *Mr.* and *Mrs. Serious* many years, while he lived at the *Interpreter's* house; and, that they were reported to walk as closely with *Immanuel*, in the pilgrims life, as any couple thereabout. He said also, that *Serious* was remarkably care-

[1] Psalm ii. 12.

ful of giving any offence, and very unblamable in his whole deportment. While *Sincere* was thus difcourfing, they came in fight of a large town, fituated on a rifing ground, about a mile to the left of the road.

The Pilgrims paffed the town, and advanced a few miles farther; when they perceived the road led them to the banks of a river; near which they faw a neat houfe, and made up to it. At the door, which faced the river, fat a venerable man, with his eyes fixed on the water, and his mind fwallowed up in reflection. As foon as he faw the Pilgrims, he arofe, welcomed them to that place, and invited them very earneftly to come under his roof. The Pilgrims were very willing to put up for the night, as it was now coming on; fo accepted the invitation. This gave their hoft much pleafure. Calling then for his domeftics, he ordered every thing that was proper for the entertainment of his guefts; after which, he fat down among them, with a moft fatisfied and obliging afpect.

Chr. You feem, Sir, to have well chofen your ground; for this is a very delightful fituation.

Medit. It is truly excellent; yet it is nothing when compared with the country farther on up this river, about the *Delectable Mountains.*

Chr. Pray, Sir, be fo obliging as to inform us, whofe houfe we are now in; and wherefore you have made this your refidence.

Medit. My name is *Meditation.* I was born and educated in *Darkland*, in the country adjacent to the *City of Deftruction.* And remember, that I had feveral good impreffions made on me, at times, while I was young; but they proved ineffectual to curb my lufts, or ftop me in the purfuit of carnal pleafures; until *Jehovah's* time came to break the infernal charm, which held me in bondage to fin. This great work was wrought when I was about thirty years of age; and in the following manner. As I was fitting at dinner in the fields, with my fellow workmen; behold, I was ftruck to the heart by an unfeen hand! and fuch a lively fenfe of my great and aggravated

vated fins filled my mind; that my whole frame trembled exceedingly[1], and I groaned with the mighty burthen that oppressed my guilty soul. I had heard of pilgrims, and knew something of the road to the *Strait Gate*, therefore I determined to set out immediately. Accordingly, I proceeded, until the *Slough of Despond* stopped me. I explored that bog to the right and left of the path, but could find no way of passing it with safety; so I returned again disconsolate to the road, and sat down on the bank of the *Slough*, quite dejected. At the same time, I saw the mountain, which I afterwards found to be *Mount Sinai*, all in a flame. I sat reflecting on the depth and breadth of the *Slough*, until I quite despaired of ever getting over it; and yet could not think of going back; therefore, was resolved to put a period to my existence, on the spot. For this purpose I drew out my knife, and was about to execute my rash purpose; when I heard a voice distinctly saying to me. " O man, work out your own salvation with fear and trembling[2]." This stopped my hand, and led me to hope, that it was possible even for *Me* to be saved. Just afterwards, one *Mr. Ignorance*, as I have since found his name to be, came up to me, and proposed to build a bridge over the *Slough*; at which I rejoiced: and we set about it directly, with what poor materials we could find in that place. In a little time, we had so well effected this work, that I judged it sufficient to conduct me over, and I eagerly ventured upon it. But, when I was about the middle, a dreadful clap of thunder from *Mount Sinai*, so shook me and the Bridge[3], that it fell with me; but, as *Our King* would have it, I fell on the steps which were just below the surface of the mire; and not perceived by me. When I found myself supported from sinking, I took courage, recovered my feet on the steps, and got over tolerably well. I passed *Mount Sinai* trembling, and was kindly received at the gate. I was very happy at the cross. And when I came to *Candidus*'s house, at the *City of Establishment*, I was so delighted with him, and his old friends, especially *Father Metaphor*, that I settled many years in that city, and acquired some of this world's good. But, being fond of a retired life, I was directed by our *Lord* to proceed to the

[1] Dan. v. 6.   [2] Phil. ii. 12.   [3] Rom. vii. 10, 11.

banks of this river, and occupy this house, for the use of pilgrims. I have lived here many years; and must acknowledge, that my *Lord* has chosen for me, better than I could have done for myself.

Sincere. Sir, we are much obliged for your free and instructing account of yourself. Permit me now to ask, whether you know any thing of a large town which we passed by, on the left side of the road? It seemed extensive, but was without walls. It is not many miles distant.

Medit. It is the *Town of Illumination*, which you mean. Within these few years past, it has had a great increase of inhabitants; but I cannot speak favourably of them. They are known among pilgrims by the name of *Antinomians*. This is so odious a name, that very few of these people will own it belongs to them; but their general practice shews that they too well deserve it. They have much light in their understandings, from whence the town derives its name; but their discipline and morals are very faulty. In short, they have disputed on grace and predestination, 'till they have thrown off all respect to the holy laws of our *King*.

Sincere. But do you imagine, that grace and predestination led them to this?

Medit. No, by no means. The depravity of our nature is so great, that it will pervert the best things to the worst purposes: so that those doctrines, which if rightly used, are to good men full of sweet, pleasant, and unspeakable comfort; are by carnal persons vilely abused, in support of that destructive position, Let us do evil that good may come of it[1].

Sincere. Do you think, Sir, that there are many persons in that town who act on such a vile principle?

Medit. There are too many who imagine, that our dear *Lord* by dying for sin, has excused them from any obligation to the moral law: and, being under gospel grace, they say, that no sin, however indulged, can hurt them.

[1] Rom. iii. 8.

Frien.

Frien. What a pity it is that such a holy religion, as is ours, should be thus grossly perverted and abused!

Medit. There must be heresies, that those who are approved may be made manifest[1]. But such an heresy as this, neither raiseth my admiration, nor greatly affects me.

Ref. I am surprized at this, for you appear to love the ways of our *King!*

Medit. I hope that I have some affection to my *Lord*, and to his interest in the world; however unconcerned I may appear about the *Antinomians*.

Ref. Do, Sir, explain yourself; for I cannot conceive the reason of your indifference respecting them.

Medit. It is thus. I am so thoroughly sensible of the horrid defection of our nature from *Jehovah* and holiness; that no scheme of opposition to religion, practised by this fallen nature, however foolish and preposterous it may appear, excites my admiration. And I am so convinced of the palpable falsehood and immorality of the *Antinomian* scheme; that I think no truly good man is in danger thereby; but, that only the abhorred of the *Lord* (in whom *Prince Paraclete* has ceased to strive[2]) will fall into such a filthy pit.

Ref. I am answered; and return you many thanks. I bless our *King*, that my own heart bears testimony with what you say; for, by what I know of the grace of *Immanuel*, it ever leads me to have respect unto all our *King*'s commandments, and to hate every false way[3].

Medit. And so you will experience it thro' every succeeding stage of the pilgrim road. Some of the *Antinomians* are so sottish as to affirm, that *Immanuel* has done all for them; not only with respect to his work of mediator and surety; but also as a head of sanctification. That he has repented, believed, and prayed for them; therefore they need not be found in such low and legal duties.

[1] 1 Cor. xi. 19.   [2] Gen. vi. 3.   [3] Psalm cxix. 104.

Sincere.

Sincere. Oh, horrible! *Immanuel*, they may further say, is gone to the *Celestial City* for them, therefore there is no necessity for *their* going thither. Nor, indeed, can I believe, that such persons have any real desire of going to that city. It is not *Immanuel*, or holiness, or the *New Jerusalem*, that they want; but a liberty to sin on, without punishment, for ever. They appear to be, what was said of old; "Hardened thro' the deceitfulness of sin[1]." In short, their sentiments are such as we may suppose a Devil's would be, if he were permitted to assume our nature. Thus they strongly manifest the exceeding depravity of their inclinations.

Medit. What you observe is just. Nor can they defend themselves against the threatnings of *Jehovah's* word. *That* law which they affect to oppose, will, by and by, play off its thundering artillery against their deluded souls: and they will find themselves as defenceless as their town appears to be.

Sincere. May *Jehovah* convince them of their impiety and blasphemy.

Medit. Amen. I see very few of them this way, tho' we are so near the town. And when any of them do straggle hither; these fruit trees, which are on the bank of the river, will not be plucked by them; nor will the water endure their touch; but both withdraw from their unhallowed endeavours. When I have seen them make these attempts, I told them they were all in vain; for, while they loved and lived under the power of sin, and pleaded for sin, they would never possess any of this fruit or water. But they generally abuse me for my admonitions, and depart, calling me an *old doating Arminian*, or a a *poor blind Legalist*.

Cler. Have no attempts been made in the town, to convince them of their shocking and impious heresies?

Medit. They have churches, and teachers among them; and their ministers will talk and preach, at times, with much apparent zeal and orthodoxy; while their practice is the very reverse to all that becomes pilgrims. The famous *George Ferridus* has

[1] Heb. iii. 13.

made

made them several visits, and was peculiarly awful among them. I have heard and seen him in their market-place, standing and blazing like another *Mount Sinai*; with thunderings and lightnings, and his voice like a dreadful trumpet; so awful, that I myself quaked and trembled [1]. Some of them were affected while he preached; as were the *Israelites* at the foot of *Sinai*; and like them they also soon forgat it, set up their idols, eat and drank; and rose up to play as usual [2]. Nor could that great man do any mighty work among them; for, he said, " He would rather preach to an *Heathen Felix*, than to an *Antinomian Drusilla* [3]."

Cler. Well, we must leave them to *Jehovah*. Let us ever pray him, to keep alive in our hearts, strong convictions of the evil of sin, tender consciences to feel it, and hearts ever averse to it. But now you mention *Fervidus*, can you tell where he is? Does he ever call on you?

Medit. I have the pleasure of seeing him at times. You must know that the adjacent river is called the *River of Life*: Its source is in the eternal hills [4], and is inaccessible to all mortals. It runs thro' the country of *Regeneration*, where is a noble port, named *Adoption*. From thence it passes thro' this country, unto the famous *City of God* [5], situated on the *Delectable Mountains*, which are about twenty miles from hence. There the river is divided into many streams, the waters of which are conveyed into every house in that city, and its mountains. As to *Fervidus*, there is a vessel called the *Covenant Transport*, which constantly plies with pilgrims, from the *Port of Adoption* to the *Port of Assurance*, in the *City of God*. *Fervidus* often sails as commander of this vessel; and, it is very probable, he may call here soon. If he comes while you are here, I would advise you to ask a passage with them.

Cler. Is there not a very safe way by land?

Medit. There is a way by land, but it is troublesome and dangerous. The famous Mr. *John Duplex* always conducts his pilgrims by land. He frequently passes by us, but will not

[1] Heb. xii. 21.   [2] Exod. xxxii. 5.   [3] Acts xxiv. 24.   [4] Rev. xxi. 1
[5] Psalm xlvi. 4.

suffer.

suffer his people to call here. He says, he has no opinion of my garden of herbs (which you may hear more of by and by) "and that I live too near the *Antinomians.*"

Cler. But what is it that makes the way by land so dangerous.

Medit. The ignorance and various passions of mankind. A true pilgrim will assuredly arrive at the hills, whether he goes by land or by water. The water is the grand and royal privilege way[1], which all real pilgrims have a *right* unto; but all do *not know*, neither *seek* to know and *enjoy* their precious privileges; therefore will not venture by water: but take the foot path, which runs along on the bank of this river. Thus, they expose themselves to many dangers. For first. They must pass thro' *Arminian-wood*; which is part of a very thick gloomy forest, of some miles extent, called *Free-will Forest*; which is infested with wild beasts. In this wood are the ruins of *Doubting Castle*; and, altho' the grim *Giant Despair* is slain; yet there are several enemies to pilgrims who lurk in the ruins of the castle. Such as the monster *Merit*, the great ancestor of the numerous family of the *Merits.* The ugly satyr *Self-sufficiency*, and the haughty fiend *Spiritual Pride*, with others, that you may hear of. To this wood succeeds a sandy desart, called *Goodwin's-Sand*; so named from one *John Goodwin*, a pilgrim, who would needs leave the common road, and go over the sand; but what became of him is not known. This *Sand* is very dangerous to pilgrims in stormy weather; for the wind raises it into clouds, which are very alarming to travellers. When they have escaped the *Sand*, they come to a long, wide, and barren heath, called *Baxter's Heath* from a famous pilgrim of that name, who, in his way to the *City of God*, lost himself on that heath; and was decoyed by a fair sorceress, named *Error*, to her habitation. There he was so intimate with her, that she had by him a strange brood of children, which he called *Aphorisms*: these are very mischievous to pilgrims, even to this day; for they always infest the heath, to perplex, rob or decoy away the pilgrims who go by land. As to Mr. *Baxter* the pilgrim, he

[1] Heb. viii. 8, 9, 10.

was, it seems, seen at the *City of God*, afterwards: but he never absolutely recovered from his shameful fall.

Prob. Kind host, I am for eating, if your supper is ready; and would fain have a drink of this fine river with our food.

Medit. I have ordered you a supper in the true taste of *Canaan*; which I am sure you will like, as you are true Pilgrims. I will order it to be served immediately.

CHAP. XXXI.

Mr. Meditation *feasts the Pilgrims.* Two Antinomians *disturb them.* Resolute *drives them away. A dialogue on the imperfections of pilgrims. An account of a remarkable garden and spring.*

MR. *Meditation* rang his bell, and they were soon presented with such fare as a stranger intermeddleth not with [1]; which was the produce of the river, and its fertile banks. The Pilgrims presently experienced the virtue of the fruits and beverage, and began to feel their hearts and tongues to be at great liberty.

Res. Why, my good host, I find that you are a man of your word; for I have not tasted such divine fare as this since I left the *Prodigal Inn*; my eyes, like *Jonathan's* are enlightened [2] by this delicious honey, and my whole man is braced up with Celestial vigour. Methinks I could now have another struggle with my old enemy, in the *Shadow of Death*.

Medit. I know that this food is animating; but I would advise you, not to trust too much on the vigour it has given; for

[1] Prov. xiv. 10. [2] 1 Sam. xiv. 27.

that may deceive you. It is not so much the *fare*, or your *appetites*, which are to be regarded by you; as the *gracious hand* from which they both proceed. Therefore, I remember, that when *St. Paul* sat at such a banquet as this, feeling its virtues, as you now do, he exclaimed, " *Now I live:*" but, reflecting on his absolute dependence on his *Lord*; he immediately corrected himself, and added, "*yet not I, but Immanuel liveth in me.*" It is, therefore, *Immanuel* who is now in your food, and strengthens your hearts. For, at another time, you may have all these dainties before you, and desire to eat as ye now do, and it may not be given you². In these respects, pilgrims do not live by bread only, but by every word which proceedeth from *Jehovah*³: that is, on the *blessing* which accompanies it, for the use of their souls.

Res. I thank you, Sir, for your seasonable caveat. I acknowledge that I am apt to ascribe too much to the food, to the manner of dressing it, or to my own appetite. But, certainly, the supper is delicate. What say you, *Sincere?* You seem to be very busy. What would you have given for a mouthful of this when you were under *Demas's Stairs*.

Sincere. Truly, brother *Resolute*, I am so well employed, that I cannot talk much; but I must confess, that at the time you mention, I was hungry enough, and deserved to have perished for want; but, my gracious *King* has not only spared me, but given me to sit at his table; thus richly spread, and surrounded with such good company.

Prob. Mr. Meditation, I now see the reason of your residing in this place. Verily, Sir, you have a goodly heritage⁴. You also look well. And, with such food, it would be a miracle if you did not. Pray, permit me to ask you; whether the taste, which so much delights us, is the genuine flavour of your herbs and fruits; or, whether there is an artificial combination of ingredients therein?

Medit. The fruits and water are in themselves excellent; but there is a way to make them still more grateful to our taste. Which art, tho' it may be *known* to the *shining ones*, who eat and

¹ Gal. ii. 20. ² Luke xvii. 22. ³ Mat. iv. 4. ⁴ Psalm xvi. 6.

drink

drink of the river and the fruits on its banks; yet, it is probable, they never *had* that exquisite relish of these things, as we Pilgrims have.

Prob. Cannot you favour us with a recipe, that we may combine them for ourselves, in our future progress?

Medit. I can inform you of this secret; but you must not think to have this river, and these rich fruits, always to refresh you. The river, as I said, runs no farther than the foot of the *Delectable Mountains.*

Prob. I was in hope that for a long while we should have been favoured with this pleasant river. However, let us praise the *King* for what we have, and trust him for what is to come.

Medit. With all my heart—So they crowned the feast with a song.

"This *God* is the *God* we adore,
"Our faithful, unchangeable friend,
"Whose love is as great as his power,
"And neither knows measure nor end.

"'Tis *Jesus* the first and the last,
"Whose spirit shall guide us safe home,
"We'll praise him for all that is past,
"And trust him for all that's to come."

HART.

While they were singing, *Mr. Meditation*, looking out of the window, saw two persons advancing towards the house; on which he said,

Medit. Yonder are two men of the *Town of Illumination*, coming this way. Their names are *Love the World*[1], and *Carnal Security*; they are enemies to pilgrims; and their design is to get into your company, and rob you of the pleasures which you now enjoy: but you are not ignorant in what manner to deal with them.

[1] 1 John ii. 15.

P   *Ref.*

Ref. Permit *me*, my brethren, to manage these gentlemen by myself. So, taking his wand in his hand, behind him; he arose, and went out to the door.

Love-world. Your servant, Sir; you seem to be very merry within. I hope you have good chear, and that you will not eat your morsel alone.

Ref. Pray, gentlemen, whence came you, and what is your business here?

Love-world. We are of the *Town of Illumination*, so famous for its nice acquaintance with, and gifts of, disputing on points of divinity; and are come to spend the evening with the master of the house, for we hear he has got some good company.

Ref. Pray, were you invited at this time?

Love-world. We like to live neighbourly, therefore have made free to call upon him.

Ref. The guests who are at this house, are more for praying, singing, believing, loving and obeying, than for disputing; so that your abilities will not be wanting among them. Besides, your townsmen have no good report among pilgrims.

Love-world. There are many slanders of us go about; but, I hope you are more charitable than to believe them.

Ref. I have your character from very good hands, and believe that you are no friends to true pilgrims, nor to their master's holy ways; so I advise you to return home again.

Carnal-security. You appear to be a very amiable young man: I could not have expected so severe a frown from *your* face. Pray, Sir, let us in this evening.

Ref. I tell you, that your company is not desired by any one here, therefore, be gone.

Carnal-s. You seem to have been well fed to day, and should not be hard-hearted to visitors, who entreat you to use hospitality. Let us in, and we will amply repay you.

Ref.

Ref. What, will you not be denied? Keep back—I tell you, that you are known; and if you intrude further, I shall chastise you.

On this, he shook his rod at them.

Love-world. Sir, you are not master of this house; we fear neither your looks nor your stick.

They pressed on *Resolute*, to force in; but he struck each of them a blow with his rod, which so affected them, that they instantly gave way, and turned their backs to go off; but *Resolute* followed his blows, and drove them from the house with precipitation. His brethren rejoiced at his success; and *Resolute*, having drove them out of sight, returned to his brethren.

Medit. Well done, good and faithful servant of *Immanuel*. I congratulate you on your victory. You treated them like a man of courage.

Ref. I knew they wanted to rob us. But who could bear to lose the good things, which we now partake of? He who will not fight to preserve such dainties, is not worthy to enjoy them[1].

Sincere. Our enemies are notorious cowards, when they are properly opposed.

Medit. That's very true: but pilgrims fight against them to great disadvantage; because they always have a party within them, which holds a correspondence with the enemy[2], and is ready to forward all his operations.

Ref. Of *that* I am very sensible; but I thank our *King*, who, by your excellent fare, had laid all that party by the heels; so that Mr. *Love the World*, and his associate, had none to help them. May our *Lord* daily refresh us in such a manner. Come, brethren, I will give out a song, and then, if you please, we will prepare for bed.

[1] Mat. x. 37. [2] Gal. v. 17.

" E'er I sleep for ev'ry favour,
" This day shew'd,
" By my *God*,
" I will bless my Saviour.
" O, my *Lord*, what shall I render,
" To thy name,
" Still the same,
" Gracious, good, and tender.
" Visit me with thy salvation,
" Let thy care,
" Now be near,
" Round my habitation.
" So whene'er in death I slumber,
" Let me rise,
" With the wise,
" Counted in their number." WHITEFIELD.

Prayer being ended, *Mr. Meditation* shewed them to their chamber, which was called *Pleasant*. It faced the river, the sweet murmuring of which lulled the Pilgrims to sleep; and there they enjoyed most refreshing rest. In the morning their host took them out to walk by the river side, which was peculiarly ravishing. The rising of the glorious sun; together with the murmuring river, the spreading trees, the harmonious birds, and the herbs and flowers pouring forth their delicious fragrance; all conspired to entertain the pilgrims. *Clericus* was so ravished with them, that he could scarcely contain himself, but burst out into rapture.

Cler. Alas, my dear brethren, and carnal friends! how greatly did you err, when ye sought to divert me from pursuing a pilgrim's life! Oh, that ye all were here, to share in these pleasures; then would ye say, " Wisdom's ways are pleasantness, and all her paths are peace¹!" Here, kind Sir, is a most delicious arbour, near the river's brink; let us enter and sit a while.

¹ Prov. iii. 17.

Medit.

Medit. Clericus, I congratulate you. You are in a right pilgrim spirit: for they wish that all their acquaintance, but especially their relations, might know the glory of *Immanuel*; and then they also would love and serve him. This is the *Arbour of Delight*, it was built by our dear *Lord*, and is endued with peculiar virtues. Sometimes I have sat thinking in it, 'till the heavens have been opened to me, and I have heard and tasted somewhat of celestial joys.

Cler. It is a refreshing bower indeed. But I must have a sip of the river.

So he lay down on a bed of violets, to drink. When *Clericus* arose, he said to *Mr. Meditation*.

Cler. Sir, I think you mentioned somewhat last night of a combination of ingredients, as an art, by which this *Water of Life* is made to taste better than it does when drank by itself. I find your observation true, for, by the draught now taken, I discern, that the water, tho' exquisitely sweet, yet is not so favoury as the beverage which we drank the last evening.

Ref. That's right, friend *Clericus!* Our brother *Probus* asked for the recipe, but the two interlopers who endeavoured to spoil our peace, diverted me from pursuing the subject at that time. I now hope that *Mr. Meditation* will oblige us, by revealing that secret; and not think me impertinent in requesting it.

Medit. There should be no such secrets among us, who have all things in common. We are directed to be helpers of each others joy[1]. To be good stewards of the manifold grace of our *King*[2]. Our *Lord* manifests his secrets to his servants[3]. We receive all freely from him, therefore we should communicate freely to one another[4].

My supper last evening was prepared in the following manner. The food, in general, was collected from the trees and herbs which grow on the banks of this river. But I have a garden of my own, adjoining to my house, wherein grows a variety of herbs[5]; which of themselves would be very dangerous

---

[1] 2 Cor. i. 24.   [2] 1 Pet. iv. 10.   [3] Psalm xxv. 1   [4] Mat. x. 8
[5] Rom. vii. 18—23.

to use; but I put them into a still, called *Repentance*, which was constructed by the famous artist *Mr. Godly Sorrow*[1]. These herbs are called by various names, among botanists, such as, *Ignorance*, *Mistake*, *Infirmity*, *Imperfection*, and many others. When distilled, they produce a liquid, which I call *Saline Water*. This I mix with my food, and find it has such a salutary effect, that the more I use it, the better I like it.

As to your drink, I have a small spring, which is ever oozing from the foundation of my house, which I carefully preserve, and cause to pass thro' my still. These I call *Drops of Demerit*; a few of which, in a glass of this water, give it a flavour which none but heaven-born souls know the relish of; and this it was that so pleased you in my supper. There must, indeed, be pain and trouble endured in preparing this water, and those drops; but, I think, a person is amply repaid all his labour, by the rich additional relish they give to his meat and drink.

After *St. Paul* had been in the *Celestial City*, and tasted the food and nectar, which the blessed inhabitants of that region feast on; he imagined, that he should in future be freed from the herbs and spring, and the trouble of distilling them. When he felt that it was not so, he begged hard of his master, to have the herbs and spring destroyed[2]: but his Lord let him know, that it would be most for his master's glory, and his own safety, to let them remain; and to make use of them as I have told you. After the Apostle understood this, he never eat or drank without some of the water and drops; and became so reconciled to them, that it was common with him to sing hymns over his cups[3]. He also recommended the water and drops, as the best antidote to preserve pilgrims from that swelling disorder, the *tympany*, or *spiritual pride*[4].

Prob. I understand you, good Sir, and thank you for your recipe. I believe that none of us need come to you for herbs and drops; for each hath a flourishing crop of his own. How is it, brother *Resolute?* Have not you a garden of these herbs?

Resolute, shaking his head, replied,

[1] 2 Cor. vii. 10.   [2] 2 Cor. xii. 8.   [3] 2 Cor. xii. 10.   [4] 2 Cor. xii. 7.

Ref. I once thought they were all dead, and foolishly strove to pull them up by the roots. As to the spring, which our friend mentions, I thought I could not find a drop[1]: but am now fully sensible of my ignorance in these respects.

Sincere. Our host says, It is dangerous to eat these herbs, or take these drops by themselves, without the preparation mentioned; and, I imagine, that it is as dangerous, to suppose we have no such herbs or spring.

Medit. I never heard of but two mere human tenements[2] that was built without having such a spring in it, and such a garden annexed to it. Many persons, especially in the present age, have vainly pretended that these herbs were entirely eradicated from their gardens, and the spring totally dried up; but, in the event, they found themselves grosly mistaken; and several of them, when returned to their right mind, have readily acknowledged their error.

Cler. May there not be too great an increase of the herbs and spring?

Medit. Undoubtedly there may. The golden rule for pilgrims is, to be sensible that they have these things; to lop the herbs[3], preserve the spring, and use them as I mentioned; but, by no means to cultivate the garden; for the herbs will grow too fast of themselves.

Cler. Pray, Sir, what effects would a total neglect, or a simple use, of the spring and herbs have on any person?

Medit. A total neglect would have fatal consequences. The herbs, if not kept under, would grow over the house, run in at the doors and windows, and absolutely cover it within and without[4], fill it with vermin, and hasten its ruin. The spring would increase, sap the foundation, and overthrow the house, as it has done thousands, and buried the inhabitants under them.

Cler. This is dreadful indeed! And would the simple use of them be destructive?

[1] Psalm xxx. 6, 7.   [2] Gen. v. 1, 2.   [3] Rom. viii. 13.   [4] Rom. i. 29, &c.

Medit. The simple use of them, without a still made by the above artist, is very dangerous. Some have taken such quantities of them, as to bring on a melancholy, which has ended in absolute despair and suicide[1]. Others, and those real pilgrims too, have used them by themselves, as they came from the still, namely, the *Saline Water* and *Drops of Demerit*; and this to their great hurt. For the nature of them, thus taken, is to relax the nerves, and lower the spirits[2]; nor should they ever be used without a good quantity of the water of this river, and the fruits on its borders.

Cler. As they may be so pernicious, I should think, that the herbs and spring had better be eradicated, and dried up, in pilgrims.

Medit. St. Paul was once of that opinion; and, as I took notice, prayed that things might be as you say; but his master thought otherwise.

Cler. Why, is it possible, that sin and imperfection can become of any good use to *Jehovah*, or man?

Medit. That is a very difficult question to answer. Sin and imperfection, as opposed to perfect holiness, are in *themselves* evils, and, as such, can never be productive of any good: but the *Being* and *Continuance* of these things in the world, and in pilgrims, may, thro' the wisdom, grace, and power of *Jehovah*, be the occasion of much good. For instance. It is greatly for the glory of our *King*, that *Immanuel* has appeared in our nature, and put away sin by the sacrifice of himself[3]: but he could not have so done, if sin had not been in the world. And as to sin and imperfection remaining in his people: it is an evil in *itself*; but the constant sense of its *Being* in us, and of our utter weakness and unworthiness on *that* account; or, our pruning these herbs, putting them into the still &c; will so operate, as to keep us humble, make *Immanuel's* sacrifice inestimable, his righteousness precious, and his salvation more and more glorious in our eyes, and to our souls.

[1] Mat. xxvii. 5.   [2] Psalm xxxii. 3, 4.   [3] Heb. ix. 26.

Chr. If I rightly underſtand you, Sir, you mean, that when the Apoſtle declares, " We know that all things work together for good to thoſe who love *Jehovah*.[1]" You think that he did not include their ſins?

Medit. I believe he did not; for that would open a wide door to licentiouſneſs. Sin, as ſuch, can never work for good; becauſe its wages and end are death eternal[2], which is the greateſt of evils: therefore, it muſt, by no means, be included in the intention of the Apoſtle, whoſe principal deſign in that declaration, was, to comfort pilgrims under the various trials which they ſuffered from the world, for their adherence to true chriſtianity.

Sincere. This is a very nice point to determine: for I know from my own experience, that my backſlidings, however deteſted by me now, yet, after my recovery, were productive of much inſtruction and good to me. And ſo it ſeemed to be with *Peter*: therefore, our *Lord* did not pray that *Peter* might not ſin, but that his faith might not fail[3].

Medit. You ſhould neither think nor ſay, that your backſlidings were productive of any good to you; but rather, with *St. Paul*, confeſs, that it is by the grace of *Jehovah* you are what you are[4]: for *that* is the real cauſe of whatever good has occurred to you. You may as well ſay, that *Lucifer* is the author of your ſalvation, becauſe he bruiſed the heel of our Redeemer, by whoſe ſtripes we are healed; as ſay, that ſin works any good to you. Our *King* is able to make even the *malice* of the *Black Tyrant* to ſubſerve his own gracious deſigns; as he does alſo the *being* of ſin in his children: and when all his work of that ſort is done, *Death* and *Tophet*; that is, ſin and all its patrons, ſhall be caſt into the *Lake of Fire*[5]. Where had you been, Sir, at this time, if you had followed your own ways? Or, what had become of *Peter*, if *Immanuel* had not prayed for him? Both he and you had fallen, and riſen no more for ever.

---

[1] Rom. viii. 28.   [2] Rom. vi. 23.   [3] Luke xxii. 31, 32.
[4] 1 Cor. xv. 10.   [5] Rev. xx. 14.

A backslider, a such, would no more return to our *King* than did *Adam* after his fall. But when the *King*, by his grace, brings the wanderer back to his duty; he has a more lively sense of his great danger, our *Lord's* rich mercy, and his obligations thereunto; than he could have experienced without such a lapse and recovery. To illustrate this, by an example. Suppose our *Lord* were to destroy the power and being of sin in one of the infernal spirits, and bring him back to partake of the joys of the *Celestial City*; do you think that the happy affections and sensations of such a restored spirit, could be felt by any of the blessed *Shining Ones*, who had never sinned, or suffered?

Sincere. I think not. Yet this way of reasoning seems to verge rather too near that horrible error, *Let us do evil that good may come of it!*

Medit. God forbid! For there is a wide difference, between a vile sinner indulging his lusts, under the delusion of rendering himself a more fit monument of grace; and the great *King* snatching abrand from the burning of *Tophet*, and magnifying his mercy by washing him in the blood of his Son. The one is an act of presumptuous rebellion, in a creature. The other an instance of sovereign grace, in the Creator. Therefore, a true convert, altho' he exalts the grace of *Jehovah*, for recovering him from such infinite jeapordy; yet he is very far from desiring to tempt the grace of *Immanuel* again; or from advising others to run such lengths in trangression as himself had done, in order to partake of such rich restoring grace: neither *David*, *Peter*, nor any recovered backslider, gives the least countenance to so vile as practice. But, on the contrary, such are always found exclaiming against themselves, for their vile practices, and base ingratitude[1]; exalting the grace of our *King* for healing their backslidings, and beseeching their brethren to learn wisdom from *their* folly[2]. In short, according to the above example, you may as well suppose a redeemed spirit, soliciting one of the blessed *Shining One*, to suffer the torments of the *Pit*, that he might taste the pleasure of a recovery; as to imagine that the grace of our *Lord*, ever leads

[1] Psal. 51. 4, 5. 103. 10. 11. 12.   [2] 1. Pet. v. 8.

its happy subjects unto acts of licentiousness. "Be sober, be vigilant," said *St Peter*, after his fall; "for I know *(by woful experience)* that your adversary the *Devil* goes about, like a roaring lion, seeking whom he may devour."

Cler. Sir, I thank you for your kind and judicious replies to my questions. I am now convinced, that it is not *Sin* that works for good, to any person; but *Grace* in the destruction of sin. So that the more of sin is destroyed, the greater is the good that is done by grace to any soul, and the more will such a soul love and praise *Jehovah*[1]. Not that he praises our *King* for permitting him to run such lengths in sin; no, but he blesses *Jehovah*[2], that when he had run the broad road, until he was just stepping on the threshold of *Tophet*; he yet has brought him back to sing in the *Celestial City*. And I believe no creature hates sin more than such a man.

Medit. You have my meaning. None but a true pilgrim, know any thing of what *St. Paul* felt, when he answered this question; "Shall we continue in sin, that grace may abound[3]? God forbid!" cried he, with an holy indignation. A *Shining One* may hate sin, but a pilgrim only, can know and loath this evil, by retaining in his mind, the bitter experience of its accursed and malignant nature.

Prob. Kind host, I have one more *Case* to state to you, the resolving of which may be of use to us all. It is this. By your recipe you seem to intimate, that a sense of our demerit and imperfections makes *Immanuel more* precious to us; if so, may it not be said, that he will be *less* precious to us when we come to the *Celestial City*? Because, we believe, that we shall there have none of these herbs or springs. Our houses from *Heaven* will have none of these appurtenances, therefore, we shall there make no *Saline Water*, or *Drops of Demerit*; consequently, our celestial fare will not have this excellent relish.

Medit. God forbid, that our houses from *Heaven* should be encumbered with such gardens, or impaired by such springs, which now make pilgrims to groan being burdened[4]! The dif-

[1] Luke, vii. 47. [2] Rom. vi. 17. [3] Rom. vi. 1. 2.
[4] 2 Cor. v. 1. 2. 3. 4.

ficulty

ficulty you have proposed, may be solved in the following manner. Altho' we shall have no occasion for our stills in the *King's Palace*, and shall make no more *Saline water*, or *Drops of Demerit*; yet this does not imply, that we shall *use* none of them in that happy state. As to the *Saline water*, I believe we shall carry none of it into that *City* with us, yet it does not appear that any of this precious decoction will be lost. Don't you remember what *David* says on this subject? He lets us know what becomes of all this water, after it has been made and used by us: for he declares, it is put into *Jehovah's* bottle[1]. And the *Lord* told *Hezekiah*, that he had taken particular notice of his tears[2]. Hence we may conclude, that all this precious fluid is reserved in the *Palace*, in our *King's* bottle; which, like the widow's cruse[3], will never fail, but a sense of its relish will be retained to all eternity.

As to the *Drops of Demerit*, altho' I trust to be totally delivered from the spring, whence they proceed; yet I can never be deprived of the drops. I have always a great number of bottles by me: and while I am this same individual person, I shall retain them, whether I am in this world, or any other. By the representation which our *Lord* gives us, of the sentiments of pilgrims, at the day of judgment; I find that they are all furnished with these drops: "*Lord*," say they, "When saw we thee an hungry, and fed thee, &c[4]". They were these drops also, which made the redeemed cast their crowns before the lamb, and say, "Thou art worthy[5] &c!" *St. John*, indeed, informs us, that "Our works shall follow us" into the *Celestial world*[6]: and another says, "Our *Lord* will not forget our work of faith, and labour of love.[7]" But still I will insist on it, that, altho' my *works* are welcome to *follow* me, if our *King* pleaseth; yet I will carry the *Drops* in *my Bosom*. My gracious Lord may condescend to remember my labour of love[7], but *I must* remember my drops. Nor shall I ever forget, what a vile and *Tophet* deserving sinner, *Richard Meditation* once was.

Prob. Dear host, I thank you for your answer. It is quite

[1] Psal. lvi. 8.   [2] Isaiah, xxxviii. 5.   [3] 1 Kings, xvii. 14.
[4] Mat. xxv. 44.   [5] Rev. v. 8, 9.   [6] Rev. xiv. 13.   [7] Heb. vi. 10.

satisfactory to me, as I hope it is to us all: and I trust that the sentiments which you have so strongly expressed, will ever live in our hearts, and influence our whole conduct.

CHAP. XXXII.

The arrival of the Covenant Transport, *commanded by* Capt. George Fervidus. *The Pilgrims embark in her. Discourse between Fervidus and the Pilgrims. Stories of* Lieutenant Newman, *and* Lord Search.

AFTER the preceeding discourse, they all retired from the *Arbour of Delight*, to breakfast. While they were at their repast, the sound of music was heard from the river; which grew louder, and was found to be accompanied with the voices of both men and women; then said the host.

Medit. My friends, ye are very fortunate. Lo here comes *Fervidus*, with another cargo of precious souls, which he is conducting to the *Delectable Mountains*. I have seen many such freights pass by, and am never more happy than when he calls here; but now as the wind is fair, and the day young, he will not stop, unless you go and ask a passage with him.

Cler. O my brethren, let us by no means miss the opportunity that offers, of being some time with that excellent man, who is an example for every ambassador of our *King* to imitate, both in his doctrine and assiduity.

So they ran to the river side, and saw the vessel approaching, under a full sail, with the *Celestial Standard*, *(a Golden cross,)* flying at the mast head. They then besought the captain to stop a little, and take them on board; with which he readily complied. *Clericus* left his chariot at the house of *Mr. Meditation*, the pilgrims all embraced their good host, and departed. They were most cordially welcomed on board the transport, by *Fer-*
vidus,

vidus, and all the company; and were soon as easy and free among them, as if they had been brought up together from their infancy. As for *Fervidus*, he was as happy as a prince: and thus addressed the pilgrims, on their coming on board.

Fer. So, so, what more fools still! I suppose you have been conversing with that old enthusiast, *Father Meditation*, until he has persuaded you to make a trip to yonder hills: and what do you think to find there?

This address seemed strange to some of our Pilgrims; but *Sincere* had seen and heard much of *Fervidus*, while he abode at the *Interpreter*'s house; therefore he well knew his free way of talking, and replied,

Sincere. How can *you*, Sir, expect any other, when you are so zealous to make such fools as *we* are? We have seen a glimpse of the *Crucified One*'s beauty, and are going to the hills that we may know and enjoy more of him.

Fer. Who is that? What my friend, *John Sincere*! I am glad to find you with us. You have been wandering about a long while, I thought to have seen you at the hills long ago!

Sincere. Every one cannot keep your vigorous pace. I have made a very poor progress indeed; however, I am thankful that I am arrived thus far.

Fer. You ought to be grateful to such a master, who is so indulgent to such idle drones of servants, as we are.

Sincere. I am, indeed, a very drone, but you, Sir, make abundance of converts.

Fer. Yes, yes, *I* make too many. You may often see *my* converts, who were very zealous for a time, reeling drunk thro' the streets, or hear them roaring in the taverns. O grace grace! Nothing else will do: to be plain with you, friend *Sincere*, the longer I preach, the less I find *I* can *do:* and yet, I thank our *King*, that I am more and more willing to spend and be spent for my master. I have again been about the towns and fields of *Stupidity*, *Resistance*, &c. and the *Lord* has given me these hedge birds, which you see in this vessel. They, indeed, are not decked in gay plumage, but they sing well: you

shall

shall hear them. Come, let us have a song, to welcome our friends on board.

"Blessed are the sons of *God*,
"They are bought with *Christ's* own blood,
"They are ransom'd from the grave,
"Life eternal they shall have.
"They are pilgrims on the earth,
"Strangers quite to this world's mirth;
"Yet they have all inward joy,
"Pleasures that can never cloy.
"They alone are truly blest,
"Heirs of *God*, joint heirs with *Christ*,
"With them number'd may we be,
"Here and in eternity." WHITEFIELD.

Fer. What think you, brethren, of my choristers? They have learned the true *Jerusalem* note. There are none in the *Celestial City* that sing better than such as are carried thither, from the dreary regions whither I have rambled after *these*.

Fervidus then fixed his eyes on *Clericus*, and said.

Fer. What, have I a brother Levite among you?

Cler. Indeed, Sir, I am a clergyman of the *City of Establishment*, but I am ashamed to own it: because I was so long ignorant of my duty, and unprofitable in executing it.

Fer. Why, Brother, it is, indeed, matter of concern, that we do so little for our divine master, even when we are called to work *by him*: but it is not to be wondered at, that we are unprofitable, when we *thrust ourselves* into his service; as too many of our profession do, for secular purposes; and therefore are of no use, but rather a hurt and scandal to the city. our *Lord's* church is his vineyard[1]: and his real ministers have the infinite honor of being called, *workers together with him*[2]. And will not the *Lord* himself choose his own coadjutors? Most certainly he will, nor should any person take this honour upon him, unless he is called of *Him*, as was *Aaron*[3].

Cler. I must confess, with shame, that I thrust myself into this work.

[1] Isaiah v. 7.   [2] 2 Cor. vi. 1.   [3] Heb. v. 4.

Fervid.

Fervid. Therefore, you ought to have been punished for your temerity. But, behold the amazing goodness of our Master! he has not only spared you, but has condescended to employ you. Come then, my brother, take up the cross, and follow *Immanuel,* your master[1].

So saying, he laid his hand on the shoulder of *Clericus,* and pressed it so hard that *Clericus* winced.

Fer. Ah! you are very tender indeed, and not yet broken into the discipline of our master! Feel here, *my* shoulder is callous like a board. The world has so honoured me, as to make me another *Simon* of *Cyrene*[2], for it has compelled me to bear a large cross. However, like the same *Simon,* I hope I am the father of some eminent pilgrims[3]; therefore, am well paid for my work. I also find his yoke easy, and his burden light [4]; therefore, I know that they are my *Lord's* badges of honour, and not my own whims.

Cler. You give me, Sir, but poor encouragement to proceed!

Fer. Poor, do you call it! I tell you it is the way soon to get an estate, and retire from business. Thus was *St Paul,* that great *Master of Arts,* instructed at *his* first setting out. I will shew him, said his master, what great things he shall *suffer* for my names sake[5]. To *suffer,* in that text, is synonimous with, to *obtain*; and so *St. Paul* understood it. For, some years after, when he began to make an estimate of his gains, he found that, tho' he was a man of figures, yet he was unable to call the mighty sum total. He, therefore, was obliged to set it down in a round indefinite way, thus, " Our light afflictions, which are but for a moment, work out for us, *a far more exceeding and eternal weight of glory*[6]. " And is not this good encouragement for preaching ourselves to death! O, I hope, that I shall die in a pulpit.

Cler. I ask pardon, Sir; I am convinced that you are right: and I beg you would pray for me, that, as I have put my hand to the plough, I may not look back again[7].

While the foregoing dialogue happened, *Resolute* was talking

[1] Heb. xiii. 13.   [2] Mat. xxvii. 32.   [3] Mark xv. 21.   [4] Mat. xi. 30.
[5] Acts ix. 16.   [6] 2 Cor. iv 17.   [7] Luke ix. 62.

very

very eagerly to some of the passengers, and *Fervidus* observed him.

Fer. Young man, is not your name *Peter?*

Ref. No, Sir, my name is *William Resolute?*.

Fer. I believe you are a *Peter*. Do not you preach?

Resolute blushed, and said,

Ref. Sir, I am apt to talk too fast, indeed.

Fer. Well, *talk* on, but take care to *walk well*. I see you have one good token with you. *That* rod is both an honour and defence to you. It was not easily obtained. Take good care of it, my son, and boldly serve *him* who so graciously bestowed it upon *you*.

Ref. I thank you, Sir. It is the earnest desire of my soul so to do.

Fervidus turning to *Probus*, said,

Fer. What is *your* name, young man?

Prob. My name is *William Probus*, from the *City of Destruction?*

Fer. Probus, honest! Pray, who gave you that fine name?

Prob. He, who, I trust, has called me from darkness unto light.

Fer. It must be so, indeed; for I know that you are of a bad family, who were all thieves[1], some of whom were hanged as such.—And you brother, (said he to *Friendly*) seem to be as little joyous as any person in the vessel. Pray, what is *your* name?

Frien. My name, Sir, is *Henry Friendly*, from *Flintshire*. I am so unworthy of any mercy, that I can hardly think myself awake, and in such good company: it all appears like a dream to me.

Fer. Mr. Friendly, you seem to be a near relation of *St. Thomas*, who wanted to be *feeling*, when all his brethren were

[1] Mal. iii. 8.

content only with *seeing*, their risen *Lord*[1].—But, look you, friend, if we insist on *worthiness*, we must all go to the bottom. As for *me*, I have a profuse spring, and a plentiful garden of herbs, to my house; of which things, no doubt, ye are well informed, by *Father Meditation*: and, if I knew of any merit-monger, or self-justifier, among us, I would either put him ashore at *Arminian Wood*, which is just by; or quit the vessel myself. But, hear what the passengers will say on this point.

On which, *Fervidus* cried aloud,

Fer. Silence there, my brethren, I have occasion to make the following inquiry, and beg that you would give me an immediate answer; if in the affirmative, hold up your right hands.— Is there any one of you, who thinketh that he does not deserve death and the pit for ever?

To this question, not a hand moved.

Fer. Are you not saved by grace, thro' faith, and *that* not of yourselves, it is the free gift of our *King*[2].

At this question, every hand was held up.

Fer. Where then is boasting of our freewill? Of our fulfilling terms and conditions of salvation?

All. It is all excluded. It is no where to be found in this transport[3].

Fer. Brother *Friendly*, you see and hear that we are all self-condemned, and have nothing to plead but *Immanuel*. Nothing to depend on but his free grace, and finished salvation. Are you of the same mind, and willing to share our fate?

Frien. O Sir! willing, willing, willing with all my soul; I never desire to be separated from your company.

Fer. Bring hither the *Cup of Salvation*.

So they brought him a large silver cup; in which *Fervidus* took up some of the river water, adding thereto a little *Saline*

[1] John xx. 25.   [2] Eph. ii. 8.   [3] Rom. iii. 27.

Water,

Water, and a few *Drops of Demerit*; he tasted it, and, giving it to *Friendly*, said,

Fer. This has the true *Paradise* flavour; beware, *Friendly*, of spoiling your cordials with too many drops. Come, take this; and whosoever will, let him take of the *Water of Life* freely[1].

Friendly took it, and while he drank, they cried out,

All. Drink, yea drink abundantly, O our beloved brother[2].

Frien. My soul already feels the chearing virtue of this living water!

Fer. Aye, aye. If I could but persuade you to drink, I knew your heart would rejoice. Now I like the lines of your face—Well, brother *Lock*, if your organ is in tune, I believe we are all musically inclined; so let *Jeduthun* set the first hymn proper for societies.

> " Who can have greater cause to sing,
> " Who greater cause to bless,
> " Than we the children of a *King*,
> " Than we who *Christ* possess?
>
> " We late were *Satan's* captives led,
> " And *Hell* had been our end,
> " Had'st thou not for our pardon bled,
> " Thou sinners only friend.
>
> " For this we ne'er will hold our tongue,
> " Nor shall our praises cease,
> " But evermore will sing that song,
> " 'The *Lord* our righteousness."
>
> WHITEFIELD.

This was a most enchanting season to our Pilgrims. For the day was fine, the organ with its solemn sound, and the sweet voices of the men and women, who were well skilled in this part of divine worship, made a kind of *celestial harmony*; unto which the water was no small addition. As for *Ferridus*, his face shone, and his heart danced for joy.

[1] Rev. xxi. 6.   [2] Cant. v. 1.

While they were finging, *Clericus* took notice of a perfon who fat near *Fervidus*; and after the hymn was finifhed, thus addreffed him.

Cler. Sir, permit me to afk, Are you not of the *City of Eftablifhment?* and were you not at one of the colleges in that city?

Newman. I am a native of that city, Sir; was at a college, were I well remember to have feen you.

Fer. This, Sir, is *'Squire Newman*, my worthy lieutenant. He is the eldeft fon of *Sir Rowland Allchurch*, of the *City of Eftablifhment*, and was educated in one of the great fchools of that city. He became early acquainted with the excellent laws of the corporation, and foon made a vifit to the crofs; where he imbibed fuch a love to the wonderful fufferer; that when he returned to the city, he fhewed himfelf a hearty friend to the people of *Church-Street*; and a bold and ftrenuous advocate for them againft their enemies.

At this *Mr. Newman* blufhed, and retired into the great cabin.

Fer. I am not forry the lieutenant is gone, as I can now fpeak more freely of his fervices in the caufe of our *King*. Not many years ago, a huge *Gittite*, named *Doctor Goliath*, who had more acquaintance with the rich and great, than with the bible; by undue influence, obtained the high office of ufher of the fchool; and became fo powerful and overbearing in the college, that he would not permit any of the collegians to be religious. Among the ftrange practices of this mighty *Anakim*; he fat in judgment, and found fome of the ftudents, namely, fix, and no more, *guilty of praying and preaching*; for which enormous crimes, thofe fix were expelled from the college.

When this proud *Philiftine* thus defied the armies of our *King*, Mr. *Allchurch*'s fpirit was ftirred up to attack him. Accordingly, he met *Goliath* in the field, and encountered him in a fingular way. Firft, he upbraided him for oppofing the known laws of the city, the college, and the examples of his

predeceffors;

predecessors; and then drew together a vast cloud of ancient writings and parchments, of laws, statutes, constitutions, &c. which *Goliath* had opposed: and heaped them up round his antagonist, in such a perplexing manner, that his strength, bulk, and weapons, were of no use to him.

Goliath stormed, and struggled to extricate himself, but all in vain; for the sacred *Genii*, both of the city and college, appeared against him, and so effectually assisted '*Squire Allchurch*, that they absolutely overwhelmed the *Philistine*; who at last sunk under the pressure. They then heaped on his dead body a monumental pile, as an evidence of his impiety and cruelty, and gave it the name of *Goliath slain*; which said monument remains unto this day.

Soon after this victory, Mr. *Allchurch* was appointed marshal of the *House Beautiful*, by the name of *Newman*; but he abode not long there; for he was directed to hasten to the *Port of Adoption*, and command as lieutenant of this *Transport*; where he has been some time, and done several memorable actions, of which, it is probable, you may hear more hereafter.

After *Fervidus* had done speaking, a person in the company thus addressed *Probus*.

Search. I think, Sir, that I have some remembrance of you, and those who came into this vessel with you. Pray, were you not at the cross together? And did you not see several persons there, while you sat near it?

Prob. Yes, Sir; and now you mention the circumstance, I recollect, that *you* was the person who opposed the hereticks, at that place.

Search. I am the same, Indeed. But I then fought in the dark, and saw not into the propriety and devotion of your behaviour. However, I found afterwards that your conduct had made an impression on me. I rode in the path you saw me take, until I came to the *City of Sensibility*, which is not far from the *Country of Regeneration*[1]. There I abode until *Mr.*

[1] Mark xii. 34.

Fervidus:

Fervidus came and preached in the city. Under him I was fully convinced, not only of the truth, but also of the inward power of the pilgrim religion. *Fervidus* advised me to hasten thro' the *Country of Regeneration*, unto the *Port of Adoption*, and embark for the hills. I took his advice, and now am swallowed up in wonder, love and praise of *that* Being, who is wonderful in counsel, and mighty in work[1]!

Fer. Your declaration, my lord, rejoices my heart. Go on Sir. Religion will still more ennoble your blood. This, my friends, is a *Real Phœnix* among our nobility. The romantic flights of the heathen poets appear even *short* of the truth, when compared with the wonders of our religion. Think, my lord, on that text, "*not many Noble are called*[2];" and it will make your bosom burn with affection to *Jehovah*, for his distinguishing grace towards you. O how will my good *Lady Liberal* rejoice to see you.

CHAP. XXXIII.

An account of the construction, crew, and service of the Covenant Transport. *Fervidus's description of* Free-will-Forest, *and the* City of Self. *John Duplex and his Pilgrims on* Goodwin's Sand. *A dialogue between them and those in the* Transport, *concerning the Covenant of Grace.*

WHILE the *Covenant Transport* was gliding gently down the river, *Clericus* thus addressed *Fervidus*.

Cler. Captain, I should be glad to know, from whence this vessel came?

[1] Isaiah xxviii. 29.   [2] 1 Cor. i. 26.

Fer.

Fer. She came, Sir, from the *Port of Adoption*, in the *Country of Regeneration*. She is called the *Covenant Transport*, and constantly plies on this river, between the above-named *Port of Adoption*, and the *Port of Assurance*, in the *City of God*, on the *Delectable Mountains*. Those who are desirous of making this passage, come to the *Port of Adoption*; and, after proper trial made of them, they embark, under the direction of some skilful pilot from the *Trinity-House*. There is no other vessel to be seen on the river, but this only.

Cler. Did she never meet with any accident? Do you think the vessel safe, and in good repair?

Fer. Repair! Oh, Sir, this is an extraordinary vessel! But, that you may not depend on *my* judgment herein, I will call such as have served an apprenticeship in his majesty's dock, to give their evidence—Tell *James Eager*, the carpenter of this *Transport*, and *Richard Ardent*, the caulker, to come hither to me.

They being come, *Fervidus* thus addressed them.

Fer. Brother *James* and *Richard*, this gentleman inquires of me, what state of repair our vessel is in? I have called you to answer him.

Eager. This, Sir, is the most singular piece of marine architecture in the universe. It has been constructed from of old, even from everlasting[1]; it has been in use almost six thousand years, and never had any repairs; yet you see how well she looks. What timber she is built of, our *Lord* only knows. I have surveyed her very attentively, and declare, that I never saw any like it, nor such excellent workmanship in any other vessel: therefore, I look on her to be of a *divine* original; and this is also confirmed by her books[2].

Ardent. Respecting my branch, Sir; I declare that she is intirely tight. I examined her well when we were at the *Port of Assurance*, and, altho' I was apprized of the excellent qualities of this vessel; yet I could but admire the beauty of her bottom, and the excellent composition with which it is

[1] Jer. xxviii. 40.   [2] Heb. viii. 8, 9, 10.

covered,

covered, which shone, and was as clean and bright as glass: nor did I ever find that it admitted any water.

Fer. Why, my friends, you seem to have a fine idle employ, for, according to your own accounts, you have nothing to do.

Ardent. I will venture to answer you, Sir, both for myself and brother. Altho' the vessel stands in need of no repairs, yet *that* is not the case with those who sail in her; many of whom are troubled with strange whims[1]; and imagine that she leaks, and is sinking; that the pumps are spoiled, the rudder lost, the masts sprung, &c. and it is our work to convince them of these errors. We being naval architects, they will listen somewhat to us; but I declare, that we have enough to do with some of them; yet, the pleasure which we have with others, and the opportunities we enjoy of drinking from this river, in seeing and hearing the wonders of *Immanuel's* grace and love; amply repays us for our trouble; and we desire nothing more than to die in this service.

While *Richard Ardent,* was thus speaking, the captain's eyes sparkled, and his heart burnt with pleasure. He replied,

Fer. Richard and James, I am satisfied; you have well answered. It is not the vessel indeed, but our poor, weak and crazy souls, which want repairing. Go, on, my friends, in your labours of love. The *Lord* bless you both therein, and grant that you may be succeeded, while this *Transport* is employed, by persons as skilful and diligent in your business, as you are— And now, *Clericus,* as to the *safety* of this passage, *I* will reply to you. Some persons say, that this vessel is likely to overset and sink, but I firmly believe, from what I have heard and seen of her, that it is impossible. Sometimes storms arise, and many of the passengers are sick and afraid; but these proceed only from want of faith in our *King,* who has told us. " That every part of this *Transport* is so well ordered and secured[2], that no weather can injure it." And as to rocks and sands, there are none in this river. For the shores are so bold and steep, that we can sail close unto either side of them, with-

[1] Psalm lxxvii. 7. 8, 9.   [2] 2 Sam. xxiii. 5.

out

out any fear of running aground. Let us praise *Jehovah* for our security.

"The oath and promise of the *Lord*,
"Join to confirm his wond'rous grace,
"Eternal power performs the word,
"And fills all *Heaven* with endless praise.

"Amidst temptations sharp and long,
"Our souls to this dear refuge flies;
"Hope is our anchor firm and strong,
"While tempests blow, and billows rise.

"The gospel bears our spirits up,
"A faithful and unchanging *God*,
"Lays the foundation for our hope,
"In oaths, and promises, and blood." WATTS.

Fer. Well, my newly arrived friends, I hope you are pleased with your quarters. I must further add, concerning this *Transport*, that she has for her crew, certain persons who are venerable for their age, and the great services they have done, by their master's commission, among mankind. Their names are[l], *Repentance*, *Faith*, *Love*, *Peace*, *Joy*, *Gentleness*, and *Goodness*. These work the vessel, under *Immanuel*; and occasionally make use of the cannon which you see on the deck, either to annoy, or defend her from our enemies.

Clkr. What, do any persons ever attack you on your passage?

Fer. Yes, Sir, but it is very seldom the case. You see that extensive *Forest* on the north-side of the river; *that* is the forest of *Free-Will*. The part of it which is nearest to the river, and is distinguished from the rest, by an appearance of order and cultivation, is *Arminian Wood*; so named, from one *Arminius*, who came thus far on pilgrimage, and was so delighted with the forest, that he settled on that spot; and cultivated those trees, and the soil, as much as their nature would permit. Many joined *Arminius*, and dwelt with him in the wood. At length, Dr. *Laud*, Patriarch of the *City of Establishment*, prevailed upon many of that corporation to resort hither, and build a city to

[l] Gal. v. 22, 23.

dwell

dwell in. This city is in *Arminian Wood*, and you may see the houses and turrets among the trees. The city is named *Self*[1], and is very populous; but, it is far from being a healthy place; for its inhabitants are very much subject to tympanies, and tumours, which often prove mortal[2]. *Doubting-Castle* stood in this forest. The ruins still remain, and are inhabited by three notable robbers, who, among others, are very troublesome to the people of the *City of Self*, and too often they make excursions quite down to the river side. Their names are *Unbelief, Fearful*, and *Suspicion*. From this vessel, we frequently see persons in their power, but, on firing our guns they quit their prey, and escape; for they cannot endure the noise of our cannon.

Cler. I think I can see the end of this wood, and a barren track of sand at its eastern extremity. I suppose *that* to be the spot which Mr. *Meditation* called *Goodwin's Sand:* and, if I am not mistaken, I see many persons travelling thereon.

Fer. You are not deceived, I can see them; and take them to be a number of pilgrims, under the conduct of my brother *John Duplex*; who chuses to travel by land, tho' his journeys are long and fatiguing. As the vessel approaches them, I see it is he. In our juvenile days, we had many disputes about our different ways of travelling, and I still believe him to be in the wrong; but I perceive that he makes use of this river, and am sure that he is made useful to souls; therefore I honour him as a laborious servant of our *Immanuel*.

Newman. I see that Mr. *Duplex* draws down towards the river, as if he would speak with us. The person who walks on *Duplex's* right hand, is named *Severe*; he is a *Levite* of the *City of Establishment*, a shrewd, sensible man, and will not let us pass by without casting some invidious reflections on us. I know him well.

Fervidus steered the *Transport* close to the shore, and when they were abreast of those on the sand; Mr. *Severe* said,

[1] Luke xviii. 9. 11.   [2] 1 Cor. iv. 18, 19, 20.

Severe.

Severe. So, captain, I see you have ventured once more with another cargo, in that antiquated veffel; which was made by no body knows who?

Fer. Yes, and I perceive that you will labour on over the fand, in your old way, notwithftanding you have had fuch abundant evidence of the fecurity of this *Tranfport.* Are not you afraid that the fand will fhift, and bury you all?

Severe. It will not, if we go on to believe in the protection of our *King.*

Fer. You deal much in *Ifs* and *Conditions*; but I have no opinion of fuch wares. I have put myfelf, and all who have been advifed by me, abfolutely into the hands of our faithful *Jehovah,* who provided this veffel for us; and I believe, that fhe will wear us out, and the world too, before fhe fails.

Duplex. You call her the *Covenant Tranfport*; but I can find no mention made of fuch a convenience, in the charter of bleffings which is given to us by our *King*; no, not any that fhould be depended on, in the manner that veffel is by you. We call this footway *Covenant Road,* and muft ufe it, and keep on in it, or we fhall never arrive at the end. I fincerely wifh you all well, but I fear that you are too merry and carelefs, and will be in great peril from the fhallows of *Licentioufnefs*, which are on each fide of the river.

Fer. Brother *John,* you are an acute reafoner; but I find that you are no geographer or pilot; for I have coafted this river many years, and never difcovered any fuch fhallows, nor any danger from that quarter. Merry we are, and have both a command and reafon fo to be[1]: and I would advife you to be as eafy and happy as we are. Come, brethren, here is room, come on board, eafe your legs, chear your fpirits, and join us in a fong of praife to our *Immanuel.*

Dup. No. This is the veffel that was made for *David,* and his family only; but you and others will infift on it, that fhe was made for you.

[1] Phil. iv. 4.

Fer.

Fer. I believe, indeed, that *David* ufed the veffel, and much approved of its conveniency and fecurity; of this he himfelf informs us. It was in this veffel, and on this river, that he failed to the *City of God*, when he defcribed both the river and city, as we find in the 46. and 48 *Pfalms*. The veffel you mention, was another of the fame name, which was made for the ufe of *David's* family [1]: but that veffel was built of materials which were perifhable; it was therefore to be kept in repair by the family. That veffel never failed on this river, but on the dangerous *River merit*, the courfe of which is different from this. Moreover, *that* bark is now decayed, and broken up[2], and the family ruined. Pray, Brother, make proper diftinctions in thefe cafes.

Dup. I know nothing of your diftinctions, nor can fee any reafon for them.

Fer. I am forry for it. However, I would remark to you, on your own principles; that, if *Jehovah* provided fuch a veffel for the family of *David*, and fo frequently pardoned their neglect, in fuffering it to run to decay; furely, he will not leave his beloved fon, and *his* family, without a fufficient provifion, to convey them fafely home. And if the *Lord* did fo patiently bear with, and fo often forgive, the provoking fins of the family of *David*, when failing on the *River Merit*, and depending entirely on their own fkill and attention; how much more of pity, grace and love, may his own family expect, from his counfels and care towards them, in our *Immanuel*; who are embarked on his own *River of Life*, and entirely depending on *Prince Paraclete* and his power, to direct and preferve them!

Dup. Your logic, Captain, may be found and lawful; but it appears to me dangerous and inexpedient. I fear, at leaft, that the veffel you are in was conftructed at *Geneva*; therefore I choofe to purfue my courfe on foot. I may be *flow*, but I believe we are all in the *fure* path.

A fine wefterly breeze fpringing up, the captain fpread his fails; and, as the veffel out-run *John* and his company, *Fervidus* faid.

[1] 1 Kings vi. 12. [2] 1 Kings xi. 33, &c. & Jer. xxxi. 32.

Fer.

Fer. Farewell, brother *John,* I muſt not loiter.

Dup. I hope you will carry no *Antinomians* to the hills: they may eaſily mingle with your high and indolent ſpirits; but *we* labour a great deal too much for *them.*

Fer. The *Lord* preſerve you all from labouring in vain.

All. Amen.

C H A P. XXXIV.

A ſtorm. It's conſequences to the Pilgrims. The Tranſport *a-breaſt of* Baxter's-Heath. *Another dialogue with* John Duplex *and* Mr. Severe, *on final perſeverance. An affecting ſtory of* King David.

IN a little time the weſterly wind increaſed to a great degree, which wafted the *Tranſport* on very faſt: but it ſo affected the ſand, that it aroſe like a cloud, and covered, for a while, *Duplex* and his company. Preſently it fell almoſt calm; when they in their *Tranſport* perceived by their glaſſes, that *John* and his people were in great perplexity, by the ſhifting of *Goodwin*'s *Sand.*

Fer. See my brethren, how dangerous it is to uſe carnal reaſon in oppoſition to *Jehovah*'s truth. The way of travelling to the hills over that *Sand* was uſed, and ſtrongly recommended, in the laſt century, by two pilgrims, named *John Goodwin,* and *Richard Baxter,* from the former, the *Sand* we have paſſed by is called *Goodwin*'s *Sand,* becauſe he loſt himſelf thereon. And the wild barren region abreaſt of us, on which you ſee not a ſingle tree for many miles; is called *Baxter*'s *Heath:* becauſe the before mentioned perſon was thereon decoyed from the right way, and brought in great danger of his life.—I think that my brother *John*'s number is diminiſhed, the *Sand* I fear has overwhelmed ſome of them.

Soon

Soon after this, a small cloud was observed to arise in the east; on which the captain exclaimed,

Fer. Now, look to yourselves, my friends. I have heard many of you talk largely of your love to our master, and the security of all those who sail in this *Transport*. But our *King* is about to try us. There is a storm at hand, therefore let us go to prayer.

They then all kneeled down; and the captain poured forth a most fervent prayer to *Jehovah*, which was confirmed with many solemn amens from the company. When he arose from his knees, his face shone like that of *Moses*, when he had been honoured with immediate access to the Divine Majesty[1]. With a voice of confidence, he said,

Fer. Let no man's heart fail him to day. My *Master* has given me every one on board this vessel[2]. I find that I have nothing here but lawful goods, nor fear I any trial. Let our friends *Eager* and *Ardent* look well to their stations, and every person trust in the *Lord*, and all will be well.

In the mean while the wind changed against them, and increased to a storm. The heavens were covered with thick dark clouds, the sea rose and broke in among them, and the *Transport* was driven backwards, at the mercy of the wind and waves. *Fervidus* kept his place at the helm, unmoved as a rock[3]. Some of the passengers, however, were in great terror; especially the women: and many were sick. *Clericus* was among the latter.—The captain and lieutenant gave them all the assistance in their power: and the carpenter, caulker, crew, and every one that was not frightned or sick, was very assiduous in assisting their friends. At length said the captain.

Fer. I find that I must have recourse to my medicine-chest. While you were at the *Port of Adoption*, and the weather was fair, ye were all good sailors, and thought not of providing any thing for this passage: but my master directed me, to take care

[1] Exod. xxxiv. 29. [2] Acts xxvii. 24. [3] Psalm cxxv. 1.

for

for the worst[1]: for he is more careful of us, than we are of ourselves. *Doctor Luke*[2], give me up the *Storm-bottle*.

The bottle being handed up, the captain added.

Fer. Here, my brethren, is the grand catholicon in such trials as now lie upon us. This is a bottle of *Immanuel*'s drops: they are of his own distilling, from herbs which grew in his father's *Paradise*. Every drop of it, is more precious than the gold of *Ophir*, I would not part with this bottle for a diamond as large as this vessel. Our *Lord* gave the disciples some of these drops, when they crossed the *Sea of Galilee*[3], and foolishly imagined that *Immanuel*, who was born to be crucified, was in danger of being drowned. *Clericus*, I am ashamed of your pitiful look. Here, Sir, smell to this[4].

He gave *Clericus* the bottle; on smelling to which, he was so revived, that he became like another man.

Fer. Hand it round among you, for most of you stand in need of it.

While it was going about among the Pilgrims, the storm abated, the clouds dispersed, and fine weather succeeded. When they were recovered from their disorder occasioned by the storm, the Captain ordered a hymn to be sung.

> " Thro' seas and storms, of deep distress,
> " We sail by faith and not by sight.
> " Faith guides us in the wilderness,
> " Thro' all the dangers of the night.
>
> " Now thou array'st thine awful face,
> " In angry frowns without a smile;
> " We thro' the cloud believe thy grace,
> " Secure of thy compassion still."   WATTS.

Fervidus and his people kneeled down, and returned the *Lord* thanks for his goodness shewn in delivering them from storm. After which, the captain desired them to seat themselves, and attend to what he had to say, on the present occasion.

[1] Mat. xxiv. 44.   [2] Col. iv. 14.   [3] Mat. viii. 25, 26.   [4] Cant. i. .

Fer.

Fer. Stormy seasons are the times to try pilgrims. I expected that we should have such a visitation, when I heard your warm professions of love and attachment to our dear *Lord*[1]. He does, indeed, much desire us to love and cleave to him; but he will not be contented with our *bare* professions; for he will try whether they are sincere or feigned: and it is best for us that we should be thus proved: because these trials are more to make us acquainted with our own hearts, than to afford any information to our *King*[2]. I suspected that you had some *Arminian crudities* in your stomachs, which spoil digestion; therefore your great and good Physician has given you a gentle puke; and I was much pleased to see the pernicious bile cast up; for now you will be the better able to receive and digest the strong meat, which your *Lord* has to give you[3]. O what pains our *Celestial Physician* is at with us! Think you, that he treats you thus for his pleasure? If you do, you are greatly mistaken. He loves to see his children fat and well to look at[4]; but they are apt to kick when they grow fat[5]: wherefore, to save them, he sends leanness into their souls[6]. He also delights to see us walk or sail in the sunshine, and in fair weather; but we are foolishly puffed up with such indulgencies[7]; wherefore he is obliged to send storms and darkness on us, to make us sensible that all we enjoy is of mere grace and free bounty. It grieveth him to treat us so; but he had rather *chasten* than loose us[8]. It is no pleasure to our father to see us miserable, but it is profitable for us to be scourged for our faults[9]. I have got more by the cross, than I have by all my preaching.

Why were ye fearful, O ye of little faith! Did you ever hear of this vessel being cast away[10]? You may as well suppose the everlasting hills to move. The shoes and garments of the *Israelites* in the wilderness[11], which never wore out, were only types and shadows of the permanent materials with which this *Transport* is built. I suppose you feared every minute that you should go to the bottom: but I have been in far worse

---

[1] Mark xiv. 29, 31.   [2] Deut. viii. 2.   [3] Heb. v. 12, 13, 14.
[4] Psalm xcii. 14.   [5] Deut. xxxii. 15.   [6] Psalm cvi. 15.   [7] 2 Cor. xii. 7.
[8] Psalm lxxxix. 32, 33.   [9] Heb. xii. 10.   [10] Isaiah xlv. 17.
[11] Deut. xxix. 5.

storms than that which has just passed over us. Yet I never thought that *Noah* was more secure in his ark, altho' *Jehovah* himself shut him in[1]; than I am in this excellent vessel. At the worst, I have recourse to the anchor which we have, both sure and stedfast; so that a storm may as easily drag *Immanuel* from his throne, as this anchor from its hold. In short, I have experienced such deliverances in this transport, that I am persuaded of the truth of what her books declare, " That she will ride out the last general storm which shall destroy all things[3]." And I firmly believe, " that neither death, nor life, nor angels, nor principalities, nor powers, nor things present, nor things to come, nor heights, nor depths, nor any other creature, shall be able to shipwreck those who are embarked in this vessel[4]." Let us sing.

" Firm as the earth thy *Cov'nant* stands,
" My *God*, my hope, my trust;
" If I am found in *Jesu*'s hands,
" My soul can ne'er be lost.

" His honour is engag'd to save
" The meanest of his sheep;
" All that his heav'nly father gave,
" His hands securely keep.

" Nor death, nor hell shall e'er remove
" His fav'rites from his breast;
" In the dear bosom of his love,
" They, shall for ever rest." WATTS.

The wind was now favourable, and the weather pleasant; when they perceived *John* and his company at a small distance before them. They had laboured over *Goodwin*'s *Sand*, and were just entered upon *Baxter*'s *Heath*; the captain, therefore, steered the vessel close to the shore, and desired *Lieutenant Newman* to ask *Mr. Severe*, how they were, after the storm; which he did.

Severe. Thank our *King*, we are well: for we had just got over the *Sand* as the storm came on; and the wind being in our

[1] Gen. vii. 16. [2] Heb. vi. 19. [3] 2 Pet. iii. 11, 12, 13.
[4] Rom. viii. 38, 39.

faces,

faces, the *Sand* was of no prejudice to us; but I thought that you were all gone to the bottom.

Newm. You never heard of this veffel foundering, nor ever will.

Severe. Whether or not *she* was ever loft, I cannot fay; but *perfons* who were in her, have, by fome means or other, been loft; by falling, or being thrown, overboard.

Newm. Brother *Severe*, it is all calumny, and the effect of your prejudice; for no fuch thing has ever happened.

Severe. Why, if there is a *Covenant Tranfport*, it was provided for *all* men; and, I believe, that *Cain* and *Judas* were as much in it, as you now are.

Newm. O fye, fye, Sir, how wildly you talk! Here are records belonging to this veffel, in which is faithfully regiftered the name of every perfon who embarks in her[1], and the time when. I have carefully examined thefe archives; and do not find that *their* names were ever inferted therein.

Severe. You take drunkards, fwearers, murderers, and adulterers, into your *Tranfport*.

Newm. I acknowledge that thofe who were once fuch finners, and, if poffible, much worfe[2]; have been wafhed, and made the voyage in this veffel.

Severe. I mean, that perfons while on board have been detected in the above crimes, and yet were fuffered to remain in her. O *Newman*, I wonder you will fail in her, fhe is defiled with the vileft pollutions; and I am inclined to think, that even *now*, there is fome rebellious *Jonah* among you[3], who was the caufe of your late diftrefs.

Newm. I proteft, that in the feveral voyages which I have made in this veffel, I never knew an inftance of fuch abominations as you flander us with. Some perfons, indeed, who had failed in her to the *City of God*, afterwards in their pilgrimage over the *Enchanted Ground*, were guilty of great turpitude; for

[1] Rev. xxi. 27.   [2] 1 Cor. vi. 11.   [3] Jonah i. 12.

which

which they deferved to die, altho' our *King* pardoned them: but you may as well fuppofe, that *Peter*, and *James*, and *John* played at cards on the *Mount of Transfiguration*; as to fuppofe, that the above enormities were committed in this veffel. O *Mr. Severe*, your fentiments on this fubject are fo contrary to *my* feelings, as a pilgrim; that they tempt me to fufpect, that altho' you have fo long travelled on the banks of this river, yet you have not hitherto tafted of the *Water of Life*.

Severe. Why are you fo uncharitable? Pray, where was *David* when he tranfgreffed fo grofsly with *Bathfheba* [1]?

Newm. David had truly made this paffage; and his name ftands with great honour in the records of this *Tranfport*; but when he committed the above crime, he was going over the *Enchanted Ground*, and was decoyed into *Mrs. Wanton*'s, who then kept a houfe of ill-fame there.

Severe. Whatever falvos you and others may provide, to excufe *David*, I believe that he was then a child of the *Black Tyrant*, and out of covenant with our *King*; and if *Repentance* had not faved him, he would have gone to *Tophet*, tho' he had, as you fuppofe, been in that *Tranfport*.

When *Repentance*, who (as has been obferved) was one of the *Tranfport*'s crew, heard *Severe* mention his name, and in fuch a manner, he replied,

Repentance. Mr. Severe, you bear falfe witnefs againft me: for I am *Repentance*, and do declare, that I never faved any finner: never made any child of the *Tyrant* a child of *Jehovah*: never put any one into the covenant of grace: but being a fervant of *Immanuel*, the furety of the covenant, am fent forth[2] according to covenant love and promife, to prepare and attend upon the heirs of glory: but I no more fave them, than you or *Newman* may be faid to fave them. I well remember the cafe of *David*, mentioned by you. I was in this *Tranfport* when he made his voyage to the *City of God*; and a fweet feafon we enjoyed, while he was with us. What with his harp and voice, and the extacy of divine praife into which he threw the whole

[1] 2 Sam. xi. 27.   [2] Acts v. 31.

company, we made the banks of this river echo, as much as they ever did before or fince. He was indeed the *fweet Singer of Ifrael*, and a man after our *King*'s own heart.—Many years afterwards, when I heard of his fall, I was exceedingly grieved; and when our *Lord* directed me to feek him, recover him again to his duty, and reſtore to him the fenfe of our *Lord*'s love; I flew after the fallen *Seraph*, and found him at the *Globe Inn*, on the *Enchanted Ground*, kept by Mrs. *Wanton*. When I touched the royal criminal's heart, he came to himfelf, and I never faw a greater penitent before. Rivers of tears ran from his eyes, the deepeſt fighs heaved his labouring breaſt, while his lips uttered fuch a fenfe of remorfe, and fuch bitter reproaches againſt himfelf; that he diſturbed all that houfe of mirth; and made even *Mrs. Wanton* fay, with tears in her eyes, " She wifhed they had not decoyed him, for fhe feared that his repentance would do more hurt to her houfe, than his fall had done good."

I got him from thence as faſt as poſſible; but, as I and *Mr. Godly Sorrow*, were carrying him along, he cried out, " Againſt thee, O my injured *Lord*, againſt thee only have I finned, and done this evil in thy fight[1]." Then he fainted, and we thought he was dead: but he opened his flowing eyes, and again exclaimed, " O *Lord*, reſtore unto me, (thy ungrateful fon) the joys of thy falvation, and eſtabliſh me with the dear *Prince Paraclete*[2]:" and then fwooned again. So that we were obliged to fupport this penitent quite over the *Enchanted Ground*, until we had brought him to *Hephzibah*, a city in the *Land of Beulah*. There we procured fome cordials, and he in fome meafure revived: but the remembrance of his folly troubled him ever afterward. And, if he knows what a vile ufe, *you*, Sir, make of his fin; it will caufe him to bluſh even in the *Celeſtial City*. His *King* forgave him his fin[3]: it does not, therefore, become *you* to rake into the filth, and expofe to contempt that eminent faint.

This relation of *David*'s recovery drew tears from all, both thofe on fhore and thofe in the *Tranſport*; and even *Duplex* and

---

[1] Pfalm li. 4.   [2] Pfalm li. 12.   [3] 2 Sam. xii. 13.

Mr.

Mr. Severe were observed to wipe their eyes. However, *Mr. Severe* replied,

Severe. So, I perceive, that you are sometimes *in* the *Covenant*, and sometimes out: in this we agree with you.

Newm. This *Transport*, Sir, is only as a tender unto *Immanuel*, who is himself, "the covenant of the people [1]:" and we know we are in him who is true[2]. Ever IN HIM. Beloved IN HIM, chosen IN HIM[3], justified IN HIM, sanctified IN HIM; we are blessed with all spiritual blessings IN HIM[4], and, therefore, shall be glorified together with him. So that we are not one day in the covenant of grace, and another out of it: one day accepted in *Immanuel*, another for what we are in ourselves; but we are ever accepted by our *King* in his beloved son. For all this *Jehovah* himself assigns a cogent reason; "even that it may be to the praise of the glory of his grace, or free favour[5]." Now, *Mr. Severe*, this being the case, we are ever in, never out of covenant grace, and everlasting love, tho' at all times we may not enjoy the comforts of this. Hence, this *Transport*, is employed, by the head of the covenant, as a blessing to all the covenanted ones; to convey them, as pilgrims, some short part of their progress to the *Celestial City:* by which they are confirmed in their privilege of, right in, and have a divine foretaste of, *Celestial* joy and glory. But in the future part of their journey, these same pilgrims may greatly suffer by the power of temptations, and their raging corruptions within them: yet, we believe, that our *King* will never blot their names from the book of life[6]. But, as in the fore-mentioned case of *David*, will send *Repentance* to humble and reclaim them.

Dup. So, Captain, your Pilgrims may fall foully, but not finally. This is a sweet syren song, indeed!

Fer. You speak very lightly about awful things. Syren song, brother, to whom? Not to a real pilgrim, I am sure. Let us try how it will operate on the company in this vessel.

[1] Isaiah xlix. 8.   [2] 1 John v. 20.   [3] Eph. i. 4.   [4] Eph. i. 3.
[5] Eph. i. 6.   [6] Rev. iii. 5.

Then

Then addressing himself to the Pilgrims in the *Transport*, he said,

Fer. My dear brethren, partakers of the heavenly calling[1], what say you to the following intelligence? Your blessed Lord and master having considered that you are formed of flesh and blood, which have a strong propensity to sensual pleasures; and perceiving that you take much pains to mortify and subdue them; is now pleased to inform you: " That he does not in future desire or expect, that you will torment yourselves in that conflict as you have done; for he gives you liberty to gratify those carnal inclinations as much as you please; and he assures you, that you can never forfeit his love, by indulging your lusts; for, notwithstanding such gratifications, he will most certainly receive you into the *Celestial City!* What say you now, will you sin foully, because grace abounds freely?

While *Fervidus* uttered the above speech, no words can describe the emotions of grief and indignation against sin, which were felt and expressed by the passengers: for, when he had concluded, they all exclaimed, as with one voice.

All. God forbid[2]! How shall we, who are dead unto sin, live any longer therein? It is not sufficient, for our dear *Lord barely* to make such a declaration of his will: for, if he means to give us up to our own hearts lusts, He must take away that incorruptible seed of His[3], which remaineth in us; for we cannot sin, in the manner you propose, because we are born of *Jehovah*[4].

Fer. Brother *John*, take the declaration of these passengers, as a full answer to all your strange sentiments. A permission to indulge our lusts is not a syren song to a gracious heart; but, even the very thought is a thousand times more ungrateful to his renewed soul, than the *American Indian's* war-whoop to a British ear. A carnal heart may be pleased with such a dispensation, but that can be no reason for us to reject the truth.

Dup. I have seen many instances of the great abuse of your doctrine.

[1] Heb. iii. 1.   [2] Rom. vi. 2.   [3] 1 Pet. i. 23.   [4] 1 John iii. 9.

Fer. But such instances do not prove, that the doctrine of the final perseverance of *true* pilgrims is false. I believe you are often misled by what happens among yourselves. Your companies are generally like *Noah*'s *Ark*, both the clean and the unclean are with you: or, like the mixed multitude[1], who followed the children of *Israel* from *Egypt*. You are not sufficiently careful in receiving persons among you. If one has a sudden qualm of conscience, he is instantly received as a pilgrim; and thus you swell your number. But such neither knowing their own hearts, nor the evil of sin; having never felt the terrors of the law, nor tasted the grace of *Jehovah*; fall into various snares and pits by the way; and then you erroneously imagine, that they are fallen from true grace, which is a blessing they never had. I perceive this day, that the *Sand* has reduced your number.

Dup. It has, and so it always did, since I have travelled this road.

Fer. You are now on *Baxter*'s *Heath*, a place notorious for robbery and murders; where, probably, you will lose many more, and yet you will persist to go on, and refuse to sail with us.

Dup. Why, brother *George*, do not *you* suffer losses of this kind?

Fer. Not in *this* part of the road. Our *King* has marvellously favoured me in this respect. I never lost one person, in all the voyages which I have made, from *Port Adoption* to the *City of God*. And, if any pilgrim hath died on his passage; then, what with the presence of *Shining Ones*, and the triumph of the departing saint; our vessel seemed to be in the suburbs of the Celestial City. In short, I have a thousand evidences which induce me to believe, that this *Transport* is of *Jehovah*'s building, and that all who sail in her, are the people of our *King*, who shall never perish, but have everlasting life.

[1] Exod. xii. 38.

Newm. And as to our harbouring of adulterers, &c. among us; it is falfe, as I hope hath fully appeared. There is, if poffible, a worfe evil among you, which has entered your camp, in the difguife of an ally. I mean that bitter *Spirit of Slander*, which *Mr. Severe* is fo familiar with, and which has prevailed on him, to calumniate us in a moft abominable manner; by putting fuch fentiments into our mouths as our fouls abhor. This he muft needs be fenfible of.

Severe. I know that many of you hate fin, and love *Jehovah* with all your hearts; but, in my late publications, I expreffed myfelf in *fuch* a manner, on purpofe to fet before your party, the horrid confequences which follow from your principles.

Newm. Will you talk deceitfully for our *King ?* We are fully convinced that our principles are agreeable to his word, therefore we are determined faithfully to preach them; and leave it to our *Lord,* either to guard them from proflitution, or to punifh the abufers of them.

Dup. There may be faults on both fides, let us therefore think and let think, as we have hitherto done. This I can fay, from my heart, I wifh you all well.

Fer. Brethren, the *Lord* blefs you. Pray for us.

So they parted in good humour. The wind now fwelled the fails, and *Fervidus* rejoiced the hearts of the paffengers, by faying, " Yonder is our defired haven, and we fhall foon be there."

CHAP. XXXV.

The Pilgrims arrive at the City of God. *They are cordially received by* Mr. Valiant, *of the* Golden-crofs Inn. *Mr. Valiant relates the extraordinary way, by which he obtained preferment in Immanuel's army.*

IN a short time the *Covenant Transport*, with a full sail, and music playing, entered the *Port of Assurance*, belonging to the *City of God*. Abundance of people were on the *Quay*, to welcome them in, and many salutations were mutually exchanged. The Pilgrims were conducted to the *Golden-crofs Inn*, in *Great-Grace-street*, which was kept by *Mr. Valiant*. The captain would not suffer *Clericus* to go to the Inn, but insisted on his attending him to the great temple, on *Mount Zion*, in the upper-part of the city; saying,

Fer. Come with me, Sir. You must not think to be idle here. I have much work for you in speculation—There are no dumb dogs[1], sleeping, nor greedy dogs, in this city.—Nay, do not linger, nor draw back.—If you have any true ambition, I will lead you to a field, where you may exhaust all your ardour. I had rather be a hewer of wood, or a drawer of water, to *these* congregations[2], than be emperor of the world. I am happy in being a servant of the servants of *Jehovah*, and yet am no *Pope*. *He*, *claims* the empty title. *I*, *feel* the sweet employ. Come, therefore, with me. I will introduce you to such singing, praying, and conversation; that you will imagine yourself very near to the *Celestial City*.

Clericus followed him, but with much reluctance; because he was fearful to appear in a public character, before such a man as *Fervidus*.

[1] Isaiah lvi. 10, 11. [2] Joshua ix. 23.

The

The Pilgrims were cordially received by *Mr. Valiant*. This man appeared as if he had been a chopping-block for the enemy, to try his strength upon: for his face, head, hands, and every part of him, were marked with honourable scars. He was blessed with a remarkable flow of spirits, a great share of true pilgrim-courage, and feared nothing. He had been cross or standard-bearer, in *Immanuel's* army, and now, being in years, was preferred to keep the *Golden-cross Inn*, in the *City of God*; a place, of which a *Shining One* might envy him the honour. *Mr. Valiant* was so sensible of the favour which his *Lord* had done him, that he never thought himself diligent enough in his office. *Mr. Fervidus* and *Mr. Valiant* were old comrades, and their souls seemed to be twins in piety and courage. When the Pilgrims came to the door, he said,

Valiant. Ye are welcome to town, my brethren. Come in, we heard you were at hand, and have provided good fare for you.—Oh, what a goodly company! *Jehovah* bless and preserve *Capt. Fervidus*, that laborious servant of our *King*, for bringing you hither.—What a busy city has this been, since *Immanuel* set him and his comrades to work! Where is your carpenter and caulker, and ship's company?—Oh, here they come—What, *Richard*, the *Gebalite*[1]! So, you have brought your old vessel once more into port?

Ardent. Brother *Valiant*, I am glad to see you. We have brought you a company of joyful souls: I have had a precious time this voyage.

Valiant. You shall all eat, drink, and abide with me, while you stay in town. I will keep open house for you. Do not fear any expence. I have been a great traveller, and very curious in my time. I have discovered a treasure of unsearchable riches[2], unto which I have free access. Wherefore, call for the best things, and the more precious the wines and dainties are, which you demand, the better you will please me: because I shall consider you, as having had a pilgrim's genteel education.

[1] Ezek. xxvii. 9. [2] Eph. iii. 8.

Sincere.

Sincere. Thank you, kind Sir: you talk well, and I am glad we have found such good quarters.

Valiant. I always entertain those whom your captain brings hither, if they have no relations or acquaintance in the city. And, I must say, that he transports hither, some of the choicest souls among us.

All this while, *Resolute* was swallowed up in admiration, at the looks, manner, and discourse of Mr. *Valiant*; and so continued, without speaking a word, until they had refreshed themselves with a comfortable supper. After which, being all set for discourse, *Resolute*, who longed to hear some of Mr. *Valiant*'s exploits, thus addressed him.

Res. Sir, you appear to have been in the wars?

Valiant. Wars! Yes, I bless our *King*, I have had some conflicts with his and our enemies. There is no being a pilgrim without fighting[1]. I believe you all know something of *that* truth.

Res. We may have had *some small* experience of it, but I can see no one, who has such a disfigured countenance as yours.

Valiant. Disfigured, do you term it! True, it is not so smooth and fair, in the eyes of men, as it was forty years ago; but, I trust, it is more amiable in the sight of my dear master.— Who, would not part with a fair aspect in the cause of HIM, whose countenance was marred more than any man's, for us[2]? I am only concerned that I have not lost an eye, a leg, or an arm in his service. I should then have had smart-money, and a pension, on which I should live more honourably, for ever. But such preferments are all disposed of at *Immanuel*'s court[3], and I am thankful for being thus far provided for.

Res. I am of your opinion, Sir; for I ever found, that when I was most closely engaged with the enemy, I had the greatest testimonies of my captain's regard.

Valiant. If a pilgrim desires to know his master's estimation of him, let him go into the field, under his colours. There is

[1] 2 Tim. iii. 12.   [2] Isaiah lii. 14.   [3] Phil. i. 29.

no fervice in the world where a foldier is more noticed, or better provided for.—When I firft entered the army, I came young from the *Land of Cowards*; of the inhabitants of which country, *Solomon* fays, "They flee when none purfueth[1]." I lived in the *Town of Trembling*; being of the feed of *Cain*, who thought every one who met him would kill him[2]; and my name was then *Magor-miffabib*[3]. At this period, I was fo fearful, that I could fcarcely look at the enemy; but in a fhort time, being encouraged by the fmiles and prefence of my Captain, and the bold examples of my comrades; I began to diftinguifh myfelf; and foon was as familiar with the whizzing of the bullets, as was *Charles the XIIth. of Sweden*. And my gracious Captain ordered me to be inrolled in our books, by the name of *Refolute*.

At this, *Refolute* blufhed, and exclaimed,

Ref. Oh, how unworthy am I of that name! I fhould be glad to hear on what account you obtained your prefent glorious appellation. You muft have feen many great exploits, and fomething fingularly heroic procured you this honour.

Valiant. I have, indeed, feen many noble feats, the doing of which would reflect glory on a *Shining One*. But our *King*'s thoughts and ways are not as ours[4]. For, I declare to you all, that the action, which, by the favour of my Captain, gave rife to my prefent name, reflects as little credit on me, as any thing I have done, fince my being a foldier. I mentioned to you, how fearful I was when I firft entered into *Immanuel*'s army. But when I beheld the noble feats which were done by many of my fellow foldiers, I became afhamed of myfelf, and prayed daily and heartily that I might be like them. My Captain was pleafed to hear me afk thus importunately, for what was fo honourable to him, and fo ufeful in his fervice; therefore, defired me to come daily unto him[6]. I did fo; and the frequent fight of, and countenance from him, ftrengthened me wonderfully, and filled me with fuch ardour of fpirit, that I thought myfelf capable of encountering with any adverfary.—At length, I began to think, that I did but weary my Captain by fuch

---

[1] Prov. xxviii. 1.   [2] Gen. iv. 14.   [3] Jerem. xx. 3, 4.
[4] Ifaiah lv. 8, 9.   [5] Heb. xii. 1.   [6] Mat. vi. 11.

frequent attendance, and as I had already received so much from him, there was no neceffity to go daily for more ftrength; but that I ought to well improve what I had already in poffeffion. For feveral days, therefore, I neglected to attend the *levee of my captain. About that time I was called upon, to encounter a ftrong party of the enemy, who came from the coafts of the *Dead Sea.* I marched againft them, with great confidence of my fuperiority ¹; but, alas! I found them far more numerous and powerful than I imagined. They furrounded my little corpfe; I laid about me ftoutly, but my arm foon waxed feeble, my fhield fell, I received many deep wounds, was left for dead in the field of battle, and had certainly been carried off by the enemy, had not *Fervidus* came to my affiftance, and drove back the adverfaries.

Frien. This was a narrow efcape, indeed! Sure you was a long time in recovering?

Valiant. Fervidus, my dear and experienced friend, had obferved my late conduct, and judged that I should be routed in the encounter; therefore, by the Captain's order, followed me at fome diftance. After he had driven the enemy from the field, he came to me, and fprinkled my face with a little *Water of Life,* which he had taken from under the throne of *Jehovah* and our *Immanuel.* He then whifpered in my ear, that the *King* had that day very gracioufly inquired after me. This intelligence brought me to my fenfes, and cheared my fpirits. He then applied to my wounds the *Balm of Gilead* ², which is our camp-medicine; and I was prefently, and perfectly recovered. *Fervidus* alfo proceeded to fhew me the error of my conduct. " My dear *Refolute*," faid he, " you cannot do worfe for yourfelf than to neglect our captain's levee. Our *Lord* hath declared, that he will be attended unto for all thofe things, which he is determined to do for his foldiers ³.—Your ftrength and mine are like the manna, which our brethren had in the wildernefs; it will not ferve us two days, without a fpecial order from our captain ⁴. We are only ftrong in the grace that is in our dear

¹ Mat. xxvi. 33, 51. ² Jer. viii. 22. ³ Ezek. xxxvi. 37.
⁴ Exod. xvi. 20, 24.

Lord; which implies, that we muſt daily go to renew our courage in his preſence. This is a great honour done us; ſince our captain has condeſcended to declare, that it is a pleaſure for him to ſee us[1]. Do not, therefore, my brother, count it a wearineſs to him, or a burden to yourſelf; but let the fatal experience of this day convince you of the contrary."

Frien. This, dear Sir, is a leſſon to me. Oh, how fooliſhly and proudly have I behaved towards *my King!* I long to hear how this affair ended.

Valiant. The next day, I waited on our royal Captain: but I cannot deſcribe the confuſion I felt, from a conſciouſneſs of my pride and folly. I entered the levee, covered with crimſon bluſhes, and ſaluted the courtiers with a ſhy air, and a low faultering voice. On the contrary, *they* were free, rejoicing to ſee me, and congratulated me on my happy eſcape. The *King* beheld my embarraſſment, and called me to him. I went, but fell at his feet; kiſſed them, and bathed them with my tears, crying, " Pardon me, *Lord*, pardon, O my *Prince*, thy vile ſervant; and permit me thus to adore thee, for ſaving me from my enemies, and calling me to thy preſence, who deſerved to be baniſhed from thee for ever."—" Thou ſhalt not die, *Reſolute*," ſaid the *King* " It was unkind in thee, to deprive me of the pleaſure which I daily had, in ſeeing and communing with thee. —I have ſhewn thee thy fault in thy puniſhment. Doſt thou not perceive it to be a greater honour and pleaſure, to come daily, and obtain ſtrength from my own hands; than to have a ſtock given thee for a month; or, to have it ſent to thee by a ſervant?" While the *King* ſpake theſe words, I lay on the ground kiſſing his footſtool, diſſolved in love to him: and, when he condeſcended to appeal to me, I eagerly replied. Yes, *Lord*, yes; and I adore and bleſs thee for ſuch a gracious permiſſion to viſit thee. " Ariſe, then," ſaid he, " take a renewal, and enlargement, of thy commiſſion." I aroſe, and ſtood before him. The *King* then wiped the tears from my eyes, kiſſed me[2],

[1] Prov. xv. 8.   [2] Cant. i. 2.

and, with a smile which I shall never forget, commanded an herald to declare his will. The herald obeyed, with a loud voice, as follows, "Be it known unto all, whom it may concern, that our trusty and well-beloved *Jonathan Resolute*, is appointed standard-bearer in our armies; and, in consideration of his faithful services, it is our pleasure, that from henceforth he be enrolled and denominated, among all our faithful subjects, by the name of *Ensign Valiant*; and let him be so respected accordingly.

The *King* then put the commission into my hand, sealed with the royal signet, and again kissed me. This marvellous grace so overwhelmed my soul, that I sunk down at his feet. He raised me, and bid me go in peace. I bowed, and retired thro' the great officers of state, who all saluted me: I silently returned their respect; but I never in my life was so abashed, as, on that memorable day.

Ref. This is not the manner of men, indeed! By what little I have felt of these things, I know that you were greatly embarrassed. Pray, Sir, how did your preferment sit upon you?

Valiant. The *Lord* forbid, that I should boast. I will only lay before you one or two facts, that you may perceive, how this grace of my *Prince* influenced me. I began to consider what service I could do for my Captain[1], in return for the honour he had done me. One fine day, therefore, I took my colours, which you know are the *Golden Cross*, and carried them flying thro' the *City of Contradiction*, where the sight of our Captain's ensign is the greatest abomination. The *Jews* did not fail to come out and lay on me most unmercifully; but I penetrated quite thro' the city, and received no material damage.—At another time, I boldly entered the *Town of Freethinking*; and, tho' they expressed their abhorrence of my colours, with every mark of diabolical malice; yet I supported my cross, and made an honourable retreat. My behaviour in both these places, induced several persons among them, to examine the reasons of my conduct, and the ground of my courage; and they have since told

[1] Psalm cxvi. 12.

me, that thefe exploits were the means of their inlifting in our army. In fhort, if my mafter had commanded me, at that time, I would have fet up my colours even on the gates of *Tophet*. There is no fear of obtaining fuccefs, under our captain. His fervice, indeed, is the moft arduous of any, yet his pay and provifions are the beft; and the affurance of victory and preferment, which he gives unto all his foldiers[1], makes it the beft fervice in the world.

Frien. Oh, that I had but a tenth part of your courage!

Valiant. My courage is nothing, nor are my exploits worthy to be mentioned, with what fome of my Captain's generals have done. I am afhamed of myfelf when I read the chronicles of our army. I have fhewn, that there is very little *natural* courage in me. Our *King* can foon perfect ftrength out of weaknefs[2].

Prob. Sir, we are all much obliged to you, for the inftructing relation of your adventures.

CHAP. XXXVI.

A further account of Mr. Duplex, *and his Pilgrims. Fervidus preaches at the great temple on* Mount-Zion. *An account of* Lady Liberal. *Fervidus fhews the Pilgrims the curiofities of the city. They review the Ramparts and the Arfenal.*

AFTER Mr. *Valiant* had finifhed his own hiftory, Mr. *Sincere* faid,

Sincere. Permit me, Sir, to afk, whether you know any thing of Mr. *John Duplex?*

Valiant. Yes, I know him well. Did you fee any thing of him on the road?

[1] Rom. viii. 37.   [2] Heb. xi. 34.

Sincere.

Sincere. We left him foon after he came on *Baxter's-Heath.*

Valiant. Aye, he had not reached fo far as the *Way of the Aphorifms*; for, at that place, he turns to the left, and does not come to our city. He is a very fingular man. In his early days he travelled to this city, and we hoped he would have been a fteady friend to our intereft. But he was foon feduced by the *Aphorifms* on *Baxter's-Heath*; who prevailed on him to make them a vifit; and, for the future, to bring his pilgrims thro' their village. So that he now leaves the direct road hither, paffes by the *Village of Aphorifms*, and goes to the north fide of this city.— There, on fome wafte ground belonging to us, clofe under our walls, between them and the *Country of Conceit* (an extenfive territory to the north), *Mr. Duplex* has fettled his pilgrims. They are now become numerous; their houfes are built of wood[1], and are very low; but, being well painted, they make a tolerable appearance. This fuburb is called *Neapolis**. *The new city.* Several great men of this city, have gone out and remonftrated againft this ftrange method of going on. They shewed *Mr. Duplex* the illegality and danger of his proceedings; but, hitherto, all their endeavours have been in vain. *Mr. Duplex* has very lately rather widened the breach, between him and the citizens, by inftituting a new order of knights, called the *Knights of the Minutes.* Their bufinefs is to defend, againft all oppofers, certain fubtle propofitions of *Mr. Duplex*, by him called *Minutes*; which favour much of *Pope Peter's* fentiments, and give great offence to true pilgrims. Of this order one *Mr. Severe* is grand mafter. Thefe knights dwell on the road to *Neapolis*, oppofite the *Aphorifms*, and unite with them in their depredations on pilgrims; fome of whom they rob, and wound; others they decoy from the right way[2], and lead into the *Country of Conceit*, from whence they feldom return.

Sincere. This fuburb, or new city, muft be greatly expofed to the enemy.

Valiant. It is moft in danger from the inhabitants of the neighbouring *Country of Conceit*, who are chiefly *Papifts, Pelagians*, &c. But thofe in the new city are fo clofe under our

---

[1] 1 Cor. iii. 12.   [2] Gal. vi. 7.

walls, that the enemy cannot injure them, unless we permit. Some time ago, an army came against us from that quarter, but our cannon played so briskly upon them, that they were obliged to retire. The balls flew over *Neapolis*, and our thundering artillery made its inhabitants tremble. *Mr. Duplex* happened then to be in the suburb, and was so sensible of the power of our batteries, that he imprisoned some of the *Aphorisms* who were with him, seemed disposed to dissolve the order of knights, went into the pulpit in *West-street*, and preached a sermon against the *Aphorisms*. From these good omens, we all hoped he was about to forsake *Neapolis*, and retire into the city. But, in a short time, he released the *Aphorisms*, and forgot all that he had said against them.

Prob. Did you ever travel hither by land? Is it not dangerous so to do?

Valiant. In my younger years, I had occasion to go to the *Port of Adoption* from hence. When we came over against the *City of Self*, in *Arminian Wood*; I desired the pilot to run close to the shore; and I fired several shot at that place, which I afterwards found did some execution. This exploit was judged to be mine, and they handed the report of it from thence to the *Aphorisms*. As I could not wait for the *Transport*, I returned by land; but was way-laid, and attacked on *Baxter's-Heath*, by the *Aphorisms*; who commanded me to stand, and deliver my coat and money. I had with me a rod of the *Tree of Life*, of the same sort as that of our friend here, (pointing to *Resolute*) and I exercised it pretty briskly on them; insomuch that they could not endure the strokes, but fled from me, altho' I was by myself.

Ref. Pray, Sir, what is the sentence wrote on *your* branch?

Valiant. This, " Surely, shall one say, in the *Lord* have I righteousness and strength[1]." This rod is a terror to the *Aphorisms*.

The night being now far advanced, the Pilgrims commended themselves to the protection of Heaven, and retired to rest.

[1] Isaiah xlv. 24.

In the morning, *Mr. Valiant* took our four Pilgrims to the great temple on *Mount Zion*; and found *Fervidus* just about to preach. He was in his proper element; for he had several thousands to hear him. His text was, " But ye are come unto *Mount Zion*, the *City of the living God*, the *Heavenly Jerusalem*[1]." This was a noble sermon. *Fervidus*'s face shone, and the hearts of the Pilgrims glowed, while he displayed the glories of the place; the difficulties which pilgrims encounter in their way to it; the assistance they receive from their *Lord* therein; and the privileges they enjoy on their arrival at the city. He boldly asserted, " That the pleasures which those citizens experience, were the same in kind as the joys of the *Celestial City*, and differed from them only, in degree and permanency."

After sermon, *Clericus* took the Pilgrims to the vestry to *Fervidus*. Here they saw *Lady Liberal*, who dwelt in a grand house near the temple. This lady is an honour to her sex and elevated situation in life. Tho' educated in the *City of Vanity*, she; for many years, has absolutely withdrawn herself from the gay, thoughtless, circles of her peers; and, like the pious daughter of *Phanuel*, departs not from the temple[2]; but incessantly serves *Jehovah*, in a series of good works, both to the bodies and souls of men: and the influence of her benevolence extends itself far and near. She was, at this time, in the decline of life; but still flaming with a most ardent zeal for *Immanuel*'s glory. *Fervidus* was her favourite chaplain, and now presented *Lord Search* to her ladyship, saying,

Fer. My good lady, blessed be *Jehovah*, I am again arrived with a large company of good pilgrims; among whom I present you with one of your own exalted rank. *Lord Search*, madam, is not ashamed to take up the cross of *Immanuel*.

Lady. Fervidus, you are most welcome to the *City of God*. My *Lord Search*, I congratulate you on your arrival here; and hope you already find, that *Immanuel*'s reproaches are no small riches[3]. You are welcome to my house, while here.

Search. Madam, I am obliged for your gracious reception and invitation. I have heard much of *Lady Liberal*, and have

[1] Heb. xii. 22.   [2] Luke ii. 36, 37.   [3] Heb. xi. 26.

too often joined in ridiculing your singular taste for religion; but *Jehovah* has convinced me, that great men are not always wise[1]. I adore him for humbling me to his will, and am happy in finding a person of your distinction, of my sentiments in these things.

Lady. We are now, my lord, come, as *Fervidus* hath been shewing, to *Mount Zion.* Here all worldly distinctions are swallowed up, in that glorious appellation, *Children of God.* Behold, what manner of love is bestowed on us[2]! Persons of our rank separate themselves from the lower classes of people, and pride themselves in an imaginary importance, and foolish distinctions; but use their fancied eminence chiefly in rendering themselves more criminal, vain, or ridiculous: for, after all, they *must* feel themselves subject to the pains, misfortunes, and propensities of the inferior classes; and, consequently, are on a mortifying level with the persons they affect to despise. But let *us* follow the great *Immanuel,* who himself was a carpenter, and went about doing good[3] to persons of all ranks. *Lord Search,* permit me to repeat to you an apostolic admonition. "Mind not high things, but condescend to men of low estate[4]." Nothing is more destructive to the spirit and practice of the world than this excellent rule.

Search. Madam, I am fully convinced of the propriety of your observations, I heartily thank you for your advice, and hope *Immanuel* will enable me to follow his great example.

Fer. I think myself happy in seeing two such exalted pilgrims. Religion puts a dignity and splendor on high birth, which is fought in vain in any thing else. Suffer me, my lord, to direct your attention to the princely son of *Amram,* who refused to be called the son of *Pharaoh's* daughter[5], that he might be a partaker of the afflictions of *Jehovah's* people. The *worst* of *Immanuel,* was more valuable with *Moses* than the *best things* the world could offer. Here appears high birth, noble sentiments, and illustrious magnanimity. His great soul was engrossed by the glorious *Recompence of Reward;* and his exalted

---

[1] Job xxxii. 9.   [2] 1 John iii. 1.   [3] Acts x. 38.   [4] Rom. xii. 16.
[5] Heb. xi. 24.

mind

mind endured as feeing *Him who is invisible.*—Now, madam, by your leave, we will withdraw to refresh ourselves; after which, I will shew our new friends this glorious city.

Breakfast being over, *Fervidus* led them thro' the city, and said,

Fer. You see how beautifully and commodiously the plan of this city is laid out. It is the work of *Jehovah*, and from thence it derives its name. This city is at perfect unity in itself[1]. Tho' the inhabitants are of various nations, and have different forms of divine worship, yet in faith and love they are quite harmonious with each other. Contention has no place in this city; the people are all of one heart, and of one soul[2]. Here is neither *Greek* nor *Jew*, *learned* nor *unlearned*, *bond* or *free*[3]. All invidious distinctions are dropped, and *Immanuel* is all in all.

Fervidus then ascended with them on the ramparts, and added,

Fero. Walk about *Zion*[4]. Consider her walls, mark well her bulwarks, that ye may inform others of her strength and perfect security.—This, my friends, is a maiden city, for it was never taken. Besieged it has often been, and so will be again; but there is no cause to fear the utmost efforts of the enemy. What the dastardly *Israelites* falsely said of the *Canaanites Cities*, may truly be applied to this; namely, "It is strong, and walled up to Heaven[5]." The ramparts we are on, are high and strong; but *that* we are now considering, is a mysterious wall; which is never seen by the enemy; nor, at all times, by the citizens. In ancient records of the city, this singular fortification is called a *Wall of Fire*[6]. It appeared in all its glory when *Elijah* was on these ramparts, and the enemy laid siege to the city, to take him[7]. In *King Hezekiah*'s reign, it was so very terrible, that only one spark of this *Wall of Fire* being darted into an army of enemies, at many miles distance, destroyed no less than one hundred and eighty-five thousand of them in one night[8].

There never was a breach made in the ramparts we are surveying, therefore, they are, with the utmost propriety called,

[1] Psalm cxxii. 3. [2] Acts iv. 32. [3] Gal. iii. 28. [4] Psalm xlviii. 12.
[5] Deut. i. 28. [6] Zech. ii. 5. [7] 2 Kings vi. 17. [8] 2 Kings xii. 35.

Walls of Salvation[1]: nor has one of these cannon ever been dismounted. The plan of the city is an exact square, for the length and breadth are equal[2]. The side we are now on, is the west, called *Revelation Battery*; because *Deists* and *Atheists* attack the city on this side. Take notice of this engine. It is named the *Apostate*'s *Reward*. From it, was thrown the ball which flew *Julian the Emperor*, when he fought against this city. The machine was contrived, and worked, by *Mr. Justice*, who is perpetual engineer of this battery[3].

We are now on the north-side, or on *Grace Battery*; which is levelled against *Papists*, *Pharisees*, and *Formalists*; who come up against this city, from the opposite *Country of Conceit*. The suburb under the wall is called *Neapolis*, and is inhabited by the people of my brother *John Duplex*; who, tho' they will not dwell in the town, yet, are indebted to this battery for their safety. This rampart will be for ever remarkable on account of yonder machine, which is the work of *Mr. Distinguish*[4], the ancient engineer of this battery. From this he threw a stone, so exactly true, amongst a company of persecutors, who were plotting against the city; that the wind of it beat *Saul*, the enraged *Pharisee*, to the ground, and yet affected no other persons[5]. *Mr. Grace* afterwards went out and brought him into the city, where he became the eminent apostle *St. Paul*.

This is the east side, and is called *Immanuel*'s *Battery*. On this side, the *Arians*, *Turks*, and *Socinians* make their attacks, they being all united against the divinity of our *Lord*. This curious sling is called *Arius*'s *Executioner*; because a shot therefrom, directed by *Mr. Truth*, the ever-living engineer of this battery[6], put an end to the life of that Arch-heretic.—Thus we have gone round the city, and are now on the south, or *Holy Rampart*, because these cannon are pointed against *Antinomians* and *Profligates*, who assault the city on this side; tho', sometimes, they are made use of, to deliver poor sinners, of that sort who are sensible of their danger, and cry to *Immanuel* for help. This artillery is remarkable for doing execution. Take notice of this bow, it is called the *Sinner's Friend*, from the following

[1] Isaiah xxvi. 1.   [2] Rev. xxi. 16.   [3] 2 Thess. i. 6.   [4] Gal. i. 15.
[5] Acts ix. 3, 4.   [6] Psalm ii. 5, 12.

well-attested fact. The *Black Tyrant* himself was dragging a Thief to *Tophet*, and was juſt at the mouth of his infernal den; but the poor ſinner cried to our *Lord*, to remember him in mercy[1]; on which, by *Immanuel*'s order, *Mr. Election*, the eternal engineer of the battery[2], ſhot an arrow from this bow; which ſo wounded this cruel uſurper, that he quitted his prey. *Mr. Vocation* then went forth, and brought him in hither: where, having tarried only a few hours, he was taken to the *Celeſtial City*, by a cohort of *Shining Ones*; and there he makes the place ring, with hallelujahs to *Immanuel*, for his wonderful deliverance.

Cler. And well he may, for there is hardly his fellow in that region.

Frien. I believe, Sir, *that* will be conteſted with him, *if I* get there.

Fer. Brother *Friendly*, let us have none of your *ifs*; they are great improprieties in the mouth of any perſon, within theſe walls. Who can doubt of his ſecurity, when he conſiders theſe ramparts, and this amazing train of artillery?

Fervidus having ſhewed them the ramparts, next took them to the arſenal of the city; where is a magazine of weapons, both offenſive and defenſive, unto which there is nothing in the univerſe to compare; therefore it is called the *Whole Armour of God*[3]. After their admiration at the firſt glance was over, ſaid

Fer. Behold this ſword! With it, *one* may chace a thouſand, and *two* put ten thouſand to flight[4]: nay, I have only brandiſhed it at the *Black Tyrant*, and he hath fled from me. The reaſon of this was, becauſe this weapon was uſed by our *Prince*, when he caſt him like lightning from the *Celeſtial City*[5]. *Lucifer* well remembers the dreadful wounds he then received, which makes the very ſight of it terrible to him. Conſider, alſo, theſe coats of mail. With one of theſe on him, a pilgrim may go thro' fire and water, without any danger. *Shadrach* and his brethren had each of them one of theſe coats, when they were caſt into the fiery furnace[6]; therefore, they walked in that

---

[1] Luke xxiii. 42.   [2] Eph. i. 4.   [3] Eph. vi. 11.   [4] Deut. xxxii. 30.
[5] Luke x. 18.   [6] Dan. iii. 23, 25.

dreadful element, with as much ease, as if they had been on yonder Terrace. Our *Prince* has promised always to attend in person[1], upon whomsoever this armour is put, as he did on the three before-mentioned heroes. In this vast arsenal are also laid up the terrible thunder-bolts, which are reserved against the last assault of this city, by the armies of *Gog* and *Magog*[2]; which will terminate in the final and eternal destruction of all our enemies.

CHAP. XXXVII.

Fervidus *conducts the Pilgrims to* Mount Promise, *the* Mountains of Spices, Mount Transfiguration, *and* Mount Pisgah. Clericus *preaches his first sermon at the* Temple.

THE Pilgrims having left the arsenal, as they went through the city, Mr. *Sincere* said,

Sincere. This city must make a vast consumption of provisions, &c. Pray, Sir, from whence is it supplied?

Fer. I am about to shew you. We are near one of the hills, from which, this part of your road is called the *Delectable Mountains.*—This, my friends, is the *Mount of Promise.* Here are the fat things full of marrow, and the wine on the lees well-refined, which are prepared for all pilgrims, by our *Immanuel*[3]. Here are the rivers of pleasure[4], the breasts of consolation[5], the hidden manna[6], the bread and the water, the meat and drink, of which it is said, to distinguish them from all other dainties, that they are, *meat indeed*, and *drink indeed*[7]. All these things, neither fail, nor waste; for there is a secret communication between this mountain and the eternal stores of the *Celestial City*, from whence they are constantly supplied; so that it is as

[1] Isaiah xliii. 2. [2] Rev. xx. 8, 9, 10. [3] Isaiah xxv. 6. [4] Psalm xxxvi. 8.
[5] Isaiah lxvi. 11. [6] Rev. ii. 17. [7] John vi. 55.

impossible

impoffible for the inhabitants of this city to be ftarved, as it is to die of hunger in the Celeftial World. Do you think that any of our citizens can be famifhed?

Ref. No, Sir; you may as well fuppofe a fifh will be drowned in the fea.

'Fer. Neverthelefs, I know a man, who, altho' he is furrounded with fuch great plenty, unto which he has free accefs; yet he imagined, he fhould ftarve, or come to the parifh. The truth is, there are in this city certain families, of the genuine pilgrim race, who are defcended from *Meffrs. Fearing, Feeblemind,* and *Littlefaith.* Thefe perfons are fubject to various infirmities, which fill them with ftrange fufpicions, both of the fecurity of the city, and the nature of thefe provifions. I have heard certain of them, in their fits, cry, " We fhall one day perifh by fome fhot from the enemy[1]. Can *Immanuel* fupply fo many of us with bread? His provifions will certainly be exhaufted, and come to an end." He will in anger either fhut up all the avenues of food, or forget to fupply us[3], and fo let us perifh with hunger!"

Frien. Ah, Sir, I am the wretch you are defcribing. I am fprung from one of thofe families you mention: but are you fure that it is only an infirmity in me? I am ready to fear that it is a mortal diftemper.

Fer. Such fears, indeed, fhew you to be a relation of theirs[4]; but, pray, how came you within thefe walls?

Frien. Immanuel brought me hither, or I had never found the way.

Fer. Then you have no mortal diftemper about you; and all your fufpicions arife from your infirmities; which, fhould be well attended to, known, and improved as fuch. But, after feeing the hills, we will call at *St. Thomas's Hofpital,* and confult the phyfician on yours, and your brother *Probus's* cafe, of which *Clericus* has told me.—Now let us afcend the *Mountains of Spices*[5], but, take care you are not overcome by them. If

[1] 1 Sam. xxvii. 1.   [2] Pfalm lxxviii. 20.   [3] Pfalm lxxvii. 8, 9.
[4] Pfalm lxxvii. 10.   [5] Cant. viii. 14.

your senses have not been exercised with these odours, I question whether you will be able to bear the fragrancy of the gardens — Now we are among them. What are the poets with their *Hesperian Gardens, Elysian Fields*, and all their Heathenish trumpery! Oh, what a wilderness of sweets is this!

Search. Good Lord! What do I see and smell! Where else can such sweetness be, as I now experience! I have read much of *Arabia the Spicey*, but this is *Eden!* this is *Paradise!* See, what roses, what lovely lillies!—Thank you, kind *Fervidus*, for this! It is luxury indeed!——

Fer. Pray, my lord, thank our *Prince*. He is the rose and the lily of this garden[1]. All these sweets and beauties flow from *him*, and unite to recommend *him*. Upon a time, a beautiful lady came into this garden, and was so delighted with a bundle of myrrh[2], that she would have it; so boldly took and put it in her bosom: nor was she reproved; but, on the contrary, the gardener was pleased with her freedom.

Ref. Brother *Sincere*, here is an apple-tree like that under which we slept so sweetly, in the garden of the house *Beautiful*. I should like a nap now, for these spices incline me to sleep.

Fer. You have too much to see at present; but while you tarry in this city, you may come, when you please, and refresh yourselves in this garden.—Let us now visit the *Mount of Transfiguration*[3]; on which have been, and still are to be seen, very wonderful things. When *St. Peter* was thereon, he saw excellent glory, and for that reason he named it, the *Holy Mount*[4].

So they all ascended up to its summit; and, while *Fervidus* was expatiating on the pleasure there is in having communion with *Jehovah*; Lo, the *Heavens* opened, and *Immanuel* appeared passing by, and proclaiming his glorious name[5]. None but favourite pilgrims can tell what these men felt at this time. *Immanuel* soon disappeared, or they had been all dead men. *Fervidus* alone supported this vision; but *he* was seen all splendor,

[1] Cant. ii. 1.   [2] Cant. i. 13.   [3] Mat. xvii. 1.   [4] 2 Pet. i. 17, 18.
[5] Exod. xxxiv. 6, 7.

being

being overcome, like another *Moses*[1]. *Lord Search* fell on the neck of *Fervidus*, in a tranſport; and the Pilgrims, fell to the ground, in holy amazement. At length *Fervidus* recovered himſelf, and exclaimed,

Fer. Oh, he is the chiefeſt among ten thouſand, and altogether lovely[2]! *Lord Search*, look up; ariſe, ye happy ſouls, for your beloved has, in tenderneſs towards you, withdrawn his glories; and you may open your eyes with ſafety.

The Pilgrims then ventured to look about them.

Cler. Oh, what a deceiver is the *Black Tyrant*, in blinding the minds of men from ſeeing ſuch glories[3]! I could not have conceived, that there were ſuch things to be ſeen and felt in religion, as I am now ſo happily convinced of. *Old Infidelity* affirmed, that they were all illuſions which pilgrims talked of, but he is a liar. Yet, if they *were* deluſions, they are the moſt extatic joys that our natures are capable of taſting; and he, who in ſuch a caſe, ſhould undeceive me, would be my greateſt enemy.

Prob. Bleſſed *Lord!* Bleſſed mountain! Dear brethren, and partakers of theſe raviſhing views of our *Immanuel!* I congratulate both you and myſelf! I find my arm quite eaſy on this mountain, and every infirmity, which I contracted in the *Caſtle of Scepticiſm*, ſeems to be removed!

Ref. This is ſomething *real!* It is good being here[4], and I ſhould like to ſpend all my days in this ſituation!

Fer. No, *Reſolute*, do not deſire to eat your morſel alone. *St. Peter* was of your opinion, when *he* was on this eminence; for he wanted to turn tent-maker and commence hermit. But, had he been humoured, he would have found it a far leſs profitable employ than his own, which was a fiſher of men. For, had that great man been indulged with his deſire, he would have gone ſneaking alone into the *Celeſtial City*, ſaying, "*Lord*, here is *Peter*, the hermit of *Mount Tabor*;" whereas, we ſhall behold him, by and by, come before the throne, with thou-

[1] Exod. xxxiv. 30. [2] Cant. v. 16. [3] 2 Corin. iv. 4.
[4] Mat. xvii. 4.

fands on his fide; and here him fay, "*Lord*, here is fimple *Peter*, who once knew not what he faid[1]: thou didft gracioufly contradict me, and now, behold me, and the many children which thou haft given me." Yes, Sirs, we muft all defcend, and go thro' many trials; but all will work together for our good; as it happened to *Peter*, and the other two favourite Apoftles.

Sincere. Am I in the body, or out of the body! I cannot determine[2].

Frien. Nor I, brother: where is *Fervidus*, and our brethren?

Fer. Here we are; and you will very foon know that you are ftill in the body! Dear *St. Paul*[3] was obliged to be well goaded, after fuch a vifion as you have enjoyed, to keep him fenfible of his weaknefs; and fo muft *you* be treated —Blefs t. ● *Lord*, brethren, for thefe manifeftations; and remember, that the *Celeftial City*, to which you are travelling, will be an eternal enjoyment of far greater glory than you have now feen; therefore, be not weary nor faint in your minds[4]. Our *Lord*'s favourites muft both watch and pray, left they enter into temptation. The eight Difciples who were left at the entrance of the garden of *Gethfemane*, were only directed, to *tarry there*[5]: but the three favourite Apoftles, who were taken nearer to the theatre of his paffion, and honoured with a view of the mighty Redeemer, in his bloody conflict; were ordered to [6]*watch and pray*. Take heed to yourfelves, therefore, my brethren. The *Black Tyrant* mortally envies the courtiers of our *King*. The *Philiftines* will furely be upon you.—Now let us clofe our vifit of the hills, with a profpect from [7]*Mount Pifgah*. It ftands well for obfervation. It may coft you fome labour to afcend it, but you will be well-repaid by what you will fee.

Search. Thank the *Lord*, we are got to the top. I was almoft out of breath in afcending hither. What a commanding fituation, backward and forward, and on every fide! I know not where to look firft. Come, kind *Fervidus*, you have often

[1] Mark ix. 6. [2] 2 Cor. xii. 2. [3] 2 Cor. xii. 7. [4] Heb. xii. 3.
[5] Mark xiv. 32. [6] Mark xiv. 38. [7] Deut. xxxiv. 1.

been here; tell us somewhat of the things which lie around us; and how we may best improve the prospect.

Fer. In the first place, take a view of the country from whence ye came [1]; there is no better method to prevent your being giddy-headed. See, yonder distant land to the west, which is under the perpetual frown of our *King* [2]. There is the rock from whence ye were hewn, and the hole of the pit whence ye were digged [3]. Behold next, the way in which the *Lord* your *King* has led you these many days. Thus did *Jeremiah*, when he stood on this spot, and cried out [4], " Remembering my affliction, the wormwood and the gall, my soul hath them still in remembrance; I consider them in my heart, and therefore I have hope." So do ye, my sons: for *Jehovah* would not have shewn you so great things, if he had not intended to preserve you unto the end [5].—A little to your right is *Freewill Forest*, in which you may perceive the ruins of *Doubting-Castle*. From thence turn and see what your *King* has prepared for you. It is a clear day, and you may plainly see the gates of the *New Jerusalem*, of which the city below us, is a figure. On this very spot stood *Moses*, when *Jehovah* shewed him the goodly land and *Lebanon*; and altho' his master thought proper not to permit that great man to enter *Canaan* [6] with *Israel*; yet he was more honoured, by visiting it many hundred years afterwards, in company with the great Redeemer [7].

Res. Oh, how glorious is yonder blessed abode! And shall unworthy *Will Resolute* dwell there for ever! Oh, my dear *Lord* [8], whom have I in that world but thee, and what is it on earth that I desire besides thee!

Fer. Ah, friend *Resolute*, you are a towering genius. You have found the very eminence on which *King David* had a sight of *Immanuel*'s glory. That is a fine air, how does it agree with you?

[1] Isaiah li. 1.   [2] Ephes. ii. 3.   [3] Isaiah li. 1.   [4] Lam. iii. 19, 21.
[5] Judges xiii. 23.   [6] Deut. iii. 25, 26.   [7] Mat. xvii. 3.
[8] Psalm lxxiii. 25.

Ref. Charmingly well! I never was so happy in my life.

Frien. Nor I, brother, for I seem in a strait[1], having a desire to be with *Immanuel* in the *Celestial City*.

Fer. Friendly, I am glad you have found that spot. It will raise your spirits. *St. Paul* never was better than when he was in those heavenly straits and difficulties. *Probus*, if you advance a little farther, I know what you will say. ——

Prob. Delectable Mountains, indeed! My soul rejoiceth with joy unspeakable and full of glory[2]. O *Peter*, you were much in the right, for I now feel what no tongue can declare!

Sincere. But you have not engrossed it all. Oh, what manner of love has the *Father* bestowed on me, that I should be called the *King*'s Son[3]!

Cler. Lord, what am I, or what is my father's house, that thou should'st bring me hitherto[4]!

Fer. Brethren, I give you joy. We seem all to be very happy: let us therefore praise *Immanuel*, in full view of our journey's end.

   " *There* we shall see his face,
   " And never, never sin;
   " *There* from the rivers of his grace,
   " Drink endless pleasures in.

   " The men of grace have found,
   " Glory begun below;
   " Celestial fruits on earthly ground,
   " From faith and hope may grow.

   " The *Hill of Zion* yields,
   " A thousand sacred sweets,
   " Before we reach the heavenly fields,
   " Or walk the golden streets.

[1] Phil. i. 23.   [2] 1 Peter i. 8.   [3] 1 John iii. 1.
[4] 2 Sam. vii. 18.

" Then let our songs abound,
" And every tear be dry,
" We're marching thro' *Immanuel*'s ground,
" To fairer worlds on high."
                                        WATTS.

Sincere. Methinks I see a very dreary region between us and the *Celestial City!*

Fer. Brother, I perceive, that you are looking too much downward; but I would advise you, to feast your eyes and heart with *Celestial* things: for, it is by looking on these eternal objects, that pilgrims are preserved from fainting in their progress[1]. You will soon enough know what the *Enchanted Ground* is; for *that* is the dreary region you mention. Your way lies across it, and there you may be tried: but, beware of sleeping there. Stand fast in the faith, and count not your lives dear unto you, that you may obtain yonder better country[2]. In imitation of your blessed *Lord*, for the joy which is now set before you, endure the cross[3], and despise whatever shame may be thrown upon you.

The Pilgrims came down from *Mount Pisgah*, and went to the temple, where *Clericus* was to preach in the evening. This was the first time of his appearing in that character before *Fervidus*, which gave him much concern: however, he came forth, trusting in the *Lord*, and made an excellent sermon from the following words, " There remaineth therefore a rest for the people of *God*[4]." *Fervidus* was observed to give frequent signs of approbation. After sermon, the Pilgrims returned with *Mr. Valiant* to the Inn, well pleased with the business of the day.

[1] 2 Cor. iv. 16, 17, 18.   [2] Acts xx. 24.   [3] Heb. xii. 2.
[4] Heb. iv. 9.

C H A P. XXXVIII.

The instructing story of Captain Intrepid. *The Pilgrims visit* St. Thomas's Hospital: *An account of the celebrated* Dr. Evidence.

MR. *Valiant* was much delighted to see our Pilgrims again under his roof. He ordered a supper, but made an apology, that as they had been so deliciously feasted that day, his fare might appear course; however, he would do his best to please them: and supper being brought, it was found much to the satisfaction of his guests. When the table was withdrawn, *Resolute*, being very desirous of hearing more of *Mr. Valiant*'s martial adventures; said,

Res. Good host, you have well replenished us with food; cannot you now tell us some instructing story, of your own, or others adventures, while you was in the army, and in actual service?

Valiant. I am here, Sirs, on purpose to serve you; and a fact occurs to my mind; which, altho' it be somewhat similar to my own case, yet may be both instructing and entertaining to you.—It is as follows: There was in our army an eminent man, named *Captain Intrepid*, who was greatly esteemed by our *King*; for he had particularly promised him, that, however warmly and dangerously he might be engaged, he would never leave him nor forsake him[1]. This officer was sent, with a chosen number of troops, on a perilous expedition into the *Land of Execration*; where he was ordered to give no quarter to any of the enemy. The captain had great success at first: at length, a prisoner was taken, who, being very amiable, was spared, and brought to the captain. The name of this prisoner was *Carnal-Reason*. He was a young man, and appeared so agreeable in

[1] Heb. xiii. 5.

person,

person, and graceful of address, in the eyes of the captain; that he not only spared his life; but, also took him into his tent to wait on him. In a short time, he so insinuated himself into his master's favour, that the captain made him his confident, and consulted him upon all occasions. *Captain Intrepid* having sent out a scouting party, they returned, and said, there was a town at a small distance, which the army might easily take. On this, young *Carnal Security* said, he knew the place well, that there was no need to use much strength against it, for a few troops would destroy it. This advice was taken. A detachment was sent, but they met with a repulse, and several were slain by the enemy.—On this defeat, *Captain Intrepid* fell into such fear and perturbation of mind, as disgraced his name, and former heroic conduct. He hastened to court, to lay his case before the *King*. I was in the levee when he arrived: he appeared in great disorder; which was a grief to all present. The captain advanced towards the throne, and falling prostrate on his face, thus addressed his sovereign. " O my *Prince*, what shall thy unhappy servant say to thee, when I, unto whom thou didst graciously promise victory, have been so foully defeated by thine enemies! Surely, it had been better for me not to have gone on this service!"

I perceived that the captain's address was not at all pleasing to our *King*; for he, with a stern look, replied. " *Intrepid*, why art thou so fearful and impatient[1]? Indeed I promised victory unto thee, but I did not say, that thou should'st receive no foils in obtaining it. Thou must acquire this triumph in the way of obedience to my orders. In vain dost thou humble thyself before me, while thou fosterest an [2] enemy in thy houshold. Thou hast transgressed against me, therefore thou can'st not stand before thine enemies[3]; nor will I any more be with thee, unless thou puttest the evil from thy dwelling." The last words of the *Prince* fell like a thunder-bolt on the poor captain. He arose, wrapped his face in his robe, and departed thoughtful, and very sad.

[1] Mat. viii. 26. [2] Psalm lxvi. 18. [3] Joshua vii. 12.

Ref. And well he might; for nothing is half so terrible to a pilgrim soldier as the frown of his *Prince*. I feel myself much interested in this case, and long to hear how the captain proceeded.

Valiant. There is a royal person at court, whose name is *Prince Paraclete*[1]. He is a near relation to, and a constant attendant on our *King*; and exceedingly kind to all the army, both officers and soldiers; for he makes it his business to serve them as a counsellor, and comforter, on all occasions. He is ever near the *King*, and knows more of his mind than any one else[2]. *Captain Intrepid* repaired immediately to this person, and told him all that had passed between him and the *King*. On which, *Prince Paraclete* desired the captain, to inform him, very particularly, of his whole proceedings in the late expedition. When the captain had so done, the *Prince* told him, that the cause of his defeat and disgrace was intirely owing to his sparing, and advising with, young *Carnal Reason*. " It is he," said *Prince Paraclete*, " who has made your enemies appear despicable unto you: not from a laudable confidence in the power of your sovereign, but from a vain consciousness of your own wisdom and courage. This is evident from your conduct. For those who confide in their *King* only, make use of *all* their strength against his enemies; but such as trust in themselves, generally make light of their foes, as you did; oppose them faintly, and meet with an overthrow: *thus* it has happened to you. My advice therefore is, 'That you hasten to the camp, and sacrifice your young favourite; then take *all* your forces, and go against the enemy, in humble confidence of the assistance of your *King*; and you may be assured of success."

Captain Intrepid stood abashed at his foolish conduct[3], while *Prince Paraclete* thus pointed out his crime and his duty; then stamping his foot, with indignation at himself[4], he bowed low, and retired in haste for his camp. As soon as he arrived, he seized the favourite, and put him to death; then took his whole corps, and made a fierce assault on the city, took it, subdued the whole country, and speedily returned to court. But,

[1] John xiv. 16. [2] 1 Cor. ii. 11. [3] Ezek. xvi. 63. [4] 2 Cor. vii. 11.

notwithstanding

notwithstanding his victory, he entered the *Presence-Chamber* very humbly; and when he made a report of his success to his *Lord*, he did it in such low terms of self-abasement¹, as I never had heard him use before. The *King* was much pleased with his deportment, and condescended to thank him for his faithful services. This was honour enough for the captain; who departed from the audience, extolling aloud the forbearance, grace and love of his sovereign; declaring all faithful obedience to him, in future; and breathing further, and eternal vengeance against all his *Lord*'s enemies.

Ref. Sir, I thank you for your edifying story. I hope we shall all remember, what hinderance *Carnal Reason* is to our victories, what an enemy he is to our *King*'s glory; and, that we have need of *all* our wisdom and strength in opposing the enemies of our salvation.

The Pilgrims then retired to rest. Next morning they waited on *Mr. Fervidus*, who had promised to attend them to *St. Thomas's Hospital*. This is a royal and elegant structure in the heart of the *City of God*. The name of the principal physician of this hospital, is, *Dr. Evidence*², a person well known in the *Pilgrim World*, and famous, both on account of his birth, age, and skill in his profession. He is known to be of a divine origin, for he is the son of the celebrated *Dr. Demonstration*³, who dwells on the other side the *River of Death*, of whom more will be said in the sequel. This physician of *St. Thomas's* has existed from the creation of the world; but, instead of growing weak, from his great age, as some people foolishly assert; he increases in strength, experience, and success every day: and those who are most familiar with the doctor, have heard him affirm, that he never was better in health, since those happy days when *Immanuel* and his father condescended to visit him, than he finds himself at present. His enemies, indeed, have endeavoured to destroy him, by assassination, poison, and other *base* arts; for the doctor is a person of such courage and skill at the sword, that they dare not attempt to engage him in a *fair* way.

¹ Psalm li. 5.   ² Heb. xi. 1.   ³ 1Cor. ii. 4.

However, all their attempts have been frustrated hitherto, as they ever will be.

This physician is a very useful person in the city; the inhabitants of which, are subject to many infirmities; especially the families of *Fearing*, &c. before-mentioned. *Dr. Evidence* is the great *Master of Regimen* to the whole city; and every week prescribes to them in that character, by appointing the proper diet for each, according to their complexions and constitutions. He has many of the faculty under him, to see that his directions are complied with; that so the health of the citizens may be preserved, and their senses properly exercised, to discern things that differ[1].

The citizens have a great regard for the doctor. They all court his favour, and tremble at his frowns. The best of the inhabitants sometimes stand in great need of his help[2]. The hospital received its name from *St. Thomas* the Apostle, who was cured of an obstinate disorder therein, which he got by not accompanying with his brethren[3]. The diseased Apostle would not suffer *Dr. Evidence* to heal him, but insisted that his father should do it, or he would not be cured at all[4]. *Dr. Demonstration* being, at that time, in the hospital, he was called to the assistance of that great but infirm man.

Mr. Fervidus and *Dr. Evidence* were very great friends. When he and the pilgrims came to the hospital, they were immediately introduced to the physician; to whom he said,

Fer. Good morning to you doctor. I have brought you a patient or two. I tried my puny art upon them; but nothing will satisfy but *Dr. Evidence, Dr. Evidence*. You are very happy, Sir, in thus winning the hearts of pilgrims; but I am not envious of you, because, I know you will direct their affections from yourself to our most worthy master.

Evidence. Friend *Fervidus*, you are welcome to me. Under the blessed *Immanuel* I owe much of my repute, at this day, to your labours. Some time since, I was quite neglected, and

[1] Phil. i. 10.   [2] Psalm xxvii. 13.   [3] John xx. 24.   [4] John xx. 25, 27.

almost

almost without fame or business; this hospital went to decay, the city was but thinly inhabited, and my precious drugs, &c. were of little more estimation in the *Pilgrim World*, than they are at *Deist-Hall*. But now inhabitants flow to the city[1], and it is very populous: they have repaired and beautified the hospital, and continual applications, from far and near, is made to me for advice and medicines. I have now very large orders by me from the *City of Establishment*, and its suburbs.

Fer. This is good news, Sir. But I beg you would look higher in this affair, than to the weak and *Tophet*-deserving *George Fervidus*; who daily feels his need of you, and who lives and rejoices only by your divine skill. I know your worth, doctor, and am glad to find that so many others are made acquainted with it. But still, Sir, I am more fond of your honoured father, and long to see him[2]. I am sorry he is gone from the city: excuse me, doctor, for I *must* think, that this is a poor, dark, and distempered world without him.

Evid. It is so. I do my endeavour to supply his place; but tho' my medicines are abundantly sufficient to preserve the *Lives*, and, in general, the *Health* of pilgrims; yet I shall never obtain that skill and success in giving florid *Health to all*, as did my father. He has a great regard for the inhabitants of this city, where he dwelt many hundred years; and told me on his departure, that he should again revisit it, and abide therein a thousand years[3]. To confirm this promise, he said, the city should never be taken by its enemies[4], and that I should never die: both which have been found true for 1700 years.

Fer. And so will continue till your father visits it in company with the blessed *Immanuel*—Now, doctor, if you please, examine these two patients, I believe they have the *Pilgrim-Evil*[5] upon them.

The doctor then, looking on *Friendly*, said,

Evid. Well, my son, what ails you? Wherefore look you so pale and dejected?

---

[1] Isaiah ii. 2.   [2] 2 Cor. v. 8.   [3] Rev. xx. 4.   [4] Mat. xv. 18.
[5] Heb. iii. 12.

Frien. Oh, Sir, I have got a bad appetite, and a worfe heart: for altho' I am come fo far, yet I am afraid that I am not a true pilgrim, and fhall never enter into the *New Jerufalem.*

On this, *Dr. Evidence* took down a bottle, on which was wrote, *Lac Amoris Fraterni*; and gave it to *Friendly*, faying,

Evid. Tafte of this, and, if you like it, drink as much as you pleafe.

Friendly tafted the milk, and found it fo fweet, that he fairly emptied the bottle. At this, the doctor fmiled, and took down another, on which was wrote, *Effentia Spiritus Veritatis*; and gave it to *Friendly*, with the fame liberty as before; and he drank it entirely off, altho' it was very ftrong. The doctor then taking his arm, laid his finger on his pulfe; and faid,

Evid. Fear not, my fon; but know, that when you arrive at the *Celeftial City*, you will be freed from all temptations to evil, and even from the very *Being* of fin[1]. Your work, thro' a long eternity, will be to ferve *Jehovah* day and night in his temple[2]; to converfe with good men, and *Shining Ones*, and to be continually growing up in knowledge, holinefs and joy.

When the doctor had difcourfed fome time on this elevating fubject; and, in the mean while, carefully obferved the pulfe and countenance of his patient; he further addreffed him, and all prefent.

Evid. There is no occafion for you, my fon, to be difcouraged at any thing you may find in you, or that can be done to you. Whatever this, your brother, my friends, may think or fay of himfelf; yet, you faw that he drank like a fifh from thofe bottles, which none but true pilgrims can relifh or endure. The firft was the *Milk of Brotherly Love*[3], and the other the *Effence* of the *Spirit of Truth*: both which were ufed by *St. John*[4], as tefts to difcover true pilgrims, in *his* days. I had this recipe from his hand. I am further confirmed in my fentiments of this patient, by the flowing of his blood,

[1] Ifaiah xxxiii. 24. [2] Rev. vii. 15. [3] 1 Johniii. 14. [4] 1 John iv. 13.

while

while I set before him the purity and perfection of celeſtial happineſs. When thus diſcourſing to *falſe* pilgrims, I have ſeen their countenances fall, and felt their pulſe grow languid; but here, on the contrary, your brother's eyes ſparkled, his face ſhone, and his pulſe quickned to a *Celeſtial Par*. All which clearly manifeſts, that his heart is ſet on the employments and enjoyments of the *New Jeruſalem*.

Frien. Sir, I thank you, and hope I ſhall ever remember your faithful and encouraging examination of my caſe.

The Doctor then, turning to *Probus*, ſaid,

Evid. And you, my ſon, what is your complaint?

In reply, *Probus* told the Doctor the ſtory of his impriſonment in the *Caſtle of Scepticiſm*, and the manner of his eſcape: he then ſhewed him the wound in his arm. On which, ſaid the Doctor,

Evid. I have a medicine, the recipe for which was given me by *Immanuel*, when he was here. He called it, *Balſamum benedictum*. It was preſcribed to *St. Thomas* in his caſe, but he made light of it, and inſiſted on the help of my father, who was then at the hoſpital. *Immanuel* graciouſly conſidered the patient's obſtinacy as a part of his diſeaſe, and ordered my father to attend him; but left the balſam with me, and his particular bleſſing, in future, on every patient who ſhould make uſe of it[1]. Some of this I will give you, but be ſure you addreſs *Immanuel* for the bleſſing, whenever you uſe it; and tho' it may not effect an abſolute cure, yet it will certainly ſecure you from any mortal conſequences therefrom. The wound may pain you, in dark cloudy weather; but it will not affect your life. Moreover, you will be ſure to find a perfect remedy at my father's, on the other ſide of the *River of Death*. And I wiſh you all a happy arrival on that *Celeſtial* ſhore.

Fer. Doctor, I thank you for this labour of love. We muſt now attend on the ſervice of the temple, ſo bid you farewell.

[1] John xx. 29.

C H A P. XXXIX.

Probus *ordered to leave his brethren, for a season. A letter from him. He returns, and they set out on their journey. They arrive at the* Globe Inn, *on the* Enchanted Ground, *kept by* Mrs. Jezebel.

THE Pilgrims continued some time in the *City of God:* but, soon after their arrival, a letter was received by *Probus,* which commanded him in the *King*'s name, to leave his brethren for a season, and sojourn in the *Town of Love,* in the *County of Regeneration. Probus* was much troubled to hear of this; for, tho' it was more honourable for him, to be employed by the *King;* yet he was grieved to leave his friends, and they were as much concerned to part with him. *Resolute,* particularly, was so affected that he wept sore; and declared, he knew not how to bear the separation[1]. *Probus* promised to return as soon as possible, and pursue his journey with them.

Fervidus returned with the *Transport* to the *Port of Adoption,* and took *Clericus* with him; and, as this was the best way for *Probus* to go to the place appointed; he departed with them, and soon arrived at his residence: from whence he sent many letters to his brethren, expressive of his warm affection for them. The following is a copy of one of those epistles of love.

Probus to his Brethren.

My very dear brethren, *Town of Love,* 14th of *June.*

THIS epistle will be a remarkable instance of the changeable situation of pilgrims, while here below. For I am now walking melancholy, in the dark and comfortless *Valley of*

[1] Acts xx. 37.

Desertion;

Desertion; surrounded with gloomy shades, haunted with hideous spectres, and intimidated with fearful and dismaying noises. O, how unlike the place from whence I came! How unlike the pure and blissful *Elysium*, where I lately breathed ambrosial sweets! Yonder, on the *Delectable Mountains*, with the dear *Fervidus*, and my precious friends, I walked at large, in full view of the gates of the *Celestial City*, which shone with bright and attracting radiance. Thus blessed, my soul was ready to nestle, and say, " I sit as a queen, and shall never see sorrow[1]. My mountain is so strong it shall never be moved[2]." But ah, how great is my mistake! Oh, what a change has taken place! How is the son of the morning fallen[3]! I am hurl'd from my eminence. My mountain is removed like the baseless fabric of a vision, and I am deeply plunged into the dismal gloom of night! Behold, I am vile! My *Lord* has left me to my wretched self, and I cannot have worse company! O, my friends, I could not have imagined, that such a contrariety to our *King* had a place in me. After so long acquaintance with *Him* and myself, how little do I know of either! The few last days of my experience have shewn me such things as surprize me! Certain *rebels*, whom I thought to be dead long ago, have revived, shewn their hateful heads, and appear to be some of the cursed *Usurper*'s chief captains. I see also, coming against me, dreadful *Anakims*, unto whom I am, indeed, less than a grasshopper[4]. Oh, *Resolute*, *Friendly*, and *Sincere*, who are better acquainted than I with the horrid dimensions of these foes, and have often engaged with them; you can guess at the situation I am now in. Nevertheless, I am not utterly forsaken of our *King*. I have a staunch loyal party with me, under the command of that divine, courageous, and incorruptible *Captain Godly Fear*[5]; who still holds my heart firm in the interest of *Prince Immanuel*, and fills me with hope, that this insurrection will soon terminate, in the total destruction of all the conspirators. O that I could hear the sound of *Immanuel*'s chariot! Make haste, my beloved *Lord!* behold thy struggling spouse is beset by vile ruffians! Like *Dinah*[6], I have paid too many car-

[1] Rev. xviii. 7. [2] Psalm xxx. 6. 7. [3] Isaiah xiv. 12. [4] Num. xiii. 33. [5] Jer. xxxii. 40. [6] Gen. xxxiv. 1.

nal visits to the daughters of this world, and thus endangered my honour: but, O my *Lord*, fetch me from *Sheckem*'s house [1], and put to death his whole generation!

This day my heart was full, and my whole man laboured under a deep sense of grief, for my separation from you, and happiness. I sought a place to weep—In my chamber, wrapped in silence and reflection, I drew near my father, my almighty Friend. He was pleased to hold out, to his trembling child, his golden sceptre. He saw that I was absorbed in grief, so he graciously took me on his knee, and permitted me to pour out my soul into his dear bosom [2]. I wept aloud. My heart almost burst with love to *Immanuel*, and my dear brethren at the *City of God*. I told my father, that I was unhappy, begged him to forgive my weakness, for I could not but consider myself as a poor banished child; and, with great energy, mentioned unto him the saying of the sweet singer of *Israel*.

" My *God*, my *King*, why should I be
" So far from all my joys and thee?"   WATTS.

I would not for all the world be without these tender passions. It is my honour, and part of my happiness, that I am counted worthy of possessing a soul, so much akin to the great *Bishop of Souls*. Oh, ye tender bosoms, to whom I am now writing, how wonderful it is, that any celestial affections should be found in us, where *Tophet*, and all its rebellion and pollution, had its throne [3]! How astonishing, that *Immanuel* should preside where *Belial* and the *Black Tyrant* reigned [4]! How blessed are we in having our stony hearts turned into flesh [5]!—May *Jehovah* make the severe providence, which now exerciseth us, to work more and more for his glory and our good. I firmly believe that I shall soon be given again unto you, for I cannot enjoy myself while absent from you. In this I may be criminal, but I am always———Dear Sirs,

Your very affectionate brother, in exile.

Probus.

[1] Gen. xxxiv. 26.   [2] Isaiah lxvi. 12, 13.   [3] Tit. iii. 3.   [4] Eph. ii. 2.
[5] Ezek. xxxvi. 26.

Many

Many other epistles were received from *Probus*, but the above may suffice to shew his fervent love for his brethren, and impatient desire of their company. At length, it pleased the *King* to order him from that station, where he seemed so unhappy; and restore him again to his brethren. Great was the joy of these Pilgrims when they met together again, and they immediately prepared to depart from the *City of God*. *Mr. Valiant* walked a little way with them: and at length took his leave as follows.

Valiant. Farewell, my dear guests. Fear no enemy. Make no parly, nor composition with, and much less yield to them: but, in whatever straits and difficulties you may be brought, do not submit, do not turn back, but press on vigorously[1] towards the glorious hill of *Zion*; where I hope soon to embrace you all.

After his departure, the Pilgrims went on their way very pleasantly, until they came to a green and extensive plain, called the *Plain of Obedience*; which they found to be, as the ways of wisdom are described by *King Solomon*, namely, " Ways of pleasantness and peace[2]." This plain is bounded on the northside, by the very extensive *Territory of Conceit*; and on the south, by the *Land of Melancholy*. These two countries run on each side the *Plain of Obedience*, and the *Enchanted Ground*, and then terminate in the unknown tracks which extend to the *River of Death*, bounding two sides of the *Land of Beulah*. In this plain, the Pilgrims comfortably walked a great part of the day. At length they entered on the *Enchanted Ground*, night spread her gloomy wings over them, and they began to feel the pernicious effects of the air on that ground. However, they roused each other, and endeavoured to avoid sleeping in so dangerous a place. As they briskly walked on, they were surprised with the sound of music[3], which, as they advanced, they found to be attended with the voices of many persons singing. The air also was illuminated, and the Pilgrims soon discovered, that the light and noise proceeded from a large house on the left side of the road, which they found to be the *Globe Inn*, kept by *Mrs. Jezebel*.

[1] Phil. iii. 14.   [2] Prov. iii. 17.   [3] Job. xxi. 12.

The Pilgrims being perceived by the people of the houfe, fome of the fervants came out, and addreffed them in a very polite manner. Walk in, Sirs, faid they, we have much company, and many pilgrims who will depart early in the morning.

Prob. Pilgrims are they! I think the found is not like the fober mirth of pilgrims.

Servant. Some are merry, and rather noify; but others are fmoaking a ferious pipe, and difcourfing in a very rational way. Gentlemen, walk in, you may be fure of good entertainment, and civil ufage.

Accordingly, as it was dark, and dangerous travelling, the Pilgrims agreed to go in until morning; but determined to keep near each other, and take care to avoid every fnare. *Refolute* grafped his rod, and they all entered into the firft room that prefented itfelf.

C H A P. XL.

The Pilgrims difcourfe with Meffrs. Lucre, Gripe, Rubicus, Bully, *and* Haughty.—*The Inn in an uproar, and the Pilgrims expelled.*

THE Pilgrims found the room to be large, and full of company, who were eager in difcourfe, and took very little notice of them. They, therefore, fat down together in a little fide box, where they talked foftly to each other, and remarked the difcourfe and behaviour of thofe in the room with them. They foon found that the fubjects of their converfation, were entirely on matters of trade, ftock-jobbing, and the method of ftriking the moft lucrative bargains. *Probus*, cafting his eye over the door, perceived, that the name of the room in which they were, was *Profit*, it being wrote in large capitals. On this,

this, *Probus* was determined to enter into conversation with them.

Prob. Gentlemen, you all seem to understand the mysteries of trade.——

Their discourse was then suspended, and they all turned their eyes towards the Pilgrims; and, one whose name was *Lucre*, replied,

Lucre. We know a little of matters; but trade is now so fluctuating, and times are so bad; that the most knowing can get but little in the fair way.

Prob. As you all seem well-disposed to adopt any profitable scheme, I can inform you of an infallible method, by which each of you may make his fortune [1].

Lucre. Say you so, Sir. I fear that you are too sanguine. You seem to be but a young man to us; therefore, I suspect, that you have taken up with some airy scheme; for we, who are in years, and well acquainted with men and things, find it a very difficult matter to obtain a plumb.

Prob. I am an entire stranger to your abilities, but I am certain that what I have said, is true, and has been found so by many.

Then they all looked eagerly on the Pilgrims for some time, at length a venerable old man, named *Gripe*, said,

Gripe. I have been starving myself and family for many years, and yet have not accumulated a sum sufficient to retire from business: and, can *you*, who are but a boy, shew any method of getting money which has not been tried already by old *Gripe!*

Prob. I believe I can, Sir: for I dare affirm, that you have never thought on the scheme which I shall propose.

Gripe. There certainly is some quirk in your scheme, or it could not have escaped my penetration.

[1] Proverbs viii.

Prob.

Prob. There is no quirk in it at all, Sir; but you may find it to be a plain, rational, and certain way of obtaining great riches.

Gripe. You feem to be ferious, indeed: but fuppofe you and I ftrike a bargain, fo that I may have the exclufive benefit of your plan.——

Lucre. Ah, old *Gripe*, are you in the monopolizing way again! You cannot leave off your old tricks. The gentleman offered it to us all, therefore keep off your clutches, and be content with your fhare.

Prob. I am willing that you all fhould reap the benefit of my fcheme.

All. Pray, let us hear it.

Prob. Why, in brief, it is this. That you all would fet out on pilgrimage.

Upon this, they all fet up a loud laugh.

Gripe. I knew there was fome trick in it. Pilgrimage, fay you! Why, we are all good chriftians already: but being Pilgrims will neither keep us, carry on our bufinefs, or acquire riches.

Prob. I dare fay, that not one of you has fairly tried my propofition; but if you did, you would be convinced, that I fpeak the truth.

Gripe. Pray, friend, how much are *you* worth?

Prob. Of filver and gold I have very little, nor hardly any thing elfe.

Gripe. You are, therefore, a very improper perfon to recommend to us a method of obtaining riches.

Prob. But we are rich in faith, and heirs of glorious promifes [1].

Gripe. Ah, child, fuch riches will not do for me. I may have them and yet go to the parifh. You are a raw inexperienced youth, indeed!

[1] Jam. ii. 5.

Prob.

Prob. But, if you possess this wealth, Sir, you cannot go to *Tophet*.

Gripe. Pho, I never had the least fear of going to that place; for, I thank God, I go constantly to our parish church.

Lucre. Yes, old Hunks, unless you hear, that there will be a collection at the door.

On which, there arose another loud peal of laughter.

Prob. Mr. *Gripe*, were not your ancestors very rich?

Gripe. Yes, Sir, their wealth far surpassed what I can pretend to.

Prob. I believe *that* person was related to you, of whom we are told, that he fared sumptuously every day[1], and refused to relieve a poor beggar.

Gripe. Probably he might: for my ancestors lived much better than I can do, and none of us have been accustomed to encourage vagrants.

Prob. But the person I speak of went to *Tophet* when he died[2], altho' he belonged to the best established church in the world.

Gripe. Oh, fye, fye, Sir, do not think so uncharitably of any man. I hope that all will be saved.

Prob. What, do you think that idolaters will be saved?

Gripe. No, no, I mean us christians. Idolators, you know, are heathens.

Prob. Then I fear that most of you are heathens. I have heard nothing talked of among you, but how to get money. *That* seems to be your idol *God*, and *St. Paul* says, that such covetous men are idolators[3].

Gripe. You are a scripture man, I perceive: but I think you had better mind your business, and leave the scriptures to the clergy; who are well paid for reading them. Many a fair pound have they had of me; which, with its interest, would have

[1] Luke xvi. 19. [2] Luke xvi. 23. [3] Eph. v. 5.

made

made a round sum by this time; but both principal and interest are gone for ever.

Prob. The parson is not to answer for your faults or mine, unto the great *Judge of all:* therefore, it is incumbent upon us to read and think for ourselves.

Worldly. Sir, I have tried your way of proceeding, but could not live in it.

Prob. Pray, Sir, what have *you* done in this way?

Worldly. I came on pilgrimage hither, but could never thrive: so I united with these gentlemen, and soon found the benefit of it.

Prob. Did you come by the way of the *City of God?*

Worldly. I came from the *Town of Vanity*, and dwelt some time at the *City of Self*, in *Arminian Wood.* From that city I came on in the spacious road, called *Arminius's Highway*, which led me far to the left of the *Delectable Mountains*, into the pleasant *Country of Conceit*, which borders on this ground. In a town of that country, named *Profit*, most of us reside.

Prob. You appear to be a lover of this world, consequently the love of *Jehovah*, and of true religion, is not in you[1].

Lucre. Gentlemen, you are very severe. You have interrupted us in our business. We have much to do, and desire that you would keep your conversation to yourselves, or retire into another room.

The Pilgrims, finding that they would hear them no further, were desirous of seeing the company in the next room, who seemed very joyous. Among them, therefore, the Pilgrims went, and were gazed at, by all those bacchanalians, with great attention. At length, one of them said, "Hand about the bowl to the new comers." But, when the Pilgrims declined to drink, they were requested to oblige the company with a song. This *Friendly* promised to do, if they would keep silence. On this offer, one of them who was master of the ceremonies, and

[1] 1John ii. 15.

named

named *Rubicus*, from his red face [1], commanded silence. Then *Friendly*, who had a clear, strong voice, began to sing a hymn, on the superiority of religious pleasure to carnal mirth.

" When in the light of faith divine,
" We look at things below,
" Honour and gold, and sensual joy,
" How vain and dang'rous too!

" The pleasures that allure our sense,
" Are dang'rous snares to souls,
" There's but a drop of flatt'ring sweet,
" And dash'd with bitter bowls.

" *God* is my all-sufficient good,
" My portion and my choice,
" In Him my vast desires are fill'd,
" And all my powers rejoice.

" In vain the world accosts mine ear,
" And tempts my heart anew,
" I cannot buy your bliss so dear,
" Nor part with Heav'n for you.   WATTS.

When *Friendly* began to sing, the company were filled with surprize and confusion: however, they let him go on to the end; then said the master of the ceremonies.

Rubicus. Sir, your song is too good for this place. We did not expect such serious things from you. We are met here to enjoy ourselves. Our time is devoted to mirth and gaiety. Every thing is beautiful in its season. There is a time for every thing [2], and few of us would care to be absent from our church on a Sunday.

Frien. You asked me for a song, and I gave you such as I had, for I know no other sort.

Rubic. What, not acquainted with one good fellowship song! O, Sir, you are a stranger to the pleasure there is in good company.

[1] Prev. xxiii. 29.   [2] Ecclef. iii. 1.

Frien. I hope I know more about true pleasure, than any of your noisy tribe. I suppose that you are all in pursuit of *that* goddess, whose name I see is wrote over the door of this room. But you are all deceived by a vile phantom, who has assumed her name. True pleasure gratifies every desire of the soul; but, is there any one of you perfectly satisfied with what you seem to enjoy? Amidst all this tumult of mirth, is not every heart conscious of a latent sorrow[1]? And do not you call for the bowl to drown the uneasy reflections of your minds?

While *Friendly* spake these words, one of the company laid his head on the table, and appeared to be much agitated: but, the master of the ceremonies, stung with resentment, exclaimed,

Rubic. A *Jesuit!* a *Father Confessor*, no doubt! But, I assure you, Sir, that you are mistaken for once: here are none for your purpose: we are, to a man, all stanch *Protestants*.

Frien. Bacchanalians rather! For shame, gentlemen, do not metamorphose yourselves into brutes. Several of you, I perceive, are already intoxicated, and most of you will be so before morning. I would advise you rather to betake yourselves to a pilgrim's life. *Therein* you will find pleasure without a sting.

Rubic. Your preachment, Sir, only spoils good company. Pray, gentlemen, who sent for you hither? None of us are disposed to follow your advice. Your absence would give general satisfaction.

Then all, but him who laid his head on the table, arose, and seemed like a herd of swine[2], disposed to rend the pilgrims: wherefore they withdrew, and entered the remaining room, which was the *Parlour of Honour*. A report of their complexion had already reached this party, so that the company was in confusion, as soon as they came in; and a *Bully* began to blast his eyes roundly; declaring, that they were men of honour, and would suffer no sneaking pilgrims among them.

Ref. Pray, Sir, have you any eyes to dispose of?

[1] Prov. xiv. 13.   [2] Mat. vii. 6.

Bully.

Bully. What mean you, Sir? I am a man of honour, and will suffer no indignity.

Ref. Nor am I treating you with any, Sir. I only asked you a plain question. If you are weary of your eyes, you had better dispose of them to some poor blind man, who knows the worth of them, than blast them in the horrid manner you do.

On this, they all laughed at the *Bully*; but he replied in a rage.

Bully. Sir, you are very affronting.

Ref. Pardon me, Sir, I meant not to affront. As you appear to be a gentleman, I hope you will behave as such.

All. We are all gentlemen, Sir, and will hear nothing of your religion.

Ref. Why, religion and good breeding are not contrary to each other.

Haughty. Yours, Sir, is not the way to shine in the world.

Ref. Give me leave to say, it is; and to shine in another world too[1]; when such honour as you pursue, will be treated with eternal contempt[2].

Haughty. Gentlemen, we hear that you have treated the company in the other rooms with great scurrility: but we, who profess the noble science of arms, will by no means suffer such treatment.

Ref. Gentlemen, true courage and honour are ever attended with sense and good manners. If you are *such* persons, you will not be offended; but, if you think to frighten us with lofty looks, and swelling words; you are greatly deceived. We are not ashamed of our profession as pilgrims, which is far more ancient and respectable than that of arms. *Your* honours and employments are transitory, but *ours* are durable and everlasting[3]. *We* have much to lose, whereas *you* possess nothing but airy phantoms.

Haughty. What, do you make us only a company of scarecrows?

[1] Matt. xiii. 43.   [2] Dan. xii. 2.   [3] Prov. viii. 18, 21.

Ref. By your appearance, you are men; but, by your reasoning, and sentiments of honour and dignity, you seem weak and childish.

Haughty. Be not affronting, Sir; we are all men of consequence, either by estate or honourable preferment.

Ref. Remember, gentlemen, the words of your favourite bard.

" Honour and fame from no condition rise,
" Act well your part, *there* all the honour lies." POPE.

It appears to me that you are out of the way to the temple of honour, and are blindly following an *Ignis Fatuus*, which will decoy you to a precipice, and there destroy you. Join with us, therefore, for ours is the only way to immortal glory, and never-fading honour[1].

Haughty. Gentlemen, be gone; you only insult us with your foolish propositions: we lately expelled *Captain Scot* from among us, because, like you, he affronted us with sentiments, which it does not become us to hear, or attend to.

Hereupon, several arose, looked very fierce, and drew towards *Resolute*; who began to redden and shew a stern countenance, saying,

Ref. Sirs, do not assume more consequence than is your due. We do not desire to continue here. You are not company for us[2]. But you may be certain, that it is the meanness of your sentiments, and not the terror of your looks, that obliges us to retire. We have already encountered the *Black Tyrant*, your lord and master, therefore we have no reason to fear any of his servants; and the less so, as we know it frequently happens, that those who bluster most about honour, have least of true courage in their composition.

So saying, the Pilgrims quitted the room, and several followed them in great wrath. They were met at the door of the inn by others from each of the rooms, who began to be very

[1] Prov. iii. 35.   [2] Gen. xlix. 6. & 1Cor v. 11.

clamorous

clamorous; infomuch, that the miſtreſs of the houſe came, and inquired, what was the matter?

Gripe. Matter! why you have introduced perſons among us, who ſay, that godlineſs is the only way to be rich[1]; which is an affront to all of our company, as it is contrary to our eſtabliſhed maxims.

Rubic. And, hark you, *Mother Jez.* If ſuch fellows as theſe are permitted to diſturb us, you may ſhut up your ſhop, and diſpoſe of your liquors ſome other way: for I proteſt, by my red face, that I will not viſit, where I am in danger of being interrupted by ſuch ſtrange mortals, as think it a ſin to drink a bottle, and ſing a good ſong.

Bully. By my honour, I feel myſelf groſsly inſulted; and, had theſe been perſons of any credit, I would have called them to a ſevere account, for thus affronting gentlemen of character. Keep ſuch ſcum[2] of the earth from our room, Mother, for the future, or you will ſuffer a total deſertion of every man of ſpirit.

Jezebel. I am ſorry, my children, that this affair has happened. I *thought* they were of the ſanctified ſtamp, but was in hopes, that ſome of you would have reconciled them to *life*, as you have, many of their brethren. This was my view in introducing them, or they ſhould not have entered my doors.

All. Pho! they are incurable by all our methods of reduction; and, if permitted to ſtay here, they will turn every one of your rooms into a conventicle.

Jezebel. Heaven forbid! for then I ſhould be ruined indeed! What, are they your *Holders-forth?*

Rubic. Aye, that they are: and, I believe, have already done ſome miſchief; for honeſt *Tom Goodman* has been in his religious dumps again, ever ſince they came into our room.

Jezebel. I am ſorry for him.—Get ye hence, fellows, or I will ſend for my friend, *Juſtice Shallow,* and have you laid by the heels.

[1] 1 Tim. vi. 6.   [2] 1 Cor. iv. 13.

Sincere. We do not intend to abide here; for we know, Madam, that you, and your children, your house, and all who are found in it, will be burnt up[1]: and this dreadful scene may happen very soon: wherefore——

Here *Sincere* was interrupted; for the whole company from the rooms united to sing a ludicrous song, made by the drunkards, on the Pilgrims, to ridicule them and their manners[2]. The Pilgrims, therefore, departed in haste, altho' it was very dark. Just as they had got into the way, a dreadful clap of thunder broke over the *Globe Inn*; which interrupted the song, and the singers all ran terrified and screaming into the house: but the Pilgrims went on singing,

" We send the joys of earth away,
" Away ye tempters of the mind,
" False as the smooth deceitful sea,
" And empty as the whistling wind.

" Lord, we adore thy matchless grace,
" That warn'd us of that dark abyss,
" That drew us from those treach'rous seas,
" And bid us seek superior bliss."   WATTS.

CHAP. XLI.

Conversation on their treatment at the Globe Inn. *The Pilgrims are joined by* Mr. Goodman. *Mr. Proteus found repairing an old Idol Temple. A dialogue with him.* Goodman *relates his adventures.*

THE song being finished, the Pilgrims entered into the following discourse.

Prob. Brother *Resolute*, the scenes at the *Globe Inn* bring to my mind those days of vanity, which you and I spent over our

[1] 2 Pet. iii. 10.   [2] Psalm lxix. 12.

bowls

bowls, in roaring out foolish and obscene songs, or playing at cards, &c. Well might a pilgrim say, the time past of our life may suffice [1] for walking in such folly.

Ref. I reflect on them with shame, to think on the depravity of my soul, at that time; and, with rejoicing, at my present deliverance. O how glad should I be to recover, if but one soul, from the ruin which I am sure they are hastening to!

Prob. I bless the *Lord* that we were enabled to bear any testimony to the evil of their ways: and, with pleasure I perceived, that one was struck with what our brother *Friendly* said.

Frien. Are those all the rooms in that Inn?

Prob. So said an experienced judge, who appears to be well informed, both of the house, the mistress, and the company [2]. He also declares, that if any man loves to sit wasting his time, in any of those rooms, neither *Immanuel* nor his *Father* will love him.

Sincere. When they all united to turn us out of doors, I thought of *Immanuel's* words. "Marvel not if the world hates you, for you know that it hated me first [3]." And of his servant's observation. "Wherein they think it strange, that you run not with them to the same excess of riot; speaking evil of you [4]."

Frien. What pilgrim would keep company with such men as hate his *Lord?*

Prob. I thank the *Lord*, that I find no inclination either to the company, or the diversions of the persons who frequent such houses.

Sincere. To one whose soul is alive unto *Immanuel*, these things must be very irksome.

The Pilgrims hearing the sound of feet behind them, turned, and perceived a man coming hastily after them: as he drew near, they found him to be the same person who laid his head on the table, when *Friendly* rebuked the intemperate sons of *Bacchus*. His name was *Goodman*. Being come near the pilgrims, he

[1] 1 Pet. iv. 3.   [2] 1 John ii. 15, 16.   [3] John xv. 18.   [4] 1 Pet. iv. 4.

fell

fell on his knees, and, with a torrent of tears, begged to be received into their company.

Prob. Arife, friend, and tell us your name, and whence you came.

Goodman. My name is *Goodman* [1], a vile backflider. And when I am a little more compofed, I will relate my whole ftory to you; but, in the mean time, permit me to walk on with you, tho' I am abfolutely unworthy of fuch an honour.

Prob. Be compofed, my friend, and prepare to acquaint us with your hiftory.

Ref. I think I perceive a building on the right fide of our road, and hear fome perfons at work thereon.

As they advanced they found it to be an old edifice, under a repair, on which a few perfons were working in the dark, directed by a man clothed like a clergyman of the *City of Eftablifhment.* When he faw the pilgrims, he came to the road, and faluted them. *Probus* then knew him to be one *Mr. Proteus*, an old acquaintance of his, and thus addreffed him.

Prob. Sir, I am glad to fee you, but am alfo forry to find you building in fuch a place and manner. Pray, what is your defign in this?

Proteus. Why, after much inquiry, I have at laft found that the *Pilgrim World* has hitherto, for many hundred years, been miftaken, as to the right object of their religious worfhip; therefore, I am determined to build a temple, in which will be exhibited the true method of adoration, of the *Supreme Jehovah, and his Chrift.* This is a difcovery of my own, and will immortalize my name. I have been fo happy as to difcover an ancient edifice erected in the apoftles days, but has been quite neglected, and lay in ruins: this I am repairing, and it will foon make a ftriking figure in the *Pilgrim World.*

Prob. Friend *Proteus,* you have fo often changed your opinion, that your credit is quite loft among pilgrims. You have fucceffively forfaken the *City of Eftablifhment, Independent-ftreet,*

[1] Acts xi. 24.

and

and the *City of God*. You are now got building on the *Enchanted Ground*, and in the dark too. A goodly reformer truly! This antiquated fabric, which you say was the work of the apostles of *Immanuel*, is no other than an old idol temple, built by *Sabellius* the idolater. How could you imagine, that the *Pilgrim World* has been hitherto deceived in such an important point, as is the right object of their religious worship? Consider, Sir, your sentiments spring from great infidelity, and lead to the grossest idolatry. Pilgrims can as soon believe that their religion is false, as that its divine author is not properly and essentially the son of *Jehovah*; or, that the whole *Pilgrim World* has been so fundamentally wrong above seventeen hundred years.

Proteus. I find you are pleading for creeds and human authorites; you must learn to look above these things, or you will never obtain a necessary freedom of inquiry.

Prob. You build in the dark; and, by what I can see of it, your edifice is destitute both of proportion and consistency.

Proteus. I follow exactly the scripture rule. I regard no one beside.

Prob. The scripture is all beauty and consistency; and, to be plain with you, I fear that you follow your own whimsies.

Proteus. You are partial. Come in, and see what we are about.

Prob. I am quite satisfied with my present faith, and like no innovations.

Proteus. I have shewn the true character of the mediator. I have proved that he is to be worshipped, but not with the same degree of worship as the supreme *Jehovah*. And I have drawn a curious line, to mark the exact degree of worship that is to be given to this *human* mediator. This has hitherto been a secret from the foundation of the pilgrim religion.

Prob. A secret indeed! And it had been happy for you not to have known it now. O, Sir, I cannot too much honour that omnipotent *Lord* who loved me, and gave *Himself* for me[1]:

---
[1] Gal. ii. 20.

therefore,

therefore, your nice diſtinctions will not ſuit me. You are fatally deceived; this ground has a bad effect on your mind. Come, leave your idol foundery, and romantic ſchemes. Call hither your journeymen, *Charles* and *Hackney*; and return back to the good old way, in which you once took ſo much delight: but, if you continue in your perverſeneſs, be aſſured, your building will fall, and bury you in its ruins.

Proteus. By no means: for tho', like you, we were once confuſed in our ideas, and talked nonſenſe; yet we now know better, and will not return to folly.

Prob. On the contrary, we think, that you are *now* deceived, and talk blaſphemy. You had better, therefore, be adviſed, and return immediately.

Proteus. So far am I from recanting, that I affirm, whoſoever does not viſit my temple, and worſhip as I direct, is guilty of rebellion againſt the *moſt high Jehovah*.

Prob. For ſhame, *Proteus*, renounce ſuch monſtrous errors. Are *you* only wiſe, and all pilgrims wrong?—But it is all in vain to talk with a man of ſuch ſentiments. May *Immanuel* have mercy on you, and forgive you.

Then the Pilgrims turned away from *Proteus*, who went to his temple laughing at, and ridiculing their ſentiments and behaviour.

Prob. My brethren, this man's caſe is very awful. He once appeared to be a very pious and uſeful ſervant of *Immanuel*; he was mighty in the ſcriptures, and remarkably ſerious and upright. But now, you ſee, that he is fallen ſo low, as to have mean thoughts of *Immanuel*, to deny his eſſential Godhead, and to ridicule thoſe who think moſt highly of him, and endeavour to keep in the good old ways of the *Lord*.

Frien. The way of ſin is down hill, and precipitated. Errors, of the nature which this man has adopted, are very pernicious, and ſtrike at the precious life of the ſoul.

Sincere. Let us leave him in the hand of *Jehovah*. And now, *Mr. Goodman*, to keep us from drowſineſs, pray oblige us with your relation.

Goodman

Goodman. I am very ready, for the glory of our *King*, to declare his wonders to my foul; altho' they fill me with confufion, under a fenfe of my ingratitude. I was born in *Dark Land*, and brought up in a country life, without any learning, not being able to read any book, nor caring at all about it. When I arrived to man's eftate, I was ftruck with a deep conviction that I was a finner againft the *Lord*, which made me very uneafy; but as I had heard nothing about religion, I knew not what ailed me; yet, became fober and ferious, and went on in a low uneafy way, two or three years. At length *Mr. Fervidus*, in his travels, came our way, and I went to hear him preach; but was aftonifhed to find, that every thing which had paffed within me, of late years, was known to him; yet was comforted to hear him fay, that many perfons had been juft as I was. After fermon, I got into the company of fome good people, and found that all the preacher had faid was true, for their experience and fentiments furprizingly correfponded with mine. Thefe people earneftly advifed me to learn to read, and to go on pilgrimage. I fet out with others, and met with a kind reception at the *Gate*, and at other places, until I came to the *City of Eftablifhment*. There I parted with my company, and grew negligent of good things, by not attending to the ordinances of our *King*. At length I came on, and was decoyed into the wildernefs of *Fear*; but got thro' it, in a bye-way, that brought me to the *City of Depravity*. From thence I came on in the new road over the *Bridge of Trial*, to the *City of Senfuality*; and fo acrofs the country to the *City of Vanity*. Thus I ftrayed from fide to fide, until I became quite regardlefs of the *King*'s highway. I had, indeed, learned to read and write, and made a little progrefs in feveral ufeful ftudies; but, to my fhame, I muft confefs, that I neither read the bible, nor prayed to *Jehovah*, for fome years. From the *City of Vanity*, I wandered thro' bye-paths, and crofs roads, afar to the left even of *Arminian Wood*, and out of fight of the *Delectable Mountains*; in a way which none know, but fuch horrid backfliders as myfelf (of which I hope there are not many). At length, I wandered near the borders of this ground, and came to the *Town of Infenfible*, in the *Country of Conceit*, and there I fixed my abode:

from

from thence I frequently visited the *Globe Inn*, to spend an idle hour, and to stifle intruding reflexions.

There I was carousing, when you came in. I knew by your dress what you were, and secretly hoped to see you intoxicated; which you certainly had been, if you had drank with us. But when this brother, contrary to expectation, began to sing a hymn, I was smote to the heart. All my backslidings appeared before me, which, with the well known hymn, tune, &c. united to paint me as a most vile and detestable deserter, of what I knew to be my greatest honour and happiness. And when he defended his conduct to *Mr. Rubicus*, I fell down slain by his words, and could no longer hold up my head. After you were retired into the next room, my companions tried to rally me out of my reverie: but I boldly told them, that I had offended *Jehovah* and my conscience, by forsaking the company of such men as you, to unite with them, who, I was sure, were in the broad way to destruction. While the rout happened about you at the door, I stole out, and retired to a private place; where I poured out my burdened soul to the *Lord*, and, like *Peter*, wept bitterly: beseeching my offended *Lord* to pardon my great sins, and enable me, for the future, to unite with his servants, and continue stedfast unto the end. I then ran after, and soon overtook you, and am heartily thankful for your receiving me into your company.

Prob. Brother *Goodman*, you are welcome among us; may a deep sense of your folly, *Jehovah*'s grace, and *Immanuel*'s love, ever abide with you; that you may no more foully draw back, and so grievously transgress.

The Pilgrims then gave him the right-hand of fellowship, and poor *Mr. Goodman* was encouraged, and began to recover his spirits.

C H A P.

C H A P. XLII.

The Pilgrims walk in great darkness. Their various trials in that state. The sun shines. They arrive at the Arbours of Worldly Ease. *Many asleep there.* Mr. Truman, *a pilgrim, discovered, and awakened.*

AFTER *Mr. Goodman* had related his story, they went on for a long while discoursing very comfortably on *divine* things; at length, they began to think the night unusually long; so one of them examined his watch, and found that it should be broad day-light, at that time. This threw them into much perturbation, which was increased when they found that instead of the day-breaking, it rather grew more dark; and, at length, the clouds and fogs were so thick, that they formed a darkness which could be felt.

A thousand ominous apprehensions, concerning this gloom, filled the minds of the Pilgrims; and boding fears, of various sorts, made their poor hearts tremble. At length, a voice broke through the horrid vail, saying, "Who is among you that feareth the *Lord*, and obeyeth the voice of his servant, that walketh in darkness, and hath no light; let him trust in the name of the *Lord*, and stay himself on his *God*[1]." This was very encouraging unto them all, but *Resolute* especially felt the power of it, and said,

Res. I was fearful that what we experienced in this place, all true pilgrims were quite unacquainted with; but now I find that a man may be a good pilgrim, and yet walk in such darkness[2],

[1] Isaiah l. 10.   [2] 1 Cor. x. 13.

I am directed to trust in the *Lord* as *my God*, and by his grace I will stay myself upon him.

However, as the Pilgrims had been so much used to daylight and sun-shine, their present circumstances were the more irksome to them, and they longed for the day, but no light appeared. Now they began to grow cold, and drowsy, and peevish with each other; nor were they, as heretofore, desirous of conversing, or being together. So they separated, and walked at some distance from each other; every man ruminating on his own dreary situation, and breathing out a sense of his distress, and his earnest desires for the return of day.

Sincere. Lord, I cannot bear this unusual eclipse of thy dear face.—My heart breaketh for the longing that it hath for thy appearing.—When shall I come and appear in the presence of *Jehovah* [1]. When wilt thou come to me, O my *Lord!* I will walk in thy way with a perfect heart [2]. O *Immanuel*, it grieves me sore to lose thy soul reviving smiles; but thou art holy in thy dealings with me, and mightest have plunged me into the blackness of darkness for ever [3].—Thou art a sovereign, and wilt visit me in thy own time: but be thy stay long or short, it is my duty and resolution, by thy grace, to wait for thee [4], and keep on in my way *Zion* ward*.

As for *Friendly*, he was inveloped in melancholy reflections, and went on weeping bitterly, because the comforter that should comfort his soul was far from him [5]. Said he,

Frien. Oh, *Lord*, the thing that I feared is come upon me. Was there ever any pilgrim's sorrow like unto my sorrow! I go forward, and cannot find my *Lord*; I look backward, and cannot see him: I turn on my right and left hand, where he worketh, but cannot behold him [6]! " Oh, for a glimpse of him my soul adores!"

[1] Psam xlii. 2.   [2] Psalm ci. 2.   [3] Jude 13.   [4] Habak. ii. 3.
[5] Lam. i. 16.   [6] Job. xxiii. 8, 9.

* This is a genuine sign of a real pilgrim: tho' he walks in darkness, yet he holds fast the truth, and holds on steady in the way of *Jehovah*.—W. M.

Prob.

Prob. Why tarry the wheels of thy chariot, sweet *Immanuel?* When shall the day break, and these gloomy shadows flee away'! Come, my beloved, nothing in *Heaven*, or on earth, can compensate for thy absence. Nothing can indemnify me for the loss of thy smiles! I will have no consolation but thee, dear *Lord:* if thou dost not appear I will go down, weeping for thee, to the grave.

Goodman. Lord, I richly deserve to be cast into outer darkness, where there is weeping and gnashing of teeth for ever. But these, thy faithful sheep, what have they done, that thou thus withdrawest from them! Oh, let not these, thy servants, suffer for such a rebellious *Jonah* as I am. Let me be cast into the belly of *Tophet*, as I deserve; but let these, my brethren, rejoice in the beams of thy countenance.

As for *Resolute*, he went on like a lion in the dark. Altho' he felt a lively sense of his loss, and had some inward conflicts of soul, yet his faith triumphed over them all. Thus he reproved and exhorted himself.

Res. Why art thou cast down, O my soul, why art thou at all disquieted within me[2]! This is a darkness of *Jehovah's* sending, and it is much better to walk in *His* darkness, than in our own light; for all who walk in the light of their own fire, shall lie down in sorrow[3]. But, O my soul, trust thou in *Jehovah*, for I shall yet praise him, who is the health of my countenance, and my *Jehovah*.

As *Resolute* went on thus struggling with himself, behold a *Fiend* of an hideous aspect met him! and said,

Fiend. Wherefore are all these womanish complaints? Why all this childish whining?

Res. Who art thou? Surely thou art of the infernal pit, or near akin to those *Fiends*, whose misery it is, to be without *Jehovah*, and not be troubled about it! Be who, or what you will, know, that I mourn the absence of my best, my dearest, my almighty friend.

[1] Cant. ii. 17. [2] Psalm xlii. 5. [3] Isaiah l. 11.

Fiend.

Fiend. Your lofs is chimerical only, for you never enjoyed *His* prefence of whom you fpeak.

Ref. Sayeſt thou fo to my face! Lying *Fiend*, begone! Thou mayeſt as foon perfuade me that I never faw the fun, or felt his beams: depart, I fay, or I fhall exercife this rod on thee, for thy prefumption.

Fiend. What is that, more than a weak reed, that I fhould regard it?

Ref. You fhall foon feel, if my *King* will affiſt me.

Upon this, *Refolute* ſtruck at the *Fiend* with all his might, and the rod fell fo heavy on him, that it made him howl, and fly away with great precipitation. Immediately, there came a voice from *Heaven*, faying, "Refiſt the *Tyrant*, and he will flee from you[1]."—As foon as *Refolute* had put his enemy to flight, he heard the voice of *Probus*, crying out in a moſt difmal manner. This roufed all the Pilgrims, and they forgot their own forrows, to haſten to the affiſtance of their brother. They found him ſtanding aghaſt, with his eyes fixed right forward, at fomething that was invifible to them.

Prob. Yonder is a moſt tremendous monſter, and it makes towards me!

Ref. *Probus*, what is the matter with you? We can fee nothing.

Prob. Oh, it is *Death*, in a moſt horrible form[*]. He looks ſternly at me, but takes no notice of any other.

Ref. You have no reafon to fear, fuppofing it fhould be him.

Prob. I was always weak on *that* fide: and he now threatens me with fome peculiar terrors.—Oh, he is near! Save me, fave me, *Lord!*———

Then poor *Probus* fell to the ground in the utmoſt diſtreſs; his brethren endeavoured to comfort him, but in vain, until a voice from *Heaven* fpoke to his foul. "Fear not, *Probus*, for I am with thee; be not difmayed, for I am thy *God*[2]." Then

---

[1] James iv. 7.   [2] Ifaiah xli. 10.

[*] This refers to the cafe of the author, as hinted in the preface.

he arose, and with some pleasure cried out,

Prob. For ever blessed be the *Lord*, my spirits revive; but the grim monster still stalks close by me.

Frien. My dear brother, *Death* should not be terrible to a pilgrim.

Prob. Nor would he be so to me, I trust, in his common shape; but this form is peculiarly terrifying. I never heard of a pilgrim being thus visited; and for one, who has been so highly distinguished, to go off in such a way, is most grievous to reflect upon—I was sinfully uneasy while separated from you, and could not submit to the will of our *King*, but thought it was the greatest trial I could endure. The *Lord* granted my request, by restoring me to you; but, by this visitation, he shews me, that he can soon imbitter all my sweets.—I am but just given unto you, and must now be snatched away, by a most terrible death.—Oh, his dart is lifted up!——

On this, *Probus* fell down in a swoon. When he revived, the horrid spectre still stood before him, ready to strike the fatal blow; which brought such a dread upon him, that he trembled in every limb. Then, behold, the voice from *Heaven* said again, "*Probus*[1], thus saith thy *Lord*, the *Lord*, and thy *God*, that pleadeth the cause of his people; behold, I have taken out of thy hand the cup of trembling, even the cup of the dregs of my fury; thou shalt no more drink it again." This sweet and precious promise, mightily strengthened him.

Res. My brother, remember your former courage, and what we have seen and felt of *Jehovah*'s care and indulgence towards us. Let this encourage you to look up in faith and hope.

Prob. Ah, *Resolute*, I once thought that I had some faith; but, alas, it fails me now. And I am more than ever convinced, that without *Immanuel*, its author and finisher, I can do nothing[2]. Pray for me, my dear friends, that *Jehovah* may increase my faith, and save me.

[1] Isaiah li. 22. [2] John xv. 5.

So they all kneeled down, and *Friendly* prayed, as did *Probus*, until he and all his brethren wept fore. A voice then broke thro' the gloom, a third time, saying, "*Probus*[1], thou shalt not die, but live and declare the works of the *Lord*."— This revived and set *Probus* on his legs, so that they all went forward; but the monster still lurked about *Probus*, and was very dismaying unto him; till the clouds parted, and the day poured its enlivening rays on the Pilgrims. Then said

Prob. The *Lord*, in this trial, has given me such evident testimonies of his peculiar favour, that, dreadful as my case was, I cannot even wish that it had not happened unto me.

The sun now shone with meridian splendour, and was the more glorious to the Pilgrims, from the suspension of his beams, which they had lately endured. They, therefore, began to sing, and express the happy sense they felt of *Jehovah*'s love to their souls.

" Our *God*, our life, our love,
" Our everlasting all,
" We've none but thee in Heav'n above,
" Or on this earthly ball.

" The shinings of thy face,
" How amiable they are!
" 'Tis Heav'n to rest in thine embrace,
" And no where else but there.

" Nor earth, nor all the sky,
" Can one delight afford,
" No, not a drop of real joy,
" Without thy presence, *Lord*.

" Thou art the sea of love,
" Where all our pleasure rolls.
" The circle where our passions move,
" And center of our souls."   WATTS.

The Pilgrims went on singing, until they came to some pleasant arbours, built by the way side, in which they saw several

[1] Psalm cxviii. 17.

persons asleep. A man standing at the entrance of one of the arbours, invited the Pilgrims to come in, and rest themselves; as it was high noon, the weather warm, and they had been travelling all night.

Ref. Pray, Sir, who are you? And who have you got asleep in these arbours? I think this is a very bad place to sleep in.

Ease. My name is *Ease*. I am a near relation to the *Lord* of the manor, who has built these booths for the refreshment of pilgrims. I have good wines, gentlemen, walk in, and sit down, until these pilgrims awake, and then you may all go on together.

Ref. Ease is very desirable to pilgrims, and never more so to us than at present; but, I do not like your pedigree. You have no intent to serve us, nor have you any connection with our *Lord*; who has commanded us to hasten off this manor, because it is not our rest[1]: wherefore, Sir, we are not for your turn. See you this wand?

Ease. Yes, and I perceive you are no friend of mine.

Then *Mr. Ease* instantly withdrew into an adjacent thicket. The Pilgrims went into the arbours, and examined the sleepers, by shaking them heartily; but they were as dead men. At length, said

Ref. Who can tell but that some *one*, at least, of these sleepers, may be a true pilgrim? I will try what effect my wand will have on each of them.

So he applied it to the eyes and ears of the sleepers, but without any success, until he came to the last; who opened his eyes, began to rouse himself, and, looking round him, exclaimed,

Sleeper. Good *Lord!* where am I? Who are ye? I fear all is not right!

He then arose, and ran out of the arbour in great haste.

Ref. Stop, friend, and take good company with you.

[1] Micah. ii. 10.

Sleeper. I cannot tarry: the *Lord* pardon me; what a wretch have I been!

Ref. Why, we are your friends, man, and will accompany you.

He then turned to them, and they all went on together. *Resolute* told the sleeper where they found him, and by what means he had been awakened. At which he was amazed, and expressed many thanks for their great kindness towards him.

C H A P. XLIII.

Mr. Truman's useful story. A Shining One *brings a message to* Goodman *and* Truman. *The affecting manner of* God's *dealing with penitent backsliders. They all enter the* Land of Beulah.

Sincere. NOW, good friend, we should be glad to hear from you, how it happened that we found you asleep in *that* place: and what is your name.

Truman. My name is *Truman*[1]. I have great reason to be thankful for your kindness to me; but my story will neither be honourable to me, nor, I fear, profitable to you.

Prob. That is more than you can tell: but do not you think that it will tend to exalt the mercy and goodness of our *King?*

Truman. That it undoubtedly will, and I am amazed that I am not in the infernal pit!

Sincere. Well then, pray let us hear what *Jehovah* has done for your soul; which I hope will make us walk more carefully over the remainder of this ground.

[1] John i. 47,

Truman

Truman. I was born in the *Town of Stupidity*, there married, and abode many years; but was notoriously immoral in my conduct; being a prophane fwearer, and grofsly propenfe to the beaftly fin of drunkennefs. This I continued to practife in defiance to the laws of *Jehovah* and man. Several preachers, in connection both with *Mr. Fervidus* and *Mr. Duplex*, vifited our town, and prevailed with many to go on pilgrimage; yet, I remained ftupidly regardlefs of whatever pafled of this fort. I never attended their preaching, nor was at all folicitous about any thing, unlefs it was how to gratify my brutal inclinations.

At length, it pleafed *Jehovah* to reclaim me, in a very fingular way, by fending to me a young female preacher. This was my eldeft daughter, about nine years of age. She was wrought on by the grace of our *King*—principally by hearing *Mr. Mether Lively*, a worthy ambaffador, in connexion with *Mr. Duplex*. This child, who had never feen nor heard any thing of religion before, grew furprizingly in the knowledge and love of divine things; and frequently admonifhed me of the danger my foul was in.

A few months after this change in her, fhe was taken ill, and faid, that both fhe, and her younger fifter, fhould die, and go to the *Celeftial City*; which accordingly came to pafs. While lying fick, fhe was continually employed in devotion, in warning and entreating me, to repent, and go on pilgrimage. After her death, I was made to hear the voice of *Jehovah* in my child; and, after fome difcourfe with *Mr. Lively* and others, I fet out on pilgrimage, and was gracioufly received at the *Gate*. Nothing very remarkable happened to me, 'till I came to *Freewill Foreft*, when I was almoft perfuaded to enter *Arminian Wood*, and refide in the *City of Self*. This inclination I believe was the caufe of the ftorm which came on me, while I was pafling by *Goodwin*'s-*Sand*. I kept clofe down to the riverfide, to avoid being buried in the clouds of fand, which were raifed by the wind. But the wind fhifted round to the north, and left me no way to efcape fuffocation, but by throwing myfelf into the river; which I did, after calling earneftly on the *Lord*. While I was in the water, I found myfelf wonderfully held up; the wind foon abated, and prefently appeared the

Covenant Transport; which took me up, and brought me safe to the *City of God*.

Prob. That was a miraculous and most gracious deliverance indeed!

Truman. It was so; and indeed, a pilgrim's life is all miracle: we are fed, and clothed, and preserved by miracle. I found afterwards, that it was nothing new to be supported from sinking in *that* river, for Dr. *Deptford* who then commanded the *Transport*, told me, that no man was ever drowned in the *River of Life*; but the more a person drank of the water, the lighter and stronger he swam.

When I came to the *Plain of Obedience*, I grew weary and whimsical; and nothing would satisfy my vicious mind, unless I examined the width of *that Plain*. I left the highway, therefore, inclined far to the left, and persisted in my search, altho' I found it not so pleasant and easy travelling as in the common path. At length, I was accosted by a decent looking man, whose name I afterwards found was *Indifference*. He appeared glad to see me. I asked him if we were in the *Plain of Obedience?* He told me, he should be very sorry if we were not; for he was going on pilgrimage, and had chosen to walk at that distance from the highway, for the benefit of reflection. I was glad to find such a companion; so we came on in a bye-road together, until we had far advanced on this ground, and were come to the *Globe Inn*. My partner would enter there; and prevailed on me to follow him into the *Parlour of Pleasure*. The bowl was handed to me, and I drank freely from a vain conceit of my ability in the art of drinking ‡ without being intoxicated: but *that* single draught was the principal cause of all my future misfortunes. The noise and obscenity of the company soon disgusted me, but my companion presently entered into their excesses, and forgot his journey. On this, I watched an oportunity, and withdrew, running as for my life, until I had got at a great distance from the house.

‡ Isaiah v. 22.

When

When I stopped to take breath, looking back, I saw a young man running towards me; he soon drew near, and saluted me very kindly, saying, that he saw me retire from the company, guessed that I was a pilgrim, as he also was: therefore, was determined to follow on, and be my companion, if it was agreeable to me. I told him that I had no objection to his company; and asked, if he knew the person who entered the Inn with me? He told me, his name was *Indifference*, and that he was employed, by the mistress of the house, to procure customers for her.

As we advanced, I endeavoured to bring my companion to some close religious conversation; but he evaded it with so much simplicity and good temper, and found so many topics of unimportant yet pleasing discourse; that I could neither contradict nor interrupt him; but grew fond of his company; tho' there was not an atom of real religion discoverable in what he said. My being thus infatuated with his discourse, I now consider as the natural consequence of my intimacy with *Mr. Indifference*, and drinking at the *Globe Inn*.

At length, night came on, and I grew drowsy; my companion observing it, proposed to sing an harmless song to enliven me. I told him, I was not used to sing or hear any thing but hymns. Upon this, he enlarged, for some time, on the harmlessness of love songs, chearful songs, loyal songs, &c. He acknowledged, that he was no advocate for obscene and impious songs; but always opposed them; he again pressed me, to hear him sing; at last I consented, and he sang such a soothing air, that I was more inclined to sleep than before.

When we came to the arbours, my companion immediately entered *that* in which you found me, crying, "Bless me, this is just what we wanted." Instantly, another likely person appeared, who, with much earnestness, desired me to come in, and sit down. I told him it was very dangerous so to do, because, the people at the *Mountains* bid me beware of sitting down on the *Enchanted Ground*. "Very true,' said he, "but you are now on the farther border of the *Enchanted Ground*, and may be said to have fairly complied with their instructions. You have endured much fatigue, and have not slept; wherefore, step in, and sit down, if it be only for half an hour, that you may enter the *Land of Beulah* in good spirits" To all this, my companion united *his* arguments, and chid me for taking every caution in the most severe sense. He said, "that pilgrims very often impose on themselves, and were more austere and abstemious than nature, reason, or religion required of them." So, with much persuasion, I complied; and the young man brought us a bottle of wine. My companion was soon very merry, and began a song, which, with the tune, I well remember seemed calculated to lull me to sleep. Just as he finished, the other person said to him, "well done, *Careless*, encore, encore." I was nodding, but at these words I roused, and, reflecting, on what company I was in, jumped from the seat, saying, *I am decoyed*; but had not walked six steps before I fell down, went fast asleep, and from that time until you awakened me, I lay quite insensible to any thing that passed. I certainly must have slept a long time', and it is an infinite mercy that I did not sleep the sleep of death, as I fear my companion will do. He told me, that he came from the *City of Vanity*.

Prob. Brother, I thank you, in the name of my friends, for this edifying story, which is full of the *Lord*'s wonders to your soul, and striking admonitions to us. Every pilgrim who wanders either to the right or left from the common *Path of Obedience*, will soon grow indifferent to his *Lord*, and weary of his holy ways. In conforming to the world he will be ensnared by *Careless Ones*, and slumber in the arbours of *Worldly Ease*, where so many sleep their last. But our *Great Shepherd* will never suffer his own sheep to be thus plucked out of his hands[2], nor to destroy their own souls. Tho' they may be sure, that our

[1] Matt. xxv. 5.   [2] John x. 28.

King

King will visit their transgressions with his rod, yet his covenant of grace towards them he will not break[1], nor suffer his truth to fail. Here is cause for watchfulness, and matter of triumph.

While *Probus* was speaking, they perceived a *Shining One*, with a scroll in his hand, coming towards them. This raised a variety of thoughts in their minds. As he drew near, they knew him to be the divine *Prince Paraclete*, and saluted him with the profoundest respect. He asked,

Prince. Which of you are named *Goodman* and *Truman?*

They then presented themselves trembling; and he further asked,

Prince. Are not you the Pilgrims who were found, one carousing at the *Globe Inn*, the other sleeping in the arbour of *Worldly Ease?*

Both. We are, indeed, the *men* who were so vile, so foolish, and ungrateful; therefore we are not worthy to be called *Pilgrims* by our *Lord*.

Prince. Your behaviour is known to your *King*, and he has sent me to inform you, that he is much displeased with your conduct[2].

These words were like daggers to the hearts of the criminals. They had only strength to say, " Thy just rebuke, O *Lord*, has wounded our hearts[3];" and then fell as dead men at the feet of the *Prince*. Their brethren ran to them, lifted them up, and they somewhat recovered; but sighed deeply, wept bitterly, and exclaimed frequently, " Behold we are vile ! Ah, ungrateful, ah, foolish *Goodman* and *Truman*, thus basely to treat your best, your *celestial* friend !"

Upon this, the *Prince Paraclete* said, with a sweet countenance.

Prince. I am also to acquaint you both, that your *Lord* waiteth to be gracious unto you[4], and has therefore sent you a form of prayer, by which you may speak freely unto him.

[1] Psalm lxxxix. 33. [2] Judges ii. 1—5. [3] Psalm lxix. 20. [4] Isaiah xxx. 18.

He then gave to each of them a paper, and difappeared. They humbly kiffed the paper, and began to read; in doing which, they were obliged to wipe the gufhing tears from their eyes. The forms were alike in both papers, and ran thus, " Take unto you words, and turn unto the LORD *your* KING, and fay unto him, Take away all iniquity, and receive us gracioufly, fo will we render the calves of our lips; the fpiritual facrifice of praife and thankfgiving¹." When the two Pilgrims had read the papers, they fell on their knees; but their hearts were fo full, they could not fpeak: they, therefore, held out the papers towards their friends, as much as to fay, Brethren, pray for us. So they all kneeled round their penitent brethren, who watered the ground with their tears, while *Probus* cried to the *King* in their favour. Prefently a light fhone on them, and they faw the fame fplendid Being as before, now flying fwiftly towards them: who, being arrived, faid,

Prince. All hail, Thus faith your *Lord*, " Behold², I have put away your fins, O *Goodman* and *Truman*, ye fhall not die. In a little wrath I hid my face from you, for a moment, but with everlafting kindnefs will I have mercy on you ³."

Both Pilgrims then fell proftrate to the ground before the *Prince*, and poured out a flood of tears, which eafed their ftruggling hearts; and they exclaimed,

Both. Oh, aftonifhing grace! But we are wretched and abominable backfliders.

Prince. I well know it, and will heal your backflidings⁴.

Both. But we can no more expect that nearnefs and communion with our *Lord*, which we were formerly fo indulged with; and this is grievous to us.

Prince. To remove this grief, I inform you particularly, That your *Lord* will receive you gracioufly to the fame communion as before.

¹ Hofea xiv. 2.   ² 2 Sam. xii. 13.   ³ Ifaiah liv. 8.   ⁴ Hofea xiv. 4.

Both.

Both. Yet, we muſt bid farewell to thoſe raviſhing enjoyments of his love, which we felt when he ſweetly ſhed it abroad on our hearts.

Prince. The thoughts and ways of *Jehovah* are not like yours, but high and godlike as becomes his glorious majeſty [1]. He knew that your tranſgreſſions would raiſe various ſuſpicions in your minds, of his grace towards you; on which account, I rejoice to inform you further, that your *King* loves you freely, and will treat you in future as if you had never oſſended him. The blood of *Immanuel* cleanſeth you from all ſin; therefore, he [2] will do all this and more for you.

All. Oh, how great is his goodneſs! How great is his beauty [3]!

Prince. Therefore is the *Lord* exalted that he may ſhew mercy on you: for the *Lord* is a *God* of judgment [4], bleſſed are all thoſe who wait for him. *Goodman* and *Truman*, be comforted. And ye *Probus*, *Reſolute*, *Friendly* and *Sincere*, men greatly beloved, ye ſhall ſoon ſee greater things than theſe [5]. You are near the delightful land of *Beulah*. Yonder, ſee how the golden gates reflect the rays of the declining ſun. I will fly and inform the guard of your approach. *Goodman* and *Truman*, be comforted. Farewell.

So ſaying, he ſpread his *Celeſtial* plumage, and left them.

The Pilgrims were now filled with inexpreſſible joy and heavenly peace. They were near the glorious *Land of Beulah* [6], the gate of which dazzled their eyes. For, over it, on a magnificent pediment, was emboſſed, in characters compoſed of ſparkling rubies, the following inſcription. *The Gate of Beulah*. On each ſide of this portal was an inacceſſible wall, which extended beyond the ſight of the Pilgrims. As they drew near, *Governor Promiſe*, who had the charge of the gate, came forth to meet them; having been informed who they were by *Prince Paraclete*.

[1] Iſaiah lv. 8, 9. [2] 1 John i. 7. [3] Zech. ix. 17. [4] Iſaiah xxx. 18.
[5] John i. 50. [6] Iſaiah lxii. 4.

On the governor's approach, the Pilgrims faid,

Pilgrims. Open unto us, Sir, this gate of righteoufnefs, that we may enter into it, and praife the *Lord Immanuel*[1].

Promife. This, Sirs, is the *Gate of Immanuel*, and only *Righteous Men* may, or fhall enter therein[2]. Thefe are my inftructions.

Pilgrims. We are *Righteous*, we are *Comely*, but it is only thro' the righteoufnefs and comelinefs of our *Immanuel* put upon us, and working in us[3]. Not unto us, but unto him be all the glory[4].

Promife. Ye are my dear children, I perceive. Thofe who are of the law are not heirs to this glorious inheritance, nor will ever enter this gate: but the *Children of Promife* are counted for the feed[5].

Governor Promife then cried aloud, EPHPHATHA[6], and inftantly the golden doors flew open to the found of trumpets, harps, and various inftruments of mufic; which filled the air with exquifite harmony, and the hearts of the Pilgrims with ravifhing delight[7]. Thus they triumphantly paffed from the gloomy, wafte, and dangerous *Enchanted Ground*, into this terreftial *Paradife, the Land of Beulah*. Their inward joy at this change naturally iffued from their lips in the following fong of praife, with which the mufic harmonioufly joined.

> " Salvation! Oh the joyful found!
> " 'Tis pleafure to our ears.
> " A fov'reign balm for every wound,
> " A cordial for our fears.
>
> " Bury'd in forrow and in fin,
> " At *Hell's* dark door we lay,
> " But we arife by grace divine,
> " To fee a heav'nly day.

[1] Pfalm cxviii. 19. [2] Pfalm cxviii. 20. [3] Ezek. xvi. 14. [4] Pfalm cxv. 1.
[5] Rom. ix. 8. [6] Mark vii. 34. [7] Ifaiah lxii. 5.

" Salvation!

"Salvation! let the echo fly,
"the spacious earth around,
"While all the armies of the sky,
"Conspire to raise the sound. WATTS.

CHAP. XLIV.

The Pilgrims arrive at the Angel Inn *in the* City of Hephzibah. *A description of the City, and* Land of Beulah, *by* Dr. Knowself, *recorder of the city. A dialogue between the* Doctor *and* Mr. Demure *a* Perfectionist.

THE Pilgrims proceeded on their way rejoicing, thro' vineyards, fruitful fields and gardens, which were free for all, both to use and walk in. The inhabitants came out to welcome them into this country, and as they passed on, joined them in their songs of praise. This whole territory is cultivated by a divine hand, and its inhabitants were celebrating a great jubilee. So that our Pilgrims went on in triumphant joy, until they arrived at the great metropolis of the land, named *Hephzibah*; which was situated on the eastern border, by the side of a broad river. The citizens gave them a joyful reception, and conducted them to the *Angel Inn*[1], in *Communion-street*, kept by *Mr. Bewley Love*, who saluted them with a glowing heart, and a shining face. A supper, in the rich stile of that delightful country, was instantly prepared for the Pilgrims; at which, having feasted high, and chaced away all their cares and fears; they set down and entered into conversation with their host. Just at this time, a lively well-looking gentleman came in; to whom said the host,

[1] Zech. xii. 8.

Love.

Love. Your servant, *Doctor.* I am glad to see you, especially now as I have these guests just arrived; who would gladly be informed of the state of our city and country, in which they are come to reside. And, who, is more capable of giving them satisfaction, than you? Brethren, this is our worthy friend, *William Knowself,* doctor of laws; whose long residence in this city, has qualified him to execute a work, which, for its usefulness among pilgrims, is justly stiled, A *Spiritual Treasury.* He is recorder of the *City of Hephzibah,* and will chearfully answer any questions you please to ask him.

Knowself. Friend *Love,* were I not well acquainted with your real sincerity, I should confider you as a flatterer. But I entreat you to be more sparing of your encomiums; for, though I live in the *Land of Beulah,* yet I am still in the body, and have too much nitre in me, to venture near such sparks as have just issued from you. If you mean, therefore, to have my company, you must no more fire off such serpents.

The Doctor then saluted the company, welcomed them to town, and seated himself.

Prob, Sir, we are just arrived in this noble city, and should be greatly obliged to you for a brief account of the town and country.

Knowself. There is a peculiar pleasure, Sirs, in describing this city and country. For I am about to give you a description, not of an *Utopia,* which exists only in the minds of *Theorists*: nor am *I* about to treat, and *you* to hear, of a territory at a distance, and the property of an unknown people: no, but in describing the *Paradise of Beulah,* and the glorious *City of Hephzibah,* I shall be only exhibiting to you, a small, but excellent part of our eternal inheritance. May *my* heart burn, and *your* souls rejoice, while I declare to you, that,

This city is named *Hephzibah*[1], because the *Lord* delighteth in it. It is the metropolis of the *Land of Beulah*; so named, because *Immanuel* has united it to himself by a solemn marriage covenant. This land was formerly a part of the *Enchanted Ground,* and was

[1] Isaiah lxii. 4.

a wild, desolate and barren wilderness; situated between two unknown worlds; for the inhabitants neither knew whence they came, nor whither they were going.

The land is four square, and not very large. On the west-side it is bounded by the *Enchanted Ground*, and on the north and south by the *Terræ Incognitæ*. It is surrounded on these three sides by a very high wall, made of the same materials as that round the *City of God*. The grand and common entrance is on the west, by which gate you came. In the north and south sides are only two small postern gates. The north postern is guarded by *Captain Eade Vigilant*, from *Baptist-street*; and the south by *Captain Bradbery Diligent*, from *Independent-street*; but the west gate is under the charge of *Governor Promise*; who is superintendent of this country, under the *Prince Immanuel*. That gentleman is much older than the world[1], tho' he looks so well; and he does not deceive us, for he is to the full as good as he appears to be. Some *Ignoramuses* indeed, give out, that he is slow and dilatory, in performing his word[2]; but I have always found him most wise and faithful; and, even in his very delays, most gracious. He has a younger brother, stationed with him at the gate, whose name is *Captain Menace*[3]; and when any false pilgrims presume to approach the gate, he only shews his terrible arms, and they flee away immediately.

The east side of the land is bounded by a broad river, which, from the person who presides over it, is called the *River of Death*. It arises in the *Land of Execration*, and runs into the *great Abyss*.

This spot of ground was formed into its present beauty, fruitfulness, and security by *Immanuel* and *Prince Paraclete*: and these divine persons have given us their covenant and oath, sealed with their signet, and ratified with *Immanuel*'s blood, that it shall no more return to its former desolate state[4]. This covenant is lodged in the archives of this city.

The country is a perfect *Paradise*. Here the *Tree of Life* grows common; and *living Water*, in a thousand meandering

---

[1] Titus i. 2.   [2] 2 Peter iii. 9.   [3] Rom. i. 18.   [4] Isaiah liv. 9. 10.

streams,

streams, refreshes the land and its inhabitants. Here are the brooks of honey and butter. This is the land of oil, olive, and honey; a land of gardens and vineyards. Here are mountains of spices, and every valley is an *Eschol*, every meadow rich with a profusion of beautiful and fragrant flowers. So that the whole land is like one great altar of incense, which is ever breathing its sweet perfume towards the munificent creator.

Here is no war nor tumult, no savage beast, noxious reptile, nor poisonous herb. The inhabitants are all righteous in *Immanuel*, and are washed from their sins in his blood. They carry in their bosom the *King*'s free pardon, the love of *Prince Paraclete* rules their hearts, and he influences and assists them in every good word and work.

As to this city; the plan, and all the buildings in it, are the work of our *Prince*. Its inhabitants, and those of the land, were all [1] orphans, desolate, afflicted, tormented, and tossed with a variety of troubles, before they arrived here. But now, they are, and know themselves to be, the sons of *Jehovah*; and each has his name enrolled in a charter of amazing immunities, respecting their everlasting holiness and happiness. These things, all true pilgrims, wherever they are, have a title to; but all *our* people have the pleasure of enjoying the knowledge of it; and, at certain seasons, they are all convened to meet in the *Court-hall* of the city, on *Mount Transport*; where I, in my place, read their charter to them. These times are always honoured by the presence of *Prince Paraclete* and his *Shining Ones*, who join their music with ours, and the joy is so great that we hardly know whether we are in, or out of the body.

The city is governed by a mayor and aldermen. Our present magistrate is the worthy *Mr. Keen*, a man of deep penetration, and tried worth. *Mr. Heavenlymind* is chamberlain of the city, and he is a person of more worth than all the riches and treasures in his custody. The excellent *Dr. William Apollos* is our bishop, and the pious and charitable *Dr. Liberal* is our archdeacon; besides whom, there are many eminent divines among us, who came from the *City of Establishment*, its

[1] Isaiah liv. 11.

suburbs,

suburbs, and various other parts of the *Pilgrim World*; who all live in the greatest harmony with each other. The city is large, unwalled, and built on several eminences; on one of which, called *Mount Preparation*[1], there are lodgings providing for you. On that hill are several delightful terraces, from which there is a commanding prospect of the goodly country on the other side of the river, quite to the gates of the *Celestial City*; the music of which place is frequently heard by us. In short, there would be no end in speaking of the pleasures and honours to which your *Lord* has brought you.

Prob. Your description, Sir, is animated and noble; but is not all this pleasure dashed, by your near and constant view of the *River of Death*, and its grisly *King*?

Knowself. He is, indeed, called an enemy to pilgrims, and the last enemy[2]. But the prospect which we enjoy of the celestial country, on the other side of the river, makes us consider *Him* as ours; that is, as our servant[3] to introduce us into those joys, which we cannot experience until he has exercised his power on us. Besides, we know that this grisly *King* is conquered by our victorious prince, and doomed to destruction[4]. This decree having been proclaimed in all the streets of this city, and thro' all the land; whenever this enemy visits the city he is despised and insulted, even by the women and children of our country.

It now grew late, and *Mr. Knowself* took his leave of the Pilgrims, with a promise of waiting on them the next day. They then retired, and spent a happy night in a room of the Inn, called the *More excellent Chambers*[5], by *St. Paul*, when he slept there.

On the next day, soon after breakfast, *Dr. Knowself* visited the Pilgrims, and informed them, that he was just going out of town, by order of the mayor; who had received intelligence from *Captain Vigilant*, at the northern border, " That there was a strange people arrived from an unknown region, who called themselves *Perfectionists*; said they were going to the *Celestial*

[1] Matt. xxiv. 44. [2] 1 Cor. xv. 26. [3] 1 Cor. iii. 22. [4] 1 Cor. xv. 26.
[5] 1 Cor. xii. 31.

City, and demanded entrance into the *Land of Beulah*; but he had refused them admittance until he heard further from the city." Upon this news, said *Dr. Knowself*, I am ordered to go and examine them. If you chuse to go with me, I shall be glad of your company.

The Pilgrims being very fond of seeing curiosities, immediately accepted the recorder's offer, and set out with him for the north postern. When they arrived, *Mr. Vigilant* opened the gate, and found these extraordinary persons, few in number, dressed very plain, their countenances remarkably reserved, and all employed in singing hymns on perfect love. The Recorder thus addressed them.

Knowself. I am deputed, Sirs, by the chief magistrate of the *City of Hephzibah*, to inquire, from whence you came, and whither you are going?

Then one of them, named *Mr. Demure*, replied.

Demure. We are perfect men. We came from the *Town of Vanity*, thro' a pleasant country, and are going to the *Celestial City*.

Knowself. By what means were you induced to go on pilgrimage.

Demure. By the preaching of that excellent *Minister of the Lord, John Duplex*. We continued with his people in our town, until we obtained a testimony from him, that we had received the *perfect gift*; and then we set out on pilgrimage.

Knowself. How is it that you came not by the good old way, which is so well known?

Demure. It was too common and unclean for us. We saw so many therein who had been guilty of great crimes; and others who complained of so many corruptions, and of so much inward impurity; that we could not bear to walk with them. So we left our city, by the way of *Fancy lane*, which brought us into the extensive *Country of Conceit*; from thence we passed into a region unknown to any but such as we are, called the *Wilderness of Imagination*; and so have come on unto this gate.

Knowself.

Knowself. Yours is a strange and round-about way indeed!

Demure. But it is a pleasant and safe way; for we met with no *Giants* in it, passed no *Shadows of Death*, nor deep humbling *Vallies*; we met with no *Fiends of Tophet*, nor trod on the *Enchanted Ground*. These things, which so many pilgrims are tormented with, we have happily escaped.

Knowself. I do not like your rout. I never heard of any *true* pilgrim taking this course. Pray, did you see any thing of *Mount Sinai?*

Demure. No, Sir, we never saw any thing of such a mountain.

Knowself. Were you never at the *City of Formality?*

Demure. As it is not far from our city, before we set out on pilgrimage, we went and sojourned some time at the *Pharisee Inn*, in that very religious place; and obtained much comfort, instruction and experience there.

Knowself. And what think you of *Immanuel*, and salvation by him?

Demure. Oh, Sir, we are always talking, thinking, and singing of him. We are in no fear of being happy with him for ever.

Knowself. What reason have you to believe that you are in his favour, that your sins are pardoned, and that you will be received into the *Celestial City?*

Demure. We have complied with all the terms and conditions of the Gospel covenant, find our hearts entirely devoted to *Jehovah*, and our thoughts ever fixed on heavenly things. We have no lusts of the flesh to trouble us: no desires of a criminal or worldly nature to perplex us.

Knowself. You seem, indeed, to have walked in an unfrequented path!

Demure. The generality of those who are called pilgrims complain much, but we sing much; they fear much, we love much; nay, we enjoy a perfect love to *Jehovah* which casteth out all fear. We are confident, and honour the gospel, by shewing that it gives us a perfect deliverance from all sin, and from all fear. There is no fear in love; but most pilgrims, who would be thought to love *Immanuel*, are, nevertheless, full of fears.

Knowself. Altho' there is no fear in love[1]; yet, you are to know, that there may be fear, and much fear to, even where the love of our *King* is; and I wish there were more fears in you, left you deceive your own souls.

Demure. Do you think that we are telling you an untruth? Lying and deceiving we hate and detest.

Knowself. I believe you speak as you feel things, and according to your knowledge; but I fear that you are unacquainted with your own hearts. Do you find no opposition in you to the will and ways of *Jehovah?*

Demure. God forbid we should: for we are born of *God*, therefore cannot sin[2].

Knowself. Then you do acknowledge the final perseverance of the saints?

Demure. No. We only believe that such as *we*, who have received the *perfect* gift, cannot sin, we being *wholly* born of God.

Knowself. It appears to me, that you know neither the nature of sin, nor true holiness: that is, you are strangers unto yourselves.

Demure. You are very censorious; and I must say, that altho' you dwell in that pure region, yet you are not made perfect in love.

Knowself. St. *Paul* prays that the love of the *Philippians* might abound more and more, in all knowledge and in all judgment[3]. Love without knowledge, such as you pretend to, is *Enthusiasm*; and knowledge without love is *Antinomianism*. Love and knowledge must unite to form a perfect pilgrim. You say that you are without sin, and yet can give no good account how you got rid of sin, or what sin is.

[1] 1 John iv. 18.   [2] 1 John iii. 9.   [3] Phil. 1. 9.

Demure.

Demure. Sin is the tranfgreffion of the law.

Knowfelf. What do you mean by the law?

Demure. I mean the moral law, or ten commandments.

Knowfelf. What, as they are explained by *Immanuel* in his fermon on the *Mount?*

Demure. Yes.

Knowfelf. And are you without fin in that fenfe?

Demure. We love *God* with all our hearts, our fouls, mind and ftrength, and are entirely dead unto fin, even in thought. Sin, both in the root and fruit is quite deftroyed; it has no being in us.

Knowfelf. Do you make any ufe of the *Lord*'s prayer; and pray for the forgivenefs of fins?

Demure. Yes, we ufe it as a general prayer.

Knowfelf. So you think that the petition for forgivenefs of trefpaffes is to you only a general, or public, not a private prayer; altho' our *Lord* recommends it as a private or clofet duty[1]. I find that your fancied freedom from fin, confifts principally in your ignorance of the nature of it. To be plain with you, I think fin has deceived you, and lies yet undiflurbed in your hearts. By your own confeffion, you never were at *Mount Sinai*, therefore you know not what fin is; for, fays *St Paul*, I had not known fin but by the law[2]. I advife you therefore to make a journey to that mountain, and then inftead of your prefent notions, you will confefs, that in your flefh dwells no good thing[3].

Demure. God forbid, that we fhould feel fuch things! *St. Paul* does not fpeak of himfelf in that chapter.

Knowfelf. Then there is no truth in the plaineft words.

Demure. If he does, it muft be of himfelf before he was converted.

Knowfelf. Suppofe it be fo, he even condemns you then: becaufe you, at no time, have feen yourfelves in fuch a light.

---

[1] Mat. vi. 6.   [2] Rom. vii. 7.   [3] Rom. vii. 18.

Demure. All men are not brought to *Immanuel* in the same way.

Knowself. All true pilgrims are, in some measure, emptied of themselves; and the weakest in grace know more of themselves than you appear to know.

Demure. I suppose you would have us complain of wandering thoughts, hard and unbelieving hearts, a body of sin, a proneness to evil, &c.

Knowself. I would have you to be sensible of these things, and then I am sure that you will complain of them.

Demure. What! are *Jehovah*'s people never to have deliverance from these things?

Knowself. You do not appear ever to have groaned under them, so that you have nothing to do with deliverance from such things as you never felt.

Demure. We make *Immanuel* a *whole* Saviour from sin, you make *Death* a greater Saviour from sin than *Immanuel* himself.

Knowself. By no means. You may with equal propriety say, That *Death*, by slaying *Immanuel* made an atonement for us, as that he saves us from sin when we die. *Death*, in the hand of our Redeemer, is only an instrument to separate us from our flesh, in which dwells no good thing.

Demure. Some of us think that they shall not die at all.

Knowself. So said one of you, in the *City of Vanity*, a few years ago; but he died a sudden, and most awful death. So said also another, a remarkable *Bell-weather*, who now is openly profane, and ridicules all professions. If you think the same, you had better keep out of this land, for, I assure you, we know of no way to the *Celestial City*, but thro' the *River of Death*.

Demure. Cannot *Immanuel* save us from all sin, and corporal death too?

Knowself. He not only *can* save his people from all sin, but he really does so.

Demure.

Demure. Aye, you mean in the *Antinomian* way of being compleat *in Him:* but I mean in *ourselves:* that is, a perfectly sinless state.

Knowself. Immanuel can do many things, which he neither has promised, nor ever *will* do for us in this world. He could save us from corporal pain and death, but we know he will not. If you are not willing to be compleat *in Him*[1], you will obtain real perfection in this world, no other way. Nor can you associate with the people of this land; for *Immanuel* is all in all to us. So I advise you to make a journey to *Mount Sinai*, and come hither in the common road, and then I shall be glad to see and receive you.

Demure. We are happy on *this* side the wall; but as we were informed, that there are no *Backsliders*, *Antinomians*, *Woulders to do good but doers of evil*[2], nor any *Complainers of a body of sin and death*, among you; we are desirous of rejoicing with you, to do more credit to religion.

Knowself. You imagine that religion is more indebted to you than you are to religion. There are no such persons among us. It appears that you can do very well without *Immanuel*, and his perfect righteousness imputed to you, wherefore we can dispense with your company. There are none among us but will acknowledge with grief, that they have often backslidden from *Jehovah*; and still find a law in their members warring against the law of their mind; so that they cannot be so lively in the service of the *Lord* as they would[3].

Demure. Is it, indeed, so with you? Then we have been misinformed: but we can shew you greater things than you have hitherto seen; and it will be useful to the service of holiness, if you receive us among you.

Knowself. Altho' a perfect freedom from the being of sin is most desirable, and what we are pressing after, yet, as we have no encouragement from *Jehovah*'s word, or the experience of the best pilgrims in all ages, to expect *that* blessing, while in this

[1] Coloss. ii. 10.   [2] Rom. vii. 15.   [3] Gal. v. 17.

world;

world; we defire not to be wifer or better than He has thought it neceffary we fhould be here. We give thanks to our *King* for promifing, that fin fhall not have the dominion *over us*[1], and we wait his time for its abfolute deftruction *in us*. This has been the uniform fenfe of the generation of *Jehovah*'s children, from the foundation of the world; nor will we condemn them, by attending to the enthufiaftic whimfies of a few ignorant profeffors of this day: who make holinefs to confift in a ftrict attendance at fome particular places of worfhip, in conftantly finging hymns, or, in certain fafhions of drefs, peculiar phrafes of fpeech, and a gloomy referve in their countenance; all which are fuperficial and merely external things; and may be found where there is not a grain of true fanctification. To be plain with you, I fear that you are defcendants of a generation which exifted fo early as in *Solomon*'s time, of whom he wrote, " That they were pure in their own eyes, but were not cleanfed from their iniquities[2]."

Demure. Sir, I wonder you are fo very fevere againft us, fince, I well remember that you firft enlifted under *Mr. Duplex* in our corpfe, at which time you contended for *Perfection* alfo.

Knowfelf. I own I was once of your company, and under your foul deceiving delufion, and fo I was alfo once an inhabitant of the *City of Deftruction*; but this is no reafon why I fhould continue either in fin or error. All I can fay is, that *Jehovah* is gracious to poor finners. He commanded the true light to fhine into my confcience, whereby I was led to know myfelf, efcape error, embrace the truth, and to glory only in, and of, the *Lord our Righteoufnefs*. It was well for me that this happened; for I could never have been admitted into the *City of Hephzibah* while in your ftate; for an ancient record of that city declares, that whofoever fays he has no fin deceives himfelf, and has no truth in him[3], nor can be a member of that corporation. So, *Mr. Demure*, you can by no means be admitted. Thefe gates are opened only to the righteous *who keep the truth*. May it be your mercy to be convinced of your errors, and taught to know yourfelves better.

[1] Rom. vi. 14.   [2] Prov. xxx. 12.   [3] 1 John i. 8.

So saying, *Dr. Knowself*, and the Pilgrims withdrew within the postern gate; and having directed *Captain Vigilant* not to suffer any of these deluded ones to enter the land, they all returned to the *City of Hephzibah*. The mayor highly approved of the Doctor's behaviour, and informed the governor of the particulars, who gave *Dr. Knowself* a letter of thanks for his wise and upright conduct on this occasion.

The habitation of the Pilgrims being now fitted up for them, they removed thither. It was in a very pleasant part of the city, on *Mount Preparation*, and the windows faced towards the *Celestial City*, whither the Pilgrims often looked, and ardently longed for the glorious appearance of *Immanuel*[1]. The mayor, recorder, chamberlain, archdeacon, and bishop of the city frequently visited them. The latter was an eloquent man, mighty in the scriptures, and a flaming preacher of the *Gospel of Immanuel*.

C H A P. XLV.

Dr. Apollos, Bishop of Hephzibah, *his reasons why pilgrims must pass the River of Death. His sentiments on the covenant love of Jehovah.*

ON a certain fine day, the Pilgrims and their friends were walking on the terraces of the city, and considering the river which rolled between them and the celestial country; when *Probus* said,

Probus. My good Bishop, wherefore is it that pilgrims are subjected to the dangerous passage of this river, at the end of their many trials?

[1] Titus ii. 13.

Apollos.

Apollos. The grand reason to be assigned for this, is, That it is the appointment of our sovereign *Lord,* the *King* of yonder city[1].

Prob. I hope that it will not be deemed impertinent, if I inquire, what other reasons you can offer, why we are to pass the river? And, whether our *Immanuel*'s death was not sufficient to redeem us therefrom?

Apollos. There can be no doubt of the sufficiency of *Immanuel*'s atonement, for any purposes it had pleased the father to extend it unto; even for the redemption from death, not only of human souls but bodies also; and not only for the elect who are and shall be saved, but for the whole race of mankind.

Probus. You seem, Sir, to rest its efficacy wholly upon the *Will of Jehovah.*

Apollos. And there it must rest, and not on a want of sufficiency in our *Lord*'s work, nor on the want of power and grace in *Jehovah.*

Prob. How then can it be said, that He willeth not the death of a sinner.

Apollos. Such words are written not to militate against the power or love of *Jehovah,* but to vindicate the rectitude and goodness of the divine government in the rational world: and they strongly imply, That all intellectual Beings, even the impenitent themselves, both men and fiends; will acknowledge at the day of judgment, that *Jehovah* has dealt patiently and equitably with them; and had a just right to expect from them, as free agents, far other returns than they made to Him; and that he will be righteous in taking vengeance on their sins [2].

Prob. But with respect to the corporal death of pilgrims, do you think it to be any part of the penal evil of sin?

Apollos. I do think it is; for the wages of sin is death [3].

Prob. How is it then that the blood of *Immanuel* appears not to be of so general good unto the elect, as sin is a general evil?

[1] Heb. ix. 27.   [2] Rom. iii. 5.   [3] Rom. vi. 23.

Apollos.

Apollos. We are too short-sighted in our views of *Jehovah's* government, to determine whether or not *Death* is an evil unto good men: that is, Whether the death of pilgrims, altho' it be a part of the curse due unto sin, may not be continued upon them, to serve some wise purpose, which shall redound more to the glory of *Jehovah*, and the good of his people, in the end; than if they, like *Enoch* and *Elijah*, had been translated to the *Celestial City*, without seeing *Death*. I am inclined to believe it is; therefore the apostle has put *Death* into the inventory of a pilgrim's estate. *Death is yours*[1], says *St. Paul*, that is, shall work for your advantage.

As to the question, Whether the efficacy of *Immanuel's* blood was sufficient to preserve us from death? There can be no doubt of it: for, if it justifies our souls from guilt, it certainly could redeem our bodies from death, from all pain and disease of every sort. But, *Jehovah* having thought fit to subject his people for a time to these trials, we may rest assured, that in the end this disposal will appear wisest in him, and best for us. And in truth, the present life is so short and vain, when compared to things of an eternal nature, that if all the possible evils that can happen unto us here, are considered as operating in the *least degree* for our everlasting good; they appear not only very light and trifling, but may be embraced with chearfulness. This consideration made *St. Paul* glory in tribulation[2]: and *St. James* to say, My brethren, count it all joy when you fall into divers temptations[3]. *This* has induced many great pilgrims to embrace the stake, and bless *Jehovah* for the flames.

Our bodies are redeemed by *Immanuel*, as well as our souls; but as the redemption of our souls, with respect to our conversion, does not take effect immediately after our birth; the elect being left under the power of sin for a longer or shorter time, as *Jehovah* pleaseth[4]; in order to serve the purposes of his will, so our bodies are, for a yet longer time, left under the burden of depravity and death, and suffer pain and disease, more or less, according to the will of *Jehovah*, until the glorious

[1] 1 Cor. iii. 22. [2] Rom. v. 3. [3] James i. 2. [4] Gal. i. 15. 16.

resurrection-

resurrection-day; and then His elect will be compleatly redeemed; that is, the scheme of redemption, by the life and death of *Immanuel*, will be then consummated. For this cause, that memorable event is called *The Adoption*, by way of emphasis. " Waiting for the adoption, that is, The Redemption of our Bodies[1]."

Prob. Sir, I thank you for this explanation. And no longer will think, that our being subject to pain and death enervates the merit of *Immanuel*'s sacrifice. But I will, by the grace of *Jehovah*, consider the trials which happen to my body and soul, and even death itself, as parts of the redeeming plan, which infinite love and power is still carrying on, by the means of *Immanuel*'s death and intercession: and which, thro' all my pains and temptations, shall continue to work together for my good; until the vast idea of the divine mind is compleated towards me, by the happy and eternal re-union of my soul and body at the resurrection.

Apollos. That is the view in which I always endeavour to see these things.

Some time afterwards the Pilgrims were honoured with a visit, from *Dr. Apollos* the bishop, *Dr. Liberal* the archdeacon, *Mr. Keen* mayor, *Mr. Heavenlymind* chamberlain, and *Dr. Knowself* recorder of the city; accompanied by *Mr. Love* of the *Angel Inn.* After a suitable entertainment, this respectable company entered into discourse as follows.

Sincere. I remember that those deluded ones, called *Perfectionists*, talked much of the love of *Jehovah*, and perfect love; now, dear Pastor, let us know your sentiments on this subject.

Apollos. You have proposed a theme that will demand the exertion of all our faculties in pursuing it. I have been long sounding this ocean, but find it to be unfathomable[2].—The love of *Jehovah* towards his creatures is divided by some, and not improperly, into covenanted, and uncovenanted love: the former is the love which *Jehovah* has to his people in *Immanuel*; the latter is the love which He has to his creatures, as they

[1] Rom. viii. 23.   [2] Ephes. iii. 19.

come

come pure and holy from his creating hands. The former love is inamissable and eternal; the latter is suspended on the obedience of his creatures.

Sincere. You believe then that there is an everlasting covenant of redemption.

Apollos. I not only believe that there is such a divine compact, but I place all my salvation[1] in it, and all my desires are drawn out to meditate on it, and rejoice therein. *Immanuel* himself, as a Saviour, is the effect of this love.

Sincere. You seem to have no idea of *Immanuel's* death causing *Jehovah* to love us?

Apollos. By no means. The scripture view of a mediator is, not that he was appointed to render the *Deity* propitious towards men; but the *Deity*, considered in three persons, are represented as establishing a covenant between themselves[2]; and appointing a mediator, by whose life and death, divine love and mercy might be extended towards sinful creatures, without any impeachment of that just and holy order which subsists between the divine attributes. This consideration made *St. Paul* say, that in our redemption by *Immanuel*, *Jehovah*[3] has abounded unto us in all wisdom and prudence. So that *Immanuel* is the *effect* and not the *cause* of *Jehovah's* love?

Sincere. And who, Sir, are the objects of this covenant love?

Apollos. Whom *Jehovah* pleases. All Beings, however intelligent, are unworthy of such an honour, even as *innocent* creatures, and much more as *sinners*. As to myself, I am confounded to think of the privilege, with which such a vile wretch as I am have reason to hope my master has invested me. For I was, the other day, a proud blind priest in the *City of Establishment*, where I was brought up, and was in great repute for learning; but not greater than my vanity thought I deserved. I preached frequently in the churches, and temple in *Arminian-street*, with great applause, and was sufficiently swelled with the idea of my own importance.

---

[1] 2 Sam. xxiii. 5.　[2] Isaiah xlix. v. 6. & Zech. vi. 13.　[3] Eph. i. 8.

But *Jehovah* was stronger than I, and soon brought down my pride, when it pleased him to reveal his son in me. On the *Lord*'s day, I was expatiating on the sufficiency and power of the human will to improve the means *Jehovah* has afforded us, and to bring about a true conversion to Him; and was warmed and elated with the imaginary force of my arguments; when lo, a voice like thunder sounded in my ears, saying, " Not of works, lest any man should boast [1]! Upon which I fell down in the pulpit as dead; from whence I was carried home, and remained insensible three days. In which time I had a clear discovery made to me of the wonderful scheme of redeeming love, and my own interest therein. On my recovery, I instantly preached the gospel which I had thus learned, and was presently taken notice of by my brethren; who soon plucked off my fine plumage, and stigmatised me as a methodist and enthusiast, and would not suffer me to preach in their churches. I therefore made a visit to the *Cross*, retired into the *Country of Regeneration*; and being appointed to command the *Covenant Transport*, I soon arrived at the *Delectable Mountains*; where I abode, until I was advanced to this most honourable See.

Thus you may perceive what reason *I* have to believe in this comfortable doctrine of covenant love; which the infernal fiends have no interest in; for *Immanuel*[2] passed by their nature. They were beloved of *Jehovah* while they kept their first estate; but as he had not condescended to bind himself unto them by covenant; when they fell, there was no provision made for their recovery, and they will never recover of themselves. The case was otherwise with us; for, altho' man fell, yet the covenant love of *Jehovah* to his elect in *Immanuel* had long before provided a remedy; and made a discovery of it by promise, immediately on the fall of our first parents [3]. By this you may perceive the immense privilege of being in *Immanuel*, in opposition to depending on our own wills, even supposing we were sinless creatures. Uncovenanted love being suspended on the obedience of a sinless being, is forfeited for ever by [4] one single transgression, as is manifest from the example of the *Shining Ones*

[1] Eph. ii. 9.   [2] Heb. ii. 16.   [3] Gen. iii. 15.   [4] Rom. v. 18.

that finned[1], and from our first parents. On the contrary, the gift of righteousness, by covenant love, is not only of *many*, but of *repeated* offences to justification of life[2]. *Jehovah*'s love not being suspended on our persons, but mediately, and as we are considered in his son; when we transgress against him, his fury does not break forth against us, as otherwise it would do; but on the contrary, his love operates to forbear and forgive us, to mortify, and at length will utterly destroy the being of sin in all his people. This is termed a being under grace; and, to be out of the covenant, is termed a being under the law; all such will be treated in a way of strict justice in their own persons, and agreeable to their own vain opinions of their abilities, and free-will: but woe be to every person who is found in those circumstances.

Trien. By what you have said, Sir, I conclude that you are a friend to the doctrine of imputed righteousness?

Apollos. I am indeed, but I must desire my brother *Archdeacon Liberal* to speak to us on that subject.

CHAP. XLVI.

Archdeacon Liberal's *sentiments on imputed righteousness. He relates his surprising adventures. An account of* Captain Hervey. Mr. Love's *discourse on the love of* Jehovah *in the hearts of Pilgrims.*

THE *Archdeacon* being thus called on by the *Bishop*, replied,

Liberal. I should be very glad to add somewhat to the pleasure and instruction of this company; and if any thing I can say of myself, or of my divine master, may contribute thereto; I cheerfully inform you, Sirs, that the doctrine of *Immanuel*'s

[1] Jude vi.   [2] Rom. v. 18.

righteousness

righteousness, imputed to a sinner for his justification, is my only hope. This robe is my defence, my beauty, and my glory. It is a garment that never wears out, nor can it ever be lost. If it had been possible for me to have been divested of it, I had been undone for ever. You must take notice, brethren, that I am a clergyman of the *City of Establishment*; there I was born and educated, and entered into holy orders, before I knew the importance of that office. I obtained my first preferment in the *City of Vanity*; to which place I removed, and preached there several years, in a manner that shewed I was better acquainted with the heathen philosophers than the pilgrim religion; but, as the knowledge of divinity was not necessary to my preferment, I procured a rich living in the *City of Establishment*. Soon after my removal thither, *Mr. Fervidus* alarmed the city with his preaching; which led me to consider more than ever the laws and government of that city, as *originally* established; and *Jehovah* was pleased to illuminate my mind in such a manner, that I determined to alter my conduct and method of preaching. I made a visit to the cross, and thus forfeited my reputation among my brethren. But I obtained a most rich equivalent from my master, who presented me with a glorious robe of his own manufactory[1], and ordered me to wear it for his sake, and set out on pilgrimage to the *City of God*. Immediately I consulted not with flesh and blood, but left the city, and had a prosperous journey until I came upon *Baxter's Heath*. On that wild desert I was taken prisoner by the *Aphorisms*, that infest the road, and carried to their village; where I was treated so respectfully, that I began to like their sentiments and way of life; and at last cast in my lot with them, and went out in their parties to rob and plunder. But, remember, I never could divest myself of my pilgrim's coat, which was given me at the *Cross*. The *Aphorisms* hated to see it, and would often give it a pull; and even foolish I myself did frequently endeavour to strip it off; but finding these attempts vain, I put the vile garments, given me by the thieves, over my pilgrim's robe, which much sullied it, and made me appear in a very singular manner.

[1] Rom. iii. 22.

With these *Banditti* I lived some time, and made depredations on the pilgrims, so that the fame of my feats and motley dress spread abroad, and became the discourse of the people at the *City of God*. At that time *Captain Hervey* resided in the city; he was a most amiable, wise, and courageous officer in *Immanuel*'s army; and *Jehovah* put it into his mind to think, that I was a real pilgrim, and detained among these robbers by some of their pernicious arts; therefore, he determined, if possible, to rescue me from them.

Accordingly, he issued forth, with a chosen corps well armed; the principal persons with him were named *Theron* and *Aspasio*. These came even to the village, and roused us while we thought ourselves secure in our strong hold. The *Aphorisms* sallied out, made one attack, and fled away: but I made a bold stand; however, I soon experienced the keenness of their swords, and fell down wounded by the captain's own hand. They conveyed me into the city, where *Dr. Evidence* soon healed my wounds.

I shall never forget the vile opinion I had of myself, when I first looked in the glass after my recovery, and perceived my glorious robe to be so defiled and stained with dung[1] and dirt, and covered with the thieves coat. I was so incensed at my folly, that I tore the coat of the *Aphorisms* from my back, and cast it from me, saying, "What have I to do any more with idols[2]." My good friend, *Capt. Hervey*, was pleased to see my indignation; and conducted me to the city fountain, where I was cleansed from all filthiness[3], and my robe appeared in its original beauty, as white as snow.

Ref. Capt. Hervey was a successful officer in *Immanuel*'s army.

Liberal. He was a man of a thousand. He had free access to our *King*, at all times. After I was washed, he took me with him to court, but I was so ashamed of my folly and ingratitude in uniting with the robbers, and plundering of pilgrims; that as soon as I entered the palace I was obliged to retire, and weep bitterly. After this, the *King* sent for me, and

[1] Phil. iii. 8.   [2] Hosea xiv. 8.   [3] Zech. xiii. 1.

told

told me, "He had freely forgiven my crimes; and that He should always esteem it as an honour done Him, if I would wear *his* livery only, and keep them clean." To this, he added, "You must set out for the *City of Hephzibah*, and there it will be told you what you are to do." When I came hither, I found that *Dr. Apollos* had received orders for appointing me *Archdeacon* of this city; but I would not believe that such a place was intended for me, there appearing so much impropriety in taking a man from a gang of thieves to fill such an honourable place of trust. But *Mr. Keen*, our mayor, said, there were several such instances on record. And the recorder affirmed, that the order for my appointment was wrote with the *King*'s own hand. So I was obliged to submit.

Ref. Was *Capt Hervey* ever in this city?

Keen. Yes; I enjoyed his company, as did *Dr. Literal* and all who are here, for some years, before he was ordered over the river. He had a lively soul, but his body was very weak.

Prob. I have heard that he was greatly favoured by his *Lord* in his passage over the river.

Apollos. Remarkably so, indeed! He had honoured his *Lord* in contending with his enemies, and *then* our *Lord* honoured him [1]. For when the day came for his going over the *River of Death*, all the other side of the river was covered with the celestial inhabitants: and a select band of *Shining Ones* came to his house, bearing an easy chair, into which the *Captain* removed, and sat smiling while they bore him, in the most gentle manner, to the river side. When they came to the brink, the waters wonderfully separated and rolled back, leaving a free passage for the saint; who was carried over the river, while he saluted his friends, and exclaimed in a rapture, *Precious Salvation! Precious Salvation!* The people on this side shouted, and those on the other side played on their harps, so that the shores rang. Even *Death*, the master of the river, was heard to say, "That he hardly ever received such an order from court, as he did about *that* officer, not to molest him in his passage." He also

[1] 1 Sam. ii. 30.

said,

said, "That himself had a particular regard for the *Captain*, because no mortal ever gave a better description of his dominions than did *Capt. Hervey.*" When he arrived on the other shore, the *Shining Ones* welcomed him by saying, "This is the man who made all the inferior creation speak to the honour of the Redeemer. Welcome, happy soul, come with us, and survey the ever verdant *Paradise of Jehovah*, and crown your labours by publishing *Reflections* on *Immanuel's Garden*, for the use of the *Celestial City.*"—The next day I preached a sermon on his passage over the river, from *Simeon's* prayer[1], "*Lord* now lettest thou thy servant depart in peace, according to thy word, for mine eyes have seen thy salvation:" Here we were again refreshed, in reflecting on the triumphant manner of his departing from us.

Frien. Capt. *Hervey* was an affectionate pilgrim, and drank deep into the spirit of *Immanuel*: I should be glad, Sir, if you would now give us your thoughts on the love of *Jehovah* as a grace in our hearts.

Apollos. Our brother *Love* who is here, will best reply to that question. He has long kept the *Angel Inn*, in *Communion-street*, and is filled with all the fulness of the love of *Jehovah*[2].

Love. My dear bishop is pleased to speak great things of me; and, altho' I dare not say, that I am unacquainted with the subject proposed, yet I will affirm, that I have nothing but what I have received from *Immanuel*: nor shall I ever forget that my original name was *Hategood*, and that I long lived in the *City of Malice*[3], the metropolis of the *County of Impenitence*, bordering on the *Infernal Lake*. There I first drew breath, altho' you now see me master of the *Angel Inn* in this city. It was the love of *Jehovah* which brought me from that dreadful region, and conducted me hither; therefore I have made it my chief study. The result of my inquiries is, that we love *Jehovah* because he loved us first[4].

Frien. Is it possible for a pilgrim to arrive at a state of perfect love?

[1] Luke ii. 29, 30. [2] Ephes. iii. 19. [3] Titus iii. 3. [4] 1 John iv. 19.

Love. If you mean by a state of perfect love, a freedom from all fear of losing the favour of our *King*, he undoubtedly may obtain it.

Frien. Then there may be perfection in this life.

Love. In *that* sense there may—but that is not a sinless state. A person may enjoy the perfect love that casteth out every tormenting fear, and yet carry about him a body of sin and death: for *St. John* does not say, that perfect love casteth out the *Being* of sin, but it casteth out *fear*[1].

Frien. Can there be sin where there is no fear?

Love. Yes, certainly. Have you at this time any fear that *Jehovah* will suffer you to become a prey to the *Black Tyrant,* and destroy you for ever?

Frien. Blessed be *Jehovah,* I have not the least apprehension of it.

Love. And do not you think that you still carry a body of sin about you?

Frien. I not only think so, but I also feel it lusting against the *Spirit.*

Love. Then you know by experience, that the *Being* of sin may consist with a fearless state. Fear hath torment: while we are in suspence whether *Jehovah* will save us or not, it is plain that our faith is weak; and, our love being ever in proportion to our faith, this suspence torments the soul. But when faith is increased to a full assurance of our salvation, then love casteth out every uneasy apprehension, and considers every dispensation of providence as the wise direction of a loving and most indulgent father.

Frien. Do you think that this perfect love may become imperfect?

Love. I do; even as, on a trying occasion, a strong faith may become weak. Experience proves, that those who enjoy great assurance of *Jehovah*'s love may become very weak in the exer-

[1] 1 John iv. 18.

cises

ces of grace. *David* and *Peter* are remarkable instances of this; and the *Father of the Faithful* himself had his fainting fits[1].

Frien. This seems to bear hard on the doctrine of the final perseverance of the saints; for that which may decrease and fail in part, may wholly perish and die. If our faith and love may thus decay, they may be totally lost.

Love. Your inference is false. *Jehovah* has no where engaged to preserve his people, while here, in a uniform state of great faith and love; but, on the contrary, he has promised that they shall not perish[2]. He has not said, That no one shall *endeavour* to pluck us out of his hand; but he has promised, that no one *shall be able* to do it[3]. He has also promised, that all our trials shall work together for our good; from whence we may infer, that a state of uninterrupted love and joy is not best for us at present.

Prob. From what you have said, it appears that grace in itself is perishable.

Love. It is no more perishable than are our souls: but, as it dwells in us, it is subject to many weaknesses. As our immortal souls by their union with our bodies are pressed with great distress; so the new man in us, altho' it is begotten of incorruptible seed, and can neither sin nor perish; yet, by its connection with our depraved nature, it is liable to much languour and imperfection: but it being the seed, and of the nature of *Jehovah*[4], it is therefore indestructible.

Prob. Sir, I am satisfied in that point; and would ask you further, What you think of the love of *Jehovah* being shed abroad in our hearts by his *Spirit*[5]?

Love. That scripture phrase shews the manner in which the *Lord* of love communicates himself to his people. You know that we have various ways of testifying our love to our wives, children and friends; but in them all, be they ever so ardent and pure, yet we feel a manifest weakness in ourselves, and often find a severe disappointment; because, with all our efforts,

[1] Gen. xii. 12, 13. [2] John x. 28. [3] John x. 29. [4] 2 Pet. i. 4.
[5] Rom. v. 5.

we are not able to move the hearts of our relations and friends. Our own bosoms may burn, and our embraces be very eager; but it is impossible for us to make the object of our love meet us with equal, nor even with one spark of affection.

This proves that our flame is corporeal and weak, and incapable of reaching the springs of love, which are in the souls of our beloved friends. But the *Being* who formed us, and blessed us with this divine affection; knows the secret wheels, and has access unto the latent movements of our souls. He that formed the ear, shall he not hear[1]? So, He who taught us to love, shall he not love? Yes; he is love essentially, and possesses the godlike prerogative of making his creatures to love him in return. When, therefore, he sheds his love abroad on our hearts by his Spirit, it is his own *Blessed Self* who then draws near unto us, and embraces us in a way peculiar to the *Deity*, who is a pure *Spirit*; and sweetly makes our souls to glow with warm returns of love to Him, who thus first manifests his love to us. It is probable that the *Shining Ones*, and the souls of the blessed, in yonder city, may have a power of expressing their love to each other, in a manner somewhat similar to *this*, by which they give and receive joys most spiritual and refined. Do not you feel a wonderful pleasure when your heavenly father thus embraces your soul?

Prob. O, Sir, it brings a joy that passeth all understanding. It is the essence of religion, and the highest exaltation of our nature!

Love. Religion would be a very insipid thing without love. What an unspeakable favour it is to be capable of the pleasure, and blessed with grace to love our heavenly Father! And what a consummate wretch is that man or spirit who cannot love his gracious creator!

Prob. I often consider it to be the quintessence of *Lucifer*'s misery, that he is for ever deprived of the pleasure of loving the author of his being.

[1] Psalm xciv. 9.

Love.

Love. Sin is a dreadful and infinite evil, becaufe it begets in the foul hard thoughts of *Jehovah*, and, in the end, an hatred of Him, which is truly diabolical. But let us dwell in love, then we fhall dwell in *Jehovah*, and He in us. Yonder bright region is the empire of love; *there this Deity* reigns, but *here* He only fojourns for a time. *There* love fits on the throne, and all His happy fubjects are continually expreffing their triumph under His government, by repeated hallelujahs.

Knowfelf. Brother *Love*, you have fpoken like the affectionate mafter of the *Angel Inn*, indeed. And that I may affift in cultivating among us this excellent grace; let me entreat this whole company to wait on me to-morrow.—For the prefent let us conclude with a fong.

" Love divine all love excelling,
" Joy of Heaven to earth come down!
" Fix in us thy humble dwelling,
" All thy faithful mercies crown.
" *Jefus* thou art all compaffion,
" Pure, unbounded love thou art,
" Vifit us with thy falvation,
" Enter ev'ry tremb'ling heart.

" Finifh, *Lord*, thy new creation,
" Pure, unfpotted may we be,
" Let us fee thy great falvation,
" Perfectly reftor'd by thee!
" Chang'd from glory into glory,
" 'Till in Heav'n we take our place,
" 'Till we caft our crowns before thee,
" Loft in wonder, love and praife."

Z 4 CHAP.

C H A P. XLVII.

The Pilgrims, with their friends, visit Dr. Knowself. *His relation of his own history. A dialogue on the submission of the heart to* Jehovah's *sovereignty, and* Immanuel's *perfect righteousness.*

ACCORDING to the aforesaid invitation, the Pilgrims next day visited *Dr. Knowself,* in company with the divines and magistrates of the city. After dinner, the Doctor took them up to an elegant and pleasant observatory on the top of his house, which was on *Mount Transport,* near the *Guild hall.* Here they were seated, in full view of the *Celestial World,* when *Probus* thus addressed the Doctor.

Prob. Sir, I think myself happy in your friendship, and in being seated on this eminence, with such a commanding prospect. I find myself better in your house than I have been for some time. Permit me now to observe, that I remember you was, some time since, challenged by the *Visionaries* at the *Postern Gate,* as having been one of them. I therefore take the liberty, in the name of my dear friends, to beg the favour of an account of your setting out on pilgrimage, and what you have met with on the way.

The whole company seconding *Probus's* motion, the Doctor replied.

Knowself. My dear *Probus,* since I knew you, I have greatly esteemed you, and can deny nothing requested by you and this good company. Yet, suffer me to observe, that the demand you make, I fear may be hurtful to me. Many are very fond of relating their own adventures. Sometimes there may be good cause for it; but too, too oft, I fear there is much of self in it, and much self-exalting sought from it. *St. Paul* seems most

clearly

clearly of this opinion, where he says, "It is not expedient for *me* to glory¹."

Prob. These suspicions come with peculiar grace from *Dr. Knowself*; but they are a further reason for our entreating to be obliged: because we are convinced, that you are sufficiently on your guard against all boasting in yourself, and well disposed to ascribe all the honour to *Immanuel*, as was that excellent apostle whose words you quote.

Knowself. With meekness and fear then I will give you a reason of the hope that is in me². But, my dear friends, while I gratify you, I beseech you to pray to our *Immanuel* for me; that I may be kept from the leaven of pride which is hid in my fallen nature; and from the swelling of self-exaltation, which I ever feel a proneness to. These, these, Sirs, we should ever watch against, for they eclipse the glory of our *Lord*; rob him of the honour and praise of his free love, rich grace, unmerited mercy, and finished salvation; and our souls of holy, humble joy in him.

I was born in the *City of Destruction*, and there continued till I was upwards of thirty years of age; but was restrained from a profligate life, and had some sense of my obligations to religion and morality. From my youth I practised both in some degree; and, on that account, was sufficiently sensible of my own goodness and rectitude, therefore had great expectations from our *King*. At length, the preachers in connexion with *Fervidus* and *Duplex* visited our city, and raised a general alarm. I went to hear them, and found that they much insisted on the knowledge of forgiveness of sins, thro' the blood of *Immanuel*. Discoursing with one of them on this subject, and observing that I could not pretend to such a privilege, tho' I had been from my youth very sober and religious;—the preacher turned short upon me, and abruptly asked, "Sir, did you ever see yourself hanging over the mouth of *Tophet*?" I was startled at the question, and offended with the proposer; but thought it must proceed from his being a stranger to my sober, righteous character; and there-

¹ 2 Cor. xii. 1. ² 1 Pet. iii. 15.

fore

fore made no reply. But the question stuck very close to me, and gave me great concern for some time. I used constantly to hear Mr. *Duplex*, with those in his connection, and sometimes *Fervidus*; and became so convinced of the dangerous state I was in, that I resolved to set out on pilgrimage. I was sweetly attracted to leave our city, and soon arrived at the *Slough of Despond*; when, suddenly, the *Heavens* were overcast, and a storm ensued, the blackest and most terrible that ever I saw or heard of. Wind, hail, and fire mingled with hail, beat upon me: at the same time *Mount Sinai* burst out into an horrible eruption; and, together with rending peals of thunder, disgorged such clouds of smoke and showers of stones, as filled the air with darkness and danger, and my poor soul with exceeding great terror. This was infinitely increased by an audible voice, roaring thro' the gloom, saying, "He that believeth not is condemned already, and the wrath of *Jehovah* abideth on him [1]." With the voice came an arrow that pierced my breast, the shaft broke of, but the barbed steel remained, and filled me with the acutest anguish[2]. I now thought of returning, but on looking back, our city appeared all in flames. Therefore I determined to wade thro' the *Slough* if possible, and hasten to the *Strait Gate*, lest I should die on the spot. But when I approached the *Bog*, my heart sunk, and the filth so affected me, that I could not immediately venture; being filled with dismaying terrors, and harrassed with dreadful suggestions, that I neither had, nor should ever have, any interest in *Immanuel*, so that it was best to finish my wretched life where I was. However, after lingering some time, my case being quite desperate, induced me to enter the *Slough*, crying to the strong for mercy to help in that time of need. And, tho' I sunk very deep, yet, found my feet had a support; this encouraged me to proceed, until I had got above half way over; when, behold! a most dreadful convulsion, attended with deaf'ning thunder, rent *Mount Sinai*, and threw a large piece of the rock into the *Slough*, so near me, that the mire flew over and almost suffocated me! In this extremity I made a desperate effort, and, by *Jehovah's* blessing, reached

[1] John iii. 18—36.   [2] Job. vi. 4.

the

the defired fhore. As foon as I was landed, I ran forward thro' the fmoke and afhes that iffued from the *Mountain*, and preffed towards the *Gate*, with thunder in my ears, and the arrow rankling in my breaft. *Mr. Goodwill* ftood at the gate, and gracioufly received me in, tho' I was covered with filth, and fainting with pain and fear. He gave me a cordial which he faid was brought from the *Cape of Good Hope*, and bid me haften to the *Crofs*, where *only*, I could have a perfect cure. At the *Interpreter's Houfe* I viewed the curiofities, but the arrow in my breaft would not fuffer me to take any pleafure from them; fo I departed, and foon came to the *Crofs*. When I beheld the glorious fufferer, I was wonderfully taken with the greatnefs of his love to men, and the fuitablenefs of his plan of falvation for finners; but I thought he frowned on *me*. I walked round and round the *Crofs*, and furveyed it on every fide, but in each fituation I could difcover no friendly glance caft towards me. I faw others received with a fmile, and go away rejoicing; but *I* was neglected. Now, alfo, the wound in my breaft feftered, and the filth on my garments ftank exceedingly, fo that I became a burden to myfelf, and wifhed rather to die than live; for I was convinced there was none could help me but the *glorious One* on the crofs; yet I could not fee my name, either on his breaft, or on his crofs.

At length came a perfon connected with *Mr. Duplex*, who feeing perfons about the *Crofs*, placed himfelf on an eminence, and began to difcourfe of *him* who fuffered on it. I drew near, and attended to him. He chofe for his fubject the cleanfing of the lepers; and fo difcuffed the point, by fhewing the exceeding finfulnefs of fin, and the abounding virtue of the Redeemer's blood fully to cleanfe it all away; that I found myfelf deeply interefted in the fubject. "Suppofing," faid he, "a perfon cannot find his *particular* name on this *Crofs*; yet the *general* name of every leprous fon of *Adam*, as a *finner*, is fufficiently evident; for it is abfurd to imagine that *Immanuel* died for *righteous* perfons." This fermon abated my pain, and hope of relief comforted my heart. When the preacher was gone, I went to the foot of the *Crofs*, opened my breaft, torn and throbbing with anguifh; and looking up, fighed with doubtful hope;"

Lord,

"*Lord*, if thou wilt, thou can'ft cleanfe and fave even *me*[1]." Inftantly I was favoured with the foul-ravifhing view of *Immanuel* as my great high-prieft, bearing the names of his people on his breaft; and ah! to my wonder and unfpeakable joy, I faw my vile and worthlefs name infcribed among them. *Prince Paraclete* alfo appeared, and took of the *Balfam of Immanuel*, and applying it to my wound, foon extracted the arrow, and healed my breaft. He then took away my filthy attire, and cloathed me with the garment of falvation; and, having marked me as *Immanuel*'s property, he difappeared. It is not in language to fet forth what fweet furprize and extatic joy overflowed my heart; and what floods of tears iffued from my eyes: at this time, I enjoyed fuch celeftial p'eafure, as, perhaps, I fhall never experience again, 'till I arrive at yonder *Celeftial City*. I came on flaming with the love of my efpoufals, thro' the *Village of Carelefs*, and was ready to beat them, becaufe they would not fee and do as I did[2]. When I came to the *City of Eftablifhment*, I inquired, as directed by the preacher, for *Arminian-Row*. There I hired a houfe on the ufual terms of keeping it in repair myfelf. I abode there about two years, and was very zealous in favour of my new friends of the *Row*, and their opinions; but was induced to leave them in the following manner.

One night as I lay reflecting on my bed, I was alarmed by a fudden crack, which fhook the houfe, and made me tremble. I inftantly arofe, ftruck a light, and fought for the caufe of the alarm, when, to my great furprize, I found that the main beam of my houfe was broken. I directly prop'd and fecured it as well as I could, and went to bed, but flept little. Next day I called in *Mr. Bungle*, my neighbour, the beft carpenter in *Arminian-Row*; who better fecured the beam, and told me every thing was very fafe. But, on obferving it from time to time, I found the crack grew wider and wider; this led me to examine the ftate of my houfe more carefully; and I perceived a general decay throughout the building. Soon afterwards *Mr. Duplex* paid me a vifit, and I laid before him what had happened. He faid, I had

[1] Mat. viii. 2.   [2] Luke ix. 53, 54.

neglected

neglected the *terms and conditions* on which I entered the houfe, by not fecuring it in time: and added, that I muft refolve to repair it, or expect to be troubled by the landlord. I remonftrated that I was not able to rebuild it, for it was totally decayed. "I am forry for it," faid he, "but terms muft be complied with, and conditions muft be fulfilled, or you will be miferable." So he left me very miferable indeed!

I was prefently after vifited by a friend who lived in *Churchftreet*, to whom I fhewed the decayed ftate of my houfe, for it was always on my mind. He faid, I muft needs live in continual fear; and obferved how very different his fituation and that of his neighbours were; who never were embarreffed with fuch diftreffing terms, and perplexing conditions in hireing their dwellings; for the landlord freely took the repairs entirely on himfelf. The next time I was in my friend's houfe, I took occafion to examine it; and found every thing fo much to my fatisfaction, that I came to as good a compofition as I could with my landlord, and removed into *Church-ftreet*. There I was fettled to my wifh, and fpent a few happy years among them; until I was called to the *City of God*; unto which I fet out with *Dr. Apollos* my bifhop, who then commanded the *Covenant Tranfport*. When we came abreaft of the *City of Self*, in *Arminian-road*; I was moved with indignation, on feeing the proud turret on the houfe of *Mr. Lofty*, an eminent ruler of that city, well known to me; and defired my captain's leave to fire at it. To this he confented, and I took fuch good aim, that I overthrew it, and raifed a general outcry in the *City of Self*—I entered deep into the ftudy of the ftatutes, ordinances, and decrees of the *City of God*; and, after a few years refidence there, by the free favour of our *King*, I was made doctor of laws, and appointed to the high truft of recorder of this city: an office of which I am the leaft worthy of all the human race. But by our *King*'s free and fovereign grace, I am what I am. This grace finks me into humility, and caufes me to exult and glory only in *Jehovah*, as the *Lord* of all grace to the loft and helplefs; and fuch I am in myfelf to this day.

Prob.

Prob. Sir, I am certain all the company, as well as myself, return you thanks for this improving account of yourself. But you have not informed us how you came by your present name.

Knowself. My original name was *Obscure*. When I settled in *Church-street*, I was called *Mr. See clear*. But when I was preferred to be recorder, I was denominated *Knowself*. Which name, I find, always goes with the office.

Ref. Sir, I am a little in the dark about your description of the ruinous state of your house, when you lived in *Arminian-Row*. I should be glad of an elucidation of that point, and doubt not but it will be pleasing and useful to us all.

Knowself. Why, Sir. I then thought, like my neighbours, that I was set up again for myself, and had a stock of what they call grace put into my hands, which I was to improve, so as to make myself inherently righteous; and that just as I succeeded therein, so my eternal state was to be determined. This was the main beam of my house; and do you at all wonder at its cracking and alarming me, so as to cause me to fly for safety? I found what *David* experienced concerning *his house*, it was defective before *Jehovah*; and he had nothing to look to and rejoice in, but the *Lord's* sure and everlasting covenant for his salvation[1].

Ref. O, I clearly comprehend your meaning now. At that time, I suppose, you had no clear views of the doctrine of the imputed righteousness of *Immanuel*, as one grand blessing of the covenant of grace.

Knowself. Clear views! dear Sir, I had scarce any view at all of it. *Mr. Duplex*, you know, opposes the doctrine, says it does immense hurt, and therefore prefers our own inherent righteousness before it. But we *must* see and know that we stand in as much need of *Immanuel's* righteousness to clothe our naked souls, as of his blood to cleanse us from the guilt of sin.

Prob. Now, Sir, as you have favoured us with this opportunity, pray inform us what discoveries have been made to you of *Jehovah* and your own heart.

[1] 2 Sam. xxiii. 5.

Knowself.

Knowself. I find daily that my nature is worse and worse. I see more and more of the workings of the pride of *Lucifer* within me. I cannot give you a more exact description of the body of sin and death which I carry about me, than the eminent *St. Paul* has given, of what was his own experience, in the seventh chapter to the Romans. And, in short, this I find true by daily self examination, that the more I know of myself, the less I like and depend on myself; which induces me to confess with shame before our dear *Lord*, that the more I know of my duty, the less strength and power I find in myself to do it.

Keen. But, Sir, how can you reconcile what you say to the goodness of *Jehovah?* That he should give us commands so disproportionate to our abilities.

Knowself. The goodness of *Jehovah*, Sir, is in this most apparent: because it is his design, and most for our good, that we should make *Him our All*. But this we never shall do, while we think we can do any thing without Him; that is, while we affect the least independence of Him, or look to any righteousness in ourselves. This is pride in the extreme! This was the ruin of the *Fallen Spirits*, and our first parents. That suggestion of *Lucifer*, *Ye shall be as Gods*, poisoned our nature, and ferments, like a most malignant leaven, thro' the whole mass of mankind, from generation to generation; and nothing but *Immanuel's* grace can destroy its fatal effects.

Keen. In this view, the whole of *Immanuel's* work may be termed, a bringing us back to our former state of dependence on *Jehovah*.

Knowself. That is my opinion, Sir; and it is a work worthy his glorious majesty, and infinite bowels of love. By nature we are afar off from *Jehovah*; that is, we act as independent of, and with no kind of respect to Him. But what is the consequence of this revolt from our sovereign, and departure from our only rest? Observe it in its most horrid extremes among the *Infernals*. What desperation, wild uproar, tormenting remorse, gnashing misery, and eternal anxiety, prey on the tormenting and tormented, in the *infernal Regions!* Turn to this *World of Vanity*, and you may see the same dreadful

ful diforders already begun among wicked men; and, by every alarming fymptom, haftening to *that fatal crifis*. Behold, the endlefs, fool fh, and vain purfuit of happinefs, where it never can be found! See, the difcontent and penury that torment the wretch whofe houfe is full of riches! Mark, the grief and difappointment that wound the heart of the ennobled *Child of Fortune*, while his face fmiles, and he is invefted with all the pageantry of honour and applaufe! In fhort, all things are full of reftlefs labour; man cannot utter it[1]. And all this wretchednefs is come upon intelligent creatures, by feeking to be independent of their great creator.

Keen. If this be true, with refpect to the *Fiends of the Pit*, and unregenerate men; it muft alfo have the fame effect among pilgrims, fo far as this fpirit is indulged: and this has been confirmed by my own experience. I had the happinefs to live long in *Independent-ftreet*, and enjoyed moft excellent means of grace; yet, after my very intimate acquaintance with *Mr. Ferridus*, attending him in his voyage to the *City of God*, and enduring various trials, until I arrived to this honourable and blefled fituation; I have found thro' all, that the more dependent I was on *Immanuel* and his righteoufnefs, the happier I have been.

Knowfelf. And thus, Sir, you will ever find it. Every fcheme of doctrine or practice, that weakens this abfolute dependence on *Immanuel* as our righteoufnefs; moft certainly wounds our true peace and holinefs. There may be an apparent peace, and feeming piety, with an independent fpirit, and vain confidence in our own righteoufnefs: but our hearts deceive us in fuch cafes; for, by nature, they are in league with *Lucifer*, againft the fovereignty of *our King*, and the one righteoufnefs of *Immanuel*, wrought out for our juftification. From hence fpring moft of the trials of true pilgrims, they being intended to break this combination, and draw us from this evil propenfity to pride and independence. A pilgrim is well repaid, when, by a moft fevere chaftifement, he is driven from this refuge of lies, into the arms of his *Celeftial Father*, and to a more firm reliance on *Immanuel* as his righteoufnefs and ftrength.

[1] Ecclef. i. 8.

Ref.

Ref. You seem to speak feelingly, Doctor, and have been in that school yourself, I imagine.

Knowself. I have so, indeed, I bless the *Lord*. The idols of self, and self-righteousness, were dear to me; but, my *Lord*, jealous of his own honour, and my happiness; tore them from my arms and heart. At this I was offended, and sullen for a time; and, like testy *Jonah*, thought I did well to be angry[1]. My indulgent *Father* then put under my declining head the downy pillow of his sovereignty; and into my trembling heart a firm faith in his everlasting righteousness; and never before did I enjoy such celestial peace, such delicious tranquility of mind!

Prob. I am happy, Sir, in finding my own feelings so similar to yours. I opposed *Jehovah*'s sovereignty, righteousness, and wise decrees, as cruel, arbitrary, and unnecessary. I refused to let him do as he pleased with his own creatures; and impiously said, I would have nothing to do with such a *predestinating Jehovah*. I now know this to be the spirit of a rebel, and the language of a fool. For, being assured, that *Jehovah* is infinitely wise and good; how perverse and blind to right reason, and its greatest interest, must that heart be, which refuses to make an absolute surrender of itself, both as to providence and grace, to the gracious disposal of such an indulgent *Father*, who, in *Immanuel*, has made most ample provision for our perfect happiness!

Keen. Those of *Arminian street* think it a degradation from their liberty, to make that submission; and an invasion of their free agency; for our *King* to assume it. They, in effect, say, "We are our own masters, who is *Lord* over us[2]." The language of their pride amounts to this, That they had rather, by having their own will, go to *Tophet*; than submit to be brought to the *Celestial City* by the sovereignty of *Jehovah*'s purposes and decrees, and thro' the perfect righteousness of his beloved Son.

Knowself. O that men were wise, that they would understand their true interest! No disposition favours so much of *Lucifer*'s, as that *Mr Mayor* has described. A life of sensual

[1] Jonah iv. 9. [2] Psalm xii. 4.

profligacy

profligacy shews a man to be of a groveling brutal inclination; but the swellings of intellectual pride, in a high conceit of moral power, and a jealousy of the infringement of the will of a *Fallen Creature*, even by *Jehovah* himself; manifests such a person, however moral his character, to be of a *Luciferian* spirit: and, as far from the kingdom of our *Lord*, as is that arrogant disposition from the submission, dependence, and docility of a child.

Apollos. Well, my dear friends, let us bless the *Lord* for teaching us better. I feel it my greatest happiness that *Jehovah* has not suffered me to have my own will. Who, but a fallen creature, would be so fond of his own moral agency, as rather to perish for ever, than have it over-ruled by sovereign grace? And who, among true pilgrims, would not rejoice to have his will so absolutely under the direction of *Immanuel*, as not to be *able* to destroy himself. It is my constant glory that I am under such powerful grace, as will not suffer me to perish by my own iniquity; nor be plucked out of my shepherd's hand by any enemy. I bless myself in *Immanuel*, and glory in him. I gave myself to my *Lord*, as a proud, wretched, diseased sinner. He has returned me *myself* again, humbled, healed, happy, and compleat in him; tho' in my flesh dwells no good thing.

Knowself. If a man desires to enjoy his own existence, let him come to, and live upon *Immanuel*. If he seeks this happiness any where else, he will surely be disappointed. In the midst of all the sensual delights of my unconverted state, my life was at times a burden, and disgustful to me: but now I bless myself that ever I was born with a capacity to know, serve, and love my dear Redeemer. I glory in *Immanuel*, who, when I had ruined and lost that capacity by sin, in infinite mercy recovered me thereto, at the expence of his own precious life. He, therefore, is my wisdom, and righteousness, and sanctification, and redemption. *Immanuel* is *Jehovah my Righteousness*. And I sweetly find the truth of that prophecy, concerning the one righteousness our *Lord* was to work out and bring in: "The work of righteousness shall be peace, and the effect of righteousness quietness and assurance for ever[1]." Thus

[1] Isaiah xxxii. 17.

standing

standing, clothed in the one perfect righteousness of *Immanuel*, I believe I am as perfectly righteous before *Jehovah* as tho' I had never sinned; and as free from condemnation as tho' I were not a sinner, nor had one sin about me. This, this, my dear friends, is the faith, the joy, the glory, and triumph of pilgrims on earth, and in yonder *Celestial World!* What think you of this *Immanuel*, my brethren? My soul feels the pleasure of your company! How is my house adorned by having so many of *Jehovah*'s jewels in it! How am I honoured by being visited by such excellent ones! But all our honour and all our excellency are derived from the matchless *Prince Immanuel!* What say you, my dear guests, will you have this illustrious *Son of David* to reign in and over you?

All. None but *Immanuel*, dear *Doctor Knewself*; we will have none but *Immanuel!* We have all said, in our folly and pride, to the *Bramble of Tophet*, "Come thou, and reign over us." But now the gracious *Jehovah* has taught us better. Therefore, let our *King Immanuel* live, and reign in and over us, and the *Celestial World*, for ever and ever.

Heavenly Mind. Hark.—do you not hear a shouting! Methinks I hear the *Celestial Arches* ring.

Keen. Yes, it is plain enough to hear—Some happy pilgrims are now entering thro' the gates into the *Celestial City*[1]. Or some vile prodigal is made to repent[2]. Or, perhaps, some new discovery is making, to those happy inhabitants, of the wonderful providence and grace of *Jehovah*[3]: which raises their songs, tunes their harps, and pours new joys into their enraptured souls.—How the music swells, and echoes over the everlasting hills!—Come, brethren, let us have our conversation in the *Celestial World*, by emulating their songs.—Yonder are three *Shining Ones* winging their way towards this city. Let us sing as they approach.

[1] Rev. xxii. 14. [2] Luke xv. 10. [3] Rev. xix. 1, 2, 3.

" Come, let us join our chearful fongs,
" With angels round the throne;
" Ten thoufand thoufand are their tongues,
" But all their joys are one.

" Worthy the *Lamb* that dy'd they cry,
" To be exalted thus ;
" Worthy the *Lamb*, our lips reply,
" For he was flain for us !

" *Jefus* is worthy to receive,
" Honour and power divine ;
" And bleffings more than we can give,
" Be, *Lord*, for ever thine.

" The whole creation join in one,
" To blefs the facred name ;
" Of *Him* who fits upon the throne,
" And to adore the *Lamb*."

WATTS.

C H A P. XLVIII.

Sincere, Goodman, *and* Truman, *fummoned away. The manner of their paffing the river. The remaining Pilgrims vifit* Mr. Heavenly Mind. *His very inftructing ftory. Difcourfe about Knowing each other in the* Celeftial City.

WHILE they were thus finging, the three *Shining Ones* came flying over their heads, fmiling to hear their mortal ftrains. When the hymn was finifhed, one of the meffengers faid, " Be happy, ye fons of *Jehovah*; and let our brethren, *Goodman, Truman,* and *Sincere*, prepare to join yonder chorifters on fuch a day."—The three Pilgrims bowed in obedience

dience to the message, and the *Shining Ones* returned to the *Celestial City*.

Apollos. My brethren, ye are happy in being first called to enter into the joy of our *Lord*.

On the appointed day, the three Pilgrims prepared to obey the summons. Accordingly, they went down to the river, accompanied by their friends; who kissed them, and wished them a happy passage over. Just as they entered the river, the sun was eclipsed, and it grew very dark; this troubled the Pilgrims: but they were far more distressed by the apparitions of *Worldly Ease, Tamper,* and *Fear*; who beset the Pilgrims, upbraided them with their backslidings, and told them, that they were coming to reside for ever with them; at which, the Pilgrims cried out in great distress.

Apollos. What troubles my dear friends? Speak, and tell your bishop of all your griefs.

Sincere. Oh, Sir, *Tamper*, the wretch who decoyed me into the *Path of Danger*, now appears, and endeavours to make me sink in these waters.

Truman. And *Mr. Ease*, who lulled me to sleep on the *Enchanted Ground*, would persuade me, that I shall never land safe on the other shore.

Goodman. Dear bishop assist me. *Fear*, my old enemy, now lays his hand on my head, and would press me under the water.

Apollos. My dear brethren, be comforted. These are only phantoms, raised by the enemy of your souls. Your backslidings have been forgiven by your *Lord*, and the pardon sealed on your hearts by his blood. Think on the infinite atonement and glorious righteousness of *Immanuel*, while we call upon him in your behalf.

Then the other Pilgrims, and all their friends, kneeled down by the side of the river, and joined with the good bishop in prayer to *Jehovah*, that he would rebuke the enemy, and shine upon their afflicted brethren. As foon as they had finished their fupplication, the Pilgrims in the river exclaimed,

All. Thank you, dear friends. They flee, they flee! The *Lord* blefs you all.

The fun then fhone out, the fpectres vanifhed, and the Pilgrims went over the remaining part of the river, crying in triumph, "O death, where is thy fting'!" They were immediately anfwered with the found of trumpets from the *Celeftial City*; and the *Shining Ones*, who had fummoned them over, now received, and welcomed them to the *Celeftial Shore*. They then clothed them in fhining garments, and conducted them, with the found of moft ravifhing mufic, up to a glorious palace which ftood near the gate of the *Celeftial City*, and is the refidence of *Dr. Demonftration*. The Doctor received them gladly, and foon made them fenfible how really, perfectly and permanently happy they now were, and ever fhould be. From thence they were conducted into the *Celeftial City*, amidft the joyful acclamations of a number which no man can number. They approached the eternal throne, and were joyfully welcomed by *Immanuel*, into his kingdom. Where we fhall leave them for a while, and return to their brethren; who departed from the river, rejoicing in the *Lord*, for giving them fuch a tef- timony of his love, by fupporting their brethren in their laft conflict.

Some time after the departure of their brethren, the Pilgrims made a vifit to *Mr. Heavenly Mind* the chamberlain of the city, who is an opulent man, and of great confequence. His houfe is on the top of *Mount Tranfport*, which is the moft elevated part of the *City of Hephzibah*. The bifhop, archdeacon, mayor, recorder, and *Mr. Love* were with them: after dinner they walked on the top of the houfe, and entered into converfation.

Prob. Honoured paftor, I am often thinking on our dear brethren who are gone to yonder *Celeftial City*, and am led to believe, that we fhall fee them again, know them, and difcourfe with them too.

[2] 1 Cor. xv. 55.

Apollos.

Apollos. You have good reason for such expectation, both from the word of our *King*, and the nature of things; but as I know that our friend, *Mr. Heavenly Mind*, has employed much of his study on this subject, I will chearfully unite with you, in desiring to have his sentiments on this question.

Heavenly Mind. You must know, my brethren, that neither my name, nor my study on this subject, proceed from any want of the good things of this world. The case is far otherwise, as you shall learn from a brief relation of my history. I sprang from the rich and honourable family of *Dives*, which resides in the *City of Sensuality*, near *Deist-Hall*, unto which my father belonged. In that city, and in the principles of its inhabitants, I was educated; and, on account of my serious air, was called *Thoughtful*. Just as I came of age, my father died, and left me in the possession of a large fortune. But, neither my wealth, nor the luxuries of that city, could prevent my reflecting on what I was, and whither I was going. I frequently used to walk out by myself, and consider the wisdom and goodness of *Jehovah* which appeared in the works of creation; I also began closely to examine the principles in which I had been educated, and found them by no means satisfactory. One day, as I was thus walking and reflecting, I was accosted, in a very respectful manner, by an amiable young stranger, whose name I afterwards found was *Grace*. He entered into conversation with me, and when he found how I was disposed, he besought me to go with him to the *Sign of the Lamb*, in the adjacent *Valley of Humiliation*. I readily complied, being very desirous of instruction. And who should be at that house but *Capt. Doddridge*, a famous officer in *Immanuel*'s army. This veteran and *Mr. Grace*, soon disarmed me of all my prejudices against *Immanuel*: I immediately became a convert, renounced my former principles, and was enrolled among the number of pilgrims. I then returned to the city, settled my affairs, and came on pilgrimage. I tarried a considerable time with *Father Meditation*, and was much profited by discoursing with that venerable man. At length I embarked in the *Covenant Transport*, and arrived at the *City of God*; where I spent much time in taking views, and making remarks on the temple, mountains,

mountains, gardens, palaces, walls, &c. of the city. On this account, the inhabitants gave me the name of *Mr. Heavenly Mind*, becaufe they did not know me fo well as I knew myfelf. At that city I found *Capt. Hervey*, and grew fo well acquainted with him, that we were feldom from each other. At length I was informed by our *King*, that I muft remove to this city. So I inftantly fet out, and paffed fafely over the *Enchanted Ground*, the air of which had very little effect on me. As I paffed by the *Globe Inn* the company came out, and laughed immoderately at me, becaufe I walked fo faft by that houfe, with my face turned up to *Heaven*. Alfo when I came to the arbours, *Mr. Eafe* came, and began to practice his arts upon me; but I ftruck him fo effectually with this rod, which I always have in my hand, that he thought proper to make off, and leave me to purfue my way to this city, where I foon after arrived.

Ref. Pray, Sir, where did you obtain that rod?

Heavenly Mind. I had it of *Dr. Evidence* at the *City of God*, he told me it was a branch of the *Tree of Life*. There is on it, as you may fee, the following fentence, " The joy of the *Lord* is your ftrength.[1]" And I have found it of great fervice to me ever fince I had it.

Prob. I am much delighted, Sir, with your little narrative; and now wait for your fentiments concerning the knowledge of our friends, when we fhall arrive at the *Celeftial City*.

Heavenly Mind. *Peter*, *James*, and *John*, knew *Mofes* and *Elias* on the *Holy Mount*. The impenitent *Jews* will fee and know *Abraham*, *Ifaac*, and *Jacob*, and the Prophets, in the *Kingdom of Heaven*. Good minifters fhall be known by their converts, and their converts by them, as their glory and crown of rejoicing[2]. Relations and friends will know each other, for, *St. Paul* comforts the *Theffalonians* with the hope, that thofe relatives who flept in *Immanuel*, fhould be brought back with him[3]: fo that as furely as thofe mourners expected to fee and know their dear *Lord*, fo furely they fhould fee and know their de-

[1] Neh. viii. 10. [2] Mat. xvii. 3.——Luke xiii. 28.——1 Theff. ii. 19.
[3] 1 Theff. iv. 14.

parted

parted believing relatives and friends. *St. John* also in his *Revelations*, represents the blessed inhabitants of yonder world, as remembering, not only that they were once in this state; but, also, as conscious of what nation they were [1], what sins they were washed from, and what trials and persecutions they endured. This opinion, moreover, is very ancient; as appears by that celebrated part of the *Apochrypha*, in which reprobates are represented, as seeing and knowing certain righteous persons at the day of judgment; to be the very men, whose manner of living (while in this world) they had counted madness, and their end to be without honour [2].

Prob. I am obliged to you, Sir, for your pertinent remarks: permit me to add, that I conceive it necessary, for the identity of our persons to be preserved, in order that we may be sensible of our great obligations to our blessed *Lord*; for, if our memories were to lose the impressions and ideas which they have acquired in this world, we could not properly be said to be the very same persons; nor could we retain such a high sense of the favours we have received from our great Redeemer.

Frien. God forbid, that we should lose any part of *that* sense: for the grand reason why I desire to be in the *Celestial City*, is; That, as this very identical *Henry Friendly*, once a most vile and filthy sinner, but washed in *Immanuel*'s precious blood; I may kiss the feet of my dear divine Saviour. I have often envied that woman her place, who wept on *Immanuel*'s feet, and kissed them so heartily. If I had been there, instead of snuffing up my nose at her, as did proud *Simon*, I would have sat down and mingled my kisses and tears with hers.

Knowself. Well spoken, brother *Friendly*, you have given us a reason for your opinion, that is worthy the mind of every true pilgrim. Nor shall you be disappointed of your hope; the *Lord*, who has given you this desire, will satisfy it.

Frien. Then I shall be satisfied: but, while I am this same *Friendly*, nothing less than paying my homage at *Immanuel*'s feet, will content me.

[1] Rev. v. 9. [2] Wisdom v. 4.

Ref. Surely, our *Lord* does not tantalize his children! For, how is it possible that we should ever have desired to see Him, if he had not inspired us with that hope? And he would not give us such an affection, only to torment us.

Prob. Torment us, indeed! A pilgrim is of all men most miserable, if in this life only he hath hope in *Immanuel* [1].

Apollos. No, no, *Probus*, *Jehovah* is not a tormentor of his creatures. We have abundant hope in our death, and our sweet and joyful expectation shall not be cut off [2].

C H A P. XLIX.

The Pilgrims summoned away. The Giant Infidelity *disturbs the house of the Pilgrims, the night before their departure.* Apollos *prays with them. They joyfully pass the river, and have an abundant entrance into the* Celestial City.

WHILE they were thus discoursing on the top of the *Chamberlain's House*, behold three *Shining Ones*, as bright as the sun, appeared in the *Heavens*.

Apollos. Yonder comes three *Celestial Messengers*, perhaps to call some of us away, that we may presently experience the sweet truths of which we have been discoursing.

The *Shining Ones* drew near, encircled the company three times, and then called *Probus*, *Friendly* and *Resolute* home to their Father's house, at an appointed day; promising withal, to meet them on the other side of the river. One of these celestial envoys addressing *Probus*, said,

Shining One. *Probus*, my beloved charge, play the man in thy last conflict.

[1] 1 Cor. xv. 19. [2] Prov. xxiii. 18.

The Pilgrim gave a sign of consent, and the *Seraphs* departed like a flash of lightning; after which the Pilgrims returned home.

On the night before the day appointed for the Pilgrims to go over the river, their house was terribly alarmed by *Probus*, who screamed out in a dreadful manner; on which, *Resolute* and *Friendly* ran to his chamber, and found him sitting in his bed, in the utmost consternation.

Res. Dear brother, what is the matter with you?

Prob. Oh, my friends, the monster *Infidelity* is just retired from my bed-side. He has been blaspheming my *Lord*, and labouring to destroy my hope in *Immanuel* with all the logic of *Tophet*.—Send for *Apollos*, I pray you.

So one ran for the bishop, who came immediately.

Apollos. My dear brother *Probus*, why are you afraid of this enemy, over whom you have obtained so many victories?

Prob. I have, indeed, often triumphed over this foe, but he is a many headed monster. I think his influence is some way congenial with my corrupt nature; for I am prone to listen to his horrid arguments, although nothing does so much distress my soul, and pain my arm.

Apollos. Our depraved nature is inclined to every evil. Each of us hath a besetting sin, and this appears to be yours. But be of good cheer, *Probus*, for this is your enemy's last onset upon you. Take, therefore, the Shield of Faith, and believe in the *Lord Immanuel*[1].

On this, *Probus* burst into tears, and cried out,

Prob. Lord, I believe, help thou my unbelief[2]. *Jehovah* knows that my hope and trust are not in the deistic scheme. I have much to lose, even the seeing, adoring, and enjoying for ever a precious *Immanuel*; and *that* makes me fear much. *He* is all the *Heaven* which my soul longs for. A *Freethinker's Heaven*, a *Jews Heaven*, a *Mahometan's Paradise*,

[1] Ephes. vi. 16.   [2] Mark ix. 24.

I defire not. It is yonder *Celeftial World* which I prefs unto. Oh, to be with *Immanuel* is the moft precious of all defirable things!

Apollos. Be comforted, my brother, all trials will foon be happily over with you.

Prob. But the monfter threatened to come on the morrow, and drown me in the river.

Apollos. He is a liar. Your *Lord* is true and faithful. *Immanuel* hath promifed, that he will come again, and receive you to himfelf[1].

Prob. Oh, if he would but come on the morrow, and blefs his trembling child with his dear prefence, in this laft trial; how would I fing his praifes in the *Celeftial City!*

Apollos. I believe he will, but we fhould afk this favour of him.

So they fpent the remainder of the night in fervent prayer unto *Jehovah*, for his affiftance on the morrow.—When the time came, the pilgrims and their friends went down to the river; and after mutual embraces, they addreffed themfelves to go over. Firft, *Refolute* entered the river, like himfelf, boldly brandifhing his rod of the *Tree of Life*. The *Black Tyrant* fhewed himfelf, but *Refolute*, fhaking his wand at him, faid,

Ref. Remember, thou enemy of fouls, the victory which my *Lord* gave me over thee, when I obtained this rod, at the very mouth of thy den. He is now about to receive me to that eternal life, which he then gracioufly promifed me. Avaunt, therefore, curfed fiend, *I am a true Pilgrim, a Sinner faved!*

On which he waded over, crying continually, " *A finner faved! A finner faved! A miracle! A miracle of grace! Vile Will Refolute is going to the Celeftial City!* Thus this intrepid Pilgrim paffed the river with joy, exhorting his brethren to follow him, until he landed fafe on the happy fhore.

[1] John xiv. 3.

Probus

Probus next came trembling to the river, dreading the fight of his bitter enemy, the *Giant Infidelity*. *Apollos* and *Liberal*, *Keen*, *Knowself*, and *Mr. Love*, comforted him, and good *Mr. Heavenly Mind* suggested to him many pertinent promises of assistance from *Immanuel*, in such times of trial. *Friendly* was remarkably joyous, at this time: so down they walked to the river; and lo, as soon as their feet touched the water, and while they were taking their last farewell of their friends; the *Heavens* opened, and a wonderful glory shone upon the Pilgrims[1]. At the same time, a voice came as from the *Celestial City*, saying, "I will come again and receive you to myself, that where I am, there ye may also be[2]." *Probus* then clapping his hands together, exclaimed,

Prob. He is come! He is come! The faithful, everlasting, long-suffering friend of unbelieving, God-provoking *William Probus* is come!

Frien. Our Lord is faithful, my brother, he cannot deny himself. Oh, *Apollos*, dear pastor, proclaim it from your pulpit, that *Jehovah* deals familiarly with pilgrims, for the dear *Immanuel*'s sake.

Prob. My feet stand sure. I shall soon praise the *Lord* for it, in yonder great city, and innumerable assembly. O my soul, thou hast now trodden down for ever the strength of *Infidelity!*

Thus mutually praising the *Lord*, and exhorting each other, they walked on the waters, to the astonishment of themselves and all their friends; for they trod *Death* and *Tophet* under their feet, and went triumphing to the other shore. There *Resolute*, and the three *Shining Ones*, received them; and having put on their crowns and fine linen, clean and white, they went on towards the *Celestial City*.

The *Shining Ones* first took them to the glorious palace of *Dr. Demonstration*, where *Probus* obtained a perfect cure of all the pains, distresses, and anxieties, which had so long, more or less, every day tormented him. There also they found their dear

---

[1] Acts vii. 55, 56.   [2] John xiv. 3.

brethren, *Sincere*, *Goodman*, and *Truman*, who were come to meet them. This meeting transported them beyond the power of language to describe; for now they were happy to find, that the purposes of divine love towards them were joyfully terminated. While they were carressing each other, they heard the found of a trumpet, and a voice rang through the palace, saying, "Come up hither[1]." This, the *Shining Ones* told them, was an order for them to attend on the *King*.

The Pilgrims therefore came forth from the *Palace of Demonstration* in shining robes, and their hearts overflowing with pleasure: immediately the everlasting gates of the *Celestial City* were lifted up, unto the found of most ecstatic music; and the Pilgrims entered amidst the acclamations of ten thousand thousand blessed beings, who shouted " Hallelujah, blessed are they who do his commandments, that they may have a right to the *Tree of Life*, and enter in thro' the gates into the city[2]."

The Pilgrims passed along the golden streets up to the glorious throne, on which sat *Immanuel* in all his glory. He beheld them with a smile of infinite complacency, and said, " Well done good and faithful servants, ye are welcome unto my palace, enter ye into the joy of your *Lord*[3]." Then all the pilgrims cast their crowns at His feet, and worshipped Him, saying, "Thou art worthy, O blessed *Immanuel*, to receive glory, and honour, and blessing; for thou wast slain, and hast redeemed us to *Jehovah* by thy blood[4], out of yonder sinful world. Wherefore, permit us thus—thus—thus—divine, precious, gracious *Immanuel*, to embrace thy feet, and adore thee."

· While they uttered these words, the Pilgrims embraced and kissed the feet of their beloved *Lord*, but the raptures which filled their hearts no language can describe, nor mortal conceive. We will leave them happy, for a while; and once more visit the *City of Hephzibah*.

[1] Rev. iv. 1.   [2] Rev. xxii. 14.   [3] Mat. xxv. 21.   [4] Rev. v. 9.

C H A P.

C H A P. L.

Mr. George Fervidus *arrives at the* City of Hephzibah. *He is nobly entertained by* Governour Promise. *Prince Paraclete summonses him away. The remarkable manner of his passing the river, and his glorious reception into the* Celestial World.

SOON after the Pilgrims had passed the river, the *City of Hephzibah* was alarmed by an unusual sound of trumpets, and other instruments of music, attended with the voices of much people, as coming from the western gate of the land: whereupon, many of the citizens ran out, to see what these things meant. As they went out, they met a messenger hastening to the mayor, with an information of the cavalcade. It was no less than *Governour Promise* himself, who had left his station for a time, to honour the celebrated *Capt. Fervidus*, who had arrived at the *Gate of Beulah*, with a large company of weak and feebled-minded pilgrims under his convoy[1], from the *City of God*. This intrepid servant of *Immanuel* in his journey over the *Enchanted Ground*, threw the *Globe Inn* into the utmost confusion[2]. For, as he drew near unto the *Globe*, the servants being ignorant of his character, invited him into the Inn; but he had no sooner entered the house than he began to declaim, in his peculiarly zealous way, against the iniquitous and vain practices that were carrying on in the several rooms.

On hearing such an uncommon voice, the company ran from each quarter, and soon surrounded *Fervidus*, who stood in the midst of them like a *Son of Thunder*[3]; and exposed the vanity, unreasonableness, and impiety of their manner of living, in such a convincing and solemn way; and, with such a tender concern, represented unto them the fearful vengeance of Jeh..h

[1] 1 Thess. v. 14.   [2] Acts xvii. 6.   [3] Mark iii. 17.

which hung over them; that a general consternation ensued[1]. Many silently withdrew, ashamed; and many others resolved to go immediately on pilgrimage[2]; insomuch, that the rooms were left almost desolate, and *Mrs Jezebel* was quite frantic with rage and vexation. In vain she called upon *Rubicus* and *Bully* to assist her in this terrible conjuncture; for *Rubicus* was half a convert, and *Bully* was silenced[3]. Those who were of most use to *Mrs. Jezebel*, and the least affected by *Fervidus*'s words were *Old Gripe* and his associates; who, at this time, shewed the truth of *Immanuel*'s saying, namely, "It is easier for a camel to go thro' the eye of a needle, than for covetous men to go on pilgrimage[4]." But *Fervidus* lost almost all his new converts in passing over the *Enchanted Ground*, and at the *Arbours of Worldly Ease*; into the latter, they would go, sit down and drink of the intoxicating wine, notwithstanding all his menaces[5]. However, *Fervidus* brought even of *them* to *Beulah*, several backsliders, and a few real converts. These were so transported with what they saw, heard and tasted of *Immanuel*'s beauty, grace and love; that they could hardly contain the joy; but hung about *Fervidus* and *Governor Promise*, with eyes full of tears, hearts burning with love, and their mouths uttering the warmest thanks for the happiness they enjoyed by their means[6]. The weak and feeble-minded also felt the salubrious nature of the air of *Beulah*, caught some celestial fire from their new and enraptured companions, and united in their triumphant songs. To crown all, and make the harmony complete, *Governour Promise*'s band of music led the choir, and the happy inhabitants united in the chorus as they passed, so that the whole country resounded with the praise.

The bishop and clergy, together with the mayor, recorder, chamberlain, &c. of the *City of Hephzibah*, went forth in their formalities to meet this respectable company, attended by a great concourse of the citizens. But when *Fervidus* saw the manner in which he was received and attended, he sighed inwardly, and said,

[1] Acts xxiv. 25. [2] Mat. xiii. 20. [3] Acts iv. 14. [4] Mark x. 25.
[5] Isaiah xxvi. 10. [6] Acts iii. 8—10.

Fer.

Fer. Alas! wherefore do you pour so much respect on such a worthless reptile as I, who am less than the least of you all? I will not suffer such ado about a poor sinner. My dear friend, turn your eyes and attention to my glorious master. It is by his grace that I am what I am. He gives All, and does All; therefore He shall have all the glory of his own wonderful work.

Fervidus was conducted with loud acclamations, notwithstanding his remonstrances, to the house of *Governor Pr——*, which is on the top of *Mount Transport*, and overlooks the whole city. The governor kept open house for all the citizens and people of the land, while *Fervidus* was with him; and invited the bishop and clergy, the mayor and all the principal officers of the city to his table, in this time of joy.—At this festival the governor brought forth some of his best stores. Whatever the rich *Land of Beulah* could afford, was plentifully served up, and some do not scruple to say, That he had certain dishes sent him even from the *Celestial City*[2]. It is very true, however, that the *Shining Ones* were often seen at the house, and the whole building was at this time so illuminated, and filled with exquisite harmony, that it seemed like a suburb of the *New Jerusalem*.

On the Saturday evening after their arrival at *Hephzibah*, the governor and his company were sitting together, in a pleasant octagon on the top of his house, and discoursing high on the glory of *Immanuel*'s person and work; when they suddenly heard a most rending acclamation from the *Celestial City*, and soon afterwards beheld a bright host of *Shining Ones* coming towards them, with the sound of exquisite music. As they drew near, they perceived at the head of the celestial band, a person of superior majesty; on which, said the governor,

Promise. Yonder is the most excellent *Prince Paraclete*, my divine *Lord*, and most opulent *Banker*[3]; who answers whatever bills I draw upon him, and who is possessed of unsearchable riches. Something of great consequence has brought him hither.

[1] Ephes. ii. 3. [2] Heb. vi. 5.——John vi. 55. [3] Eph. i. 1,

Then they all arofe, and as the *Prince* drew near, they bowed themfelves towards the ground.

Prince. All hail, O men greatly beloved: and thou *Fervidus*, my faithful fervant; I am come to inform you, that your labours are nearly finifhed, and you are foon to enter into your eternal reft.

Fervidus then bowing low at the *Prince*'s feet, replied.

Fer. Good is the word of my moft gracious *Lord*; but wherefore fhould the *Prince* of the *Celeftial World* thus regard fuch a vile wretch as I am? I rejoice in your gracious approbation of my poor fervices, and am willing to continue them; but as it is my *Lord*'s pleafure to call me hence, if fuch a defpicable worm may choofe, permit me to finifh my labours and trials on the morrow, it being the *Lord*'s day of reft.

Prince. Fervidus, your requeft is granted. To-morrow thou fhalt pafs the river, nor fhalt thou be deftitute of my affiftance; wherefore be ftrong, and play the man againft the laft enemy[1].

Then *Fervidus* and the company again bowed low, and the *Prince* directing his band to play, they ftruck up fuch a divine tune, as filled them with a pleafure they never felt before. The *Prince* perceiving the ftrong emotions of their fouls, left it fhould overcome their mortal frames[2], fpread his divine plumage, and returned towards the *Celeftial City*; leaving them all in a tranfport of feraphic joy.

The fucceeding night was fpent in various expreffions of love between *Fervidus* and his friends; who were grieved at his fudden departure from them; but *he* rejoiced at the will of his mafter, and faid,

Fer. I was immortal 'till my work was done. Many attempts have been made to take away my life, but all in vain, for my mafter's time was not come. But now, as he has fo honourably fignified his bleffed will to remove me; I leave his fweet work

[1] 1 Cor. xv. 26.   [2] 1 Cor. xv. 50.

to other servants much better than myself, whom my *Lord* will send forth into his harvest.

Early on the *Lord*'s day morning the *Celestial City* appeared peculiarly illuminated with glory, the everlasting gates were wide unfolded, and the whole distance from the river to the gates was covered with an innumerable company of *Shining Ones*. The sun also arose with unusual lustre to make the scene more splendid. *Death*, and him who hath the power of death[1], foreseeing for whose honour this uncommon apparatus was intended; burnt with envy at it, and were permitted to indulge their malice on this occasion; wherefore, the river was suddenly swelled to its utmost height, and the *Black Tyrant* himself appeared, to oppose and trouble *Fervidus* in his passing the river.

The eminent ambassador of the *Celestial King* now prepared to attend the court of his divine sovereign; and, accordingly, was accompanied to the river by the officers of the *City of Hephzibah*. He was supported by *Governor Promise*, and *Mr. Heavenly Mind*, his old and familiar friends. The inhabitants of the city also crowded to the river side, being desirous of seeing the last of this great man; and were much comforted for the loss of him, in beholding the honours with which his master dignified him.

As soon as *Fervidus* came to the river, the *Black Tyrant* raised an horrible tempest, which blew the waters into a dreadful commotion; but the hero stood undaunted on the brink; and, with his face stedfastly fixed towards the *New Jerusalem*, he cried, saying,

Fer. O *Prince Paraclete*, who didst never fail thy servants, I beseech thee, remember the word which thou didst yesterday promise unto thy unworthy creature; and, in consequence of which, I now hope for thy presence, to assist me in this last conflict with my enemies.

No sooner were these words uttered by *Fervidus*, than a triumphant shout was heard among the hosts of *Shining Ones*; and *Prince Paraclete* was seen, with his magnificent attendants, flying towards *Fervidus*. When he was come near, he embraced

[1] Heb. ii. 14.

the *Man of God*, kissed him, and then commanded his standard-bearer to spread his colours. Immediately the glorious ensign of the blood-royal of *Heaven* waved in the wind, in which was wrought with divine art, the mysterious cypher of *Redeeming Love*, and the destruction of *Death* and *Hell*. As soon as these enemies of *Fervidus* beheld the terrible standard, they fled away with great precipitation[2], and the river immediately became calm and quiet.

The standard-bearer then advanced to the river, and the *Prince* taking *Mr. Heavenly Mind*'s place, he and *Governor Promise* supported *Fervidus*, while the waters divided[2] before them, and left an easy passage unto the opposite shore. As they went over, there appeared, issuing from the city, the flaming chariot of *Immanuel*; which drove down thro' the shining ranks, and met *Fervidus* as he ascended from the river[3].

Immanuel ordered a splendid white robe to be put on *Fervidus*, then took him up in his chariot, and kissed him. Prince *Paraclete*, *Immanuel* and *Fervidus* sat in the chariot, and *Governor Promise* returned to *Hephzibah*. While this passed, the concave was rent with the joyful acclamations of myriads of happy beings. As for *Fervidus*, he was all in extacy, but could not be persuaded to ascend the chariot, until *Immanuel* let him know it was his absolute will, that thus it should be done[4] unto all such as he delighted to honour.

Just as the chariot was moving towards the city, a large body of pilgrims made perfect[5], came near and besought *Immanuel*, that they might be permitted to go next his chariot, in the procession. These were the spiritual children of *Fervidus*, whom he had been the happy instrument of bringing to that blissful region[6]. They were all clothed in white robes, and had the ensigns of victory in their hands[7]. Their petition was immediately granted, and they followed the chariot singing the following song, while all the rest kept a joyful silence to hear it.

Pilgrims. " Salvation to our *King*, to *Prince Immanuel*, and to *Prince Paraclete*, who are worthy to receive all ascriptions of

---

[1] Isaiah lix. 19.   [2] Joshua iii. 16.   [3] John xiv. 3.   [4] John xiii. 6—8.
[5] Heb. xii. 23.   [6] 1 Cor. iv. 15.   [7] Rev. vii. 9.

glory, honour and majesty, for their wonderful love to us, and blessed be our glorious *Jehovah* for thus honouring his faithful servant, and our dear father; who, with indefatigable zeal, followed our lost and wandering souls into the highways and hedges[1] of yonder lower world, and compelled us to come in to this joy of our *Lord*. Welcome, thrice welcome, dear *Fervidus*, to this thine everlasting rest!"

Fer. Cease, ye happy souls, from thus honouring a poor unworthy instrument, whose services were far over-balanced by his infirmities and sins. Rather behold, and celebrate the praises of this precious *Lamb of God*, by whose blood and righteousness alone both you and I enjoy this amazing honour and happiness; the abundance of which at present so overwhelms me, that I am hardly capable of supporting it.

Immanuel. O ye, my precious *Redeemed Ones*, with whom this my servant, and your parent, did travel in birth until you became my true pilgrims[2]: I accept with delight the regard you shew unto him in this *Celestial World*, for he is worthy[3]. Go on, therefore, to love and honour him as your glorified affections shall incline you.—And you, *Fervidus*, my faithful servant, consider those souls as your glory and crown of rejoicing[4]. In this manner I honour every one of my ambassadors, on their arrival here; for I know that both you, and the children which I have given you[5], are so thoroughly purged from pride and self-seeking, that you will never give or receive any honours derogatory to my imperial crown and dignity. Wherefore, eternally live and love each other, and I shall rejoice in beholding and increasing your mutual affection[6]: to which end now, *Fervidus*, enter into the joy of thy *Lord*[7].

On this, the chariot of *Immanuel* moved onward, and the children of *Fervidus* followed, giving an amazing loud shout of joy, and the whole host united in the high applause. Thus they entered the pearly[8] gates of the *New Jerusalem*, and proceeded on to the eternal throne, which was surrounded by a most brilliant

[1] Luke xiv. 23. [2] Gal. iv. 19. [3] Rev. iii. 4. [4] 1 Th. ii. 19, 20.
[5] Isaiah viii. 18. [6] Jer. xxxii. 41. [7] Mat. xxv. 21. [8] Rev. xxi. 21.

rainbow.

rainbow [1]. *Immanuel* afcended the throne, *Fervidus* drew near and proftrated himfelf before the throne, with all the expreffions of adoring love. He was commanded to rife, and *Prince Paraclete* led him, all aftonifhment, quite up to *Immanuel*, and placed him at his left hand on the throne. Then filence being made, faid,

Immanuel. Be it known unto all the thrones, dominions, principalities and powers of our angelic hofts; as alfo to our dear brethren of the human race; that this perfon whom *Prince Paraclete*, according to our promife by Him made [2], has placed as an overcomer on our throne; is, by name, *George Fervidus* [3], my faithful fervant, whofe abundant labours in feveral parts of the earth, have, thro' our grace, been fo fuccefsful in bringing many of you to this city, and who, in a little while, will be joined by many others. It is therefore our will and peafure, that he who has fo greatly improved his talents, fhould receive diftinguifhed honours; wherefore, ye our bleffed martyrs and confeffors, behold your worthy compeer, and let him have a place in your exalted fituation.

The *Prince* then paufed, and all the celeftial company fignified their joy in the royal decree with ten thoufand times ten thoufand, and thoufands of thoufands of bleffed voices [4]; and with all the inftrumental mufic of that world of harmony. While this grand concert was playing, *Fervidus* arofe from the throne, with his mind full of fuch fentiments as appear in thofe who cry out, "*Lord*, when faw we thee an hungry and fed thee, &c. [5]" and again humbly bowed down himfelf before the throne, and then was, by the whole company, welcomed to his eternal home. To compleat his joy, fome of his dear fellow labourers and friends, who had arrived before him, prefented themfelves unto him; nor was it the leaft part of his pleafure to find *Probus*, *Refolute*, *Friendly* and *Sincere* in the number of his fellow-citizens of the *New Jerufalem*.—While *Fervidus* and his friends were congratulating each other on their happy arrival, one of the great minifters of ftate made the fignal for filence in *Heaven* [6]. Then fpake the glorious *Prince*.

[1] Rev. iv. 3.   [2] Rev. iii. 21, 22.   [3] Rev. iii. 5.   [4] Rev. v. 11.
[5] Mat. xxv. 37.   [6] Rev. viii. 1.

Immanuel.

Immanuel. Forasmuch as, on such happy occasions, as the present, we have been accustomed to make further discoveries of the mystery of *God*, and of the *Father*, and of *Immanuel*; and to make known our counsels, unto our dear brethren and servants; we are, with pleasure, about to honour the arrival of our beloved friend, and faithful ambassador, *George Fervidus*, in the same manner.

Immediately the refulgence of the *Triune Deity* shone with amazing glory in the face of *Immanuel*[1], which, like a most powerful magnet, so attracted the surrounding audience, that they all pressed nearer the throne, and were held in the most blissful and profound silence and attention; while the great and illustrious *Son of God* proceeded.————————But this oration was delivered so much in the elevated stile of that glorious world, and the substance of it was of such a sublime nature, that no mortal could understand it[2]. Let it suffice, therefore, to add, that every one of that vast congregation fully comprehended it; and, at the close, returned thanks to *Immanuel* for his great condescension, with such loud acclamations as seemed like the sound of many waters; which, as the music swelled, became like the voice of mighty thunderings[3]: and yet the following rapturous exultation was distinctly heard." "Let us be glad, and rejoice, and give glory to our *Jehovah*, and *Prince Immanuel*; for all this display of glory and experience of love." And again they shouted, *Hallelujah*, which filled the vast concave of the *Celestial World*, and resounded over the everlasting hills. Silence being again commanded, said,

Immanuel. I see of the travel of my soul, and am abundantly satisfied[4]. I rejoice and glory in those sufferings which have made you thus happy. Ye are my brethren and near kinsmen. Members of my body, of my flesh, and of my bones[5]. Come near unto me, therefore, my dear children, that I may bless you, and dismiss you from the present solemnity.

Then arising from his throne, He stretched out, over his numerous and happy family, his blessed hands, adorned with

---

[1] Heb. i. 3. [2] 2 Cor. xii. 14. [3] Rev. xix. 6, 7. [4] Isa. liii. 11.
[5] Ephes. v. 30.

the fears of his wond'rous love; and with a loud voice pronounced the following benediction upon the assembly.

Immanuel. Blessed, for ever blessed be ye, my beloved bride and faithful friends! Ye are my portion, my glory, and my peculiar treasure! I rejoice over you with joy. I rest, and am happy in my love[1]; and will never cease to love you: but will go on eternally to bless you, and do you good, with my whole heart[2], which was pierced for you; and my whole soul, which was sacrificed to redeem you! Behold these arms which were nailed to the cross, are now extended to bless you; and this my glorious kingdom pours forth all its honours and joys upon you, to make you for ever, and for ever, compleatly blessed!

Immanuel then sat down on his throne, with a smile on his face that inflamed with seraphic love every heart in the audience. The assembly then broke up, and dispersed to rest in their *magnificent mansions*[3]; or to walk the *Golden-streets* of the *Celestial City*[4]; or to repose on the flowery banks of the river, under the *All-healing Tree of Life*[5]: and, whether solitary or social, to make the glory and love of *Immanuel* the subject of reflection and discourse. In this happy state the once wearied Pilgrims find perfect rest; waiting for the arrival of their brethren, and the *Great Adoption*, that is, the *Redemption of their Bodies*[6].

[1] Zeph. iii. 17.   [2] Jerem. xxxii. 41.   [3] John xiv. 2.   [4] Rev. xxi. 21.   [5] Rev. xxii. 2.   [6] Rom. viii. 23.

F I N I S.

www.ingramcontent.com/pod-product-compliance
Lightning Source LLC
Chambersburg PA
CBHW032009220426
43664CB00006B/189